To Karen, with love + blessings, Gordon Davidson Corinne McLaughlin

More praise for *Spiritual Politics*

"This book challenges the reader to re-imagine the world and to think in new ways about both politics and spirituality."
—DAVID SPANGLER
AUTHOR OF *EMERGENCE: REBIRTH OF THE SACRED*

"This inspiring book shows us a way to move from global breakdown to social synergy. It infuses politics with spirit and is essential reading for those engaged in personal and social transformation."
—PATRICIA ELLSBERG
SOCIAL CHANGE ACTIVIST
BOARD MEMBER, WORLD POLICY INSTITUTE

"To create something new calls for courage, imagination and inspiration. I feel this is what these two very courageous authors of *Spiritual Politics* are doing, and I'm sure millions of readers will agree."
—EILEEN CADDY
COFOUNDER OF THE FINDHORN FOUNDATION

"*Spiritual Politics* clarifies what it means to be truly human in a rapidly changing world. Hopefully it will be widely read by leaders in all spheres of life since its principles provide for us the ▓▓▓▓▓▓—the ethical guidance system which is so necessar▓▓ ▓▓▓▓▓ ▓▓logical civilization."
—NOEL BROW▓
DIRECTOR
UNITED NA▓▓▓▓ ▓▓▓▓▓▓▓▓▓▓ ▓AM

"Eye-popping! Addresses more que▓▓▓▓ ▓ ▓▓▓▓ ever thought to ask about forces underlying today's po▓▓▓▓ events and actors. Political science will never be the same."
—HAZEL HENDERSON
AUTHOR OF *PARADIGMS IN PROGRESS*

"*Spiritual Politics* is destined to become one of the great 'in' books of our time. It's *in*spirational, *in*tuitive, *in*formative, and *in*telligent. The authors have taken the available truth from ageless wisdom and translated it into the politics of now. It's *in*novative, *in*sightful, and *in*structive. Read it through your intellect, but listen to your heart."
— ROLLAND G. SMITH
TELEVISION JOURNALIST

"Some readers will find some interpretations they cannot accept, and some claims they cannot believe. But I would advise even the critical and skeptical reader to pay attention to the main theme: New metaphysical assumptions are taking over and the modern world will never again be the same."
— WILLIS HARMAN, PRESIDENT
INSTITUTE OF NOETIC SCIENCES

"This book will appeal to anyone who yearns for a way to apply their spiritual insights to urgent public problems. The authors are virtually encyclopedic in their coverage of groups utilizing spiritual insights in politics and in their recitation of spiritual interpretations of public events."
— PROFESSOR LESTER MILBRATH
STATE UNIVERSITY OF NEW YORK

"*Spiritual Politics* leaps beyond wishful thinking and speculation about the mind–body–spirit connection. With a resounding 'yes' to our wholeness and with an astounding synthesis of facts and possibilities, this book invites, prods, and encourages us to become practical participants in evolution's big leap."
— GLORIA KARPINSKI
AUTHOR OF *WHERE TWO WORLDS TOUCH: SPIRITUAL RITES OF PASSAGE*

SPIRITUAL POLITICS

Changing the World
from the Inside Out

◆ ◆ ◆

Corinne McLaughlin
and Gordon Davidson

Ballantine Books • New York

Sale of this book without a front cover may be unauthorized.
If this book is coverless, it may have been reported to the
publisher as "unsold or destroyed" and neither the author
nor the publisher may have received payment for it.

Copyright © 1994 by Corinne McLaughlin and Gordon Davidson

Foreword copyright © 1994 by His Holiness The Dalai Lama

All rights reserved under International and Pan-American Copyright
Conventions. Published in the United States by Ballantine Books, a
division of Random House, Inc., New York, and simultaneously
in Canada by Random House of Canada Limited, Toronto.

Grateful acknowledgment is made to the following for permission to
reprint previously published material:

Lucis Publishing: Excerpts from *The Externalisation of Hierarchy* by Alice Bailey. These extracts may not be reprinted except by permission of the Lucis Trust, which holds copyright.

Jack G. Shaheen: Excerpt from "Our Cultural Demon—the 'Ugly Arab' "
by Jack G. Shaheen, professor emeritus of Mass Communications,
Southern Illinois University at Edwardsville.

David Feinstein and Stanley Krippner: Excerpt from "Bringing a Mythological Perspective to
Social Change," *ReVision,* Vol. 11, No. 1., published by Heldref Publications.

The Washington Post: Excerpt from "Why We Hate Politics" by E.J. Dionne.
Copyright © 1991 by *The Washington Post.*

Excerpt from "A Turning Point in History," an editorial in *The Washington Post National
Weekly Edition,* August 26–September 1, 1991. Copyright © 1991 by *The Washington Post.*
Reprinted by permission.

Library of Congress Catalog Card Number: 93-90881

ISBN: 0-345-36983-1

Cover design by Susan Lovelace

Cover photograph © Uniphoto Picture Agency

Manufactured in the United States of America

First Edition: August 1994

10 9 8 7 6 5 4 3 2

*To M and DK
and to all the Warriors of the Spirit,
that they may awaken to the fire in their hearts
and hear the inner anthem calling them
to the Great Work.*

Contents

◆

Foreword

◆

In our present state of affairs, the very survival of mankind depends on people developing concern for the whole of humanity, not just their own community or nation. The reality of our situation impels us to think and act properly. Narrow-mindedness and self-centered thinking may have served us well in the past, but today will only lead to disaster. We can overcome such attitudes through a combination of education and training. On the basis of love and kindness towards our human brothers and sisters, we need to develop a sense of universal responsibility.

Attempts have been made in the past to create societies that were more just, whose members were more equal. Institutions have been established with noble charters to combat anti-social forces. Unfortunately, too often such ideals have been cheated by selfishness. Today, we can see more clearly than ever before how ethics and noble principles become poisoned by self-interest, particularly where politics are concerned. Politics devoid of ethics contribute nothing to human welfare, and life without morality reduces humans to the level of beasts.

Civilization is founded on such human qualities as honesty, morality, compassion, and wisdom. But these qualities must be cultivated and sustained through systematic moral education in a conducive social environment. Normally such qualities should be inculcated from childhood. However, we cannot wait for the next generation to make the change. We need a revolution in our commitment to and practice of universal humanitarian values right now.

A real "new world order" is not a question of economic or political adjustment, but a realignment of our motivation. To begin with, we can avoid harming others in any way, whether directly or indirectly, on an individual or international level, and pause to examine how we can help them.

The end of the cold war may have removed one kind of threat, but we are still faced by the problems of environmental degeneration, overpopulation, and ethnic strife. This timely book, *Spiritual Politics: Changing the World from the Inside Out,* sets out ways for developing a new approach to creating a happier, more peaceful world. The authors have done well to produce it, but the success of their efforts will depend on whether readers put their advice into effect.

—The Dalai Lama
December 1, 1993

Acknowledgments

◆

So many people have helped in the creation of this book that any list is filled with omissions. However, we would especially like to thank George Christie for the commitment and time he has given to reading and discussing the book with us; Congresswoman Claudine Schneider, Nancy Seifer, Jan Van der Linden, Dr. Jeff Fishel, Dr. Ted Becker, Dr. Christa Slaten, William Bloom, Shepherd Bliss, Mark Satin, and Sue Kennedy for reviewing parts of our manuscript and offering feedback. We would also like to thank members of Sirius Community and the New Fusion group for their thoughts, inspirations, and discussion of these topics over the years, along with our many students in the Sirius School who have provided us with a forum for our thinking and valuable feedback and encouragement to write this book. We also thank Steve Kane, Judy Dean, Don Karp, and Cindy Pauley for help with word processing, Allen Gold for his loyal personal support, and Libby and John Farr for their help. Many thanks are also extended to manuscript editor, Barbara Shor, and editorial assistant Leah Odze. We especially appreciate our editor, Cheryl Woodruff, for her support and contributions to this project from its inception in 1987 to its completion in 1994. A special acknowledgment is also due for all the help we received from those in the spiritual dimensions who provided continual inspiration and opened many doors.

That which is called God by the Christians,
Jehovah by the Jews,
Ultimate Reality by the Hindus,
The Buddha Mind by Buddhists,
Allah by Mohammedans,
And which the Chinese call the Tao—
That is the Real Self
And is all-pervading.

Spiritual Politics

INTRODUCTION

*Few are willing to brave the disapproval of their fellows, the cen-
sure of their colleagues, the wrath of their society. Moral courage
is a rarer commodity than bravery in battle or great intelligence.
Yet it is the one essential, vital quality for those who seek to
change a world that yields most painfully to change.*

*Each time a person stands up for an idea, or acts to improve the
lot of others, or strikes out against injustice, [s]he sends forth a
tiny ripple of hope, and crossing each other from a million different centers of energy and daring, those ripples build a current
that can sweep down the mightiest walls of oppression and resistance.*

—ROBERT F. KENNEDY[1]

Our passion for politics and concern for world events was initially sparked
by John F. Kennedy's presidency. Politics became all consuming for us as
activists in the 1960s. Although it would be some time before the two of
us met, our experiences were remarkably similar. Both of us were politically
active, one in Berkeley, California, the other in Amherst, Massachusetts.
The 1960s were tumultuous and powerful. It was a time when our generation felt we could change the world. Yet it was also a very painful and
confusing time for those of us who cared deeply about what was happening
to our country—moments of triumph and euphoria mixed with horror and
despair. Like many others, we felt we had to do something about the senseless killing in Vietnam, the degradation of life in inner-city ghettos, the destruction of the environment, the oppression of women. So we both took
to the streets and demonstrated and organized.

Looking back now, we feel the radical political movement of the 1960s
helped accomplish certain things—racial and sexual inequalities lessened to
some extent; U.S. troops finally withdrew from Vietnam; and the voting
age was lowered to eighteen. Yet great injustice and corruption still per-
sisted in the United States. By the early 1970s we both felt ineffective and

burned out. Seeing faults in the leaders of our movement, we asked ourselves whether it was really possible to create a new society. Or were we merely replacing the old social order with another one that was just as repressive and conformist in a different way? Like many others of our generation, we slowly began to realize that something had been missing in our activism.

Finally, after much soul-searching, we each in our own way took time out for a retreat, realizing we had to turn within. We had to begin the inner journey and confront our own shadows, our own darkness—instead of seeing evil only outside ourselves and blaming the government and big corporations for all our problems. We had marched for peace in the world yet did not feel peace in our own hearts. We confronted injustice in our government yet did not want to admit our own injustices to others.

We finally realized we had to begin to perform the inner alchemy of transmutation on ourselves, to work to change our own negative patterns. Slowly and painfully we began to let go of our fears and our old, limited ways of perceiving the world. And this, in turn, allowed us to see things in a more expanded context. We also learned new skills for becoming more effective and for communicating with those holding different views without creating conflict. Most important, we learned that only a changed person can be an agent of change.

We both walked away from the political movement around the same time to explore the other side of the 1960s—the inner side—of personal growth, humanistic psychology and spiritual teaching of all types. These two camps seemed forever at odds in the 1960s, each believing it alone had the most important truth. Everyone was on one side or the other and lived in separate worlds. Years later we discovered that at the time a good friend had run a drop-in counseling center just down the street from where one of us had worked at a political magazine, but our worlds had never touched. The political activists felt politics was the only road to help people and to change the world. The personal growth contingent and those devoted to Eastern gurus said, Don't worry about the world—change yourself first. We felt we had a foot in both worlds.

As we each continued our inner work on ourselves, and explored many spiritual paths, we came upon the "Ageless Wisdom" (often called "the Perennial Philosophy" or "the Sacred Science"),[2] and something resonated within us. Finding this teaching was like meeting a long-lost friend. At last we had found the missing threads we had been looking for—the ones that linked our inner spiritual journey to our outer journey as political activists. We discovered a conceptual framework in the Ageless Wisdom that bridged the two worlds, which still seem separate to so many people today—the spiritual transformation groups and the political activist groups. The Ageless Wisdom is the golden thread connecting the hidden, mystical teachings within the major religious traditions. Although this tradition of perennial wisdom has been known to the great initiates of many faiths and cultures, it is quite new to most people today. Plato and Pericles, for example, during the Golden Age of Greece, were initiates of the Mysteries of Eleusis, and the great Athenian democracy reflected many of the principles of the Ageless Wisdom.

The two of us were raised as Christians, one a Catholic and one a Baptist. This gave us a solid spiritual foundation based on faith in God and living an ethical life. But it left many questions unanswered—such as the seeming lack of justice in the world. We were only able to resolve these issues later, as we began to understand the principles of karma and reincarnation as taught in the Ageless Wisdom.

Through the power of meditation we developed the ability to contact Spirit. We found we could transcend the illusion of duality, of inner growth vs. outer activism, because at last we could see their interconnection in the evolutionary process. The oneness of all life became an experiential reality for us. We found a new meaning, a broader context, in which all the pieces of our lives began to fit together, revealing more clearly the purpose of life and human evolution.

Not long after this, the two of us finally met—at the Findhorn Foundation in Scotland, a well-known spiritual community based on a modern application of the Ageless Wisdom. There we discovered how similar our journeys had been.

Spiritual Politics represents our understanding of the Ageless Wisdom tradition applied practically to world events. The insights shared here have grown out of our experience of putting these principles and techniques to work in our own lives and from our intuitive insights and meditations as well. Gordon had worked for four years with the Lucis Trust in New York, which publishes teachings of the Ageless Wisdom, and both of us taught spiritual studies for several years at Findhorn in Scotland. In 1978 we founded Sirius, a spiritual community and ecological village in Massachusetts, where we've lived for over fifteen years.

Recently we've begun dividing our time between Massachusetts and our university teaching and business in Washington, D.C. We've worked with several groups that have experimented with a new political and economic paradigm, including the New World Alliance, the New Synthesis Institute, the Greens, the Social Investment Forum, CERES, and Ally Capital (an environmental finance company). Living in several alternative communities for over twenty years has helped us free our minds from a great deal of social conformity and old ways of thinking. It has also helped us to continue experimenting with new approaches on both inner and outer levels.

All through our years of spiritual growth we have been working to develop and trust our intuition, which was dramatically tested as we tried to research the metaphysical aspects of America's founding. Then, suddenly we had a glimpse of viewing the world from a vast expanse of wisdom and experience. We felt as though we were looking back on the present from centuries into the future and seeing the small, distorted versions of truth passing for wisdom in the world's greatest halls of learning. We knew then that if we were to tread the higher way of wisdom, we must trust our own intuition and inner guidance, for the world's secular "authorities" have yet to see with clarity the inner side of life.[3] We observed the historical pattern that what passes for mysticism today often becomes tomorrow's common sense.

OVERVIEW OF THE BOOK

Our intention in this book is to offer you our experience of the spiritual and material dimensions of life as they join in service to the pressing needs of our planet. Politics has been given a bad name because what most of us mean when we say "politics" is "partisan power struggle." But politics is really the art of governance, a science that synthesizes opposing views into a higher level of understanding. Spiritual politics responds not just to competing interests and the demand for rights, but, rather, focuses on the next evolutionary step in growth for each individual and group. It directs resources and structures institutions to help citizens meet their own needs, while learning to embody the virtues common to all religions and systems of ethics—compassion, honesty, and the sharing of skills and resources.

We feel the time has come to unite that which has been separated for so long—politics and spirituality. Politics—local, national, and global—must be lifted beyond power-tripping, deceit, and manipulation and restored to its highest purpose: addressing the greatest good for the greatest number. This is the deeper meaning of politics.

As our founding fathers rightly understood, we must avoid the dogma and dominance of a state religion. Spirituality is not limited to organized religion. True spirituality is found in honoring our highest ideals as human beings, as well as the transcendent Divinity. Spirituality today must go beyond concern for personal salvation to help others in need, and to address the crises in the world.

Spiritual politics sees the Soul, the highest potential, in each person, whether friend or adversary, while not being blind to individual personalities and problems. It is an approach that turns inward for understanding and inspiration from the spiritual realms, and then brings this inspiration into the world to create new, more effective forms and institutions.

Although many religious thinkers through the ages have stated the need for ethics and values in our political life, there has been little of the deeper metaphysical perspective in political thought or writing. For example, there hasn't been much discussion of the karmic causes of global crises, their effects on planetary cycles, or the deeper symbolism of world events.

In *Spiritual Politics* we address the split in the social change movement between political activists and those who are spiritually minded. We offer new insights into the practical application of spiritual ideas for those concerned that the spiritual movement is preoccupied with personal, rather than planetary, growth.

In *Spiritual Politics* we seek to transform the world from the inside out—rather than from the outside in. Our aim is to shift the focus of political dialogue from the outer level of physical forms and activities to the inner, causal realm of consciousness. "Consciousness precedes being—not the other way around," noted former Czech President Vaclav Havel in his 1990 address to the U.S. Congress. The human mind is not simply a reflection of prevailing social structures—it creates form. The interplay of human and Divine thought creates all personal and social reality.

We advise you to use your own intuition in evaluating the ideas we are presenting here, as we do not insist on ultimate authority for them. We know that each of us needs to individually discover what rings true and then to follow that truth.

It is our intention to provide you with a context for examining data in a new way and to introduce you to the metaphysical concepts and tools you will need to do this. We also discuss a number of practical applications for these concepts. It is our hope that you will pursue the metaphysical sources listed here in more depth. If our reflections on these subjects bring you any new insights, inspire you to greater service for humanity, provide a sense of hope for the future—or at least present you with new food for thought—then we are satisfied that our purpose has been fulfilled.

In part 1, "The Book of Life," we outline the philosophical framework of *Spiritual Politics.* Chapter 1, "Reading the Book of Life," begins by encouraging readers to cast off the old blinders of "consensual reality" to explore the deeper causes of events. We then introduce the Ageless Wisdom as a map for exploring the inner realms. The interconnection of everything through the planetary web of life is discussed, and new scientific research is presented to illustrate the effect of thoughts and feeling on our personal health. We then explore what our collective thoughts are doing to our collective health as a society.

In chapter 2, "The Symbolism and Significance of World Events," we explore the inner forces at work and the lessons presented in such events as the Persian Gulf war, the collapse of communism, and the reemergence of feminine energy.

In part 2, "Evolutionary Governance," we explore a new type of political process.

Chapter 3, "The New Transformational Politics," and chapter 4, "Politics as if People Mattered," outline a new political paradigm rooted in the Ageless Wisdom tradition and offer successful examples of political groups based on this paradigm.

Part 3 outlines "The Hidden Causes of World Events." In chapter 5, "Form Follows Thought," and chapter 6, "The World Is Our Mirror," we survey specific types of positive and negative emotions and thinking, such as nonsystemic linear thinking or shadow projection, which have created either positive or dysfunctional results in the world. Chapter 7, "Many Lives, One Soul," explores causes of world events generated by the human soul, through karma and reincarnation.

In part 4, "The Divine Hand Behind Human Affairs," we explore more universal influences.

Chapter 8 discusses "The Invisible Government" of the world and the spiritual guidance given to humanity from the time of ancient Greece to the founding of America. In chapter 9, "The Cosmic Causes of World Events," we explore the forces of Light and Darkness, the Devas or Angels, and changes in astrological and ray energies. Although many of the ideas in these two chapters are not yet acceptable in most traditional circles, we suggest approaching them with an open mind and reserving judgment. If you find the rest of the ideas in the book convincing or plausible, the material in chapters 8 and 9 may very well emerge in a new light. In fact, this information may fill in missing blanks left by most theories of social science, making sense out of a world that often seems hopelessly confusing.

Chapter 10, "The Soul of Nations," may offer a new perspective for many readers, for we discuss nations as though they were individual personalities with positive and negative character traits. We also offer suggestions for ways each nation might fulfill its highest potential.

In part 5, "Creating a New Planetary Order," we ground spiritual principles in the world.

Chapter 11, "The New Planetary Economics," and chapter 12, "Planetary Stewardship and Human Empowerment," provide practical applications for new economic ideas emerging from the inner side—the current emergence of a new socially responsible form of economics that views the entire planet Earth as our household.

In chapter 13, "Inner and Outer Work for Planetary Evolution," we present many techniques for what each of us can do on inner and outer levels to help the world—such as visualizations and thought-form building.

We feel that much of what we are presenting in this book are ideas whose time has come—or, more accurately, ancient wisdom applied to modern problems. We hope this wisdom will continue to contribute to the shift toward a new political and social paradigm. According to John Naisbitt and Patricia Aburdene in their book *Megatrends 2000*, researchers are reporting that 5 to 10 percent of the American population—with up to 15 percent in some East Coast and West Coast cities—have adopted some of the "new paradigm" thinking we are presenting in this book.[4] Since, in a democracy, major change generally happens through shifts in public opinion—and since politicians spend a vast amount of time and money to see the results of the latest opinion polls—our work is aimed at helping to bring about a profound change in the way the public thinks about issues. From this opening to Spirit will come much wiser solutions to the many problems we face as a nation and as a human family on this small planet.

We hope, too, that the new insights in this book may inspire social scientists to do careful studies in some of these areas to verify such things as the effect of negative thoughts and emotions on political events. But more important, it is our hope that this book will catalyze further and deeper reflection and assist in the birthing of a vast field of inner research, reflection, and thought. The true purpose of *Spiritual Politics* is not so much to provide metaphysical information as it is to encourage you to begin examining what goes on in our world from a spiritual perspective. In this way you will discover for yourself even deeper and more profound understandings of the ways things really are. This book is only the beginning.

Gordon Davidson and Corinne McLaughlin
Shutesbury, Massachusetts
January 1994

Part 1

◆ ◆ ◆

THE BOOK
OF LIFE

♦

Chapter One

READING THE
BOOK OF LIFE

All things by immortal power
Near or far
Hiddenly to each other linked are;
Thou canst not stir a flower
Without troubling a star.
—FRANCIS THOMPSON

Spiritual forces are moving deeply and powerfully behind the scenes of world events in ways that are not always obvious on the evening news. Today's headlines, viewed with the right consciousness, can be seen as a living alphabet through which humanity comes to know itself and God. A deeper meaning is revealed.

Native Americans call this "reading the Book of Life." They have traditionally interpreted what they observed in life as a reflection of an inner reality that had a deep message for them. The timing and direction of their walks through nature would bring activities to their attention that had great meaning. Perhaps a particular animal would cross their path that represented a certain quality in their belief system, such as courage—reminding them what they needed to call up in themselves to solve a problem. Each event they encountered in life added to their understanding until they became increasingly adept at this kind of reading.

Medieval monks also saw the world as *liber mundi*—the book of the world, which was to be read and interpreted. The ancient Druid bards or priests, who advised the kings of Ireland, were also trained to read the Book of Life in this fashion, as were the Vedic priests of India.

Our Pilgrim forefathers had a similar perspective—viewing an epidemic or an Indian attack as a message about their lives. When such disasters occurred, they would call for a day of fasting and prayer to examine why they had attracted the experience to themselves. They would search out and discuss the attitudes or actions they felt must be out of alignment with God's will, and that they needed to change.[1]

Our personal experience has also led us to see that everyday life is our greatest spiritual teacher. At Sirius, the ecological community we founded in Massachusetts, members have learned to view difficult experiences with a detachment that asks: "How did I create this? Why did I attract this to me? What can I learn from it?"

Where do we find the answers to these questions? Where do we find the key that unlocks the mysterious living alphabet of the Book of Life? Deep within ourselves!

But in order to truly understand the world in a new way, we first have to throw off the blinders of "consensual reality." This old perspective says that only our physical senses—what we can see, hear, touch, smell, and taste—can tell us what is real. That nothing inner or subjective is real or important or has any effect on the real world. With such training from birth, few of us give much time or attention to our personal inner life, and even less to our collective inner life. As a result, the inner dimension has come to hold little reality for most of us.

Yet we all repeatedly come up against brick walls as we keep trying to solve complex national and global problems from a materially oriented consensual reality. Surely it has become abundantly clear as the millennium approaches that for new, workable solutions to emerge we must find a way to bridge both dimensions. How can we reestablish communications with the inner realm? How can we bring together the inner and the outer, the spiritual and the material, to create a new, more fully awakened consensual reality?

THE AGELESS WISDOM THROUGH HISTORY

The Ageless Wisdom tradition, as it developed in the West, bridges this gap and offers a profound synthesis of spirituality and politics. We have found that the code for understanding the next step of human evolution is present in these teachings.

This tradition demonstrates that society can be transformed not only by our outer actions, but also by working on the inner, subjective levels with meditation, thought-form building, and the transmission of spiritual energy. In the West, the followers of the Ageless Wisdom tradition have usually worked to transform society as well as themselves. The Western esoteric tradition does not view physical life as simply "maya" or illusion to be transcended, as in some teachings of the East, but rather as a field for service and active reform. Unjust systems and institutions need to be transformed to enable consciousness to evolve and be expressed more fully. Students of this approach have not just been recluses in monasteries or ashrams. Very often they have been reformers—like Annie Besant, an early president of the Theosophical Society, who led marches for women's rights and for Indian independence in the early part of this century, long before these issues became popular. Leaders in the Western esoteric tradition have been politicians, businesspeople, artists, and scientists—not just religious leaders.

The Ageless Wisdom is said to have existed on this planet for millions of years. It has been described as the "golden thread" that connects the esoteric or hidden teachings that underlie the ancient Chaldean, Egyptian, Hebrew, Hindu, Greek, Chinese, Buddhist, Christian, and Islamic traditions—as well as some indigenous teachings the world over.

Although the outer forms and popular teachings of the many religious perspectives on this planet may appear, on the surface, to be in conflict with one another, when the symbols, mysteries, and inner teachings of their various founders and prophets are studied in depth, a remarkable harmony and correlation can be seen. All the great teachers of the major religions are thus transmitters of the same fundamental truths under the veil of local symbols, appropriately presented to suit the time and culture. All true religions and spiritual paths teach universal values of compassion, unity, truthfulness, fairness, tolerance, responsibility, respect for, and service to, all life.

For centuries, the Ageless Wisdom in the West was shielded from an unprepared public, veiled in the original teachings of Hermes Trismegistus, the geometric symbols of Pythagoras, the alchemical formulas of Paracelsus, the diplomacy of the Count St.-Germain, and the writings of great initiates such as Apuleius, Jakob Böhme, John Dee, and Francis Bacon. The unveiled truths were handed down only orally by individual teachers to tested disciples or by certain religious groups and secret societies, such as the Kabbalists, Druids, Essenes, Sufis, Knights Templar, Rosicrucians, Freemasons, and others who carefully guarded the teachings down through the centuries. A study of these secret societies would reveal powerful influences on the history of nations.

MORE RECENT BLOSSOMING OF THE AGELESS WISDOM

Over the last hundred years, the Ageless Wisdom has spread widely in the West, beginning with the work of the Russian Helena Petrovna Blavatsky. Her seminal book, *The Secret Doctrine*, published in 1888, synthesized Christian, Jewish, and Islamic mysticism with the Eastern teachings of

Hinduism, Taoism, and Buddhism, showing their common roots and comparing their sacred texts.

During her extensive travels in the East, Blavatsky worked directly with several Indian and Tibetan masters who helped her record and explain the Ageless Wisdom for the West. With Colonel Henry Steel Olcott, Blavatsky founded the Theosophical Society in New York in 1875, which soon grew into a worldwide philosophical organization with thousands of members.

Several other major movements branched out from the original tree planted by Theosophy. The Anthroposophical Society, founded in Germany in 1913 by Rudolf Steiner, added a stronger emphasis on the central role of Christ and grew into a worldwide movement. The Agni Yoga Society, founded by expatriate Russians Helena and Nicholas Roerich in 1920, presented the teachings of "Living Ethics," a synthesis of all the forms of Yoga from philosophical to physical.

The next development came through the teachings of an Englishwoman, Alice Bailey, a former member of the Theosophical Society. In 1919 Bailey was contacted by a Tibetan master, Djwhal Khul, who asked her to write a series of books with him telepathically that would continue Blavatsky's work. Over a period of thirty years, Bailey received eighteen books from him on the nature of the cosmos and the human being, outlining principles for individual spiritual growth and humanity's next evolutionary steps. In 1923 Bailey founded the Lucis Trust to bring the teachings in her books to the public. A year later she began the Arcane School. The books were written to apply to several levels of consciousness at once and thus can be read by both beginners and advanced students. Her works have been especially helpful to the two of us in our own spiritual growth and have provided much of the inspiration for *Spiritual Politics*.

PRINCIPLES OF THE AGELESS WISDOM

These teachings are called "ageless" rather than "ancient" because, rather than rigid dogma, they are a living expression, continually being revealed and expanded through people's lives and experiences. Although much of this wisdom is thousands of years old, it is often "new" to mainstream thinking. However, as the old French saying goes: "Everything begins in mysticism and ends in politics."

From our perspective, "New Age" teachings are popularizations of the Ageless Wisdom, and like all popular versions, some are wise, culturally relevant applications, while others tend to be somewhat watered down or distortions of truth.

Rather than dogma, which requires unquestioning belief, the Ageless Wisdom tradition is based on a more scientific approach, offering a series of postulates that can be applied by anyone to daily life and tested for their truth. Basically, it teaches us to think in terms of energy, rather than form. For most of us, the true understanding of these teachings is the work of a lifetime. However, since the major principles of this wisdom form the foundation of our exploration of world events in *Spiritual Politics*, we would like to introduce a few basic concepts. These principles will be explained in more depth in later chapters, where we apply them to current political events and issues.

LEARNING DETACHMENT: THE STANCE OF THE OBSERVER

The Ageless Wisdom tradition encourages the development and use of the mind, especially the abstract or philosophical mind. It teaches that we individually and collectively create the reality we experience through our thinking, so we learn to become detached observers and consciously direct the workings of our own mind in a more positive direction. We also learn detachment from our desires and our emotions in order to see the world and its problems more clearly and dispassionately. Pain comes from attachment to forms—material things, places, and people—as well as to attachment to beliefs—our own version of truth. The Ageless Wisdom teaches us to transcend duality and provides training in paradoxes, so we can see the truth in both sides of any issue—which has major political implications. We learn to see personal and world events as the interplay of energies and the outworking of inner causes.

Developing Compassion and a Commitment to Service

Opening our hearts in order to develop true compassion for all living beings is essential in this approach, as is learning self-responsibility for our own problems. This helps us appreciate the spiritual values found in both the compassion of liberalism and the self-reliance of conservatism. The Ageless Wisdom also teaches methods for aligning our personal will with the Divine Will. It is from this alignment that we develop a sense of clarity about our purpose and service to the world, making our social activism more effective.

Trusting Inner Guidance

Unlike the Eastern approach, spiritual seekers in the Western Ageless Wisdom tradition often have no outer teacher or guru. We cultivate spiritual self-reliance by learning to trust our own inner source of guidance—the

Soul—and by applying these teachings to our daily lives. In this tradition the emphasis is on group work—serving in groups made up of inwardly guided individuals. Today some of the most effective and innovative political work is being done by inspired groups.

Embracing the One Life

The Ageless Wisdom teaches that all life is interconnected, joined together by the heartbeat of the One Great Universal Life—One Energy, moving at different rates of vibration. Spirit is matter at its highest point; matter is spirit at its lowest point. What this means is that all life forms from galaxies to algae are essentially energy functioning at different levels of manifestation. Divinity incorporates all opposites and all possibilities. It is the transcendent Creative Principle. And it is also the Indwelling Spirit (God Immanent) that exists within each of us. This is expressed by the major religions as:

"The Kingdom of God is within you" (Christian - Jesus)

"Look within, thou art the Buddha" (Buddhism - Buddha)

"By understanding the Self all this universe is known" (Hindu - The Upanishads)

"He who knows himself knows his Lord" (Moslem - Muhammed)

"Man, know thyself and thou shalt know the universe and the gods" (Ancient Greek).

Divinity is present in all of life. But at the same time it is beyond self, beyond duality, beyond all form. This recognition radically transforms how we treat nature and how we relate to people of different races and cultures.

The Divine Soul Within

The Ageless Wisdom teaches that all of manifested Life contains within it the spark of the Divine Spirit, or the One Life. When this Divine Light expresses itself through matter, it creates consciousness. This is the principle of the evolving Soul.

The purpose of life is the redemption or spiritualization of matter and the evolution of consciousness in all forms. Our Divine Soul incarnates into matter and through our effort and invocation eventually infuses the matter of our physical bodies and our personalities with Divine Light. Ultimately we will return to the Divine Source from which we came, with all the accumulated growth and creative potential we have gleaned from our experiences on Earth.

Here, in this "schoolhouse of the Soul," we learn the lessons of individuation, creativity, love, and self-transcendence. Meditation, study, and service to the world are seen as the primary methods for spiritual growth in this approach, which is also called the "Yoga of Synthesis."

Expansion Through Initiation

Our spiritual development proceeds through many lifetimes as we learn to purify, perfect, and control each aspect of our personality. We reincarnate each time in new cultures and new bodies to learn different lessons. Our position, character, abilities, and problems are the result of karma we've set in motion in our previous lives. The Law of Karma teaches that "as we sow, so shall we reap." The Soul, the immortal part of us, gradually infuses our personality through a series of expansions called initiations. The more we learn to control our physical desires (the first initiation), to stabilize our emotions (the second initiation), and to develop our higher mind and intuition (the third initiation), the more the power and energy of the Soul become available to us. Much of the power, inspiration, and vision of great political leaders can be understood as the expression of individuals who have taken higher initiations.

The Masters of Wisdom

Those humans who have fully achieved the integration of Spirit, Soul, and personality, and have graduated from all the lessons of earth life, are seen as Masters of wisdom and compassion—the Enlightened Ones. They form the true spiritual Inner Government of our planet, serving as protectors and guides of human evolution. They include the founders of the world's great religions—Krishna, Moses, Buddha, Jesus, Mohammed—as well as many others, including women, who are less well known. In addition, all physical life forms are in the loving care of the Angelic energies in the subtle realms who provide unconditional love as well as inspiration and help. These beings are known as the "Devas" in the Hindu tradition and "Kachinas" in the Native American, and can be of help in solving our environmental problems.

A NEW POLITICAL PARADIGM BASED ON INNER CAUSES

Spiritual Politics seeks to articulate a new paradigm for politics based on the Ageless Wisdom. The word *paradigm* comes from the Greek root *paradeigma*, which means "model" or "pattern." A paradigm is a set of assumptions or beliefs about the nature of reality. During our lifetime, these beliefs are repeated and reinforced over and over again on a daily basis until we come to accept them as "the way things are." A paradigm explains the world to us and helps us predict behavior and the most likely eventualities.

Since our particular paradigm defines us and our place in the world, we tend to have a deep emotional investment in its continued existence. We continually filter our consensual reality through both our cultural and personal paradigms, and we maintain it by sampling only a small number of cues when seeking a comfortable match for our conceptual maps.[2]

The powerful global changes of the last ten years have shown us very clearly that the time has come to explore a new political paradigm, one that allows us to see and learn from the inner side of world events. Using the principles of the Ageless Wisdom, we would like to propose a new map of reality, based on the principle that consciousness creates form. The outer material world of physical forms in which we invest so much attention is only a reflection or outer symbol of the inner subjective world. The new paradigm reflects a whole new way of seeing politics and economics. It moves from an outer, form-related perspective to an inner one focussing on deeper causes.

The old separative, linear approach to politics is transformed into an interconnected, whole-systems view based on mutual causality. In this way, problems can be seen as interrelated, reflecting the fundamental unity of the social fabric. In this realization lies the secret to creating real and lasting solutions that keep eluding our grasp, to societal problems such as crime or cycles of economic crisis.

Our current tendency to rely solely on rational, quantitative solutions to problems is transformed into a broader approach that includes an intuitive and psychological understanding of political issues. We note, for example, how "shadow" projections affect our foreign policy and how low self-esteem is a basic problem for many welfare recipients.

The usual political strategies—winning at all costs, triumphing over adversaries, achieving more power—are transformed into a concern for the good of the whole and into win/win approaches to conflict. Once the inner causes of events are recognized, policy discussions can focus on the moral lessons being learned and how humanity is growing and evolving in this schoolhouse called planet Earth. With such a focus, decisions about war and peace, for example, take a very different direction, and conflicts are resolved for mutual benefit.

The old approach to politics as a dirty business dealing merely with the exercise of power is transformed into a new one that elevates governance to a science of synthesis. When the underlying inner unity of humanity is honored, it is then possible to create harmony out of apparent diversity and conflict. Race, sex, religion, and political beliefs will then be seen as merely outer forms of difference, adding to a rich and creative diversity that strengthens the whole.

Seeing one side of an issue as more correct or more popular is transformed into a greater wisdom that understands the best in both sides and synthesizes them into a new policy reflecting a higher truth. A whole new synthesis of liberalism/conservatism, hierarchy/equality, globalism/decentralism, and idealism/realism then emerges. From this more enlightened perspective, issues such as abortion need no longer tear the country apart.

Overreliance on archetypically masculine expressions of energy, such as dynamic will and power, is transformed into a balanced masculine-feminine expression that enhances the nurturing, intuitive, and inclusive qualities in both men and women in order to solve the global problems we face.

Seeing money as a commodity for keeping score and measuring personal value is transformed into an understanding of money as a shared energy to be used wisely as a social responsibility and a sacred trust.

Passive dependence on political leaders is transformed into personal empowerment—a realization that each of us has the power to cause change. When we follow our own inner guidance and understand the collective power of thought, we see ourselves as citizens in charge of our democracy, just as the ancient Greeks did, rather than just as "consumers." Our spirit is reunited with our power. Both the mystic and the warrior can then join hearts and hands to renew our nation and our planet.

Outmoded and limited notions that humans are the only political actors are transformed into an understanding of the transhuman causes of events—such as the role of Divine guidance in the founding of the United States or in the defeat of Adolf Hitler in World War II. Once we realize that help is always available to those whose intention is to serve the highest good, the world situation is no longer seen as hopeless and unchangeable because of human weakness.

Our outgrown perception of nations as a collection of competing interest groups dominated by a particular leader or party is transformed into a view of nations as distinct entities—each with a self-involved personality and a selfless, compassionate Soul—both vying for control while evolving in consciousness.

To create this new political paradigm, we must first understand how the inner, subjective worlds affect the outer worlds.

THE INTERCONNECTEDNESS OF ALL LIFE

Understanding the interconnectedness of life—a truth long held by the Ageless Wisdom—is one of the first doors that opens onto the inner workings of world events. Recently many eminent scientists are discovering, through their investigations into matter, the deeper truth of this interconnectedness. Physicist David Bohm, a colleague of Einstein's and a student of Krishnamurti's, said that modern physics reveals a universe that is "continuous and indivisible . . . an undivided and unbroken whole."[3] Bohm believe that each of us holographically contains the whole, thus sharing one consciousness. A change in one person's level of being can thus begin to change all others.[4]

Mathematician John Bell's theorem demonstrates that everything in the universe is connected, and that phenomena cannot always be explained in terms of causes in the immediate space-time vicinity. It demonstrates that the local world we perceive "is in actuality supported by an invisible reality which is unmediated, unmitigated, and faster than light."[5]

Scientist Rupert Sheldrake, a Theosophist, speaks of a "morphogenetic field"—an invisible matrix or organizing field that connects all life and all thought on earth, with each aspect affecting all others. Thus this field becomes a blueprint for new forms struggling to evolve. Biologist James Lovelock writes about the "Gaia" theory—how living organisms coordinate their activities around planet Earth to affect the land, water, air, and climate to keep everything in balance within the narrow range of conditions that support life. Physician Deepak Chopra, a student of Transcendental Meditation, reminds us that every breath we take probably includes at least a few molecules breathed out by an ancestor of ours thousands of years ago, as well as those breathed out by someone halfway around the world some time before.[6]

MIND OVER MATTER: CONSCIOUSNESS IS CAUSAL

Princeton University scientists Robert Jahn and Brenda Dunne, as well as others, have conducted experiments that verify the influence of mind over matter (psychokinesis) and the accurate prediction of future events (precognition).[7] A study reported to the U.S. House of Representatives' Committee on Science and Technology noted as follows:

Recent experiments in remote viewing and other studies in parapsychology suggest that there exists an "interconnectiveness" of the human mind with other minds and with matter. A general recognition of the degree of interconnectiveness of minds could have far-reaching social and political implications for this nation and the world.[8]

Physicists have found that the classical Cartesian/Newtonian notion that matter consists of solid objects does not adequately reflect reality. Electrons sometimes behave like waves and sometimes like particles in different situations. The more precisely one dimension, such as position or velocity (momentum), is fixed by the physicist's observation, the more the other becomes uncertain. The exact relation between them is defined by the "uncertainty principle" developed by physicist Werner Heisenberg. This means that neither the electron nor any other atomic "object" has any intrinsic properties independent of its environment or of those observing it.

In quantum theory there are only relationships, interconnections, and processes—no isolated "things." This finding has major implications for our social and political reality. For example, as historian William Irwin Thompson notes, "If you know the momentum of a global economic transition, you cannot locate it; if you can locate it—a deal in New York or a new product in Japan—you cannot know its economic momentum."[9] It also illustrates how we can't solve social problems in isolation from everything else—all is related.

Physicists at the National Institute of Standards and Technology in Boulder, Colorado, recently found that attempting to measure particles at the atomic level can alter the very characteristics that are being measured. The phenomenon is called "the observer effect," or "the quantum Zeno effect," after the Greek philosopher. Scientists found that continuous observation of unstable radioactive isotopes prevented the isotopes from disintegrating radioactively.[10] So, theoretically, if a nuclear bomb were observed intently enough by powerful enough minds, it might not explode. The immense power of our minds to affect the world around us—long a tenet of the Ageless Wisdom—is finally being discovered by science.

In addition, scientists are now able to demonstrate that our thoughts and emotions do indeed affect the health of our bodies. Dr. Candace Pert, formerly of the National Institute of Mental Health, and a researcher in the new field of psychoneuroimmunology, says that "the mind is what heals the body. Literally, your body is the outward manifestation of your mind." *Newsweek* notes that "psychoneuroimmunology will become . . . the most important medical field in the 21st century. Healthy thinking may eventually become an integral aspect of treatment for everything from allergies to liver transplants."[11]

The New York Times reported that Dr. Redford B. Williams found that angry, cynical people are five times more likely to die under the age of fifty than people who are calm and trusting.[12] Dr. Herbert Benson of Boston's Deaconess Hospital and author of the best-selling *The Relaxation Response* has found that 80 percent of the patients to whom he taught meditation and prayer were able to reduce either their blood pressure or their drug use.[13] Researchers at both Harvard University and the University of California-Riverside have shown that people who think positively are healthier, maintain better relationships, and have better jobs.[14] Patricia Norris, a researcher at the Menninger Clinic, points out that a number of studies have all demonstrated the capacity of the immune system to respond to intentional behavioral strategies and mental visualization.[15]

As the ancient Greek philosopher Socrates once said, "There is no disease of the body apart from the mind." Human thoughts and emotions are actually energies that pour through a person's etheric, or energy body, and tangibly affect the etheric body of everyone and everything in the environment. Positive, loving thoughts are health-producing. Negative, fearful, hateful thoughts aid the disease process.

Energy Follows Thought

This is a well-known metaphysical truth that we have personally verified in our daily life, and we invite you to test it out for yourself. Try setting aside one day in which you think only negative, critical, worrisome thoughts. Then observe what happens that day. The next day try thinking only positive, loving, hopeful thoughts, and again observe the experiences you have. This should be a very effective experiment in demonstrating how we "create our own reality."

The idea of an individual mind's ability to affect other minds is becoming widely accepted. Over 67 percent of Americans report having experienced ESP, according to the National Opinion Research Council of the University of Chicago.[16] Since the publication of *The Secret Life of Plants* by Peter Tompkins and Christopher Bird in 1973, thousands of people have duplicated Clive Backster's initially startling discoveries of the effects of human thoughts on plant growth.

In Russia, the power of the mind and Spirit to heal the body is widely recognized. Since scientists claim that we are apparently using only a very small percentage of the capacity of our brains, perhaps the rest of the brain is involved in this more subtle arena of awareness.

If our personal thoughts and emotions affect our own health and life so dramatically, we'd need to explore how our collective thoughts and attitudes affect our collective health as a nation and planet. And just as we are moving towards a preventive ethic in our personal health, so must we in our collective political health. To deal with the causes of the problems in the world, we believe it is necessary to explore the thoughts and emotions that gave rise to them. The workings of the Law of Correspondences—"As below, so above; as above, so below"—taught by the ancient metaphysician Hermes Trismegistus thousands of years ago, can help us understand the effects of the microcosm (the individual) on the macrocosm (the larger society), as well as the effect of society and the universe on the individual. By studying either one in depth, we begin to gain a deeper understanding of the workings of the other. Once we realize the collective effect of our smallest thoughts, we may be motivated to use our Divine powers more consciously and carefully.

Pattern in Chaos

In "chaos theory," which is becoming increasingly popular in scientific circles, "the butterfly effect" explains how a tiny cause, such as the movement of a butterfly's wings somewhere on our planet, can create a chain of tiny causes and effects that eventually results in a major effect, such as a typhoon, thousands of miles away. The seeds of a major event—like the *perestroika* revolution in the former Soviet Union—are sown far ahead of its actual occurrence. Mikhail Gorbachev and his foreign minister, Eduard Shevardnadze, for example, seriously studied the new paradigm thinking that had been brought to the Soviet Union many years before by a few pioneering citizen diplomats from the United States, and they saw the need to totally transform their society.[17] One event builds quietly on another until the final outcome erupts on the front pages of our newspapers. At the heart of the most random or chaotic event lies order, pattern, and causality, if only we can learn to see it in a large enough context.

THE PLANETARY WEB OF LIFE

The more deeply one studies the inner workings of life, the more wonderful and expansive they become. The more one studies the outer, the less it means and the more ignorant become those who engage in it solely.

—BENJAMIN FRANKLIN[18]

How does this interconnectedness of life work? Modern physics sees matter not as autonomous particles acting and reacting against one another, but rather as a network of relationships. All matter in the universe is connected like the strands of a spider's web. Even the tiniest movement in one place sends a wave all around the world, back to where the movement started. Each actor is thus also acted upon. The Lakota Sioux have a word for this—*mitak' oyas'in*—"all my relations," which acknowledges the individual's relationship to all of life.

Even political leaders are beginning to acknowledge this interconnection. Mikhail Gorbachev called for "the formation of an integrated universal consciousness," which he described as "a form of spiritual communion and rebirth for mankind." He said, "For all the contradictions of the present-day world, for all the diversity of social and political systems in it, this world is nevertheless one whole."[19]

According to the teachings of the Ageless Wisdom, every aspect of life, from the smallest organism up to a human being, affects all the other aspects of life through the planetary "web of life," the "etheric body." This body, which contains the "vital" or "life force," is the subtle energy field or framework upon which the physical body of an individual or a planet is built. It affects an individual's body through the endocrine glands. This energy body is a web of energy streams, lines of force and of light that sustain the whole and provide the patterning for the physical body. The human energy body is, in turn, fed by energies from the planetary and solar energy systems. This network of infinitely intricate energy lines nourishes, controls, and galvanizes the nervous system and carries the life force or vitality. The etheric body is strengthened or vitalized by fresh air, sunshine, physical exercise, rest, and positive thoughts and emotions.

Sir Isaac Newton, an initiate of the Ageless Wisdom, accepted the idea of this universal medium, which he called "aether." Consider the following, which he wrote in his *Principia Mathematica* in 1687:

> A certain and most subtle spirit . . . pervades and lies hid in all gross bodies, by the force and action of which spirit, the particles of bodies mutually attract one another at near distances, and cohere if contiguous; . . . all sensation is excited . . . by the vibrations of this spirit, mutually propagated along the solid filaments of the nerves.

The constant circulation of human, planetary, and solar life forces through the etheric bodies of all forms is the basis of manifested life and the expression of the essential nonseparateness of all life. All forms are interrelated and interdependent through the shared planetary etheric body. Everything is energy moving at different rates of vibration. Lines of light pass from form to form, constantly circulating energy, some moving slowly and some more rapidly, depending on the level of consciousness. The only differences among forms are the levels of consciousness, which affect the rates of vibration of the etheric body.

Vibration quickens and consciousness expands as form progresses through each higher kingdom. In the mineral kingdom, the vibration is slow and dense and expresses itself through radiation. In the plant kingdom, sensitivity and color are developed, and in the animal kingdom, movement. In the human kingdom, there is the principle of self-awareness, which is now developing into group and planetary awareness. Humans act as a bridge between the realms of nature and of Spirit, for we contain elements of the mineral, plant, animal, and spiritual kingdoms within our makeup.

Many traditional religious teachings also reflect this interconnection of life, within an omnipresent Divine Being. In the West, the Bible tells us: "In Him we live and move and have our being" (Acts 17:28). In the East, the Bhagavad Gita states: "Having pervaded the universe with a fragment of Myself, I remain." Zen Buddhism teaches: "One Nature, perfect and pervading, circulates in all natures." In the medieval alchemical manuscript *The Book of the Twenty-four Philosophers*, God is defined as "an infinite sphere whose center is everywhere and whose circumference is nowhere." The Oneida Indians say: "Everything is alive, everything is related, everything is connected, and everything affects everything else."

Interestingly, physicists call the smallest particle that holds the atom together the "charmed quark," and its symbol is a heart. From a metaphysical perspective, this is very accurate, as it is the energy of love that holds all of the universe together. In all the world's major religions, God is love.

THE DIVINE PURPOSE BEHIND HUMAN EVOLUTION

"God governs in the affairs of men," Benjamin Franklin told our First Continental Congress two hundred years ago. Our Founding Fathers understood something of the Divine Purpose that fires the heart and unveils the future, bringing insight into the mystery of world events.

We can reclaim our power as a people by aligning ourselves with this Divine Purpose as a catalyzing fire within our hearts and within the heart of the body politic. In our work we have found that an immense amount of help is available from spiritual dimensions if we but ask for it. However, we also have to be willing to do our part—by changing our dysfunctional patterns of thought and taking practical action where needed. We can work as co-creators or partners with the Divine, rather than thinking we have to work entirely alone or just be passive receivers of spiritual guidance or help.

This awareness has been tremendously helpful for us personally in starting our community and in writing this book. We know that there is a role each of us can play, on both outer and inner levels, in aiding human evolution. The impact of even one spiritually motivated individual in effecting political change can be seen clearly when viewed on an inner level. The light and love generated by individuals and groups radiates throughout human consciousness like waves of sunlight, lifting the spirits of depressed people and giving new hope, vitality, and strength to those who are seeking truth and striving to live in harmony with Spirit. Understanding this is tremendously empowering, for it helps us to realize that we no longer have to be victims of powerful political forces we don't fully understand or control. What we do, and what we think, affects every other living being in the web of Life.

As the two of us have journeyed through the inner landscape, looking behind the scenes of events, we have personally found that there is much cause for hope—despite the dire crises on the evening news. Examining each event from the inner side, we can begin to see in each the larger context of an evolving Divine Purpose—an outworking Will that fosters the evolution of consciousness as well as the evolution of physical forms. History is simply the record of this unfolding Divine Purpose. It is the record of humanity receiving—and either expressing or resisting—each new Divine idea for human evolution. It is the Will of Divinity that we human beings have personal free will, which gives us the freedom to choose to live according to spiritual law or not. But we also must live with the consequences of our choices over time. However, if we develop our capacity to use our free will wisely and carefully, the benefits of choosing to align ourselves with Divine Will become abundantly clear.

Viewing human history from an inner perspective gives us a very different understanding. One of the things we begin to notice is that great spiritual initiates have conditioned whole civilizations for centuries. For example, Moses brought us the concept of Divine Law. Jesus taught us about the need to love one another and not meet violence with more violence. We're still trying to live up to His teaching! Very often these great souls are ahead of their time, and many are abused and oppressed in their own countries, but then, years after their death, they are revered as heroes and saints. Nevertheless, the evolution of consciousness always moves in the direction of greater love, inclusiveness, tolerance, synthesis, freedom, and empowerment, however slowly and painfully.

According to the Ageless Wisdom, growth proceeds through building and then destroying what we've created: "In the shattering of forms lies hid the secret of evolution." The life or consciousness within a form shatters it when it has outgrown its usefulness, because the indwelling life is too powerful for the form. At each step, a new form (physical, emotional, or mental) is created by the ability of the evolving human consciousness to more adequately express itself. This can be a new physical body or structure, a new emotional expression, or a new idea or belief system. But eventually each new form will become limiting and hold us back from taking the next step in our growth. At this point it must in turn be destroyed, or withdrawn from, and a new form created. Physical, emotional, and mental forms need constantly to be destroyed to allow the life within to evolve. Great reformers appear time and again when consciousness is held in bondage by form, to help humanity break free of our self-created prisons. Abraham Lincoln, who broke the bonds of slavery in the United States, is an example of such a great leader.

As our knowledge of the physical sciences grows, events that were once strange and mysterious to our ancestors are now understood by means of the insights science gives us into the physical laws of nature. In a similar fashion, we believe it is now possible to apply a new paradigm—a metaphysical science, with its own metaphysical laws—to understand the causes of unexpected political or natural crises that have until now been seen as mysterious "acts of God" or the result of random causes.

As this new, yet ancient, metascience expands, we will eventually understand what is today incomprehensible. The evolution of human consciousness can be viewed as a gradual awakening to these laws, and the outworking of Divinely inspired ideas in human life.

Chapter Two

◆

THE SYMBOLISM AND SIGNIFICANCE OF WORLD EVENTS

It is the light of symbolism that shall outshine the light of the torches of the siren, Commercialism.

—LEO TOLSTOY

The Chinese character for "crisis" is made up of two ideograms, "danger" and "opportunity." The crises in the world today—crime, racial and ethnic violence, skyrocketing debt, environmental devastation, the increasing numbers of poor and homeless people, the breakdown of the family, the rapid spread of AIDS—are very dangerous, yet they also provide great opportunities for our growth as a human species. The Ageless Wisdom teaches that crises become opportunities when they are read symbolically in the Book of Life and understood for the lessons they offer. Life on earth is a "programmed learning environment" where everyone receives the specific lessons they need for their growth.

Just as we as individuals often reflect deeply on our lives and make major adjustments after an illness or family crisis, so social crises can be used as opportunities for all of us to take stock of what's really important to us and make needed changes. Each of the global crises that we experience collectively as citizens of planet Earth has something of major importance to teach us if we are willing to take the curriculum and learn the lesson.

For example, Hurricane Andrew, which devastated the Florida coast in 1992, helped many people return to an appreciation of what is most important in life—their inner strength and love of their family and friends, not their lost possessions. One of the victims said, "We know that the wind was God talking to us. I think He was saying you have to get closer to each other, learn to work with each other better. . . ."[1]

THE SPIRITUAL LESSONS OF CRISES

Our use and abuse of free will on this planet offers many opportunities for growth. Each of the crises we encounter in the "school of hard knocks" serves a higher purpose by helping us grow and evolve toward greater love, cooperation, and understanding of our place in the universe. On a spiritual level, it may be that our Higher Selves viewed these negative experiences as the only—or fastest—way to wake us up so we can begin to make needed changes in our consciousness.

The glaring problem of homelessness, for example, is confronting Americans with the limitations and injustices of the social system we've created—with its vast gulf between the rich and poor in this country. We are becoming painfully aware that this gulf has widened in the last decade, for we can't avoid seeing the homeless everywhere we go on our city streets. Perhaps some of the homeless are Souls who inwardly choose to make a major sacrifice to teach us about the inequities of our system. However, on a deeper symbolic level, homelessness also confronts each of us with our feelings about what constitutes our true home and about the transiency of any material sense of home and security not rooted in a deeper experience of our eternal Selves. Floods, earthquakes, and hurricanes provide us with opportunities to learn detachment from material things and places, and break up crystallized thinking.

It seems sometimes that humanity grows and learns only through pain. According to the Ageless Wisdom, pain as a teacher is more relevant to Earth experience than any other place in the universe. When we experience pain, it serves an important purpose in making us more sensitive to the needs and pain of others and more aware of changes that are needed in our attitudes and behavior. We have found that pain can thus catalyze spiritual growth. Philosopher David Spangler notes:

[A] profound planetary spirit of love and goodwill is at work, using the instability and the individuals that emerge from it as a farmer uses a plow, to turn the soil and prepare it for new seed and a new harvest. Everything happening in the world now represents a cry from humanity for a transformation; a cry for help in achieving another step toward its destiny. It is the separativeness of humanity that will be challenged, often by being highlighted.[2]

From the perspective of the Ageless Wisdom, the meaning of the word *spiritual* is far broader than a specific religious connotation. "Spiritual" applies to anything that relates to the expansion of consciousness; that drives an individual or society forward toward some form of development—

physical, emotional, mental, intuitive—and that develops greater under-standing, love, or beauty.

This transformative process of learning through pain that we, as human-ity, seem to use takes place through the events in our individual and col-lective lives. In both physics and metaphysics, events can be defined as the end result of the intersection of energies of different frequencies. These fre-quencies of energy represent the culmination of a vast combination of causes that produce the outer event.

The Four Levels of Events
Events can be viewed from four different levels or perspectives:

1. *The level of information*—facts and data, our usual human response.
2. *The level of symbology*—what the symbols of names, places, and events tell us about the inner forces and energies at work.
3. *The level of meaning*—what events mean to us when seen through the eyes of a compassionate heart that understands the love and growth of-fered by spiritual lessons.
4. *The level of significance*—how the event relates to the fulfillment of the Divine evolutionary Will and the outworking of the purpose for our planet.

When we view them symbolically through the mind, it seems that all physical events are shaped by consciousness, and their names may even symbolize some of the inner forces at work.

For example, Colonel Oliver North's name symbolizes "El Norte," as Central American people often call North America and its policies of op-pression and manipulation. The British ferry *Herald of Free Enterprise* sank in 1987, with much media attention, perhaps symbolizing the sinking state of the British economy at the time.

When we approach events with a compassionate heart, it becomes possible for us to identify with all the actors on the world stage, to stand in their shoes and see the world as they do. The great Mississippi floods of 1993 gave the entire nation an opportunity to experience sudden, unexpected loss and to open their hearts by seeing how people helped each other, contributing food and other needed aid from around the country. The inner meaning of an event is then revealed as we come to understand how love is present or being developed within the circumstances of people's lives.

The significance of an event is determined by its relationship to the dy-namic of Divine Will, the power of Deity that holds the perfected comple-tion of all evolutionary activity as a timeless, already accomplished fact. Thus, an event—whether it seems positive or negative in the short run—is significant to the degree or extent that it helps us all evolve to higher consciousness and realize the unity and purpose of life. Thus, an event involving the United Nations, an organization that symbolizes our aspirations toward global cooperation, is usually more significant than a purely local event. As we grow in our understanding of significance, we can then use our free will to choose to align with God's will.

A symbol is an outward and visible sign of an inward and spiritual reality. Events, circumstances, and physical phenomena of every kind are simply symbols of what is occurring in the inner worlds. They allow us to see the conditioning energies in the environment as energies in action.

A symbol opens the door to the eternal and brings our individual lives into relationship with the unchanging whole. Symbols are tools that allow us to read the secrets of inner realities by focusing the mind and introducing into it certain associated ideas and feelings. Symbols, like great art, trigger a deeper level of understanding.

Asking the New Questions

To recognize the symbolic message in events, we can work to empty our minds of preconceived opinions about events. A good beginning is to release the thought-forms created by newscasters analyzing the news in the ordinary way. We need to keep viewing events in a fresh light, letting go of the heavy baggage of our preconceived opinions and partisanship. One helpful approach to doing this is to meditate regularly, as this develops the stance of an "objective observer." To do this, try sitting quietly and reflecting. Ask yourself the following questions:

• What are the inner forces at work here behind the scenes?
• Do the names involved in this event offer any clues to its *symbolic* meaning?
• Does the timing of this event tell us anything?
• Are there other people or events that this event seems "coincidentally" tied to? Does this offer us some deeper hints about what is really going on?
• What is this event teaching all of us through the experience of the people involved? What do we need to let go of?
• Can we understand the *meaning* behind all of this by compassionately identifying with each of the actors involved and trying to see the world from their perspective? Can we drop our sense of separateness and see our interconnection as one human family? What is the underlying call for love in this crisis?
• How does this event serve a positive *purpose* in helping humanity's evolution in some way and so fulfilling the Divine Plan?

As we were writing this book, we were invited to speak on this theme to a conference in North Carolina, and on the trip back to Washington we experienced an amusing incident that we felt was symbolic for us. Some of the manuscript for this book was in Corinne's briefcase, and as we were leaving the plane, an older man kindly offered to help carry it. Since it wasn't particularly heavy, the help was politely refused, but he insisted. He picked it up and proceeded to walk quickly straight ahead to where his car was waiting. But it wasn't in the direction we needed to go, so we followed him and finally got the briefcase back. When he introduced himself, we looked at each other knowingly. He was Senator Strom Thurmond (R-SC), one of the most conservative members of the Senate.

Most people would simply have found it interesting to meet an actual senator in person and then would have written the incident off. But we'd been thinking about symbolism for too long to let this one pass. Perhaps it was a reminder that those with old, crystallized belief systems will always march straight ahead on the path they've always followed. They will insist on their version of old-fashioned values without thinking about the needs of others—even when they're honestly trying to be of help. It was also interesting to note that he was attracted on some unconscious level to the manuscript in our briefcase and seemed to want to have it with him.

Another interesting symbolic event that we experienced was noting the particular slide that just happened to get stuck in the slide projector when we were showing "The Spiritual Heritage and Destiny of America" in Britain for the first time, after showing it in the U.S. hundreds of times without incident. The jammed slide pictured the American colonists toppling a statue of King George. When we laughed and explained what happened, a British man stood up and gently said, "You just can't show that slide here!"

As we begin to see the world through a symbolic lens, we also notice events all around us in a new way. For example, the covered plaza at the headquarters of the Federal Reserve Bank in Washington, D.C., has become a favorite spot for the homeless, and even *The Washington Post* noted that many critics see this as a perfect symbol for the failure of capitalism. The Statue of Freedom atop the U.S. Capitol dome captivated many as it was taken down to be cleaned for the first time ever in May 1993, symbolizing our need as a nation to clean up our collective expression of freedom, and learn the difference between freedom and license.

Television commentators pointed to the symbolism of Federal Reserve Chairman Alan Greenspan being seated between President Clinton's and Vice President Gore's wives at the first State of the Union message to Congress. They wondered if this symbolized that Greenspan was in the new administration's pocket—while others feared that maybe it was a message to everyone about the power of the Federal Reserve and all the nation's banks it represents.

Architect Pierre-Charles L'Enfant, who drew up the original plans for Washington, D.C., had designed Pennsylvania Avenue to be a straight line from Congress to the White House. However, since President Jackson decided to put the Treasury Building on the corner and the road has to jog around it, we can note the symbolism of the Treasury's location, and the effect of money on the relationship.

THE SYMBOLOGY OF NAMES

The following analyses of events are offered as examples to help catalyze your thinking and to encourage you to try your hand at creative interpretations of the symbolism and meaning of events. First we will explore the names of some events, as they sometimes provide interesting clues about the deeper forces at work. Then we will explore the deeper meaning and significance of additional events. The following are just a few examples, to help you pay attention to names:

Love Canal: Poisoning the Birth Canal
In 1976 it was discovered that for years, toxic chemicals had been dumped in upstate New York in the Love Canal by Hooker Chemical Company and others. A "hooker," or prostitute, distorts the true sense of love for profit, just as the chemical company prostituted the "love canal" (symbolic of the birth canal) into a place of poison and fear for financial gain. On a deeper level, this distortion of love by a "hooker" harms the birth canal of the mother—Mother Earth—and so damages her children. The destruction of our environment by chemicals is a grave threat to human health and the delicate ecological balance of our planet. It affects future generations yet unborn who may have to enter a poisoned birth canal.

The Atlantis Space Shuttle: Misusing Power
Atlantis was the name of a space shuttle that carried a secret military cargo on its first mission in December of 1988. Atlantis was also the name of the legendary island kingdom that is said to have blown up and sunk beneath the ocean because of misuse of power. Many people believe the United States has misused its military power to protect its economic interest around the world, and that it is trying to extend its military dominance into space in an inappropriate way. In case the name was not enough to evoke a resonance, *The Washington Post* reported that "in keeping with the

mission, the voice of *Star Wars* character Darth Vader, with the theme from the movie as background music, provided the five-man military crew with their wake-up call this morning."[3] Darth Vader was the leader of the evil forces, "the Empire," against whom the film's heroes were fighting. Why did the U.S. military choose to use this voice, and why was this one of the few details revealed about the secret shuttle?

Korean Airliner 007: Creating Your Own Reality
In 1983 a South Korean airliner, suspected of being on a mission to spy on Soviet missile bases with cameras and test Soviet border protection, was shot down by the Russians. That flight was numbered "007"—the code number of Ian Fleming's famous British spy character James Bond. The code meant that the agent was "licensed to kill." Among the passengers killed on that airplane was Rep. Larry McDonald (D-GA), chairman of the anticommunist John Birch Society. Coincidence? Or is there a symbolic message reflecting the inner reality here? Could it be that years of fearing and hating communists drew to him what he feared most, and thus he helped create his own reality?

Peter Haze: Creating Pollution
Sometimes a person's name can give their whole game away. We nearly fell off our chairs laughing one evening when the manager of a chemical plant in Colorado named Peter Haze was being interviewed about reports that his plant was polluting the environment. His name was on the screen while a noticeable *haze* was visible in the sky in the background, yet he was denying with a straight face that his plant had caused any pollution.

National Health Care: Do We Care About Real Health?
Our national debate on health care is symbolic of deeper questions than insurance coverage, cost containment, and doctor's fees. It's about whether we see health related only to our physical body, or to our whole being—body, mind, and spirit. Can we take individual responsibility for our health, preventing "dis-ease" through conscious living, rather than seeing our bodies as machines we can abuse and then have repaired at the medical "body shop" with everyone paying the bills.

The health care debate on a deeper level is really about what creates a healthy life. And it leads us to ask if we can be truly healthy and free of disease if we are living lives of greed, anger, fear, and selfishness. It also raises the issue of whether we can be healthy individuals in a morally degenerating, crime-ridden society. Can we recognize that individual health is connected to the health of all?

THE DEEPER SYMBOLISM AND SIGNIFICANCE OF EVENTS

Events can also be analyzed from a deeper symbolic level to understand their metaphysical meaning and significance and to explore the deeper lessons they offer in the school of life. Here are some examples from recent years:

The Assassination of John F. Kennedy: Confronting the Issue of Evil

For both of us personally and for most of our generation, John Kennedy's sudden and violent assassination was of major significance and left a lasting impression. It was probably one of the defining moments of the century, and it still remains a festering sore in the American psyche. It marks the beginning of broad public distrust of our government, since so many people believe they have not been told the truth about it, and their rage and grief has hardened into cynicism. Thirty years later the assassination continues to unfold as a far-flung and intricate murder mystery—a tale of good and evil, with the true identity and motive of his killer(s) still a key question for most Americans.

Perhaps the worst legacy left by the two Kennedy assassinations and that of Martin Luther King, Jr., was the overwhelming violation of our faith in leadership and in the system, hitting us hard with the message that if you speak up and confront those abusing power—the Mafia, the military, the CIA, the oil, steel, and banking industries, and racists, as they did—you will be silenced.

Michael Lerner, editor of *Tikkun* magazine, noted that the assassinations defeated our national sense of optimism and our sense that social movements could be successful in bringing about change. Coeditor Peter Gabel pointed out that the real tragedy of JFK's death was "the sudden, violent loss for millions of people of the part of themselves that had opened up, or begun to open up, during his presidency." Berkeley professor Peter Dale Scott charged that blaming one crazy, lone gunman gave the nation a nonpolitical account of the assassination, leaving us in collective denial, pretending that our political democracy still worked.[4]

Some spiritual teachers have said that John Kennedy was only just beginning his work, that he had a greater global work to do beyond the United States in implementing a universal vision of peace, justice, and racial equality. His famous words at the Berlin Wall, *"Ich bin ein Berliner—I am a Berliner"*—were a powerful expression of humanity's essential oneness and evoked a tremendous response. Some of the 1960s generation were Souls who had incarnated to help him with his global work. The real tragedy was how his untimely assassination so confused and angered them that they withdrew their energy from constructive change in the world for many years.

Although he certainly had a number of human flaws himself, especially in the obsessive way he related to women and sex, in some areas Kennedy may have been too far ahead of his time for people who were mired in their inertia and fear of change. Many people weren't ready to face the spiritual challenges he posed for them: "Ask not what your country can do for you, ask what you can do for your country."

JFK's assassination has been a central allegory in the history of our nation and one whose final moral message is up to us as a people to write. Since the facts surrounding his death have still not been proven to the satisfaction of most of us, we are forced to deal with a monumental issue we'd rather avoid: the question of evil on a grand scale. Was the assassination the work of an evil conspiracy to take over our government? This idea confronts the very foundations of our democracy: the right of citizens to know the truth and to be in control of their own government. Perhaps Kennedy's Soul took on martyrdom for a larger purpose than we can yet see. Perhaps his death was intended to motivate us as citizens to take back our government from the evil manipulators of power, money, and covert influence.

The Ageless Wisdom teaches that there has been organized evil throughout history, and that these Dark Forces have always had their cycles and times of triumph when hatred, cruelty, chaos and violence ruled many lands—only the specific identities and roles have changed over time. However, their true purpose in the Divine Plan is always to challenge us: to test us and strengthen us until we recognize them, call them by their true names, and overcome our fear by standing up to them.

Fletcher Prouty, who was featured as Mr. X in Oliver Stone's movie *JFK* and who worked with the Joint Chiefs of Staff from 1955 to 1964 to provide military support for the Secret Service and for covert CIA operations worldwide, spoke openly in an interview about what he fears is happening to this country. He believes the assassination was basically a coup d'état by a secret group so powerful that world leaders must deal with it. He said that in 1963 Secretary of Defense McNamara told General Prulac that he needed approval from a certain powerful but mysterious civilian before he could order withdrawal of personnel from Vietnam—and this was refused.

Prouty claims that the main point behind Kennedy's assassination was not only to eliminate him because he was about to order withdrawal from Vietnam, but rather to deliver a powerful message to the world that "if we can kill a U.S. president—as well as over 150 witnesses to his death—we can certainly kill you."[5] Kennedy had presented a proposal to the UN called "Blueprint for the Peace Race: A Treaty on General and Complete

Disarmament" on September 25, 1961—which no doubt threatened the military-industrial complex. Lyndon Johnson, quoted in *The Atlantic Monthly* in July 1973, said that the U.S. government had been running its own "Murder Incorporated," plotting the death of foreign leaders like Fidel Castro of Cuba, who were seen as a threat.[6]

As Abraham Lincoln wisely noted, "you can't fool all the people all the time." The public's intuitive wisdom said that despite the Warren Commission's cover-up, there had to be something much larger and more evil than a lone assassin. A December 1991 *Time*/CNN opinion poll (taken *before* Oliver Stone's film *JFK* was released) found that 75 percent of Americans believe there was a conspiracy around Kennedy's death, and 50 percent believe the CIA was somehow involved. Stone's popular film, based on the premise that there was a megaconspiracy and coup d'état, has helped build public pressure to have the assassination archives reopened—which is at least a beginning.

As writer John Welwood sadly noted recently, most of the U.S. media has been behaving more and more like a dysfunctional family on the subject of the assassination, engaging in characteristic denial. The media offensive against both Louisiana attorney Jim Garrison, who brought a suspected assassin to trial, as well as against Oliver Stone for his film, resembles the attacks of abusive parents against their children for exposing the family secrets.[7]

Perhaps there is significance for our nation in the fact that we remember John Kennedy on November 22—the date of his death—rather than on his birthday, May 29. We celebrate his death—not his life. To honor his life and what he stood for, perhaps we need look again at the ideal that was key to him: courage. He not only wrote an award-winning book on the courageous decisions of political leaders (*Profiles in Courage*), he saw politics as a noble profession and the best way to solve our common problems. This may have been the central meaning of Kennedy's life and death—that we must internalize the courage we admired in Kennedy and look evil squarely in the face to find his true murderer(s), and that we must *demand* political courage of our elected officials today more than ever—and stop denying our problems.

JFK's assassination may also offer many of us (especially those who came of age at this turbulent time in the '60s) some deeper lessons about life and death—universal lessons that all Souls eventually need to learn. Many idealists see the death of a great leader as a loss, and they feel victimized and confused, lost in their personal drama of sadness. They are often unable or unwilling to see the larger pattern or purpose of a death that may in the end prove more necessary than continued physical life (e.g., Kennedy's civil rights program moving more quickly through Congress because of his death). Detachment from the form—the physical body—is always a key lesson in the Soul's journey.

A healing of the psychic wound left by Kennedy's death may be currently underway in the national psyche—symbolized by the positive ending in a recent film on an attempted assassination called *Line of Fire*. A secret service agent (representing Everyman) overcomes his own sense of guilt and failure over not protecting President Kennedy, and effectively stops another assassination attempt thirty years later. Just as the agent had to stop blaming himself for Kennedy's death and resist the twisted guilt-tripping of a would-be assassin, today we too are transcending our fears that good leaders will always be destroyed by evil that we can't stop. We are restoring our faith in the ultimate triumph of good.

(For more on Kennedy, see also chapter 5 on Prophecy and chapter 9 on the Forces of Light and Darkness.)

The Vietnam War: Painful Lessons on All Sides

The Vietnam Veterans Memorial in Washington, D.C., is a perfect psychological symbol of the war. Unlike past glorious war memorials, this one is dark, low to the ground, listing thousands and thousands of names on a plain, mirrorlike surface that reflects the faces of the visitors who pass silently by. It overwhelms people with the huge numbers of casualties, greatly deglamorizing the mystique of war. Escalating swiftly after John Kennedy's assassination, the war was a dark mirror for us as a nation, reflecting the inner war in our national psyche—a split between generations and between conflicting views of authority.

The older generation, growing up with the glory and moral certitude of World War II and years of anticommunist indoctrination, could see only "evil" communists in Vietnam, exactly the way they had viewed the "evil" Nazis. The younger generation, (including the two of us) could see only how they or their friends were being forcibly drafted to fight an unpopular war in a remote part of the world. The ferocity of the protests and the entrenchment of the governments headed by Presidents Johnson and Nixon created a deeply divided nation. The inner war in the American pysche struggled with the meaning of Vietnam, the true nature of patriotism, the need for courage to speak out against unwise authority, and the need for loving understanding of those with different opinions.

On the level of meaning, the Vietnam War, like many other wars, provided a testing ground for those who served, in courage and in overcoming fear of death. But another test in courage was faced by those who refused to go to Vietnam—the courage to speak out against a war they believed to be unjust, as many people did. Vietnam probably helped catalyze the feminist movement as well, as a reaction to the macho calls to defeat communism and defend "the American way." The shallowness of this, and its cost in terms of lives lost on both sides, soon became too high a price to pay. For a time after Vietnam, war was no longer seen as a glorious arena in which to prove one's manhood. After all, despite all our great firepower, a simple peasant people had defeated us. Since Americans had previously believed that God was always on our side in a war, and we were always in the right, Vietnam was the perfect setup to deflate our national ego and erode confidence in something we were inordinately proud of—our military prowess.

Ironically, many who went to war to prove their manhood ended up losing it, coming home crippled or castrated, as was painfully dramatized in the popular film *Born on the Fourth of July*. In the debate over the invasion of Iraq in 1991, the humbling experiences of Vietnam continued to haunt us. We didn't want to face another defeat by a Third World country or endure the loss of thousands of American lives.

From the suffering on all sides during the Vietnam War, a deeper meaning and significance unfolded. Like the fire immolating the Vietnamese monk who protested the war but whose pure heart did not burn, the fires of passion about Vietnam scorched this nation for many years. But our hearts are finally being purified. In recent years there has begun to be a healing of the old wounds as each side honestly evaluates the wisdom of the other.

A true healing will only be complete when the U.S. achieves reconciliation with Vietnam and its people, just as we have with other former enemies. Karmically, we must help end the continuing suffering of Vietnam's people, because we have contributed so much to its cause.

The wisdom of the antiwar youth proved prophetic as the situation in Vietnam became more and more like quicksand for American troops. Even the prowar supporters finally acknowledged it as a mistake. As a result, the voting age was dropped so young people would have some voice in possible future wars. The draft was abolished, and a volunteer army was developed. Many began to wake up to the unrestrained, self-serving power of the military-industrial complex that President Eisenhower had warned us about.

On the other side, antiwar protesters saw what a mess the communists made of South Vietnam when they took it over, and they realized their own naiveté. To make up for past insensitivities during Vietnam, many former protesters made a point of supporting and honoring individual Americans in the Gulf war, while still criticizing the policy of war itself. Some Vietnam veterans have felt inwardly moved to return to Vietnam and help rebuild the nation they destroyed. Others have formed support groups with former Soviet veterans of the Afghanistan war, to share their similar, painful experiences.

Nuclear Energy: A "New Clear" Message

The word *nuclear* sounds like "new clear." Because the threat of nuclear weapons is still so frightening, it makes issues very clear: nuclear bombs are not weapons—they are tools of self-annihilation.

On the level of meaning and the unfoldment of love, the issue of nuclear war tells us something about our individual as well as national tasks. Since "the macrocosm reflects the microcosm," the international issue won't be solved until more of us are able to create love and peace on a personal and interpersonal level. Both the physical and the psychological weapons that we use against one another must be reduced. On the level of significance or purpose, it is clear that the nuclear issue is forcing humanity to learn to coexist with diversity and with political and economic systems that are different from our own. This, ultimately, will allow us to live as one united, human family.

On a deeper level, the nuclear issue can help us explore where our true security lies. Will we ever feel secure, no matter how many weapons we have, if we constantly fear an enemy who is also insecure? Does focusing all our fear on an exterior enemy merely help us avoid dealing with our disowned shadow—our own inner aggression that we project on others? Is there anything we can do outwardly in the world that will bring us all peace of mind? Or has the time come to find security on the only level where it is truly possible—inwardly, within our own hearts and souls, trusting in God's evolutionary purpose? We then can begin working together to find win/win solutions to our problems. Only *mutual* security—security for all, rather than *national* security—will make us truly safe.

The major application of nuclear energy today is based on fission of the atom—separation and division. This is symbolic of the basic problem we are facing today—the sense of separateness, among nations, among groups, and among individuals. In splitting the atom, we have lost the sacred fire of unity itself at its most basic level—the essential energy that holds our physical world together. This atomic fission has caused innumerable problems—poisonous radiation from nuclear accidents such as Three Mile Island and Chernobyl, fear of total destruction by nuclear war, and problems with disposal of nuclear waste—"poisoned fire"—which will be contaminating planet Earth for generations.

But there is another process for releasing the power of the atom—through fusion rather than fission, a method that has been predicted in the

Ageless Wisdom as the energy of the future for humanity. Scientists may have discovered some clues to this in experiments with low temperature nuclear fusion, which brings atoms together rather than splitting them apart.[8] Fusion energy would create almost no harmful waste, unlike the nuclear fission process, and could be healing rather than destructive. Since the main ingredient needed in the process is seawater, fusion could provide unlimited cheap power and would not perpetuate global warming or acid rain.

In 1991 the United States, Japan, Russia, and the European Community agreed on a joint project called the International Thermonuclear Experimental Reactor program, which has very positive potential from a symbolic level, as it involves cooperation, a kind of fusion, among many nations.[9] Significantly, the United States hired 116 of its former enemies, Russian nuclear physicists, to work on the project, which heats isotopes of hydrogen under immense pressure until they fuse into helium and release energy. This project seems an appropriate symbol for the human process that the Americans and Soviets went through during the Cold War. We were overwhelmed with the psychological pressure of facing each other's nuclear warheads. In fact, "Mutually Assured Destruction," MAD, was the actual name of the U.S. nuclear program. This situation became so hot that there was nowhere to go besides blowing ourselves up—or fusing our efforts and finding new ways to solve humanity's energy needs together.

The Moral Re-Armament group says, "A chain reaction of forgiveness unleashes the power of fusion within societies, rather than the threat of uncontrolled fission. It is the energy source for social revolution in the 1990s."[10] The fusion process of bringing atoms together is symbolic of the energy of love, a powerful magnetic, fusing energy which unites the worlds. Our evolutionary purpose is to experience the greater benefits of love and healing that result from joining together in unity rather than splitting apart in separateness. Here, the processes of the microcosm embodied in the atom accurately reflect the macrocosm—the larger forces operating in society. Scientists note, however, that it would probably take thirty to forty-five years to make any fusion process usable—symbolic of the time it will probably take humanity to begin fusing or uniting together in consciousness as one people.

Chernobyl: A Border Meltdown

The former USSR was notoriously overprotective of its borders, terrified of being invaded, not letting ideas or people in or out, believing it could remain isolated. Some people have compared the former Soviet Union to a battered mother who was abused many times, lost her children, and became so terrified that she locked herself in her heavily protected home. But the fallout from the

Chernobyl nuclear accident on April 28, 1986, which was carried by the global wind well past Soviet borders, was painful and embarrassing. And it was symbolic of the larger reality that no nation can long remain separate from others or keep anything major a secret. Again, the "new clear" energy made things very clear. The post-Chernobyl Soviet policy of *glasnost*, or openness, was an appropriate change in response to this development.

Chernobyl ultimately became the worst nuclear accident in the world, with the deaths of over eight thousand people and the poisoning of vast areas of the Ukraine and Scandinavia. It is also interesting to note that in the Russian Bible, *chernobyl* is the Russian word for "wormwood," the name of the star that fell to earth and poisoned the waters in the Book of Revelation.[11]

Space Missions: Yearning for Heaven

The international effort to reach into space, "the final frontier," is symbolic of humanity's aspiration to reach "heaven." It produced the first photographs of planet Earth from space, the first symbolic rendering of human unity transcending national boundaries, which are invisible from space. In addition, many of the cosmonauts and astronauts, such as Edgar Mitchell and Rusty Schweickart, have had transformative spiritual experiences while in space and as a result returned to Earth with a powerful commitment to work for humanity as a whole, not just for their own nation.

About the time that man first landed on the Moon in 1969, the women's movement suddenly exploded. Could there be some deeper meaning in this? The Moon has symbolized the Great Goddess and the feminine polarity—just as the Sun has represented the masculine—in most ancient culture. Men standing on the Moon is symbolic of males finally beginning to see the Earth from a feminine perspective—as a unified whole—rather than the masculine view of it many separate parts. With this act humanity suddenly became self-reflective. This shift has had a tremendous influence on the thinking of the human race in the last twenty-five years, a period in which many men have been learning to love and respect their own feminine, nurturing side as they search for their own wholeness.

The human longing for heaven has too often been translated merely into a technological effort, linked to military goals. We have used space to compete, to achieve superiority over our opponents. The proposed U.S./ Russian space station is one of the first signs of the new consciousness reaching our attitudes toward space.

Interestingly, according to a public opinion survey, the explosion of the space shuttle *Challenger* on January 28, 1986, was the event that people said had the most impact on their lives in the last twenty years because it destroyed their faith in technology.[12] Perhaps this was the spiritual significance of the event—the need to break humanity's overreliance on technology to handle all our problems. We need to learn to deal with the human dimensions of problems, using technology as a tool rather than as a god. Space missions are a rather "macho" approach in the first place—a symbolically phallic rocket "penetrating" space. The explosions of several rockets, including the *Challenger*, at a time when the United States was focusing on its Star Wars technology in space, may have communicated a strong message about our overreliance on aggressive military solutions to problems.

Much media attention was focused on the death of the female civilian teacher, Christa McAuliffe, in the *Challenger* explosion. This reinforced the idea of the damaging effects of an excessively masculine approach on the feminine principle. Christa's name is significantly a feminization of Christ—symbolically pointing out her sacrifice for humanity. She also happened to be a teacher—and her death certainly taught us something. Many ordinary citizens could identify with the civilian schoolteacher who was killed and thus could reflect on the cost in human terms of our Cold War in space. The increasing militarization of the space program, and the planned Star Wars defense initiative, suffered a considerable setback from this cosmic message.

Several months after the *Challenger* shuttle exploded, three other American rockets—the Air Force Titan 34D, the Delta, and a third rocket over New Mexico—also exploded, thus reinforcing the message. The Delta's project manager even reported that the sharp cutoff of the engine occurred "almost as if it were a commanded shutdown."[13] Three of the twenty-two plutonium-carrying space missions have ended in disaster.[14] Another Titan rocket exploded in August 1993, followed by the loss of a weather satellite, and then the Mars observer. It seems clear that our space exploration will be limited until we deal with human problems on Earth.

The dramatic dysfunctioning of the mirrors on the Hubble space telescope in June of 1990 was another symbolic message. As the atmosphere of earth itself prevents us from seeing clearly into the heavens, placing a high-powered telescope in space seemed to be the answer. Scientists had hoped to see how black holes—collapsed stars—are formed. "We're blind from the ground," one of the scientists reported. "But when we get above the atmosphere, the universe opens up." Apparently, however, we took the distortions of our earth atmosphere with us, as there was no clear mirror to reflect the light emitted by the distant realms of the universe, caused by a greedy company's refusal to correct its known manufacturing error. Perhaps humanity is not yet ready to perceive a new view of God's universe, as we are still relying too heavily on our outer technological "mirrors"— rather than using our intuitive faculties to perceive spiritual truth.[15]

As if to make sure we got the message, another problem with flawed mirrors showed up the next month on advanced weather satellites orbiting the earth, leaving forecasters without the vital images they need to track storms and hurricanes—a situation that constituted a national emergency.[16]

Symbolically, an innovative Russian experiment in 1993, which showed a positive use of technology called "Operation Banner," used mirrors—not to view the heavens, as did the U.S. project, but to reflect the sun's rays back to earth as a stellar spotlight to light up sun-starved polar areas or blacked-out cities.

Early in 1988 the Congressional Office of Technology Assessment released parts of a study concluding that Reagan's Star Wars defense would probably fail "catastrophically," due largely to computer unreliability. Just as the House of Representatives was ready to vote on Star Wars funding, the computerized voting system in the House failed, and the vote had to be counted by hand.[17] Unfortunately, the House funded the program for another year, and the obvious symbolism was missed—that technology alone cannot solve our international human relations problems and provide security.

The Environmental Crisis: The Sacredness of All Life

The environmental crisis is symbolic of our lack of connection to the natural world and of the centuries-old split between spirituality and materiality. Too often spirituality has been interpreted as being otherworldly and disconnected from daily life, or religious doctrine has been used as a rationale for exploiting the biological systems of the planet with little regard for the consequences. Many traditional religions have sought to transcend nature and so have neglected the physical world. For example, the Hindus see the physical world as "maya"—illusion, while some Christians see it as the devil's arena for tempting humanity.

The Ageless Wisdom takes the view that we are both spiritual and material beings and we must honor all dimensions of ourselves. To do this we need to maintain awareness of the third principle—the Soul—which is the bridging consciousness between Spirit and matter. The Soul has the wisdom to keep Spirit and matter in balance. As the Soul, we would not become so detached from the world as to ignore humanity's need for help, nor would we become so overidentified with material reality as to forget our true spiritual identity.

The environmental crisis provides an opportunity to redefine the balance between Spirit and matter with a new ethic based on the sacredness of all life. With polluted water and air and toxic dumps affecting the health of many people directly for the first time and fears of global warming receiving front-page treatment, this crisis dramatically illustrates the sacred interconnection of all life. We are beginning to see that everything we do affects everything else. We can no longer attempt to solve a problem in an isolated way—without paying any attention to the whole context in which the problem occurs and without dealing with the long-term consequences. Polluting the rivers or the air affects others miles away and years later. Acid rain doesn't recognize national borders—pollution from American factories is carried in the rain that falls on Canadian trees. Recognizing and dealing with these problems requires love and concern for the effects of our actions on others.

From major floods as well as widespread drought, we learn humility because we come face to face with our dependence on nature and God for our sustenance. During the drought of 1988, the evening news showed farmers joining together in prayer and ceremonies for rain, reminiscent of Native American "rain dances."

The environmental crisis is motivating humankind to change its attitude about taking nature for granted and thereby "fouling its own nest." The deeper significance of this crisis is to help humanity recognize its purpose of incarnating Spirit on earth by renewing our bond with the natural world and seeing it once again as part of the sacred circle in which all life is one. We then see our role as a co-creator with nature, rather than as a dominator of the earth.

Pollution may also serve as a catalyst in bringing together the nations of the world to develop joint policies to cope with environmental threats. These conferences are helping to break down barriers of barbed wire and ideology, such as the 1979 Convention on Long-range Transboundary Air Pollution, the 1988 Intergovernmental Panel on Climate Change, and the 1992 Earth Summit in Brazil.

In 1992, during the major confrontation in the Pacific Northwest between lumber companies and environmentalists trying to preserve the old-growth forests, an attempt was made by the environmentalists to use the protection of an endangered species of bird to save the ancient trees. Although national attention was focused on this one bird, the northern spotted owl, it was unfortunate that few seemed to notice the deeper symbolism. For centuries, in most cultures of the world, the owl has symbolized wisdom. Perhaps a physical embodiment of this ancient symbol was needed to focus public attention on the tragic loss of giant, irreplaceable, ancient trees. The owl is symbolic of death in Native American and Celtic cultures. Similarly, America's national symbol, the eagle—a symbol of the soaring Spirit in many of the world's religions, as it flies highest in the heavens—is now an endangered species. Due to pollution and illegal hunting, this symbol of America's spiritual vision and values is being endangered.

The environmental dilemma also confronts everyone with the issue of overconsumption and built-in obsolescence, leaving us with the demanding issue of identifying our true material and spiritual needs. Solutions to the carbon dioxide, ozone layer, and global warming crisis will not come through a few new recycling programs. They require dramatic changes in life-styles as well as in national political and economic priorities. In the deeper sense, the outer environment is only a reflection of the inner environment—our inner values, thoughts, and feelings—and it is just as necessary to avoid generating emotional and mental smog to create a healthy, beautiful world. (See chapters 5 and 6.)

The Valdez Oil Spill: Addiction to Consumption Spoiling the Environment

One of the worst ecological disasters in history—a huge 10,080,000-gallon oil spill in Valdez, Alaska, in 1989—dramatized our urgent need to move beyond dependence on fossil fuels and all their problems. The Exxon oil tanker that ran aground symbolized some of the major problems in our economic system today. The drunken captain of the ship was symbolic of the drunken captains of industry who let their own addiction to power and greed destroy companies through huge debts and corporate takeovers. The heavy black oil spilling from the ship symbolized uncontrolled industrial growth polluting the pristine waters, the symbol of Spirit. Not only humans were affected; the creatures of the wild—fish, birds, and otters—became stuck in the heavy, sticky oil and died.

Our disconnection from the beauty and purity of the natural world gave us a big message—miles wide. If our obsession with consumption and materialistic pursuits continues unchecked, we too will be coated in a heavy black muck, unable to free ourselves to the flow of the Spirit. Through the eyes of love, we can feel a deep compassion for the pain of the wildlife and natural world affected by the oil spill. But seen from an evolutionary perspective of significance, this great disaster may have been the shock needed to wake up humanity to the vast destruction of the environment occurring everywhere today.

Exxon itself didn't seem to get the message and make needed changes. Even though it was heavily fined, the company was responsible for two more oil spills within a year of the Valdez accident. Other companies caused additional major oil spills as well, such as the huge spill off the Shetland Islands in January 1993.

Illustrating how good can result from negative events, environmental groups around the country reported increased public response and offers of financial support following the Valdez spill. Together with leaders of the social investment movement, they created a corporate code of environmental conduct called the Valdez Principles.

Tearing Down the Berlin Wall: Releasing Fear and Separateness

The Berlin Wall served for decades as a major symbol of the cold war between the East and the West, and the tearing down in 1989 of this "concrete" reality that had pierced the heart of the nation produced a great release in the Soul of humanity everywhere. The reuniting of the people of East and West Germany struck a great blow for the freedom of the human spirit. As the images were carried around the world on satellite television, tears filled the eyes of millions of onlookers. In that the wall was a symbol of the separation among people everywhere by imposed belief systems, its destruction was a significant step toward "unity in diversity" and the "synthesis of opposites"—both major goals of human evolution. The wall's destruction also signaled a release of fear and tension at a key spot where the friction of opposites might have caused an explosion.

On the inner level, the tearing down of the wall meant we all had taken a step toward wholeness and global integration by reowning the "shadow projections" of each side. This symbolic gesture signaled an end to seeing the "other" as aggressive and deceitful and therefore needing a wall for protection. Old thought-forms about the inevitability of conflict and war were powerfully transformed by this one incident. On the deepest level, the destruction of the wall symbolized the ultimate triumph of good and the highest aims of the human spirit, sending a message of hope to an often cynical world.

However, if the deeper root causes symbolized by the wall are not dealt with—the ingrained sense of separateness that may spur us to create new enemies if the old ones become friends—then new walls will be erected. We have already begun to see this in all the ethnic violence in Eastern Europe—for example, the Serbs and Croats fighting each other in a devastatingly bloody war now that they no longer have the Soviets to fear.

On New Year's Eve 1989, as four hundred thousand people wildly celebrated their freedom at the opened Berlin Wall, a large videoscreen collapsed, injuring over one hundred people. Defying police orders, some people had climbed up the scaffolding of the videoscreen to reach the top of the Brandenburg Gate, causing the screen to fall on the crowd. The incident reminded us symbolically of the blindness sometimes caused by the euphoria of embracing freedom without responsibility. This event was a dramatic reminder that until people everywhere develop the capacity to be responsible to the whole, some regulations and limits on freedom will continue to be necessary.

The Persian Gulf War: The Need for a New Enemy

In late 1989 the world looked as if it were miraculously transforming. The Berlin Wall had come down. Eastern Europe seemed to be managing a peaceful transition to democracy. The United States and the former Soviet Union were warily becoming friends. Yet while there was a great joy, there was also a certain unease here at home. No longer having a major enemy—an "evil empire" onto which we could project our unowned shadow (the unconscious elements that contain all the aggression and deceit we deny in ourselves)—Americans collectively needed a new bad guy.

Suddenly a former "friend," Saddam Hussein of Iraq, conveniently obliged us by acting out the part of a new "Hitler," delighting many with the opportunity to try out our fancy new military technology.

Saddam's Iraqi invasion of Kuwait in August 1990 provided a symbolic "Rorschach test" for the world. Like the famous ink blot around which clients create stories so psychologists can observe their subconscious patterns, the Iraqi invasion provided ample opportunities for projections. To World War II veterans, it brought up renewed fears of what happened when you tried to appease an aggressor like Hitler. To 1960s antiwar activists, it looked as though the United States were repeating the mistakes of Vietnam. To the oil industry, it signaled the opportunity to raise prices and ignore environmental concerns about drilling in the fragile Alaskan ecosystem and off the shores of California. To environmentalists, it provided a strong message to develop alternative sources of energy. To the defense industry, it was proof of the peril of cutting the defense budget. To supporters of Israel, it provided further evidence of Arab aggression. To Arabs, it brought to the surface many hidden feelings and conflicts among their nations.

The United States's particularly military response toward Iraq was symbolic of a deep insecurity in the American psyche. When someone threatens our "way of life"—that is, our overreliance and addiction to an oil-based life-style—we respond with great fear and defensiveness. Instead, we might have seen this as a message from the universe for us to change our life-style and thus begin to lessen our vulnerability. As oil is essentially the stored energy of the past nurtured in the earth, it is symbolic of our reliance on the past. An alternative approach is to direct more money into research on energy efficiency and the development of solar energy, which had been cut during the Reagan era. The sun is symbolic of Spirit in many traditional cultures, as it radiates and purifies. Thus solar energy is truly the energy of the future.

Although the war was fought to protect "strategic" oil reserves, the Iraqis destroyed billions of barrels by burning as many Kuwaiti oil fields as possible and pouring untold gallons of crude into the Persian Gulf, creating a monumental ecological disaster. Symbolically, the message seems to be that if our motive is only to protect oil, we may lose it anyway. The pollution of the environment was so dramatic that we couldn't miss it.

Initially, the Persian Gulf war symbolized a major paradigm shift in the world of international relations, strengthening the UN and shattering the myth of Arab unity that had cloaked major differences. It was also a reminder that the energy of violence and aggression in the world, which feeds the rationale for the arms buildup in almost every nation, is far from overcome. And while U.S. forces in the Gulf took a principled position to turn back naked aggression, they faced missiles that U.S. companies had manufactured and sold to Iraq—symbolic of our facing the karmic shadow of our own militarism and greed.

Spiritually, the Persian Gulf conflict also symbolized a deeper issue, one of form vs. consciousness. Was the loss of lives any worse than the continued poisonous atmosphere of hatred and separateness in consciousness so widespread on all sides in the Middle East? There is an equal danger that if peace is maintained at any price in order to continue vast injustices and materialistic, wasteful life-styles, then spiritual death may be the result. Physical death is only of the body, the form nature, which according to the Ageless Wisdom will be reborn again in another form. We must be cautious about a stubborn idealism that loves the ideal of peace more than it loves humanity's evolution. We can become so enamored of peace that it leads to inertia, stagnation, and, above all else, an attachment to material comfort. Peace and war are not the true opposites—peace and change are. War is only one form of change, and often the least effective.

Yet there is a role for the right use of destruction when it is used against rigid and crystallized forms of thought and cultural patterns that prevent Life from evolving to its next step. After the horrors of World War II, people became exhausted with war as a way of solving conflict, and the forty-five years of peace that followed laid a foundation upon which a united European Community could finally be built. A similar exhaustion with war may have been the necessary precursor to the resumption of Middle East peace talks, and the Israeli–Palestinian peace agreement, which occurred after the Persian Gulf war.

Sometimes wars provide major spiritual lessons in learning to transcend self-centeredness and to make sacrifices for the good of the larger whole. However, we will have truly grown in consciousness when we can extend our willingness to sacrifice to more than just the good of our own nation. We cared greatly about the loss of American lives—but little about the huge numbers of "enemy" lives lost.

Stationed in the hot, empty deserts of the Middle East, with no possibility of escape into alcohol, drugs, or sex with local people, U.S. troops were symbolically offered the opportunity of what many spiritual traditions refer to as "the desert experience." All familiar trappings and circumstances of their daily lives had been stripped away. They were forced to face themselves and their possible death alone in the vast emptiness of the desert, an experience that can be purifying and transforming. These Souls who chose to participate in the war may also have learned from its horrors, so that in the future they will use their warrior energy only in defense of the highest principles and the good of the whole.

In the Islamic world, the war held karmic overtones of the Crusades, which to the Arab mind happened only yesterday and still permeates the present. Saudi agreement and pan-Arab assistance in the multinational force constituted a major realignment of the Arab world with the West. This is one of the more significant aspects of the crisis, since Western troops and dependents living within Arab borders for an extended time may have been another leavening agent that will help to eventually modernize the Arab world and integrate them into the family of nations. The freeing of women and the modernization of feudal Arab states is a necessary step toward the developing planetary awareness of humanity.

The United States hoped for a neat, conclusive war with few American casualties. However, the bloody aftermath of U.S. withdrawal—the civil war and thousands of Kurdish refugees fleeing Saddam and dying in the mountains—symbolized a new lesson in the failure of war to solve complex human problems. Although pictures of the gruesome killing of more than one hundred thousand Iraqis by U.S. troops and the suffering caused by the Western embargo were censored from American television, our media soon showed the pain and death of thousands of Kurdish men, women, and children. These tragedies illustrate that a price must always be paid for violence.

Clearly, a more systemic view of the whole problem in the Middle East is needed. Instead of seeing the issue as merely an isolated greedy invader, injustice in the whole region—including help for Palestinians—must be addressed in order to create lasting peace. We have to realize that humans will always have conflict. By symbolically stating we are like this, and not like that, conflict seems to be the method we each use to define our identity. Our evolutionary growth comes when we manage conflict to increase tolerance, understanding, and coexistence through negotiation rather than war.

One positive consequence of our guilt at killing so many thousands of people—many of them women and children—from a culture we know little about has been a new interest in understanding Arab and Islamic perspectives and their positive contributions to the world over the centuries. Although couched in fundamentalist and often fanatical terms, the Islamic emphasis on following the will of Allah, of God, is a much needed value in our Western materialistic culture. Five times a day all business and other activities cease in the Islamic world, while people kneel, face Mecca, and pray for the mercy and justice of Allah.

The intent and meaning of the aftermath of the Gulf war was revealed in the love expressed by U.S. troops helping Kurdish refugees in Iraq. Green Berets, with years of training in combat operations, said that assignment was the most ennobling they had ever drawn. "This is the best thing I have ever done in my military career," said one. "Helping people—not helping them fight, just helping them."[18] Another Green Beret commented prophetically, "I hope one day we'll be able to do the same thing for people starving in the Third World, in Ethiopia and Sudan."[19] And later, Somalia provided that opportunity.

The Clarence Thomas Hearings: National Psychotherapy

The Senate hearings in the fall of 1991 to approve Clarence Thomas for a seat on the U.S. Supreme Court became one of the most riveting events of the decade in America. Charges of sexual harassment by one of his former female co-workers, law professor Anita Hill, contributed to a vast public drama and guessing game of who was telling the truth. Symbolically, Anita *Hill* had to climb Capitol *Hill* to testify. And her testimony made it crystal clear to millions of women that this was a male stronghold, unresponsive to a woman's point of view. On the positive side, however, the hearings catalyzed many new women into running successfully for Congress in the following year.

Since both Thomas and Hill were seen by most as reputable people, the event reflected the psychological projection of partisan beliefs—both political and sexual. It demonstrated quite clearly how our perceptive lenses are strongly filtered by our own belief systems—we see what we want to see. Republicans were convinced that Thomas was telling the truth; Democrats were convinced Hill was. Men believed Thomas; women believed Hill. Whites saw black promiscuity, as they have always projected their shadow— particularly denial of their own sexual obsessions—onto black people. No one wanted to see that there might be a more subtle reality at play in the hearings, rather than only one side telling the truth and the other lying. The reactions to the hearings made the "war of the sexes" seething just beneath the seemingly placid veneer of public life much more visible. The significance of this event was that for the first time, publicly, a black woman (doubly oppressed as a black and as a woman) courageously confronted the sexual abuse of black women by black men, rather than allowing racial solidarity to contribute to the denial of dysfunctional behavior in classic co-dependency.

The entire process was a kind of national psychotherapy on the theme of sexual harassment. Here were two African Americans unconsciously playing out the drama for the world to see, as they discussed intimate sexual occurrences before millions riveted to their TV sets. It sensitized both men and women to the issue and helped clarify what is considered improper behavior. Many new programs were established in workplaces around the country as a result of the hearings. Anita Hill became a heroine to many for having the courage to discuss this sensitive topic and freed many other women to do the same. Several of our friends who are therapists told us that the trial brought many women into their offices wanting to talk about sexual abuse they had experienced, but never before discussed.

Thomas appeared to be in trouble with Hill's credible testimony until he suddenly switched to the victim scenario, using loaded terms like "high-tech lynching." Then, as *Newsweek* commentator Mark Whitaker noted, "Senate Democrats backed off, African Americans closed ranks, and millions of whites felt sorry for him." But the trouble with the victim game is that it is ultimately self-defeating.[20]

If Americans still didn't get the message about this sexual exposé of "he said/she said," it was replayed again several months later in 1992 in the William Kennedy Smith rape trial. Democrats believed him—Republicans believed her. Men believed him—women believed her. The issue came to national attention once again when Gennifer Flowers charged in the midst of the campaign for the 1992 presidential nomination that she'd had a long affair with then Governor Bill Clinton of Arkansas. And then Senator Brock Adams (D-WA) resigned because of sexual harassment charges and Senator Bob Packwood (D-OR) was also charged with sexual misconduct. Perhaps the symbolic intent of all these events was to point out that most women are still overidentifying as victims and need to find their collective voice. As a result, many women and women's groups are now empowering themselves to reframe these debates into a collective referendum on abusive and chauvinistic behavior in men.

The Two Kings: The Rage of the Dispossessed
It may have been more than coincidence that King is the name of both African American men who were the catalyst for two major riots (or rebellions, depending on your point of view)—Martin Luther King, Jr. in 1968 and Rodney King in 1992. The first King was an inspirational leader, but the second King is just an average guy, a Mr. Black Everyman, suddenly

thrown into the limelight. Archetypically, the blood of the king is said to restore the "wasteland"—and the lives of black people in the ghettos today couldn't be more in need of help.

During the riots that resulted from the first acquittal of the police officers who beat him, Rodney King tearfully pleaded to the nation, "We're all stuck here for a while. Can't we just get along?" This was a profound metaphysical statement, truly symbolic of the whole problem humanity faces, since we're all "stuck here" on Earth until we "get the message," and learn how to not only get along, but even love and help one another.

During the riots, a group of angry black men pulled an innocent white truck driver out of his vehicle and began to beat him just the way the white police had beaten Rodney King. But then the white man was rescued by a group of blacks, so no one could say all blacks didn't care or were violent and hated whites.

Significantly, the first trial took place in the white enclave of Simi (pronounced "see me"!) Valley, California, home of the new Ronald Reagan Presidential Library, symbolically pointing out the result of Reagan's disregard of the underclass and his cutbacks of government programs. The significance of Rodney King's two trials was that a racial injustice that is common, but usually hidden, was recorded on videotape and shown around the world. The reaction to the injustice of the first verdict finally forced a second trial and justice triumphed. Metaphysically, Los Angeles, whose name means "City of the Angels," is the heart center of the country, clouded over by the smog of inner and outer pollution. It is the place where universal love is trying to express itself by bringing to the surface all the darkness that blocks it. Los Angeles is now the most ethnically diverse city in the world, according to Tom Bradley, former L.A. mayor, and some see it as the first true "world city."[21]

The evolutionary significance of all this is that for the first time in decades people are talking directly about the issues that divide them. Finally they are beginning to look at the deeper causes instead of blaming each other, and they are finding new solutions that synthesize the issues of the Right and Left. New alliances are springing up in surprising places, between warring L.A. gangs—such as the Crips and the Bloods—who contributed to the violence. Despite fears, polls taken within a few days of the riots found that blacks and whites were agreeing; 86 percent of the whites and 100 percent of the blacks said the first verdict acquitting the white policemen was wrong, and a majority of both blacks and whites believed the violence was unjustified.[22] The meaning of the event is a dramatic illustration of the desperate need of the poor and minorities in even the most affluent trend-setting "world city" and for compassion on all sides.

The Rio Earth Summit of 1992

The United Nations Conference on Environment and Development (UNCED; pronounced "unsaid") left a large number of issues "unsaid"— issues that were not given the attention they deserved, reflecting the state of the world's consciousness at the time. These include $1 trillion in annual world military expenditures, population growth and its impact on the developing world, corruption, patterns of consumption sustainable only with exploitation of developing countries, the impact of racism on North/South relations, and the widening gap between rich and poor worldwide.

The significance of the conference was reflected in the tension between two opposing paradigms—one in which the United States and other wealthy nations dominate the world economy and manipulate systems for their own advantage, and the other where the welfare of all members of the family of nations is of primary concern. This was symbolized in the debate over the Global Warming Treaty and the Earth Charter. Although the United States, under the Bush Administration, blocked the adoption of any real enforcement provisions, as it did not want any international controls on its right to pollute, President Clinton later signed the Global Warming and the Biodiversity treaties.

For the first time in international power relations, however, the underdeveloped world has a bargaining chip of great value to the West—their cooperation in preserving the global economy's environmental support systems and reducing pollution. They can now ask for something in return: the help of affluent societies in dealing with life-threatening poverty. People facing starvation today are not likely to worry about the effects of climate change tomorrow. We can no longer separate the issue of the future habitability of the planet from the current distribution of wealth.

As a result, the potential now exists for what is called the Grand Bargain, an agreement that provides financial help from the developed northern countries in sustainable development in underdeveloped southern countries, who would, in turn, agree to limit their use of fossil fuels and CFCs and work to preserve their natural ecosystems. Although this type of consensus was not fully achieved at the Rio summit, progress was made by European nations and Japan, which agreed to contribute more financial aid to underdeveloped nations toward these goals.

The presence of thirty-five thousand activists from around the world, representing nine thousand nongovernmental organizations (NGOs) and indigenous peoples, created planetary networking of historic proportions. The summit was a significant event because so many people and governments were addressing basic human and planetary needs without the preoccupation of cold war politics. A redefinition of security is under way, from military to ecological and economic security, as well as a redefining of sovereignty, determining which resources belong to one nation and which belong to all.

The Earth Summit was a mirror of our collective consciousness. It was clear that wealthy nations are not yet ready to strike the Grand Bargain with developing countries. The Rio Declaration is a statement of principles to guide actions of governments, and Agenda 21 describes what is needed to address environmental and developmental challenges into the next century in areas like achieving sustainable living, working toward efficient resource use, managing fragile ecosystems, sharing global resources, and managing wastes. However, the consciousness of the world's leaders allowed them to take only a small step in implementing these goals.

The United States, which has the most powerful influence on life-styles around the world, has a human obligation to express a new set of values and behaviors to the rest of the world. Developing countries have great difficulties agreeing to actions that will require sacrifice on their part (like not exploiting their natural resources to the fullest), if they don't see a similar willingness on the part of the United States to limit consumption and pollution and redirect some of its vast wealth to human development all around the planet.

The Earth Summit highlighted the issues that will form the crux of the great planetary debate that will take place at this hinge of history through the millennium. World forums like this allow us to struggle for agreement over the environment, development, equitable sacrifices, and sharing of resources for all people of planet Earth. There is no question where the evolutionary direction lies.

The Early Clinton Presidency: The Beginnings of a Transformational Approach

A significant outcome of the 1992 elections is that Americans responded positively to the themes of hope, healing, and reconciliation emphasized by Bill Clinton—underlining the symbolism of both his birthplace in "Hope," Arkansas, and his middle name of "Jefferson." In losing his real father before he was born, Clinton carries a personal wound similar to his generation, which arguably lost its last real father figures and leaders with the deaths of the Kennedys and King. Clinton had to grow up with an alcoholic stepfather and deal with co-dependency and denial issues, so he is well suited to confront the basic co-dependency in the national psyche that tries to deny major problems like the escalating debt and racial divisions. *Newsweek* called Bill Clinton the first "New Age President" because he is the first sensitive male chief executive who has attended family therapy sessions and "can search for the inner self while seeking connection with the greater whole."[23] *The New York Times* refers to the yearly Renaissance Retreats in South Carolina that he enthusiastically participates in as "New Age Retreats."

Clinton's stepfather abused his mother, symbolic of the macho attitude in this country that has harassed women and denigrated feminine qualities. But Clinton found the courage to confront and stop his stepfather's behavior. His inner journey to assume a balanced expression of positive male leadership and feminine compassion, and to find his true voice despite hoarseness and media attacks, may be symbolic of the step we all must take to rescue our nation from the abusive use of power.

Unlike many radicals in the '60s who became very angry over John F. Kennedy's and Martin Luther King's assassination and withdrew from society, Clinton instead acted in a constructive way, bringing food and medical supplies into the burning ghettos, and working within the system. Instead of blaming his opponents when he lost elections in Arkansas, or was attacked by the media, he tried to change himself and find better strategies for winning. Unlike the last of his Democratic challengers, Jerry Brown, Clinton wasn't angry and polarized against the system, but rather optimistic about working within government to change it.

Clinton assumed the role of holding his dysfunctional family together, just as he has now symbolically attempted to hold the national family together and keep all parties at the negotiating table—environmentalists and loggers, gays and the military, free traders and protectionists, etc. He is one of the first national leaders to model the beginnings of a transformational approach to politics—a non-adversarial, win/win approach that listens deeply to both sides of an issue and attempts a higher synthesis. Beginning with his Economic Summit in Arkansas before he took office, Clinton has modeled collegial leadership—compassionate listening and skilled synthesizing. His conference in the Pacific Northwest bringing together loggers and environmentalists to find common ground on old growth forest issues was another move in the right direction. However, his first strategy in trying to get his economic bill through the Senate took the opposite approach—a very partisan, confrontational approach spearheaded by Senator Byrd (D-WV)—which barely passed. Clinton seems to have learned from this, and took a more bi-partisan approach that successfully passed NAFTA, a crime bill, and other legislation. He also thinks systematically about policy, unlike most people in Washington, and understands how deficit reduction, job creation, health care and government reform all fit together and affect each other.[24]

President Clinton is also modeling a transformational approach in his sensitivity to the psychological dimension of policy-making. In his first Cabinet retreat he brought skilled facilitators to encourage Cabinet members to open up, trust each other and tell revealing stories about themselves. This approach might have been earth-shaking for those in government and the media, but facilitated meetings for trust-building and teamwork are actually very commonplace among leading edge businesses today.

According to a report in *The Washington Post*, Clinton confronted dysfunction by spending "three gut-wrenching hours together with Russian President Yeltsin talking over the pain of family abuse and drug dependency and inspiring him to summon the willpower to tackle his drinking problem." Clinton reportedly calls Yeltsin twice a week to make sure he is maintaining personal discipline.[25]

Each president sounds a certain note and holds a particular vision for the country. Clinton's greatest spiritual gift seems to be his evocation of community, a vision that is very close to his heart and a key aspect of a transformational approach. The theme chosen for his Inauguration was "An American Reunion," which he described as not only a physical reunion but also a spiritual one. In his first State of the Union Message he said, "The test of this [economic] plan cannot be, 'What is in it for me?'; it has got to be, 'What is in it for us?' "

His genuinely inclusive spirit seems to indicate a more open heart center—unusual for a president. Our own experience in meeting and talking to him in person several times also confirmed his remarkable ability to be fully present with each person in a way that transcends traditional politics. Out of sight of the cameras, he put his arm around a homeless man and walked back to the White House with him to hear the man's personal story.

Unlike traditional liberals, Clinton emphasizes matching rights with responsibilities—the right to college loans, for example, but the responsibility to do community service in exchange. In a much-publicized talk at Cooper Union School, Clinton said, ". . . [We] are a community and we're all in this together, going up or down together. Whether we like it or not, that is clearly the truth." He realizes that government can only make changes from the outside, and that other answers must come from the "values and voices that speak to us from within . . . the Spirit, the Soul," as he said in his 1993 speech at Mason Temple Church in Memphis, Tennessee. His transformational approach represents a third way between Left and Right, synthesizing an activist government with personal responsibility.

A deep honoring of feminine energy and women's contribution to public life is another keynote of a transformational approach, and Clinton symbolizes this when he says that his wife, Hillary, is smarter than he is, or that she's a better lawyer. He has appointed several very outspoken women to top Administration positions, and seems genuinely unthreatened by strong women, and thus centered and confident of his own masculinity.

President Clinton often invokes the power of faith, saying, "Today, we are seeing too much cynicism and too little faith . . . always pointing out the pain of change and never embracing its promise . . . If you don't remember anything else I say, I hope you'll remember this: the human condition in the end changes by faith."[26] He seems also to understand the importance of wholeness—a key aspect of a transformational perspective: "I think serious people, the older they get, try to achieve a certain integrity in their lives. You try to put your mind, your body and your spirit in the same place at the same time."[27]

However, the President apparently still has some learning to do (as we all do) in embodying his belief that, "If we only have faith, we can define ourselves from the inside out, rather than the outside in, as most people in Washington do" (Inaugural Prayer Breakfast speech, January 19, 1993). He doesn't always distinguish between listening to all sides and trying to please all sides. He sometimes avoids difficult decisions and demonstrates too great an attachment to popularity. Thus his greatest weakness is in trying to be all things to all people, and not always making political hard choices and fully standing up for them when needed, although he admirably models a collegial, community-building approach.

THE REBALANCING OF MASCULINE/FEMININE: THE DEEPER MEANING OF FEMINISM

Life today is out of balance. The Hopi Indians, who see themselves as Earthkeepers, call this *koyaanisquatsi.* Today's escalating violence, pornography, and environmental destruction are symbolic of a deeper imbalance between the primal energies—the masculine (yang) and feminine (yin) principles—which the Ageless Wisdom refers to as the "sacred Dual Origins of the Universe." This is a root cause of many of the social and political crises in the world today. The feminine principle within each person, man or woman, is in tune with the heartbeat of earth—our deepest biological roots as humans. The cause of much of our human pain is our alienation from these deep roots. Many people today are orphaned from the Great Mother, out of touch with nature and their own human nature, destroying the earth and the ecological balance. They are often afraid to lose rational control and express their softer, intuitive, feminine side. This overemphasis on the masculine principle has been at great cost to men as well as to women.

The movement to restore the balance has led to a symbolic reawakening of the Goddess within each person—to reconnect with the sacredness of the physical body, the beauty of nature and the earth as Mother—honoring the web of relationships among all of life.

The masculine and feminine energies are seen as essentially *within* each person, regardless of their gender. The primal masculine or "yang" principle expresses qualities of dynamic will, rationality, authority, discipline, and justice, while the feminine or "yin" principle expresses the qualities of receptivity, intuition, flowingness, spontaneity, and mercy. Through the yang vertical line, hierarchy and rank ordering are established; through the yin horizontal line, equality and inclusiveness are embraced. The yang emphasizes goal, product, accomplishment; the yin focuses on relationship, process, emotional support. We see these principles in dynamic tension in all our institutions today.

The sacred balance of masculine and feminine is disrupted at our peril. But, fortunately, in the cosmic design of the Universe, neither polarity can be overemphasized for long. Sooner or later inner forces erupt, causing change and movement toward the rebalancing of these two great principles. In the sacred yin/yang symbol of the East, the two polarities are hanging in a dynamic balance, a dot of one nested within the other. Only together are they whole—a complete circle.

These two polarities are primarily principles of consciousness, related to the cosmic Divinities of Solar Father/God and Earth Mother/Goddess. This is the primal source from which the new Goddess-centered feminism and generative, myth-centered men's movements are emerging.

In most of the metaphysical teachings of the world's religions, Spirit or Father/God, the spark of the Creative principle, impregnates the Mother/Goddess, as the matrix or eternal womb of matter (the substance of the Universe), and from their Sacred Marriage comes the Divine Child, Consciousness, or Light. To us, this Sacred Marriage is of major significance to understand today, as it helps us see more clearly the path needed in the future to rebalance the two sacred principles of masculine and feminine. The correspondences are as follows:

FATHER (CREATOR)	+	MOTHER	=	CHILD	
SPIRIT	+	MATTER	=	SOUL (CONSCIOUSNESS OR LIGHT)	
CAUSE	+	FORM	=	RELATIONSHIP	
POSITIVE POLE	+	NEGATIVE	=	ELECTRICITY	

The nature of the Mother (matter) is to receive the seed of the Father (Spirit) and nourish the growth of the child in her womb. Likewise, our physical bodies (which are part of the Divine Mother) receive the seed of Spirit implanted within each of us, and through guarding and nurturing this union of Spirit and matter, we create Consciousness or Light, which is called the Soul or Christ principle.

Only through incarnating in matter do we as spiritual beings evolve—through the Mother/matter. Only through living fully in the material world and painfully learning its lessons do we develop in consciousness or wisdom and unfold the seed of the Soul or Light within. By learning first to love and embrace the Mother—the material world, including nature and our physical bodies—we draw forth its beauty. To be more fully in touch with the Divine Feminine within us is to more fully incarnate and embody the Light, to bring heaven down to earth. "If life and the soul are sacred, the human body is sacred," writes poet Walt Whitman in "I Sing the Body Electric."[28]

When spirituality is seen only as something transcendent, removed from daily life, and the world is seen as evil—"the flesh and the devil" or "*maya and illusion*"—it creates a terrible split in consciousness. We then neglect our bodies, the natural world, and the political world around us. The temple—the body of the Mother, which houses Spirit—is thus defiled. When spirituality is removed from the physical plane, the world is held hostage to the expression of blind power, to be pillaged and plundered by those whose sole pursuit is self-interest and greed. We can see the devastating results of the overemphasis on transcendent divinity all around us when "spiritual" people refuse to get involved in "dirty" politics. Reawakening to the Divine Feminine helps us to honor God Immanent—the inherent sacredness of life—in ourselves and our world. It is symbolized by the ancient Sanskrit greeting *"Namaste"*—"I salute the Divinity within you."

From an inner perspective, feminine values are beginning to permeate the substance of our society in far more profound and subtle ways than just the battle for equal rights for women. The myth of the Goddess is re-emerging everywhere in the world today. Like the Goddess Isis, who found and restored all the lost pieces of her husband, Osiris, many are restoring the unity of all life, bringing together the separate parts of humanity—different races, religions, and cultures. Many are also restoring a sense of unity and wholeness within themselves by reowning denied aspects of their psyches.

The peace movement, the women's movement, and the ecology movement are all restoring important feminine elements that have been missing in our strategic thinking and policy making. The women's movement began with a different approach from most movements—more of an inner, personal journey—as women gathered in small support groups to listen deeply to each other's stories and share pain and anger. The growing concern for the environment, for "Mother" Nature and "Mother" Earth, and the huge response to Earth Day, April 22, 1990, also reflect the growing feminine energy. Ecological thinking is a diffuse, feminine awareness of how everything is linked to everything else—an intuitive sensing of the whole system.

Many other popular interests today reflect the influence of the feminine principle or the Goddess: the new emphasis on nurturance in relationships and the widespread popularity of psychotherapy; the powerful use of intuition to complement reason—now much admired in top corporate executives; the natural and gentle birthing techniques such as LaMaze; fathers staying home to nurture their children. The new attention to holistic health, health foods, the fitness movement, and the wisdom of the physical body are all part of the reawakening of the Goddess archetype, for the body is seen as the vessel of the Mother in all the ancient religions. The mounting public pressure to end the sexual harassment of women reflects the growing strength of the Goddess energy—respect for women and sexuality. The election of many women to Congress in 1992 was also a reflection of this energy, as was the selection of more women for cabinet posts by President Clinton and the growing public acceptance of First Lady Hillary Clinton's dynamic leadership. This is also evident in the election of many female heads of state around the world in the last few years.

The abortion issue is so controversial today because it is part of this rebalancing toward the feminine. Both sides of the abortion issue represent concerns sacred to the Goddess or Great Mother. The right-to-life side wisely honors the sacredness of human life—the forms embodying the energy of the Great Mother. The freedom-of-choice side rightly restores choice to the woman as representative of the Goddess—who was said to be the "guardian of the gates of birth and death." Thus birth and abortion are related not only to the feminine principle, but also the politically controversial "Right to Die" movement—where those kept alive artificially at great expense to their families are given the right to die. Also connected are the increasingly reported "near death experiences," where those in life-threatening situations report seeing a blaze of white light and angelic guides who help them evaluate their lives and then return to the conscious state.

In *Woman: Earth and Spirit*, Helen Luke points out that our abuse of money is symbolic of our abuse of the feminine principle today. We forget that the sacred origin of the word *money*—from the Latin *moneta*, meaning "mint" or "money"—was originally the name of the Roman Goddess in whose temple money was coined. Money is an abstract representation of the exchange of *material* resources, that is, the resource of the Mother, ma-ter, matter—the Divine Feminine.[29]

Significantly, it is the Virgin Mother—rather than Jesus Himself or male saints—who has been appearing miraculously to thousands of people in modern times—at Fatima in Portugal, Lourdes in France, Garabandal in Spain, Zeitun in Egypt, Medjugorje in Yugoslavia, and Tickfaw in Louisiana.[30] There have also been miraculous appearances of the Virgin Mary to the public in Ireland, Italy, China, Nicaragua, Rwanda, Ecuador, Korea, Japan, Ukraine, and Czechoslovakia—mostly areas where there has been denial of religious freedom or strong intolerance of other religions.[31] A Catholic Pope, John Paul (who only held office for a month before he died in 1978) said, "God is not only your father, but your mother"—thus honoring the feminine aspect of Divinity.

Although many gains have been made by feminists in guaranteeing women greater equality in legal matters, in the workplace, and so on, there are still huge inequities worldwide. In recent times there has been a backlash against feminism, chronicled in numerous articles as well as in the best-sellers *Backlash: The Undeclared War Against American Women*[32] and *The War Against Women.*[33] Author Susan Faludi documents the rise of a highly effective, often insidious campaign to discredit the goals of feminism, distort its message, and make women question if they really want equality.

There may be more women in business and political office today, but the real revolution is in consciousness, not just in women's equality in roles. A new feminine form of leadership is beginning to emerge, in both men and women, that is inclusive, nurturing, and intuitive, and which emphasizes the relationships, connectedness, and obligations among people first—the "sociocentric values." The masculine pushes to make things happen, but the feminine allows the process to unfold on its own and lets go in order to achieve. The feminine principle is the ground of being that creates a protective and nurturing field within which form is created. It is the body of the Mother— the safe, loving environment or context in which something constructive can be conceived and cared for. The womb of the Mother nurtures the seeds of the new world. It embraces and supports, helping people relax and feel their inherent connection with each other.

By returning a quality of heart and nurturance to politics, the feminine or yin principle supplies the missing key needed to create healing and unity among groups and among nations. The balancing effect of the feminine will complement the necessary masculine or yang qualities of purpose, dynamism, action, and courage.

We have presented these historical and current events as examples of how a new type of symbolic thinking could be used to help us explore the deeper forces at work behind the scenes and to understand the spiritual lessons and significance of these collective experiences. We challenge our readers to watch tonight's evening news in a new way. The more of us who work on seeing the inner side, the greater will be the collective wisdom to help us deal more consciously with our national problems.

Part 2

◆ ◆ ◆

EVOLUTIONARY GOVERNANCE

◆

Chapter Three

THE NEW TRANSFORMATIONAL POLITICS: WHOLE-SYSTEMS THINKING

Put your politics in one hand and Spirit in the other, and fold them together.

—LORRAINE CANOE, MOHAWK INDIAN LEADER

Politics is usually the last frontier in the process of cultural transformation. Our traditional but narrow definitions that view politics simply as "the pursuit of power," "the authoritative allocation of values for a society," or "the rallying of wills toward some cause" are part of the problem. Transformational politics is a more wholistic approach, promoting a symbiosis between personal and social change. Because form follows thought, we have found that changes in consciousness are needed to create a truly new politics.

A new paradigm reflecting the principles of the Ageless Wisdom is being developed by those whose minds and hearts have been opened through their own evolutionary development, and/or through the discipline of meditation or other consciousness training. Many of these innovators have not consciously studied the Ageless Wisdom, although their work clearly reflects its principles. They are working out prototypes for what we have come to call "transformational politics"—in which both individuals and society are transformed on a deep level. The new political institutions they have created are early, partial responses to the inpouring of new ideas. To more fully understand and embody transformational politics, however, requires much personal, inner work in consciousness—a deep process that doesn't happen overnight and may take months or years to develop.

This new paradigm is related to emerging ideas in quantum physics, chaos theory, family systems therapy, and Eastern and Western spiritual traditions—all of which embrace a worldview in which everything is interconnected. This perspective embodies a nondualistic approach to politics—a whole-systems approach. The new political groups we highlight in this chapter and chapter 5 provide successful models of some of these new ideas.

For the last fourteen years the two of us have been actively engaged in formulating a new politics and have been networking with other political innovators around the country, and especially in Washington, D.C., where we have spent about half of our time in recent years. Since early 1991 we've been hosting salons (informal discussion groups) in our home in Washington, exploring policy issues and current events from a new paradigm perspective. Some of the founders of the more innovative groups that we present here have been participating in these biweekly salons, along with innovative thinkers in government and academia.

Shifting the Old Paradigm

A key tenet of the new transformational paradigm is "the personal is political, and the political is personal." This involves a kind of moral accountability where private lives must be lived in accordance with publicly stated principles. We must transform ourselves if we intend to transform the world. This perspective holds that everything we think, say, and do has political implications—from consumer choices to personal growth work to how we compost our gardens. "The political is personal" also means that our public policies often reflect our collective psychological issues.

"Politics is the way we live our lives," stated an early new paradigm group called the New World Alliance, which we helped cofound with forty other leaders in 1979. "It is not just running for office. It is the way we treat each other, as individuals, as groups, as government. It is the way we treat our environment. It is the way we treat ourselves. Politics has to do with where we shop, what we eat, how we maintain our health. It has to do with the kinds of schools we create, the energy we use, the neighborhood organizations we build, the work we do. Politics involves our way of seeing the world, of developing our consciousness, of awakening our whole selves. It has to do with our attitudes, our values, our innermost dimensions."

The old political paradigm assumed that events were caused solely by political leaders and public policies. The new emerging paradigm could be called "politics as if people mattered." It addresses causes inherent in our own human psyche, our thoughts and feelings, as well as in the karma of groups and nations.

The old political paradigm was based on the concept of economic growth, in which societies were thought to be doing well if they were at peace and growing economically. But the new political paradigm is a postmaterialist one, based on the image of healthy human growth. A successful society is one that places the physical, social, and spiritual health of the people above all else. This is reflected in the ancient wisdom of the Chinese, whose word for "governing" is the same as for "healing." A good politician is a healer of collective ills.

Those creating a transformational politics are exploring the deeper causes behind problems because they want solutions that are long-term and sustainable, not just "quick fixes." This new transformational paradigm is based on certain key ideas, which have long been part of the Ageless Wisdom tradition:

- Respecting the interconnection of all life.
- Creating a synthesis out of adversarial positions.
- Transcending old definitions of Left and Right.
- Synthesizing the best of hierarchy and democracy for real empowerment.
- Matching rights with responsibilities.
- Promoting government initiatives to develop self-reliance.
- Reframing the context of the debate.
- Searching for common ground and the good of the whole.
- Thinking in whole systems.
- Creating nonviolent, win/win solutions to problems.
- Building cooperative relationships that respect the highest in each person.
- Learning to truly listen to other points of view.
- Examining the psychological roots of problems.
- Releasing enemy images.
- Enhancing self-esteem.
- Using intuition and "attunement" in decision making.
- Shifting from a mechanistic toward a spiritual, value-oriented perspective.

This new political approach requires a "psychotectonic" shift, as UC Berkeley professor Robert Fuller calls it—a dramatic change in the psychological plates of consciousness, analogous to a shifting of the tectonic plates of the physical planet. It's a shift of our deepest assumptions about ourselves and what it is to be human. A psychotectonic shift is to the realm of moral understanding and human behavior what a paradigm shift is to scientific understanding and behavior. This is the kind of shift that the U.S. Bill of Rights created—a new consciousness that ordinary human beings, not just kings and lords, had rights. A similar shift was the one surrounding the issue of slavery.

Transformational politics requires a similar shift in contemporary consciousness: a truly open mind; a willingness to see the humanity in our opponents and the good in their point of view; a measure of humility and compassion; a letting go of being a fanatical "true believer"; and training the mind to be comfortable with paradoxes.

Seeding the Mainstream Culture

Transformational political groups seed the mainstream culture with a new paradigm function very much like the inoculation of a culture in a biological experiment. As Dr. Joan Halifax put it in an interview we did with her for our first book, *Builders of the Dawn*: "If you're a visionary . . . you inoculate your culture with your vision, and it will take a few weeks or months (or years). You create the template, the key, the pattern for the organism's development. Now frequently, when you inoculate, the organism appears to die. . . . [But] actually a little while later it comes back to life in that pattern. . . . You've created a track in the field."[1]

The New World Alliance was one of the first groups to articulate aspects of the new transformational politics, especially the idea of creating a new synthesis of left and right, which later was reflected in mainstream institutions, such as the Progressive Policy Institute and Heritage Foundation's joint conference called "Left and Right: A New Politics for the 90s?" Although the Alliance's pattern-shifting work ended twelve years ago, it advocated a new approach to politics based on a complete transformation of the society and the individual. Ten years later the key values of the Alliance were incorporated into the Transformational Politics Section of the American Political Science Association, the prestigious national professional association of political scientists—to end traditional divisions in political science and political life (normative/empirical; personal/professional; theory/practice; liberal/conservative; global/local; secular/spiritual) and to seek a new synthesis.[2] Pioneer Republican Congresswoman Claudine Schneider (RI) began introducing new paradigm ideas in Congress in the early 1980s, and President Clinton in his presidential campaign called for "a third way between welfare-state economics and laissez-faire capitalism—transcending the old left-right divisions with a new synthesis."

Transformational political scientists have a dual focus. One is on empirical research—such as Boston University's Dr. Betty Zisk's extensive participant observation of numerous local environmental and peace groups (1992). The other focus is on theoretical research, such as that of Auburn University's Dr. Theodore Becker, who edited a book called *Quantum Pol-*

itics, which outlines a new theory of politics based on quantum physics. One of the authors, Dr. Christa Daryl Slaton, explores how proven principles of uncertainty, complementarity, randomness, and nonlocal causation are linked to such transformational political principles as direct democracy, deep ecology, nonadversarial conflict resolution, relational property, and the strength of networks over hierarchies. She says there is an emphasis on process and on permeable interaction, not just on structure; and on randomness and change, not just on order and stasis.[3]

Corinne regularly presents papers in the Transformation Track of the American Political Science Association, which sponsors some of the more innovative thinkers at their yearly conference. And since the transformational approach embraces the whole person—emotions as well as mind—the track offers the only ongoing support group in the conference of several thousand. It is an opportunity for political scientists to share their personal feelings and experiences of the conference in a nonacademic, noncompetitive atmosphere.

REFRAMING

> *The real voyage of discovery consists not in finding new lands but in seeing with new eyes.*
>
> —MARCEL PROUST

Sometimes, those creating a new political paradigm may figuratively stand on their heads to see something in a new way, or perhaps they will attempt to stand in someone else's shoes. This process is called "reframing" an issue. People who use this approach are dedicated to exploring the larger context in which problems occur and then working to reframe the questions being asked. The Ageless Wisdom teachings encourage the freeing of our minds so that we can transcend rational thought and be open to intuitive insights from the Soul. The new political groups we found that were most able to reframe old problems were all started by people who've been involved for years in a great deal of consciousness-expanding work, meditation, and/or personal growth work.

The new approach of transformational politics can be symbolized visually by the simple connect-the-dot puzzle below. Draw four straight lines connecting all of the nine dots without having your pen leave the paper or double back:

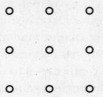

The solution to the puzzle is found only when we realize that we have to *reframe* our perception of the puzzle. To connect all nine dots, we have to look *outside* the frame and see the space around the dots as territory into which we can extend the lines:

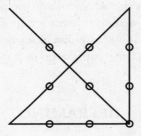

The same is true of transformational politics. We need to look beyond the established boundaries, beyond the conventional framework, to see a problem in a new light and thus find new solutions.

Another way of thinking about this new political paradigm is to expand our perception of the figure/ground image so that the background becomes the foreground and a whole new perspective comes into view. For example, in the drawing below we can see either a goblet or two profiles:

To find creative solutions to problems of governance, those creating the new transformational politics are working on listening with new ears and seeing with new eyes. They are creating an expanded context, one that gives a new meaning to the same facts and circumstances commonly perceived in the old ways. A more creative map of reality or a new gameboard is used, so that participants have to shift their thinking and behavior. In a sense they are "remapping the mind"—discovering and recording whole new territories—and releasing the need to defend their existing ideas and opinions. They are creating innovative metaphors for the changes we need to make—such as seeing world governance as a question of "imagination building" rather than "institution building" as Anthony Judge of the Union of International Associations in Brussels suggests.

The Foundation for Global Community (formerly called Beyond War), based in Palo Alto, California, with local team project groups, began in 1982 to encourage people to reframe their thinking about nuclear war, to see it as obsolete, because no one could win a nuclear war. They believed war could only be ended by changing our view of the earth, by realizing that we all live together on one planet with one life-support system. They said we must reframe how we see ourselves and our "enemies" and begin identifying with the whole. Just like the story of the blind men feeling different parts of the elephant and trying to describe what the animal is, each of us has a narrow frame of reference and finds it difficult to see the whole picture. Credence must be given to what others have experienced because understanding all viewpoints is required to reach a clearer perception of the true situation. Since photos of planet Earth taken from space dramatically demonstrate our oneness and interdependence, one of the Global Community teams distributed over fifteen thousand of these photographs to classrooms around the United States and in more than thirty countries.

Members of the Foundation for Global Community see that all life is one—interdependent—but that diversity among the plants and animals and the different races, cultures, and religions is the rich mulch that fuels the creativity also inherent in earth's nature. They believe that the challenge for humanity is to reconcile these two realities of unity and diversity. The foundation offers educational programs and training in this new way of thinking organized by grass-roots members all around the country. Their goal is to have 20 percent of the world's people committed to the long-term well-being of our global living system by the year 2010. This approach is based on studies that found an idea becomes a dominant way of thinking when 20 percent of the population adopts the idea.[4]

Search for Common Ground, a pioneer new paradigm group in Washington, D.C., begun by John Marks, a former Foreign Service officer, began reframing national security issues in the early 1980s by asking, "How can we have a military that makes us secure without making other countries insecure? How can we create a 'common security' for all nations?"

Common Ground sometimes uses a physical exercise in demonstrating the concept of reframing. For example, if person A grabs person B's finger, person B usually tries to escape by pulling his finger out, which only makes person A grab harder. A new approach would be to push instead of pull in order to escape—a contrasting notion that reverses the psychology of the situation. This is a reframing of conflict.

Another process that helps reframe the conflict among those of different views is to show films made by each side about the same issue. For example, to a group of conservatives and liberals, members of Common Ground showed five minutes each of a pro-arms film and a disarmament film. The pro-arms film tried to scare people about the Russians so they would send in money to support the arms race. After the screening, the liberals pointed out these fear techniques. But then Common Ground showed the disarmament film, which used the same fear techniques to scare people about the conservatives and raise money. This film also smugly suggested that it had all the answers, just as the pro-arms film did. By the end of this experience, each side found it hard to hold on to the certainty of its own position and to feel it had all the answers. As a result, both sides were more open to the possibility that there might be another way.

Opportunities often evolve out of crises. Since the status quo was destroyed by the Persian Gulf war, Search for Common Ground has taken the initiative in reframing issues in the Middle East. They have launched a new nongovernmental, multitrack diplomacy effort in the Middle East based on the successful Helsinki Conference on Security and Cooperation in Europe and have developed possible terms for an Israeli-Syrian settlement. The new initiative includes several former ambassadors and assistant secretaries of state and is working to create an overarching vision of a peaceful, cooperative Middle East based on new ways of thinking and new mediation technologies. This initiative reframes the negotiation process through its inclusive approach, working collaboratively with private groups and official government groups, giving reality to the synergistic idea that the whole can be more than the sum of its parts. Common Ground has done similar work in Russia and Macedonia to reduce ethnic conflict.

Additionally, Common Ground has established a network for Life and Choice to move beyond the polarization that characterizes the abortion debate and establish a working model that can be replicated in other cities. Through facilitated dialogues, retreats, and TV programs, they help pro-life people find ways to work together with pro-choice proponents on mutually chosen projects.

The reframing work of many new paradigm groups actually anticipated the radical transformation of the old comfortable business-as-usual framework that formed our worldview up to 1989. These groups understood the new possibilities inherent in the upheaval brought about by the ending of the cold war, the collapse of communism, the breakup of the Soviet Union and its Eastern European satellites, and the sudden Persian Gulf crisis of 1990 that made the traditional Left-Right, hawk-dove arguments and automatic responses totally outdated. Conservatives no longer had an evil empire to fight. Socialists saw many of their most deeply held values suddenly being discredited. The old analogies, pieties, and shibboleths could no longer stand up in these new situations. Many pacifists during the Vietnam War later favored military intervention in Iraq and Somalia. Few "leftists" could feel comfortable saying that Saddam Hussein was mobilizing the true Arab spirit in Iraq and that the United States was as usual backing the tyrants, moneybags, and decadents. Many traditional foes suddenly found themselves on the same side, and many traditional friends found themselves pitted against each other.[5] The ability to avoid traditional mind-sets and reframe our problems is clearly what is needed in this country today on a large scale, and the new transformational groups are pointing the way.

SYSTEMS THINKING

When we try to pick out anything by itself, we find it hitched to everything else in the universe.

—JOHN MUIR

Transformational politics is based on "systems thinking"—a key tenet of the Ageless Wisdom. This approach is a political application of general systems theory, popularized by biologist Ludwig von Bertalanffy, who was in turn inspired by the fifteenth-century cardinal and mystic Nicholas of Cusa. Systems thinking is a way of seeing patterns and whole pictures more clearly—a kind of "ecological thinking" applied to more than just the natural world. It means moving beyond our old narrow and separative viewpoints. It means seeing relationships rather than only linear cause and effect chains and seeing processes of change rather than snapshots of change, as management consultant and author Peter Senge notes.[6] It means realizing that political life is complex because all the parts are interconnected, so it is often difficult to treat a problem as an isolated case, as fixing it may cause short-term benefit but long-term malaise. Systemic thinking helps us find the structure underlying complex situations and thus organize complexity into a coherent approach that addresses causes and solutions.

"Evolution is not just adaptation to environment," notes physicist Fritjof Capra in his film, *Mindwalk*, "but rather an organism and its environment evolve together. Likewise, in music, the essence of a musical chord lies in relationship. Even subatomic particles are not discrete and separate." From this perspective, all of life is a living system. Living systems are self-organizing, self-maintaining, self-renewing, and self-transcending, says Capra. They act as self-regulating feedback loops. When changing environmental conditions disturb one link in an ecological cycle, the feedback around the cycle's loop will tend to bring the situation back into balance. Variables in ecological cycles undergo continual interdependent fluctuations.

The Elmwood Institute, which Capra founded in Berkeley, California, sees that none of the major problems of our time can be understood in isolation. A systems approach is needed, as all our problems are interconnected and interdependent, facets of one single crisis—essentially a crisis of perception. This crisis is part of a cultural shift from a mechanistic worldview to a holistic and ecological view, from a value system based on domination to partnership, from quantity to quality, from expansion to conservation, from efficiency to sustainability.

A Psychology of the Whole

A systems approach to politics offers a broader perspective on how we are all interconnected and are thus affected by decisions made within the system. Rather than encouraging the pursuit of narrow self-interests and developing top-down hierarchies with one-way communication, a whole-systems approach strives to maximize participation and interaction among all the parts. When we lose track of the whole, we actually work against our self-interest.

The lack of a systemic approach leads to the "tragedy of the commons," based on the English common pastures experience, where each individual acting in rational self-interest creates a catastrophe for the community as a whole. In this example, many farmers growing more crops to earn more money will collectively lower the price because they produce a larger supply.

Instead of an adversarial approach to political differences that targets enemies, the new approach often borrows from psychology and family systems therapy. It goes beyond blaming an individual for causing a "problem" and instead looks at the dysfunctional "problem system" created by all the players. Representative Dick Armey of Texas brought systems analysis, which he'd learned from his wife's family systems therapy practice, to issues before Congress. "Aberrant behavior is never going to be in an individual alone," he said. "You've got to get at the family—the system the individual operates in." So Armey is trying to break the system of "log rolling" in Congress that allows members to trade favors for votes, ganging up on each other's pet programs. Armey was successful in brokering an agreement in 1988 to close eighty-six outmoded military bases and later pushed a bill to bar federal subsidies to farmers whose net income was more than $100,000.[7]

A Systems Approach to Health Care

A typical example of a crisis reinforced by lack of systemic thinking is found in our health care "system." Many uninsured patients do not see a doctor until they are so sick that they must go to a hospital emergency room, where treatment is least effective and most costly. Since hospitals treat uncollectible emergency fees as overhead, this raises the average cost of health care and therefore the cost of health insurance. Higher insurance rates then result in more uninsured people. An even more subtle and delayed consequence occurs when the higher rates American companies pay to insure their employees raise production costs, thus reducing our competitiveness in the global marketplace.

Drexel A. Sprecher, Jr., developer of the new discipline of generative political leadership, told us in an interview that an effective approach to health care cannot be found in either more reliance on the market or more government control of health costs. The role of government here is to change the rules and incentives so that our connection to those who are uninsured is recognized earlier by decision makers. Eventually these old ways of doing things will be seen clearly as expensive and often fruitless exercises in misplaced compassion. It is not enough to relieve pain and suffering when it is too late to heal.

A much more effective approach would offer incentives to make it possible for these people to get into the system early on so that our institutions can plan to respond to them. Without incentives it is very difficult to shift resources from high-pain, low-return crises to low-pain, high-return opportunities. Our models of cause and effect are primitive. We have not learned to detect subtle causes and their delayed effects, so we overact to the immediate causes of pain. This is not compassion, it is distorted seeing. True compassion neither leaves people on their own nor accepts full responsibility for them. True compassion would spend less on someone's pain and suffering and invest more in their capacity to participate responsibly in our society.

A Systems Approach to Forestry

Some forward thinkers in the U.S. Forest Service are beginning to adopt a "new environmental paradigm"—a whole-systems approach that recognizes the role of forests as havens of biological diversity and as indicators of the general health of the planet. The Forest Service is moving toward an interdisciplinary approach that focuses more on the total environment and understanding the interplay of species and less on growing more trees faster.[8]

A Systems Approach to Peace and Diplomacy

A whole-systems approach to diplomacy is being pioneered by Ambassador John McDonald and Dr. Louise Diamond in their Multi-Track Diplomacy Institute (of which Corinne is a board member). They have recently worked on mediation in Cyprus and the Middle East, and with the Dalai Lama and the Tibetan government-in-exile. McDonald and Diamond see that there is a living system, a web of interrelated parts in a circular rather than linear relationship, all operating toward a common goal of peace. Their approaches cover official "track one" diplomacy efforts, as well as citizen tracks—professional mediators, citizen groups, business, media, religious organizations, educational institutions, and the funding community. They feel that the value of a whole-systems approach is to give us an effective tool for self-examination and reflection. These groups exist together with numerous areas of overlapping and complementary activities where resources can be shared and cooperative networks built.[9] Most international conflicts are not structured to yield to easy resolution by track one official diplomacy. The value of unofficial citizen diplomacy efforts pioneered by people like Jim Hickman, Michael Murphy, and Joe Montville was roundly applauded by Mikhail Gorbachev in helping to break down the Iron Curtain.

Pathways to Peace in Larkspur, California, is an NGO at the United Nations that brings people together to plan a project each year for the International Day of Peace on September 15, the date of the opening of the UN. Peace groups on the left as well as the right of the spectrum—from disarmament to "peace through strength" approaches—are invited to work together on commonly decided task teams. By planning an event relating to peace, participants have to try to embody peace and create a peaceful process among themselves. Being with such a diverse group united around a higher purpose helps people learn to really listen to each other and look for the grain of truth in each position. And it helps to develop whole-systems thinking.

Pathways to Peace founders Avon Mattison and Sheldon Hughes say that peace is a dynamic, not a static, process that reconciles diverse forces and produces a temporary state of harmony and serenity. This temporary harmony is eventually disturbed again by something new that must be reconciled, and thus what is most important is to have peaceful processes.

Sheldon and Avon are very close colleagues of ours who are also dedicated students of the Ageless Wisdom.

The Mo Tzu approach, advocated by U.C. (University of California) Berkeley professor Robert Fuller, was named after a fifth-century Chinese peacemaker. "We need to find what we love in what we hate," says Fuller. A systemic approach places great value on the gifts each culture brings to the human family, believing that we complete ourselves through each other by incorporating the empowering truths that other people and other cultures embody and exemplify. This implies a willingness to see our own culture and a rival one as complementary, each bearing an aspect of larger truth that embraces both and compromises neither. Just as diversity strengthens an ecological system, so we should celebrate and learn from different points of view politically. For example, we might sometimes hate another country or ethnic group, but we can also remember what it is we love about them and use that as a handle to hold hatred in its proper, subordinate place. Fuller calls this "completion."

The minute we find what we love in someone else, we become bigger ourselves and more powerful. Fuller notes that "as the sense of threat diminishes, we redesignate our former 'enemies' as 'adversaries.' With the first hint of positive mutual value, 'adversaries' become 'rivals,' a term which acknowledges each as a secret teacher of the other. Eventually 'rivals,' recognizing their mutual dependence, come to see themselves as 'partners.' " Mo Tzu members have traveled to the world's trouble spots, such as the Middle East, Ireland, Poland, and Kenya, immersed themselves in situations to learn about them, and then set out to see what might be done to broker a better relationship between "partners" in a conflict.

The more perspectives that can be incorporated in our thinking, the more powerful will be the results. Whoever can hold more will be the greater, the Ageless Wisdom teaches. Meditating on the vastness of the starry skies helps to put things in perspective. As journalist Mark Satin wrote in *New Options*, "Coming up with a solution is not a matter of adopting correct political beliefs. It is rather a matter of learning to listen— really listen—to everyone in the circle of humanity, and to take their insights into account. For everyone has a true and unique perspective on the whole. Fifteen years ago the burning question was, How radical are you? Hopefully someday soon the question will be, How much can you synthesize? How much do you dare to take in?"[10]

WIN/WIN SOLUTIONS

The new politics seeks a nonadversarial "win/win" solution, rather than a "win/lose" solution to problems, in resolving conflicts either in an intentional community or in the international arena. Rather than the old "zero sum game" in which one party's gain exactly equals the other's loss, the new approach is a non–zero sum approach, where both parties strive for highest spiritual gain. Win/lose is really illusory, since the losers simply lick their wounds and wait for an opportune time to reopen the conflict in the mistaken hope that they will win the next time. The conflict is not resolved. All that the winners have won is a period of time during which they can mistakenly pride themselves on having won.

Although most people think of conflict resolution as working primarily on an emotional level to overcome anger and create harmony, it is really a more mental level approach. It lifts the emotional issue by offering a positive way of thinking about conflict as an outgrowth of diversity that can enrich us and enhance relationships.

Win/win is a more sustainable approach, and it reflects an important teaching of the Ageless Wisdom on karma. If we don't solve our personal and collective conflicts now, they'll just keep coming back to us later in this life—or in others as our karma, until we learn our lesson. In our community, Sirius, we've been learning to resolve all our conflicts effectively from this win/win approach for over fifteen years.

The value of this approach was confirmed dramatically by deposed President Aristide of Haiti, who said that after his election he didn't think about the losers—those threatened by the changes he represented. But they were the ones who eventually forced him out of the country. He noted, "I have learned something . . . and would do it different next time. I would include the losers in the process of rebuilding the country. I would give them a place."[11]

Win/win approaches are derived in part from the Eastern martial arts such as aikido. Instead of resisting an opposing force, we join with it and guide it to a higher level.

One example of a win/win approach is the "debt-for-nature" swap, where Third World countries are relieved of their liabilities in exchange for commitments to improve conservation practices, such as Brazil committing to protect its rainforests. Another example can be seen in the protecting the environment vs. protecting jobs conflict. More intense, managed forestry could be encouraged on private lands, as Gregg Easterbrook suggested, in order to protect lumber jobs and allow higher production of sustainable timber. This would then reduce the need to log Forest Service lands, which could be strictly preserved.

A win/win approach to the school prayer conflict would allow for prayers by adherents of the majority religion, but would respect minority views by allowing one day a week for their prayers (or humanistic ethical statements, if atheist). This could provide an educational experience of other religions.

Project Victory, based in Palo Alto, California, believes that the danger we face in common requires an "evolutionary shift of mind"—a massive reframing of global issues. Founded by Craig Schindler and our friend Theo Brown, who has participated frequently in our biweekly salons, Project Victory sees that there must be a "Great Turning" in the way nations manage conflicts, and that a shift toward nonviolence will come about through "smaller turnings in the lives of individuals and groups." Through the use of psychology, conflict resolution techniques, and the ethical precepts of the world's great religions and philosophies, they have developed a strategy that includes both personal and political transformation.

At Los Alamos National Labs, for example, Project Victory brought together over 350 peace activists and nuclear weapons designers—the entire political spectrum from the Left to the Right. Their approach was to shift the process in the room to one of reciprocity, mutual respect, and practice of the Golden Rule.

"Because the people there really listened to each other, and weren't preoccupied with making their own case or trying to prove the other person wrong, they each discovered new insights," commented Schindler. "New options emerged that otherwise would not have because there was a broader understanding." People are taught to identify with their own center, the "observing self" within, rather than with the content of their mind. Then, when someone disagrees with their point of view, they don't generally get defensive, which they would if they still believed they *are* their position.

Project Victory has organized conferences and training sessions to teach conflict resolution in over fifty cities around the country, including many schools. The whole notion of one political viewpoint "winning" and all the others "losing" may be an anachronism, says Craig Schindler. In a dangerous, complex, and interdependent world "it is in our own best interests to turn our conflicts into mutual gain," he notes. To achieve this approach, Schindler adds, "we don't advocate any 'content' solution. What we strongly advocate is a shared commitment to change the process [by which] we make political decisions. . . . The participants in a [true] dialogue may prefer a certain position at the outset. But he or she must be willing to listen to other perspectives. . . . Instead of people facing each other as adversaries, they start sitting together facing the problem. They start sitting on the *same side* of the table facing the problem, which is on the other side of the table."

The approach is not so much to come up with a better political *platform* as to come up with a better political *discourse* . . . one that forces all sides to listen to and learn from each other. Each side must restate the other's position to their satisfaction, to be sure they really hear each other, rather than think ahead to prepare their own defense. Out of this new discourse, a better political platform may emerge.[12]

Project Victory has organized policy dialogues among adversaries such as liberals and conservatives. For example, in the spring of 1991 they brought together corporate representatives and environmentalists on the issue of reducing toxic waste while maintaining a strong economy in the Silicon Valley. The purpose of these dialogues was to promote a model for future programs of nonadversarial communication around the country and to identify specific strategies for how individuals and organizations of diverse views can work together more effectively.

The problem, they found, is that our society lacks the "community ethic" necessary to sustain an adequate balance between our economic and environmental needs. Over thirty-five findings about the current impasse and creative solutions to help reduce toxics and maintain a strong economy resulted from the meetings, helping to break the deadlock.

The project also has been holding a series of dialogues on chemical demilitarization with army officials and community environmentalists in Maryland, exploring the best way to dispose of chemical weapons. Project Victory is developing a series of interracial dialogues to bring together people of different cultural and ethnic backgrounds for increased understanding. This kind of person-centered approach, learning to listen deeply to each other, was first pioneered by humanistic psychologist Carl Rogers.

The Center for California Studies of California State University at Sacramento created a "Growth Management Consensus Project" in 1991 involving "stakeholders"—representatives of environmental groups, developers, and government—in a win/win approach to development that would be sensitive both to the environment and to economic concerns. The series of dialogues was carefully designed to encourage all sides to more fully understand each other and to discover new creative solutions that would take all their concerns into account. The resulting landmark consensus was then presented to a special joint committee of the California State legislature.

The Tin Wis Coalition in Vancouver, Canada, created the first working coalition of timber industry workers, Native Americans, and environmentalists in 1988. They found some solutions to competing claims on timberland, seen by some as an economic resource and by others as a sacred ancestral home and an irreplaceable wilderness. The common ground for all three groups was developing long-term sustainability plans and creating educational programs about the fragility of local biosystems and about the effects of corporate control and deregulation.[13]

Win/Win on Capitol Hill

Win/win ideas are even filtering up to Capitol Hill and the White House, as some members of Congress phrased proposals, such as a free trade bill with Mexico and Canada, in "win/win" terms.[14] President Bill Clinton noted that after a bad experience as governor with a task force on timber management, he would no longer pursue an agenda solely from an adversarial position. He wanted to adapt his leadership style to one of conciliation, appreciating "the importance of bringing adversarial parties together to make real change happen instead of polarizing people and choosing up sides, which often results in paralysis of government programs and not progress."[15] The realities of polarized politics in Washington have obviously been a challenge to Clinton's ideals, and may be the reason many criticize him for not taking a definitive stand on some issues.

Frustrated by failures of the executive branch to produce rules that implement its laws, Congress finally passed a law in 1990 to encourage the use of negotiation. This has been effective in some areas, as representatives of traditionally warring sides—oil industries and environmental groups—recently reached a win/win agreement to supply cleaner-burning gasoline to the smoggiest cities, starting in 1995, using this recommended "regulatory negotiation." American Petroleum Institute vice president Bill O'Keefe said, "When people who are traditional adversaries sit down and work out these problems, they see the other point of view and see the benefits of accommodation instead of thrashing out their differences in court." David Doniger, the Natural Resources Defense Council representative, added, "What each side wanted was compatible with what the other side wanted. We wanted cleaner gas, and they wanted certainty and flexibility."[16]

Senators Sam Nunn (D-GA) and Richard Lugar (R-IN) demonstrated a partnership rather than partisan approach in what has been called "one of the most successful new political ventures of recent congressional history," breaking deadlocks and passing legislation on demilitarization and long-range policy for dealing with the former Soviet republics.

Principled Negotiation

"Negotiation on the merits" to achieve a win/win solution has been developed at many conflict resolution centers around the country. In their best-selling book, *Getting to Yes*, Roger Fisher and William Ury of the Harvard Negotiation Project recommend putting oneself in the shoes of those who hold an opposing point of view and trying to understand their perspective, rather than just seeing all the merits of one's own case and the faults of the other side's. This helps both sides move from an attitude of blaming to one of problem solving. They recommend the following:

• Separate the people from the problem—see both parties working side by side, attacking the problem, not each other.
• Focus on future concerns rather than on past grievances and on interests rather than fixed positions, since interests motivate people and can often be fulfilled by a variety of other solutions.
• Invent options for mutual gain through brainstorming techniques.
• Insist on using objective criteria and fair standards.[17]

For example, the Camp David Treaty of 1978 between Israel and Egypt demonstrated the usefulness of looking behind positions to interests. Both countries' positions were totally incompatible, as Israel insisted on keeping some of the Sinai and Egypt insisted that every inch of the Sinai be returned to Egyptian sovereignty. However, Israel's interest was in security—they didn't want Egyptian tanks on their border—while Egypt's was in sovereignty—as the Sinai had been part of Egypt since the time of the pharaohs. So both agreed to a plan that would return complete sovereignty to Egypt yet demilitarize most of the territory to assure Israel's security.[18]

An Israeli group, **Shalom Achshav** (Peace Now), started by three hundred officers in the army and now one of the largest grass-roots movements in Israeli history, has continued a win/win approach to Israeli/Palestinian conflict with a program of dialogue called "Building Bridges with the Palestinians."

Wallace Warwich of the George Mason University Conflict Clinic recommends that mediators also explore the deeper levels of conflict underneath the rational level of positions and interests. The nonrational level includes values (such as respect and belonging) and basic human needs (such as food or shelter). In his many years of experience with conflict resolution, Professor Warwich has found that if these values or needs are not addressed directly, no successful outcome can be reached.

For example, in the Azerbaijani/Armenian conflict, citizen negotiators Rama Vernon and Max Laffer found that the real need of the Armenians was not for peace or land, but an apology for the 1915 massacre by the Turks. The negotiations over the future of Northern Ireland have stalemated because Protestant leaders tend to ignore Catholics' need for belonging, recognition, and being treated as equals. Catholic leaders often appear to give too little importance to the Protestants' need to feel secure.

The **Natural Step Project** in Sweden, founded by Karl-Henrik Robert, M.D., successfully applied a win/win approach to create a national consensus among artists, scientists, and politicians about causes and cures for environmental problems. Robert suggests that potential enemies be asked for advice in solving the problem under consideration. When their advice is followed, they are partly responsible for the solution. The Natural Step Project generally approves of the advice given, as most people have good ideas.[19]

Fine-Tuning

Another technique for creating win/win outcomes is to get people on each side of an issue to fine-tune their differences. For example, in a recent conference, William Ury, director of the Harvard Negotiation Project, asked conservative Elliott Abrams, then Assistant Secretary of State for Human Rights, and liberal Dick Clark, former U.S. senator (D-IA) to carefully explore their differences on peace and security issues. They were finally able to realize that a "major" difference between them was that Abrams believed that the East/West conflict should take precedence over human rights issues 80 to 90 percent of the time, while Clark believed that it should be more like 60 to 70 percent. So there was actually not that much of a difference, and in fact they had more in common than they realized. The implications of this for public policy could be immense.

A similar fine-tuning would greatly help the explosive abortion issue, as Rushmore Kidder, founder of the Institute for Global Ethics, suggests. Both sides agree on most things—believing that life is important, that freedom of choice in a democracy is important, etc. They only disagree on the exact point at which life begins—whether at conception or during gestation.

The Spiritual Approach

In addition to the conflict resolution faculties at a growing number of universities, there are many spiritual groups such as the **Quakers**, the **Baha'is, Pax Christi, Fellowship of Reconciliation**, and **Moral Re-Armament** that have successfully facilitated negotiated settlements in many countries around the world over the years through the application of spiritual principles. These groups have been far more successful in resolving conflicts that are nonideological or nonterritorial than traditional diplomats because they better understand nonmaterial "identity-based" conflicts involving race, nationality, or religion. The **Religion and Conflict Project of the Center for Strategic and International Studies** in Washington, D.C., is also researching and promoting this approach.

Changing the Media

Some of those interested in creating win/win solutions to conflict, such as Search for Common Ground founder John Marks, have also been trying to change the adversarial quality of the media. Search for Common Ground has produced shows on finding common ground on energy, abortion, and the Middle East and South African conflicts for American and foreign TV. Business-as-usual media believes that good reporting of "hard news" is rooted in conflict and involves the chronicling of clashing personalities and forces—reflecting the political process itself, with opposing parties, ideologies, lobbyists, and lawyers. The very structure and definition of news coverage may actually prevent conflicts from being resolved. To begin to change this situation, meaningful amounts of time and space should also be given to covering solutions in addition to covering the strife.

CREATING SYNTHESIS OUT OF POLARITY

Many great truths are paradoxes, according to the Ageless Wisdom. Training in paradoxes is one of the secrets of metaphysical development. Transformational politics seeks to transcend apparent duality and paradox and raise issues to a higher level of synthesis. This is the heart of a new political paradigm.

Compromise is distinct from synthesis. It usually includes some of this position and some of that and can be seen as the midway point on a line between two polarities. But true synthesis is different. In synthesis we have to go to a higher level and transcend the polarities—going to what psychologist Carl Jung called the "creative function." Just as hydrogen and oxygen need a spark to create water, so two opposites require the spark of higher consciousness to create synthesis of the best of both at a higher level.

One of the best-known Western philosophers to articulate synthesis was Georg W. F. Hegel in the early nineteenth century. It was Hegel's view that all things unfold in a continuing evolutionary process whereby each idea or quality (the thesis) inevitably brings forth its opposite (the antithesis). From their interaction, a third state emerges in which the opposites are integrated, overcome, and fulfilled in a richer and higher synthesis. This synthesis then becomes the basis for another dialectical process of opposition and synthesis. Instead of seeing opposites as logically contradictory and mutually exclusive, as have most Western philosophers since Aristotle, Hegel believed that the creative stress of opposing positions was essential for developing higher states of consciousness. In the moment of synthesis, the opposites are both preserved and transcended, negated and fulfilled.[20]

This is not a new idea, but rather an ancient one that was part of the training for initiates of the Ageless Wisdom: "The pairs of opposites distract the eyes . . .Only the single eye directs the steps of the initiate upon the Way."[21]

To visualize the distinction between compromise and synthesis, Roberto Assagioli, an Italian psychologist and student of the Ageless Wisdom, suggested that we draw a triangle from the ends of the line (with the two polarities on opposite ends) up to a point above, the point of synthesis.

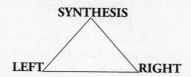

Perhaps a fuller expression of this concept would have to be multidimensional, or a hologram, as there may be more than two competing points of view that need to be raised to a higher level of synthesis.

To move into a position of synthesis, we must be willing to see the good in an opponent's position and to realize that each one only has a partial view. It also helps to distance ourselves from the problem and to develop a more impersonal perspective in order to move beyond equating our position with our identity, which can then be threatened by any change. However, by focusing on the positive elements of each side, and by raising them up to a higher, intuitive level and holding them in the Light, they can unite to create a synthesized solution.

The mind and the emotions always function in polarity. Wherever there is one idea, there is an opposing one; wherever there is a positive feeling, there is also a negative one. Only through intuition can we transcend polarity and realize true synthesis.

Synthesis as a Way of Life
Synthesis is a life-changing concept. Once we personally began to work with it in a deep way, we found it so profound and universal in application that it continues to have repercussions in our lives. Finding it difficult in most circumstances to think any other way, we no longer feel at home with a purely liberal perspective, for example, and have taught university courses entitled "Transcending Left and Right." Once we began working with this theoretical model, it greatly affected not only our politics, but also our lives and our view of conflict, helping us develop a new respect for those with opposite views.

This shift was dramatically illustrated for us when we were invited to one of the first "Space Bridges" in Washington, D.C., a few years ago—a live television satellite link between members of the U.S. Congress and the former Supreme Soviet (parliament). It was very moving to experience these "enemies" begin to communicate and see each other as human beings. This breakthrough, which seemed to help melt the walls of opposition and fear, was a powerful experience that brought tears to our eyes.

When it was over we walked outside and joined a major march that was in progress down Pennsylvania Avenue to protest President Bush's policy in Central America. It was the first large demonstration we'd participated in for many years, with hundreds of thousands of people from all over the country. But somehow we just couldn't get enthused emotionally about the march in the way we used to. Even though we agreed in principle with the positions of the marchers, we had just experienced an inspiring transcendence of polarity and opposition. Returning to an angry, polarized demonstration seemed a step backward. Although we still felt marches of this kind were very important and necessary to get the government's attention and to change policy, and we respected the courage of those who marched, we realized it was no longer our approach.

Instead we began working to create a higher synthesis of opposites. For example, capitalism vs. socialism (individual ownership vs. state ownership) can be synthesized into the example of worker-owned cooperatives that operate in a free market. Investment based solely on highest return vs. outright donations to good causes can be synthesized into social investment— investing in companies that express good values. "Doing well by doing good" is the slogan of the social investment movement. Rather than making a trade-off between economic concerns and environmental concerns, "Good business practices can serve the environment, and the environment can provide good jobs," as Maurice Strong, director of the 1992 United Nations Conference on Environment and Development noted. Rather than pro- and anti-law and order views on crime, we can have volunteer and police "neighborhood foot patrols," which are proving to be very effective.

A Unitive Approach to Abortion

A nonpolarized approach to the right-to-life vs. freedom-of-choice issue might honor the ethical complexities of both sides. It would look at what each side has in common—not wanting abortions to occur, discouraging unwanted pregnancies, and promoting some form of birth control. Each side holds sacred a different principle: the pro-choicers honor the mother's life and principle of freedom above all; the right-to-lifers honor the life of the fetus as most sacred.

A unitive approach would synthesize the best of both sides—the sacredness of both mother and fetus—rather than continuing the emotionally devastating battle over abortion. Instead of focusing all the arguments between each side on exactly when life begins and whether abortion is murder, the focus could be shifted to conscious conception. This could be aided by dissemination of information on preventing unwanted pregnancies through a national educational campaign funded by the federal government. Both sides could find a whole range of options on which they could work together, such as promoting adoptions, reducing infant mortality rates, promoting women's and children's rights and male responsibility. However, a truly higher synthesis from a spiritual level would be to develop the intuition to control conception so it would reflect the highest good for both mother and child. Then there would rarely be a need for abortion in the first place.

A Synthesis of Liberalism and Conservatism

> We are suffering from a false polarization in our politics, in which liberals and conservatives keep arguing about the same things when the country wants to move on. . . . We are encouraging an "either/or" politics based on ideological preconceptions rather than a "both/and" politics based on ideas that broadly unite us.
> —*Washington Post* writer E. J. Dionne[22]

"Liberal" and "conservative" are two polar energies that are always present in the public arena, as they provide checks and balances for each other. Liberals, or progressives, archetypally push for changing what is outworn and no longer needed in a society, while conservatives archetypally preserve what is best in a society. Progressives guarantee that evolution will proceed and inertia won't set in. Conservatives guarantee that progressives won't change things too fast and create problems. Until we recognize and appreciate the contribution of each of these basic energies, we will remain in polarized positions and won't be able to draw out the best of each to create a higher synthesis.

The Economics vs. Values Debate
One philosophical dividing line between conservatives and liberals is a disagreement over whether social problems result more from economic factors (objective factors) or from a breakdown in individual values (subjective factors). Conservatives argue that if our problem is with values, then more spending will do little good. Liberals argue that having good values doesn't help if equal economic opportunity is not available for all. Conservatives believe the State must promote a virtuous citizenry. Liberals believe the

State must redistribute the wealth and fix social problems. Policy deadlocks in Congress are often the result of trying to separate economics and values from each other, with neither the conservatives nor the liberals admitting any wisdom in the other's perspective. As E. J. Dionne noted in *The Washington Post:*

> Conservatives love to talk about "values," but usually fall silent when their values and the market collide. That's why they prefer to keep politics focused on symbols ... and away from problems. ... Liberals support energetic government intervention in the nation's economic life. ... Yet when the talk turns to what values or what forms of personal behavior the welfare state should encourage, liberals fall strangely mute. So fearful are liberals of imposing "values" on anyone that they act as if billions in government money could be spent in a "value-free" way.[23]

Liberals see the private sector as the problem; conservatives see it as the solution. Liberals see the public sector as the solution; conservatives see it as the problem. Liberals promote government control of the market; conservatives promote the free market. Liberals argue for environmental protection; conservatives argue for job protection. Liberals find protection through equality; conservatives seek protection of rewards. Liberals want the State to redistribute wealth; conservatives want no government intervention. Liberals value greater government spending on programs for the disadvantaged; conservatives value private initiatives for them. Liberals emphasize compassion for the disadvantaged; conservatives emphasize personal responsibility. Liberals say poverty breeds crime; conservatives say crime creates more poverty. Liberals want to protect individual rights; conservatives want tougher crime bills. Liberals promote judicial activism; conservatives advocate judicial restraint.

Liberals believe people are born virtuous but are corrupted by institutions. Conservatives believe people are born sinful and have to be restrained by the institutions of society. Creating a synthesis between liberalism and conservatism brings together liberty and virtue, community and individual initiative, compassion and self-reliance, altruism and accountability to create a more successful and democratic civic culture. Author John White calls this synthesis "liberative."

Cornel West, director of the African-American Studies Department at Princeton University, remarked: "We must acknowledge that structures and behavior are inseparable, that institutions and values go hand in hand. The economy and politics are not only influenced by values, but also promote particular ideals of the good life and good society." For example, although the poor may suffer from some of their values, such as smoking, more than the rich, they also suffer from inadequate diets and a lack of access to health care, both of which can be partly cured by government spending.[24]

National Service

Rather than harping on big government vs. no government, a left-right synthesis reframes the role of government as a catalyst and partner with both the business and the nonprofit sectors. It distributes opportunity rather than outcomes. Government tries to expand the opportunities and then holds individuals responsible for seizing them. A policy example of this approach, initiated by President Clinton, is The National Service Program, helping the sick or the homeless, as a way for young people to give something back to the community in return for receiving college loans. He noted, "My experience as governor brings me up against the limits of politics all the time, as we spend more and more money to fix broken lives that should have been kept whole. I don't think there is a program for every problem. . . . [Government initiatives] have to operate within a receptive culture where everybody is willing to assume some responsibility for the future."[25]

Law and Order

Conservatives demand more law and order to deal with rising crime, believing human nature is inherently uncivilized and needs to be restrained. Liberals' solution is more economic aid to the poor and crime-ridden areas, believing people are inherently good but social institutions have failed them. A higher synthesis recognizes that humans are all progressing and yet are at different levels of development at any given time. Conservatives realistically see the current mass level of development, and liberals see a future mass level of human development. A policy strategy of synthesis would be geared to the present and future development of specific individuals, as well as to the mass of society as a whole. It would include a focus on both restraining negative behavior and developing institutions for self-help.

For example, prisons could be created as small-scale, supportive communities/colonies where inmates could be taught practical skills, teamwork, and techniques of self-improvement. This would be the path of wisdom, for when criminals are not helped to reform themselves, but instead are repressed or executed by society, they often return to the world even more angry and violent to wreak further havoc.

Housing, Education and Welfare Reform

The notion of empowerment is a synthesis of left-right ideas that links government assistance to personal responsibility. For example, it establishes a program that would allow the poor eventually to buy the government housing now provided for them. When people own their own homes, they usually feel responsible for them and keep them safe and clean. This approach was promoted by both a conservative U.S. Department of Housing and Urban Development (HUD) former secretary (Jack Kemp) and by groups of welfare mothers. A friend of ours, Gloria Cousar, has worked closely with this empowerment project at HUD, which is called HOPE, and is encouraged by the results.

A similar idea is a system of government-funded educational vouchers that allow parents to choose their children's schools and thus make them more competitive. The key idea is to make the consequences of choice be generative, not punitive, so schools will be motivated to improve. This concept is already being tested in several states—Minnesota, Idaho, Arkansas, Iowa, Nebraska, and Ohio. To counter criticisms of unfairness, some— like President Clinton—recommend that the vouchers be valid only in public schools.

The idea of "workfare" instead of welfare ties welfare payment to jobs or job training through a variety of tax breaks for the working poor. This helps the poor restore their self-respect and enter the working world, which gives them a better chance to improve themselves. Welfare reforms such as emphasizing the responsibility of divorced fathers to support their children, as well as the Earned Income Tax Credit, rewarding low-income working families, are both examples of a synthesis of left-right approaches. Marketplace routes to social equality also might represent a new synthesis.

The New Paradigm in the Mainstream

Some of these ideas have been promoted as the "New Paradigm" by former president Bush's advisers James Pinkerton and Edith Holiday and by former HUD secretary Jack Kemp.[26] Republican as well as Democratic supporters of these ideas formed the New Paradigm Society, with monthly meetings to discuss new policy proposals from this perspective.[27] Democratic supporters of the New Paradigm, or what some call the "New Mainstream," such as Will Marshall, Elaine Kamack, and Robert J. Shapiro, created the Progressive Policy Institute of the Democratic Leadership Council, and worked to "deconstruct" their own thinking—letting go of old habits of thought to find what works. They applied a new left-right synthesis to various policy issues like crime and drugs—and then took this concept into the Clinton administration.[28]

Senator Daniel Patrick Moynihan (D-NY) noted, "Most liberals talk about the economic pressures on families and neglect family values; most conservatives talk about the values and neglect the economics. Liberals tend to reach for bureaucratic solutions even when they are counterproductive; conservatives tend to reject government responses even when they would work. Both are wrong. . . . Surely each group is seeing part of the truth and can find common ground in accepting one another's perceptions."[29]

In 1991 we were invited to a landmark conference called "Left and Right: A New Politics for the 90s?" in Washington, D.C., which we found very exciting, as it was co-sponsored by a liberal and a conservative think tank and presented New Paradigm ideas in a mainstream policy context. Progressive Policy Institute director Will Marshall described the New Paradigm synthesis of left and right as "a more catalytic role played by government" in establishing creative public-private partnerships. He says the New Paradigm emphasizes responsibilities as well as rights and entitlements; a restructuring of markets rather than of government; a new focus on results and output rather than on input—how much money to spend on public assistance; government *by* the people rather than *for* the people; decentralized rather than centralized approaches; family-centered tax relief; the primacy of work, family, and education.

Reinventing Government

David Osborne, author of the seminal *Laboratories of Democracy* and (with Ted Gaebler) *Reinventing Government*, has been applying key aspects of the New Paradigm pioneered by states and cities to the Federal government. "The fundamental goal," says Osborne, "is no longer to create—or eliminate—government programs; it is to use government to change the nature of the marketplace."

Osborne says, it's not a question of more or less government, but rather that we need better government. Economic growth must be our major priority, he says, but it can be combined with equity, environmental protection, and other social goals. Whereas interest group liberals put their social goals first and conservatives put growth first, the New Paradigm realizes that in today's economy, growth requires both equity and environmental protection. (However, unlike advocates of a sustainable economy, Osborne never questions the wisdom of growth as an end in itself.) Osborne's New Paradigm emphasizes investment rather than spending, redistribution of opportunity rather than outcomes, and a search for nonbureaucratic methods.[30]

In *Laboratories of Democracy*, Osborne noted that in the 1960s the primary focus was on bringing the poor into the political process through civil rights legislation, community organizing, and federal efforts such as the Community Action Program. Today's efforts, however, focus primarily on bringing the poor into the economic process—through education, training, employment, and investment. The old paradigm's approach was to increase spending by public bureaucracies.[31]

In *Reinventing Government* Osborne and coauthor Ted Gaebler describe a New Paradigm of "entrepreneurial" government that synthesizes left and right. Such an approach would be

- *catalyzing* (steering rather than rowing)
- *community-owned* (empowering rather than serving)
- *competitive* (in service delivery)
- *mission driven* (transforming rules)
- *customer driven* (not bureaucracy driven)
- *enterprising* (earning rather than spending)
- *anticipatory* (preventing rather than curing)
- *decentralized* (from hierarchy to participation and teamwork)
- *market-oriented* (leveraging change through the market)[32]

Senator Joseph Lieberman (D-CT) noted, "[T]he old assumptions of the Left and the Right are no longer working." The political system needs to embrace "a new consensus that drops ideology and replaces it with rationality," he said.[33]

Mark Satin, author of *New Options for America*, notes that the rugged individual has been the conservative model of the American citizen—ambitious, assertive, and entrepreneurial, believing strongly in the notion of personal freedom, even if making money is done at the expense of the community or environment. By contrast, says Satin, the collective individual is the liberal model—identified primarily with a work, ethnic or sexual group, believing in social justice even at the expense of oversize government. The synthesis he envisions is the "caring individual" who cares deeply about self *and* others, about self-development and social change, about individual freedom and social justice.[34]

The liberal urge to help the poor and the conservative emphasis on entrepreneurship and accountability can be synthesized into such private sector ideas as **FINCA** or the **Grameen Bank** which give the poor of the Third World very small loans to start businesses, and depend on peer relations to pay them back. These creative ideas could be adapted for use by government, seeing its role as catalyst providing small loans to be repaid, rather than outright support. (See chapter 11 for more information.)

Most people intuitively respond to a right-left synthesis even when they don't realize that's what they are hearing. This is why, for example, John F. Kennedy's inaugural address was so immensely popular—it was a masterful synthesis of liberal and conservative perspectives, emphasizing collective and personal responsibility, peace and strength. Similarly, President Clinton's campaign for the presidency was successful because he synthesized liberal ideas of an activist government and conservative ideas of self-responsibility in what he called "A New Covenant."

A Synthesis of Hierarchy and Democracy

> *These ... builders of the new world ... will sweeten and clarify the political situation and present those ideas which will eventually lead to a fusion of those principles which govern a democracy and which also condition the hierarchical methods.*
> —Alice Bailey[35]

The Ageless Wisdom teaches that the synthesis of hierarchy and democracy is the next evolutionary step for humanity. Synthesizing these principles was perhaps the most important lesson we learned about leadership at Sirius, the community we co-founded in Massachusetts. Having previously experienced only oppressive, top-down hierarchies in our lives, we naturally became involved in the iconoclastic, anti-leader politics of the 1960s. At first we refused to assume or acknowledge our own leadership, trying instead to distribute power equally among all members, even when newly arrived. But through painful experiences of holding too high an expectation of others' abilities and willingness to shoulder responsibility, we finally began to learn the necessity for a balance of hierarchy and democracy.

We recognized that although we all may be theoretically equal in potential, not all of us are at the same level of actually manifesting our full potential. This perception avoids burdening people with unrealistic expectations that can cause guilt, anger, and resentment if they are not able to live up to them. An obsession with equality can come from a lack of self-worth, as it is a subtle demand for reassurance that we are just as good as everyone else. It also can come from a fear of accepting our own leadership responsibilities. Overemphasis on equality can lead to a lack of motivation for developing our own potential, as no greater rewards accrue for this, and others tend to view greater abilities with jealousy. This can lead to what's often called "the tyranny of the structureless group," where no one is empowered to take initiative on behalf of the group, and there is an anti-leadership bias leading to stagnation.

On the other hand, as we are all well aware, overemphasis on hierarchy can lead to arrogance and abuse of power, as well as missed opportunities for new creative impulses. The limitations of the leader or leadership group can become the limitations of the entire organization. This can lead to immense frustration, with a continual threat of rebellion or at least passive resistance and subtle sabotage.

The Best of Hierarchy and Democracy

When a transformational synthesis is applied to this age-old conflict of hierarchy vs. democracy, it takes the best aspects of hierarchy—love and responsibility (rather than power and dominance)—and the best aspects of democracy—participatory inclusiveness (rather than the lowest common denominator)—and raises them to a transcendent level. The principle of hierarchy acknowledges *current* abilities, quality, and excellence (*actualized* potential). Authority is matched with skill, energy, and ability to take responsibility. The principle of democracy acknowledges *future* potential and empowers its development. Equal opportunity, political rights, and voting power are bestowed on all so that individuals may develop their full potential.

From a reincarnational perspective, democracy is spiritually validated, because we all began with the same potential and will all eventually achieve the same development—but some of us may take many more lives to achieve it, if we learn slowly from our mistakes. When we transcend time and observe the whole, we see only our equality as Souls. But in any given moment within time, a hierarchy of abilities is always present, as people develop at different rates.

In the new synthesis of hierarchy and democracy, as individuals take more responsibility for the good of all, they are then given commensurate authority and power—not the reverse. This approach takes the best of democracy—giving people the maximum freedom to grow and develop— and the best of hierarchy—providing models of the highest expression of what people are striving to become. Democracy provides opportunity and encouragement; hierarchy recognizes ability and accomplishment. Democracy provides the container to hold and nourish people's development; hierarchy provides the direction to grow into. Democracy values inclusiveness, relationship, listening, compassion. Hierarchy values leadership, purpose, direction, vision, efficiency. Each of us must learn to recognize "the great chain of being"—discovering whom we can serve (recognizing responsibility) and whom we can learn from (developing humility), by recognizing those who are more advanced than we are.

Different types of people learn about leadership in different ways. Conservatives usually respect authority and model themselves after a men-

tor, who grooms them for leadership. Radicals often rebel against established authority in order to discover their own identity and exercise leadership in their own created sphere.

Transformational Leadership

Where there is a good synthesis of hierarchy and democracy, leaders accept
only as much authority as people are willing to give them. Work gets done
through inspiring people with vision or purpose, rather than bossing or
dominating them. There is an encouragement rather than a suppression of
feedback, since good leaders know how to listen and will invest a great deal
of energy in developing good relations with all members of the group.
Transformational leaders allow other people to make mistakes so they can
learn from them. They win support and love from others by giving them
support and love.

The transformational approach creates "power with" rather than "power
over"—a cooperative blend of leadership and empowered equality, where
leadership relates to function and to "focalizing energy," rather than to personality. Individual learning and responsibility are fostered, as is a sense of
team spirit and ownership by all members. The new type of leadership is
educative rather than directive. It inspires responsibility rather than creating dependence. Based on the assumption that people already have the potential wisdom and creativity within them, the task of leadership is mainly
to encourage and draw this out, helping people to develop their skills and
sense of self-worth. Organizations and processes are structured so that people are inspired to do things for themselves and others, to make their own
decisions and to take on more responsibility. They are helped to develop
self-confidence and a sense of self-worth. Negotiation rather than pure authority is the basis of relationships. As the ancient Chinese sage Lao-tzu
said, "Leadership is best when the people say, 'We have done this ourselves.' "

Political scientist James McGregor Burns offers a good example of this
style of leadership: "The transforming leader looks for potential motives in
followers, seeks to satisfy higher needs, and engages the full person of the
follower. The result of transforming leadership is a relationship of mutual
stimulation and elevation that converts followers into leaders and may convert leaders into moral agents."[36]

Using Intuition

Native Americans say that for someone to really understand something, it
must be heard by the left ear (the rational mind), the right ear (the intuitive mind), and the heart. Transformational leaders express both analytical,

left-brain thinking and intuitive, right-brain thinking and problem solving. The major limitation of concrete, analytical thinking is that it can relate individual data only to other data. But once this is done, the intuition can rapidly assimilate and relate the detail to the manifesting whole. This approach can result in creative solutions to problems because it's able to take in the whole system, the evolutionary context.

David Spangler, formerly co-director of the Findhorn Foundation in Scotland, describes this approach as "a feeling into and becoming one with the process of unfoldment in the life of a person, a group, or a nation." At Findhorn, for example, members first discuss an issue analytically, reviewing all information and facts in a logical, fact-based manner. Then they shift to an intuitive approach, using prayer or meditation to contact an inner source of guidance—the infinite wisdom accessible within each person.

Heterarchy

A good synthesis may function through a rotating system of leadership, with different people taking turns at leadership at different times or for different functions. The person with the greatest skill at a certain function would serve as leader in that area. In this "heterarchy," as futurist Donald Michael calls it, the locus of authority varies with the task, and autonomy is dependent on the effective operation of the whole system and vice versa.[37]

A good synthesis increases the creativity that is the best aspect of democracy and the structuring of accountability and boundaries that is the best aspect of hierarchy. One of the best examples of this synthesis is the **Foundation for Global Community,** which evolved into a new approach after seeing the limitations of overreliance on a charismatic leader. We first met with leaders of the group in 1991 when we gave a lecture at their Palo Alto, California, headquarters about our work with New Paradigm groups in Washington, D.C., and later when Corinne attended local group meetings and some of their annual conventions. We found them to be among the most inspirational and enthusiastic people we'd met, with a remarkable degree of group consciousness and teamwork. Most of the work of the foundation occurs in decentralized local teams that take on projects of their own choosing, such as the environment. National coordination is done by a leadership team, chosen by the entire membership on the basis of their proven abilities, and these serve on a full-time, nonsalaried basis.

Focalizing

A new type of leadership functions in some other transformational political groups through "facilitators" or "focalizers" who are chosen for each work area or project. A "focalizer" is not a leader or a boss in the traditional sense of the word—someone who is responsible for keeping the organization running and who reports to someone higher up in the organization's hierarchy. Rather, this person is a kind of facilitator of energy who holds the focus for the group, thus synthesizing hierarchy and democracy. In a sense, the focalizer is the servant of all.

For example, a focalizer of the maintenance department at the **Findhorn Foundation**, the international educational community in Scotland where we lived, described her role as being like "a funnel through which one pours water into a bottle. A funnel directs water into the bottle, but the energy for the action is not in the funnel, it's in the water. It's a service you are providing, a particular input into a circle of people." A focalizer does not insist that someone do something, but rather shares in an open and clear way the reasons why it should be done. This way participants in the group gain a broader awareness of the way an entire system operates and how their contribution is an essential part of the whole.

This type of leadership is neither aggressive nor dictatorial. Rather, it works to draw out the natural leadership and awareness in others. Sometimes a quiet, nonleader type of person is asked to focalize a work department at Findhorn in order to develop that person's strength and potential leadership abilities. Similarly, a naturally strong person who likes to take charge is sometimes asked to take a more supportive role to learn patience and listening skills. Focalizers of various work departments meet together regularly, as does a central Core Group of rotating members, which takes responsibility for maintaining the long-term purpose and vision of the community. In decentralizing governance functions, the principle of leadership is not eliminated, but becomes a creative synthesis of hierarchy and democracy.

Creating Consensus

Consensus is often used in transformational groups to achieve the best thinking of all members. It is a process by which the whole group reaches an agreement on the general direction of a decision, with no serious objections or blocking. It is experienced intuitively as a sensed unity within the group on an issue. The advantage of consensus decision making over traditional majority/minority voting is that everyone feels they "own" the decision and is thus personally responsible for carrying it out, rather than having a minority harboring resentments.[38] (See our book, *Builders of the Dawn*, for consensus-building information.)

Institute for Cultural Affairs (ICA) members were able to effectively teach participatory techniques of governance and consensus building to people in poor neighborhoods and Third World villages because these were the tools they learned in their own work on themselves. Members of the ICA, a fairly racially diverse group, were already living in a community environment of shared houses and learning how to plan and make decisions together, blending hierarchy and democracy. In each of ICA's sixty-five ecumenical centers worldwide, two to three people were designated by the larger global body to "be first among equals." Their job was not to "be in charge" in the usual sense, but to "monitor and symbolize the consensus of the group" and assure the continuity of decision making. Responsibility for many of the practical aspects of daily life was shared by all members.

The consensus process at ICA honors each person's insights regardless of his or her culture. The contribution of a black African villager carries as much weight as that of a white American professional. ICA members don't believe that you need to have every member of a group present to create a consensus, because it's each person's responsibility to hold the perspectives of those not present. The primary value inherent in the consensus process is that each contribution be appropriate to the situation and to the vision of a planetary society.

The process of forming consensus begins in each group, where issues are first discussed that will be addressed in the yearly global meetings. The front line of decision making is local because members believe that the local group is a microcosm of the whole body and consensus is built on behalf of the whole body. In turn, the local group is responsible for the implementation of the consensus of the planetary network. Consensus agreements made at the global meeting then come back to the local group. If a local group disagrees with the intent of the consensus (not just the form), then it can feed this back to the global group, and a new process will ensue until there is consensus between the local and global groups.

A Synthesis of the Individual and the Collective: Rights and Responsibilities

In order to function as part of a community, members must learn to identify with the whole and act in awareness of the group, while at the same time honoring their own individuality and freedom. They must be responsible and give back to the whole at the same time that they are demanding their personal rights. From a transformational perspective, there is no conflict between the needs of the individual and those of the group. The Ageless Wisdom has always taught that when one is in Soul consciousness, the individual and the group are always in harmony. Eva Pierrakos, co-founder of the **Pathwork Community** in upstate New York, put it this way:

> True group consciousness does not level off uniqueness, but furthers it. The group is no longer used as a crutch because the self cannot handle life. Nor is the group an authority that one needs to rebel against. . . . The highest organization of group consciousness is that within which each individual has found . . . autonomy.[39]

Transformational groups such as the Findhorn Foundation, the Pathwork Community, and the Institute for Cultural Affairs are giving members practical experience in the synthesis of collective and individual approaches and the balance of rights and responsibilities. Members of these groups have learned to trust other people to be aware of them as individuals and to include their needs and rights, while they themselves give to the whole. At the same time, members have learned to maintain their individual integrity so that they're not overwhelmed by an overidentification with the group, too much dependency on it, or too much control by it. Martyrs, who get burned out by giving too much to the group and not nurturing themselves, as well as passive participants who easily fall into dependency patterns and don't do their share of the work, are dysfunctional patterns.

Both individuals and groups go through cycles of individualism and collectivism. Each change in the cycle can move upward on a spiral, with a higher level of development experienced. Lessons learned in a cycle of individualism can strengthen the whole group. Lessons learned in a cycle of strong group identification can be applied to an individual's growth. Most successful groups have alternated cycles of individual expression and creativity with group responsibility.

The **Communitarian** movement, spearheaded by Professor Amitai Etzioni of George Washington University and others, promotes a synthesis of rights and responsibilities. Communitarians support both the love of liberty and the sense of community, encouraging "responsibilities" to balance the demand of "rights" and entitlements and to develop a sense of obligation and commitment to the community, the social whole. Americans, Etzioni notes, demand the right to a jury of their peers, but when asked to serve on a jury themselves (fulfilling their responsibilities of citizenship), they often evade it. Communitarians want to strengthen families and neighborhoods as a community response to preventing drug abuse and crime. Communitarians also encourage moral education at all school levels and the overhaul of divorce laws to apply the principle of "children first" (in other words, responsibility) to property settlements and support awards.[40]

The Communitarian platform developed by Professor Etzioni, Professor Mary Anne Glendon of Harvard University, and others was presented at a "Communitarian teach-in" that we attended on Capitol Hill in 1991. Communitarians point out that liberals overemphasize rights and entitlements, and conservatives glorify unfettered market forces. This polarization has created a political gridlock and left pressing problems unsolved. The Communitarian movement notes that if you have a strong community, you don't have to worry as much about big government or rely as much on the government. "We have to move away from the simplistic notion of it's either the state or the individual [solving social problems] and recognize the social realm and the moral realm as major factors," says Professor Etzioni.[41]

At their conference on the new Communitarian ideals, Professor Jane Mansbridge of Northwestern University, author of *Beyond Adversary Democracy*, noted that our most effective industrial relations are those that appeal to altruism as well as to financial incentives. What is needed is a return to the importance of "public spirit," she said.

Professor Mansbridge noted that most people act responsibly to the social whole when they can immediately see the direct results of their behavior—when a situation is structured so that they can see the hurt they cause. Pollster Daniel Yankelovich noted at the same conference that "altruism flourishes when people are invited to act responsibly." It is when they are not given this opportunity that they often regress to selfishness.

A SYNTHESIS OF VISION AND PRAGMATISM

The new political paradigm is centered around the vision of creating a better world through small, practical, replicable steps that can be taken today—synthesizing idealism and realism, vision and pragmatism, the mystic and the technocrat. This approach is about "thinking fundamentally and acting realistically."

As the Ageless Wisdom tells us, "Without vision, the people perish," because vision provides the direction and forward movement. Pragmatism, however, regulates the speed of the movement and the rate of growth, which helps to prevent burnout. From a metaphysical point of view, this is the action of the new incoming energy, bringing Spirit (vision) into matter (practicality), which is growing today. Ideals are used as a guide for action rather than a shield against action, for the louder and more insistent the words are, the greater may be the gap between ideals and actions. The most advanced Souls are always those who embody a synthesis of idealism and pragmatism.

One of the ways transformational groups have learned to develop pragmatism is to start with a vision and grow slowly and organically (rather than growing too big too quickly), taking each successive step when the time is right. Most of the New Paradigm groups we've written about here, such as Search for Common Ground and Project Victory, began on a grass-roots level and have grown slowly into successful models on a larger scale. This has been a proven way of working for us as well.

RESULTS, started by our friend Sam Harris in Washington, D.C., envisions a high ideal of ending world hunger, but has a very down-to-earth strategy for grass-roots lobbying. It focuses on helping people break through the belief that "I don't matter; I can't make a difference" in order to create the political will to end hunger. They teach people how to be articulate on issues, how to write op-ed pieces for local papers, and how to call or to lobby their congressional representatives on visits to the home district. Instead of the old model in which people around the country send money to hire people to lobby members of Congress on specific issues, RESULTS reverses the flow and sends out information to local groups around the country, empowering them to lobby their local congressperson. Harris believes they have "created a format that is usable by any group working to create the political will to accomplish anything." The key, he says, is a willingness to make our democratic institutions work for us by becoming the lobbyists ourselves, as he notes in his book, *Reclaiming Our Democracy*.

Local members of RESULTS participate in a national telephone conference each month that links all the groups with an expert on the current issue. They then listen to a tape produced by RESULTS on how legislation moves through Congress, studying the particular issue being addressed and practicing speaking on the issue. Next they organize a local gathering to show a videotape on the issue, inviting the public to attend. Attendees then write letters to their elected officials and/or local papers about their concern. Members of Congress pay special attention to letters received locally, so RESULTS has an effective strategy for getting action on global issues.

RESULTS has grown to over one hundred local groups in thirty-four states, and has had over three hundred editorials printed in papers around the country—a better record than any highly paid lobby group. They've been successful in getting government funding for three national hunger bills, low-cost immunizations for the world's poor, inexpensive housing for people with low incomes, and microloans to help Third World cottage industries become self-sufficient. They are often called "the most effective lobby on Capitol Hill per dollar." In September 1990 they successfully coordinated thousands of people in seventy-five countries around the world in candlelight marches for the United Nations World Summit on Children.

The Better Way Project of the **Foundation for Global Community** is a grass-roots effort with a larger vision that brings together small groups of people to creatively brainstorm better ways to solve a particular social issue decided on by group consensus. For example, participants faxed or mailed their best solutions to each of the presidential candidates in 1992. The candidates' response was very encouraging, saying this process can contribute to the well-being of an effective democracy. One campaign director said he included the Better Way program in their volunteer offices. There are always things that can be done to achieve a larger vision if the group proceeds step by step and doesn't bite off more than it can chew. The key is to become "realistic idealists," consolidating and grounding each step in growth before taking another.

A SYNTHESIS OF GLOBALISM AND DECENTRALISM

Both globalist and decentralist approaches are synthesized in transformational political groups that are "thinking globally and acting locally," as bacteriologist and author René Dubos put it. This is a critical key to their effectiveness.

Global Communities is a Washington, D.C., group that works toward global peace by helping to create local municipal foreign policies—bringing together seemingly opposite concepts of "municipal" and "foreign." While most peace groups believe that the tinder for war is being laid by the "military-industrial complex" and its "imperialist ideology," most national security groups used to blame the prospects of war on "communist expansionism" and "Marxist-Leninist ideology" and now blame fanatical Arab leaders.

Whatever strands of truth exist in these views, Global Communities' founder Michael Shuman believes that the deeper, more fundamental cause of war is a widespread sense of powerlessness. Global Communities feels that if the rigid nation-against-nation conflicts could be transformed into fluid relationships among the cities of different nations to form joint alliances on some issues and disagree on others, there would be a better chance of creating a more complex global politics where no one disagreement can lead to war between large geographic blocs of nation-states.

By making communities a basic building block of international diplomacy, local governments infuse their foreign affairs activism with money and legitimacy. During the 1980s, the federal budget allocated to cities was reduced by 75 percent and reallocated to defense. In response, municipal foreign policy became a way for cities to further the cause of peace. For example, the city of Minneapolis broke its contract with an international law firm because it was doing public relations work for the Salvadoran government, which had connections to military death squads that have killed a total of over seventy thousand people. The firm lost something like $500,000 each year on the contract.

With hundreds of billions in investments and annual expenditures at stake, local governments are beginning to awaken to their enormous economic power. For example, over 100 cities have now divested money from firms doing business in South Africa, 160 cities have banned nuclear weapons production within their borders, and over 1,000 cities have passed nuclear freeze resolutions. Several dozen have even begun to ban production and use of CFCs and other ozone-depleting compounds.

More than 1,400 U.S. cities now have "sister" relationships with cities abroad, and a growing number of these are with cities in adversary nations such as China. San Francisco and Seattle passed resolutions protesting the Bush administration's policy in Central America. Teaneck, New Jersey, lobbied for human rights in Brazil.

Transformational political groups also make great use of "networking"— creating and nurturing connections among peers. Unlike traditional institutions, which often become overly hierarchical, bureaucratic, and crystallized, many of these new groups rely on informal and decentralized information links with those of similar values, which often prove more effective in getting the job done and create a bridge between global vision and local focus.

All of the above are practical examples of groups that are transcending the usual dichotomies of left-right, hierarchy-democracy, and the like, and demonstrating the tremendous energy and effectiveness that is released when this is done. But it is not enough to just think in a new way, in a whole-systems approach, to create a new politics. We also have to change our negative and dysfunctional emotions and pay attention to the psychological side of events and policies. Let us now explore part two of this New Paradigm—the psychological dimension.

Chapter Four

◆

POLITICS AS IF PEOPLE MATTERED: THE PSYCHOLOGICAL DIMENSION

I believe in the convergence of the personal and political . . . since my personal and political struggles now share the same focus—how to grow healthy human beings—what I learn in one is invariably related to what I learn in the other. I want to help develop and legitimize a more humanistic and holistic politics.
—John Vasconcellos, California State Assemblyman[1]

The new transformational paradigm explores the whole context in which politics operates—especially psychological and spiritual factors, for nothing operates in a vacuum. Just as we must understand the economic context of a political problem, so must we understand the psychological context, because the political mind is a reflection of our psychological state, according to the Ageless Wisdom. The better we understand human nature, the more effective and enlightened our politics will be.

For example, psychologist Jerome Bernstein accurately predicted the collapse of communism seven years earlier through a psychological analysis based on the work of Carl Jung. But publishers rejected his book as too radical, until history confirmed his findings in 1989.[2] There is now a whole professional society exploring psychological issues—the International Society for Political Psychology. Corinne presented a paper at their annual meeting in 1992.

EXPLORING OUR INTERNAL POLITICS

Most political and social issues contain a large psychological element—the underlying psychological dynamics of a policy issue are often similar to our personal inner dynamics. Self-awareness increases political effectiveness because it helps us understand the issues more clearly and act with emotional detachment. Our ability to affect a problem in the world is often directly proportional to our own awareness of—and ability to solve—the same problem within ourselves. The New Paradigm in politics focuses on not just the transformation of public policy, but the transformation of self.

For example, in a New World Alliance seminar called "Political Awareness," which we developed some years ago with our colleagues, participants were asked to pair up and role-play their feelings toward their political adversaries and then to reverse roles and play their adversaries. Many deep insights resulted, with participants discovering that they themselves often had problems similar to the ones they accused their adversaries of having. A person who accused the communists of being very authoritarian, for example, discovered that he had well-disguised authoritarian tendencies in himself, especially when he was being very self-righteous about his views and dominating others.

"A people get the government they deserve," Thomas Jefferson reminded us two hundred years ago. It's important not to blame everyone and everything outside of ourselves, including our government, for our personal problems. We can begin with the humility to take responsibility for our own contribution to problems—our aggression, power trips, and selfishness. A good example of this willingness to look honestly at oneself was given by former California governor Jerry Brown, who said he learned a "painful truth" about his years in office:

> I forgot about the basic building block of any powerful institution: shared effort, shared philosophy, and caring—not just about political goals, but about the persons right in front of you. I knew where I was going, but too often I was going there by myself.[3]

By honoring the Law of Correspondences, as taught in the Ageless Wisdom: "As above, so below; as below, so above"—as in the macrocosm, so in the microcosm—we can help ameliorate world tensions. We can begin by exploring our internal politics—our own inner "defenses" and willingness to "disarm." For example, in an article in *ReVision*, Deena Metzger, a California psychotherapist, has found fascinating parallels between an individual and a country. In working on herself and her clients, she found that each of us comprises multiple selves whom we govern as nations are governed, with the same problems and issues arising. Within us there is often a repressed minority that is dominated by a "dictator" in power—aligning with the "establishment," the "church," and so on—to promote production and efficiency. The "nation" may suffer from the delusion that it can destroy one segment of its population and remain intact or thrive. Often there are internal revolutions and terrorist acts on both sides, with power lines sabotaged and energy shortages. The talents of the repressed minority are often coopted while they are forced to work as slaves at cultural tasks or menial labors.

The internal government sometimes calls in "impartial international advisers" to deal with internal problems. At times there may be drops in "exports" causing economic problems, or individuals may live in "armed camps" with ongoing wars with external enemies, invasions, and a need for disarmament talks.

Metzger offers "Personal Disarmament" workshops where she asks participants to consider themselves as a nation and ask the following questions: "Who governs my country? What form of government is used? How does the ruler stay in power? Who is oppressed in my country? What are my borders? Do I exploit other countries? Who are my enemies? What are my defense systems and weapons? Am I willing to disarm? Am I willing to share power?" This is an excellent exercise for personal meditation.[4]

Some powerful work in this area was also done by the late psychotherapist Naomi Emmerling, who brought together groups of Jewish and non-Jewish Germans in the United States and Germany to release their fears, anger, grief, and guilt about each other and to work on forgiveness. Jews worked to release a victim consciousness in themselves, and Germans worked to release feelings of superiority. Participants were able to reown their negative projections on each other, discovering the dictatorial Hitler type, the obedient Nazi, and the victim Jew all within themselves. They learned about the patterns of prejudice and blame and feelings of guilt they'd been carrying, which resulted in a great emotional healing for all participants. Emmerling believed that just as damage to the individual psyche from early childhood can be healed, so can wounds within our collective history.

Moral Re-Armament (MRA) is a global movement begun in 1938 by Frank Buchman that is based on the principle that to change the world we must change ourselves. There is a famous story told about Madame Irene Laure, a member of the French parliament who had been a leader in the French Resistance during World War II and found she couldn't even be in the same room with Germans when she saw them at a conference sponsored by MRA. After an intense inner struggle during which she locked herself in her room for three days, she finally realized she had to ask the Germans to forgive her for her hatred.

Her breakthrough really affected the hearts of everyone at the conference, and thereafter she and others from Moral Re-Armament traveled throughout Europe, telling their story. Their example affected thousands and is credited with helping to rebuild Europe psychologically after the war. Today we are beginning to see the emergence of the European Community and a united Europe. MRA members say, "You are as close to God as you are to the person from who you feel most divided." Whenever there's a conflict, they remind people, "It's not who's right, but what's right." Recent MRA conferences have been to heal ethnic strife in Eastern Europe and racial strife in Richmond, Virginia.[5]

In analyzing the **Green Party**'s stinging defeat in the 1990 West German elections, late cofounder Petra Kelly stated that the more they attempted to raise issues ignored by the major parties, the more the internal differences within the Green Party itself came to the forefront. Kelly found that the greatest hurdle to overcome in establishing themselves as a political force was the disrespectful and abusive way they treated each other—which turned off voters. A similar perspective was voiced by Christa Slaton, professor of government at Georgia Southern University, who worked with and studied the Greens in the United States. She was concerned that Greens carried "mistrust into most of their political interactions with each other . . . name calling and insults are routinely exchanged."[6]

As political commentator Mark Satin noted, the irony was that the Greens made a point of saying how important it was to treat people well, yet he found that they sometimes treated each other worse than people in traditional political parties. The Greens' experience shows how difficult it is to change our own consciousness and to personally embody our ideals, but a least they're trying to be honest in their self-critiques and are committed to doing better.

It's the psychological mind-set that often leads to a political group's ineffectiveness—a strong victim consciousness ("they" did it to us), for example, and at the same time an overly self-righteous attitude that only that group itself has the truth (this is typical of the fundamentalist Right as well as the radical Left).

Some lawyers are beginning to include the psychological dimension in their work, transforming themselves from win-at-all-costs hired guns into practitioners of the healing arts, helping clients deal with the inner conflicts that led to the dispute. Bill Van Zyverden, founder of the **International Alliance of Holistic Lawyers**, calls their approach "client-oriented law from the heart," which promotes holistic, long-range problem solving rather than short-term litigation to resolve disputes: getting a client charged with drunk driving to stimulate him to overcome drinking, for example.[7]

RELEASING ENEMY IMAGES

As psychologist Sam Keene suggests, "Depth psychology has presented us with the undeniable wisdom that the enemy is constructed from denied aspects of the self."[8] The denied parts of ourselves are called the "shadow"—or "the Dweller on the Threshold" in the Ageless Wisdom tradition—that which blocks our movement forward. Shadow projection is clearly the deeper cause of racism and sexism, for example. If we don't want to admit our own laziness or weakness, we project it onto blacks, women, and the like. Any time we find ourselves getting self-righteous and worked up emotionally about the bad qualities of our enemies, it's usually a sign to stop and look a little deeper inside ourselves at our own "shadow projection." (See chapter 6 for more on shadow projection.)

Since public opinion is very much influenced by psychological factors, there are now many psychologists who are helping to clarify the psychological distortions projected onto public leaders and policies. **Psychologists for Social Responsibility (PsiSR)**, a national association based in Washington, D.C., is an active network of clinicians and academics who are doing this kind of work. PsiSR was officially included in the professional association of psychologists, the American Psychological Association, in 1989 as the Division of Peace Psychology. PsiSR analyzes the psychological causes and consequences of war and destructive conflict, by identifying the psychological mechanisms that shape public attitudes and maintain the war-focused system. PsiSR also provides educational programs to decrease enmity and increase empathy and compassion. They've most recently worked on the Bosnian conflict and with Muslim rape victims, and have written a brochure in Croatian and Serbian to recommend ways to deal with the severe emotional effects of war trauma.

PsiSR pointed out a number of culturally and psychologically insensitive moves on the part of the United States during the Persian Gulf war. For example, a woman ambassador was appointed to a country where women traditionally do not take such roles, thus ignoring the cultural fact that the basis for trust in Arab society depends mainly on establishing relationships. The U.S. government then not only refused to listen to Saddam's concerns, it insisted upon ultimatums—an especially dangerous move in the shame-oriented Arab culture. Equally dangerous was insisting on deadlines, for there is a different perspective on time in Arab culture.

One of the projects of Psychologists for Social Responsibility is to defuse exaggerated images of the "enemy." According to several studies, enemy images lead people to selectively attend to and remember negative aspects of "enemies" more than friends. Dutta Kanungo and Freiberg (1972) studied English Canadians and found that when questioned on material read previously, the subjects remembered more unpleasant adjectives about French Canadians than they did about English Canadians. When they studied French Canadians, the reverse was true.

A similar study by Taylor and Jaggi (1974) found that Hindu office clerks in southern India attributed friendly behavior by fellow Hindus in various situations to their personalities and unfriendly behaviors to circumstances, while they attributed the opposite to Moslems. When they studied Moslems, the researchers found that Moslems attributed friendly behavior by fellow Moslems to their personality and unfriendly behavior to circumstances.[9]

Psychological studies show that enemy images have a deep effect on people's attitudes and actions. Such images lead people to predict hostile behavior from enemies and to act in a hostile manner toward them based solely upon this prediction. They will also lead people to exaggerate the level of hostility of enemy actions compared with similar actions performed by nonenemies, to encourage ignorance about enemies, and to be biased in attributing motives for actions of enemies. In a study by Plous and Zimbardo (1984), U.S. readers of *Psychology Today* magazine were unable to differentiate between the unlabeled aggressive actions of the United States and those of the former Soviet Union.

Psychologists for Social Responsibility is working to increase public awareness of the enemy images that aggravate racism, conflict, and war and to help people understand the psychological principles underlying peace and justice. Enemies are dehumanized and stereotyped by creating oversimplified views of them and by overlooking their human qualities and depicting them as subhuman. Enemy images are useful to governments because of several short-term benefits: they divert attention from domestic problems, stimulate economic activity by increasing military spending, and provide a sense of moral order and legitimacy for some international actions.

PsiSR has created a number of exercises in their publication to help people understand enemy images—for example, recognizing the universality of these images across time, place, and leadership. Participants are asked to identify which sketches of enemies from popular posters and cartoons are from which nation—and very few can tell the difference, as each nation's enemies look like the same monsters.

During the Persian Gulf war, for example, PsiSR documented how the great majority of movies and television shows in the United States demonized Arab characters, portraying them either as ruthless terrorists, corrupt sheiks, or seductive harem dancers. Professor Jack Shaheen charges that "the sheik image parallels the images of the Jew in Nazi-inspired German films. . . . [Just as] the Jew was made the scapegoat of Germany's problems, [so] today the Arab lurks behind the misfortunes, evils, and imbalances in our own economic and cultural life. . . . Few critics, scholars, or politicians speak out against the stereotypes [because] [t]hey fear public condemnation of 'ugly Arab' portraits could be construed as being pro-Arab and anti-Israel."[10]

Living Politics
Consultant Michael Goldberg and Anne Anderson, national coordinator of Psychologists for Social Responsibility and a member of our biweekly political salon, gave seminars in the early 1980s called Living Politics, in which participants were asked to get in touch with and express the feeling of a particular nation or organization in a major conflict. They might play political groups, like the Sandinistas, or political objects, like the Korean airliner that was shot down. Once the drama is established, they move back and forth between the political drama and "reality"—their personal lives, examining each in light of the other.

In one of their workshops people were asked randomly to choose one of three groups—the Palestinian Liberation Organization (PLO), Israel, or Lebanon—and act as if they were members of this group, intuiting what their positions would be. Each group was to create a consensus about what it wanted to bring to the conference table to discuss with the other two groups.

The most powerful and telling part of the exercise was when participants were told to "take your space"—arrange themselves physically in the room, individually or with their group, according to how they perceived their role. Each group had a unique expression—their body language markedly reflecting the actual country. The PLO was very noisy, passionate, and disorganized and never even sat down together. The Israelis immediately formed a tight, highly organized group, which was very defended psychologically. The Lebanese acted very depressed and couldn't get their group together, complaining that the instructions given for the game were impossible. They felt they weren't even a country (and this was the day before the headlines in the papers actually proclaimed LEBANON NOT A COUNTRY). Each participant later noticed how the experience of who they role-played reflected exactly the issues in their own personal lives. Surprisingly, most participants said they had "randomly" chosen the group most opposed to their own political beliefs, and this created much food for thought.

Learning the Stance of the Observer

Simply presenting two different points of view on an issue is not enough for most people to be able rationally to assess each position and make an informed choice. Since our psychological mind-set tends to keep most of us locked in to our own preformed prejudices, making it very difficult to hear an opposing point of view, PsiSR members have provided "meta-cognitive interventions." Before the presentations they point out the psychological mechanisms, such as "selective perception" and "defenses," that are often at work in such situations and invite people to observe the workings of their own minds while they're listening to the presentations. Anne Anderson says they have found this to be very helpful in developing the stance of the objective observer, so the content of our own consciousness could be observed. Both sides could then truly be heard, new insights gained, and informed choices made.

Reconciliation

A number of transformational groups are working to reconcile traditional enemies and bring a spirit of healing to the process. According to Tama Pearson at the University of Arizona, several factors contribute to creating shifts in an antagonistic relationship. There needs to be some acknowledgment of the other group's humanity—their basic human needs, their suffering, their historical legitimacy. People need to be willing to take risks, to allow themselves to be vulnerable. And there needs to be some symbolic component, such as when President Anwar Sadat of Egypt went to Israel.

This reconciliation work has recently spread to many conflicted issues. The **Public Conversations Project**, directed by Laura Chasin in Boston, is a group of family therapists working to create a "demilitarized zone" between pro-choice and pro-life adherents on the abortion issue. They noticed that the public arguments in American political life resembled the "stuck conversations" of troubled families, with each side locked into hostile, fixed positions. Under the ground rules, people joining these dialogues are not allowed to try to convince each other, only to talk and listen and explore their stereotypes of each other.

Afterward each side was able to see its opponents as more compassionate and principled than they had previously believed. They also uncovered shared concerns about the well-being of both mothers and children, the need for preventing unintended pregnancy, and the advisability of sex education. Both sides agreed that using abortion as a form of birth control was wrong. Groups similar to Public Conversations now exist in Missouri, Wisconsin, Texas and California.[11]

The **Victim-Offender Reconciliation Program**, directed by Reverend Louise Stowe Johns in Montgomery, Alabama, involves crime victims and offenders in a process of restorative rather than retributive justice based on Judeo-Christian principles. Referred by a criminal court, the parties meet voluntarily with a trained mediator, and both agree upon restitution. Rather than the justice system incarcerating the offender, victims have an opportunity to vent their feelings with the offender and then offer forgiveness and so positively affect the life of the offender. This new movement is meeting with tremendous success.

A reconciliation project has also been organized in East Germany between former members of the Stasi, the repressive secret intelligence organization, and their victims. To bring healing to their country, the ex-Stasi wanted to talk about why it all happened and what the consequences really were—a process of confession and self-examination.[12]

The work of all these groups in finding effective nonviolent solutions to conflicts is providing a major evolutionary shift and laying the groundwork for future mediation and reconciliation for all human conflict.

SELF-ESTEEM

The promotion of individual self-esteem is unambiguously at the core of a healthy nation.
—JACK KEMP, FORMER SECRETARY OF HOUSING AND
URBAN DEVELOPMENT IN THE BUSH ADMINISTRATION

The Ageless Wisdom emphasizes the importance of self-knowledge and self-respect, for within each of us there is an indwelling Divinity. Self-esteem builds faith in ourselves and our own innate capacities, and enhances our inclinations toward becoming constructive, life-affirming, responsible, and trustworthy citizens. Self-esteem helps us own and exercise our power and take charge of our lives and our society. But according to a Gallup/*Newsweek* poll, 10 percent of Americans believe they personally suffer from low self-esteem, and more than 50 percent say someone in their family suffers from it.[13]

According to some psychologists, lack of self-esteem is a chief cause of many of our social problems—especially drug addiction, violence, teen pregnancies, school dropout rates, and low work productivity. In a 1993 letter to an education conference in Santa Clara, California, President

Clinton wrote, "In a world where guns and drugs are too often a part of the landscape, the cultivation of self-esteem may be the greatest protection available to a child."

Nearly all American institutions seem to promote personal helplessness to foster greater dependency on themselves and other institutions. But the quality of life we experience is often more a function of what we think of ourselves than what institutions do for us. Greater self-esteem can promote greater self-reliance (which used to be an American virtue) and lead to greater productivity.

Developing people—our human capital, the untapped potential and gifts of all our people—is a key not only to economic development, but to building community, as only someone with self-esteem can relate comfortably across lines of race and gender and therefore help build a multicultural democracy. When we begin to feel comfortable in ourselves, we will no longer need to have everyone else be like us. Although it's clear how low income and a poor home environment lead to lack of self-esteem, it's also true that low self-esteem continues to perpetuate the cycle, and this makes it difficult to find a good job. Even those from upper-income families who lack self-esteem experience failure in their careers.

Some see low self-esteem as a metadisease, a state of mind that seems to underlie and perhaps cause a wide range of physical and emotional problems, from bulimia to performance anxiety. Self-esteem is fostered by developing a sense of security, identity, belonging, purpose, and competence. There is also an interdependent system between evolving a healthier Earth (called "eco-esteem") and fostering healthy self-esteem. People who don't respect themselves are less likely to respect the environment or to feel a sense of responsibility toward caring for it.

The concept of changing society by raising personal self-esteem is transformational. It reframes the political dialogue to include both the conservative ideal of self-reliance and the liberal idea of helping people improve their lives.

The effect of low self-esteem engendered by childhood experiences on the character of political leaders has often been explored in psychological literature and is now gaining wider acceptance in other circles. Feminist Gloria Steinem, for example, has written about how her own lack of self-esteem affected her politics.[14]

Gail Sheehy, in her controversial book *Character*, analyzed the relationship between the early psychological experiences of all the major contenders in the presidential primaries of 1988 and their politics. She noted, for example, that none of George Bush's family or friends could remember a single instance of his disagreeing with, or standing up to, his father or anyone else—and drew a parallel to his inability to take definitive stands on anything before he saw public opinion polls.[15]

The Self-Esteem Task Force

California Democratic assemblyman John Vasconcellos, one of the most powerful men in the assembly and chairman of the Ways and Means Committee, is a good example of the effectiveness of personal self-esteem work, according to Professor Jeff Fishel of the American University. Fishel notes that Vasconcellos has developed a reputation as "the conscience of the legislature" because of his "absolute honesty and personal integrity with colleagues, lobbyists, voters, and everyone else." A colleague commented that he is "extraordinarily patient, empathetic, and understanding." He has made friends with, helped out, and won over some of the crustiest, stiffest, most conservative Republicans in the assembly. He can bridge and transform differences among some of the most unlikely people, setting aside his ego, ideology, and power stakes to help others reach "win/win" solutions. He is one of the few members of the assembly to whom all factions turn when the going gets rough.[16]

In 1986 Vasconcellos was instrumental in getting the state of California to establish the Task Force to Promote Self-Esteem, to hold public hearings across the state and to issue a report on its findings. It explored the correlation between self-esteem on the one hand and on the other, crime, drug and alcohol abuse, teen pregnancy, child and spouse abuse, chronic welfare dependency, and the failure to achieve in school. Vasconcellos believes that welfare recipients aren't the only ones lacking self-esteem. He feels that this lack is reflected in all levels of our society, which is focused on competitive pursuit of wealth, power, and status. Researching how to nurture self-esteem and how to rehabilitate it, the task force received more requests for appointments than any commission in the state's history and helped spin off forty-seven (out of fifty-eight total) county-level self-esteem units.

According to task force member Jack Canfield, all graduating students of Los Angeles schools are now certified that they have learned teamwork, cooperation and conflict resolution as a result of self-esteem training. Eight inner-city schools in the San Jose School District of California that implemented self-esteem programs are now in the top 5 percent of California schools on achievement tests, with 99.7 percent attendance and only 5.4 percent dropout rate (compared with 16 percent in other nearby schools). Violence and drug abuse have been eliminated.[17]

California teacher credentialing now includes self-esteem criteria. Over 175,000 California welfare recipients will go through a three-year self-esteem training program to teach them how to move through their personal barriers to success, how to become gainfully employed, and how to achieve their goals—something needed more than ever in the aftermath of the Los Angeles riots. All legislation in California is now examined for a self-esteem component. Maryland, Louisiana, and Virginia have created similar task forces, and twelve other states are moving in that direction.[18]

In addition, a National Council for Self-Esteem has been established with chapters in more than sixty cities, and an International Council for Self-Esteem has chapters in more than eleven countries. National legislation on Social and Economic Esteem has been drafted to establish national criteria and offer incentives of matching federal funds for local districts to provide self-esteem training in education, welfare, and other areas.

Vasconcellos reframed the issue around his Self-Esteem Task Force from a project that needed taxpayers' dollars for support to one that would save taxpayers' dollars. To get the support of the governor of California, he showed how developing self-esteem among population groups that are likely to become drug abusers and pregnant teens would make the need for welfare much less likely in the long run: people who have developed high self-esteem are far more likely to grow into productive, self-reliant members of their communities and are therefore less likely to need government handouts.

Vasconcellos says, "This is truly grass-roots revolution . . . wherein each of us comes to know that we need no longer look to the government or other agencies and/or authorities for solutions to our human problems. We can and should, instead, look deep into our selves. [It is] the ultimate truly populist revolution, for instead of being a reaction against authority and/or wealth, it is truly pro-active, pro-person."[19]

Local and International Projects

Another successful example of the application of self-esteem to poverty, drug abuse, and crime is the Modello Housing Project in Miami, Florida, which had been one of the worst examples of public housing in the country. But when Roger Mills began holding classes on self-esteem and community leadership training, he got the cooperation of the local Department of Housing and Urban Development as well as a local crime prevention group. He helped project residents see that the root of their problem was their self-image. Within two years school delinquency dropped by 80 percent, child neglect by 60 percent, and drug trafficking by 75 percent, and parent involvement in schools increased by 500 percent.[20]

The D.C. Service Corps, an effective project to develop self-esteem, was founded in the nation's capital as part of a sixteen-city project to put young volunteers to work helping the community. The program provides a substitute for the many negative experiences of urban school dropouts—drugs, delinquency, violence, poverty—by offering such positive experiences as renovating homeless shelters, restoring playgrounds and parks, and assisting the elderly. This helps young people develop the good work habits, skills, knowledge, and self-confidence they need to prepare them for jobs with a future.[21]

The Teen Institute of the Garden State, based in New Jersey, enables inner-city teenagers to fend off the pack mentality of drug and alcohol abuse by raising their self-esteem through "sharing time" and "process groups."

Self-esteem training has been growing in the corporate sector as well. The personal development classes provided to the managers of the national chain of Hardees restaurants, for example, was so effective and popular that families of Hardees employees have asked to take the program.

In the summer of 1990, educators, psychologists, and health care providers from nine countries, including the former Soviet Union and other countries of Eastern Europe, met in Oslo with veterans of the California experiment. They had concluded that self-esteem—with its conviction that each of us is important and makes a difference—was necessary for the success of the new democracy in their countries. They looked to the self-esteem work to help reduce prejudice, child abuse, alcoholism, and other destructive behavior. The first meeting of the Soviet National Council for Self-Esteem was scheduled to meet in Moscow in August of 1991, where the minister of education was planning to introduce self-esteem programs into the schools. At the same time as the meeting, the Soviet coup was being defeated by Boris Yeltsin's challenge to the people to resist—in a remarkable example of rising national self-esteem.

However, like everything else, this new emphasis on self-esteem can also become distorted. In some schools kids are given so many awards and honors for routine accomplishments that it becomes trivialized. In other schools the F grade for failing has been abolished, so kids get no useful feedback when they're not even trying. There needs to be a balance in developing self-esteem so it is not taken to such extremes that people become arrogant, with no real-world connection to their actual abilities and achievements. But, overall, most self-esteem programs are providing just the right amount of support to build students' self-confidence and optimism.

COOPERATION AND COMMUNITY

Cooperation is a state of mind. There is little hope of real progress until we make this discovery and act upon this knowledge.
—THOMAS JEFFERSON

An important foundation in the new transformational political paradigm is a spirit of community, of healing and cooperation, rather than of competition. There is something in the human condition that eternally yearns for a greater sense of connectedness with others. Working to create a spirit of community helps to overcome the feelings of isolation and separation so prevalent in the West today. Community is a way to begin to heal past hurts. As the Foundation for Global Community group offers, "Global community is a genetic idea of the future." The Ageless Wisdom teaches that cooperation is the innate attitude of the Soul—it is naturally group conscious rather than individually self-centered.

Cooperation is a process that makes it easier for us to face the complexity that often forces people into hard-line positions. Cooperation can reposition the players on the board in such a way that they're able to look at a problem in a new light and find the higher ground. As Fran Peavey says in *Heart Politics*, cooperation is about learning to act politically out of a sense of connectedness with others, rather than out of a fixed ideology.[22] We move toward cooperation by developing our sense of group identity, so that even if an individual cannot win every time, he or she may get satisfaction from benefits accruing to the group.

Reciprocity

In computer tournaments featuring the famous Prisoner's Dilemma game—where two prisoners face the choice of informing on each other (defecting) or remaining silent (cooperating) without knowing what the other will do—the winning strategy is one of simple reciprocity. By cooperating on the first move and then doing whatever the other player did on the previous move, unnecessary conflict is avoided by cooperating as long as the other player does. Thousands of computer games, and corroboration from many real-world examples, illustrate that cooperation based upon reciprocity can develop even between antagonists. For cooperation to emerge, the interaction must extend over an indefinite or at least an unknown number of moves, and the importance of each encounter must be great enough to make defection an unprofitable strategy.

The tournaments also demonstrate that it is actually better to respond quickly to defections by responding in kind, in order to avoid sending the wrong signal—that defections pay. In this case the foundation of cooperation is not trust, but the durability of the relationship. The value of reciprocity becomes self-reinforcing—once it gets going, it gets stronger and stronger.[23]

In *Breakthrough: Emerging New Thinking of Soviet and Western Scholars*, Robert Axelrod writes, "A concrete example of this theory was the case of the 'live and let live' system that emerged during the trench warfare of the western front in World War I. Frontline soldiers often refrained from shooting to kill, provided their restraint was reciprocated by the soldiers on the other side—which actually violated orders from their own high commands."[24]

Although Westerners assume that the emphasis on competition is universal, in fact cross-cultural observers have confirmed that our competitive society is the exception rather than the rule. From the Inuit Indians of Canada to the Tangu natives of New Guinea, from the Iroquois in North America to the Bathonga of South Africa, from kibbutzniks in Israel to farmers in Mexico, cooperation is prized and competition generally avoided. Professors David and Roger Johnson at the University of Minnesota reviewed 122 studies conducted from 1924 to 1981 and found that 65 studies showed that cooperation promotes higher achievement than competition, 8 showed the reverse, and 36 showed no statistically significant difference. Recent studies by Professors Robert Helmreich of the University of Texas and Teresa Amabile of Brandeis University also confirmed the power of cooperation.[25]

Creating a Framework of Equality

The mission of the **Institute for Social and Economic Policy in the Middle East**, directed by Leonard Hausman at Harvard University's John F. Kennedy School of Government, is to bring together Arabs and Israelis to seek common ground for cooperation in education, health, welfare, and business. The institute sponsors a program on Economic Transition that explores trade arrangements, the development of joint industries, and cooperative arrangements with seaports, water supply, and utility systems. Senior economists—twelve Israelis, twelve Jordanians, and twelve Palestinians—participate in short-term meetings and then coauthor a paper on the results.

The institute has a small fellowship program that brings together Arab and Israeli health and human service professionals to study at Harvard for a year and develop joint projects. The number one ingredient of the program is that the fellows not only take courses together, but also experience a sense of community by living together with their families in the same dormitory, eating together, shopping together. This helps Jews and Arabs move beyond seeing each other merely as stereotypes. It is from this deep human contact that understanding and trust are built between former enemies. As members of the institute note, "People make peace; politicians can do it only on paper."

Another cooperative effort is a successful Arab-Israeli kibbutzlike community called **Neve Shalom/Wahat al-Salam** (Oasis of Peace) in Israel, started by Father Bruno. Over seventy Jews and Palestinians of Israeli citizenship live and work together in this kibbutz, and their children are taught to respect each other's cultures. The aim is to create a social, cultural, and political framework of equality and mutual respect in which residents are able to retain their own heritage and identity. In the kibbutz's School for Peace, Arabs and Jews confront one another and learn nonviolent skills for solving personal and social conflicts. In this process they use their lives as examples of cooperative coexistence, manifesting their long-term commitment to justice and peace in the Middle East.

Earthstewards Network, based in Washington State with local chapters all over the country, is a volunteer effort to improve cooperation, sharing, and understanding among people from different countries. They've sent U.S. teenagers to the former Soviet Union and to Northern Ireland to help melt the walls that exist between cultures, and they've brought together Russian, American, and Indian youth to reclaim the deserts of India and to work in the rain forests of Costa Rica. They've also brought together U.S. veterans from Vietnam and Soviet veterans from Afghanistan for technical and personal support in healing the emotional wounds of fighting an unpopular war. Both veterans groups have now started a factory in Siberia together to produce much needed wheelchairs.

Their Urban Peace Trees project has helped to train inner-city youth in leadership skills by tearing up concrete and planting trees alongside young people from other countries. As they worked together, sweating and dirty, the young people discovered how very much alike they are and how interdependent our planet is. They have also organized visits to the Middle East to live in both Arab and Israeli homes.

R and D in Cooperative Living

There are thousands of alternative communities around the world that function as research and development centers for society, experimenting with cooperative forms of living that can be studied and adapted for use elsewhere. In the area of governance, they provide some of the more viable models of the new political paradigm available for the public to observe. Their cooperative, participatory forms of governance are based on commitment and trust rather than on hierarchical discipline and material motiva-tion. There is a quality and a spirit present in these groups that is almost nonexistent today in most organizations. Honesty, caring, listening, and good interpersonal communication help make cooperation possible.

There are few rules in these communities. Rather, each person is ex-pected to be responsible for the good of the whole. **Findhorn** in Scotland, **Auroville** in India, **Alpha** in Oregon, **Lama** in New Mexico, and **Sirius** in Massachusetts are all good models of a cooperative form of governance. These communities and many others are pioneering an evolutionary step for humanity, when their work can be adopted on a larger scale. (For more information on communities see our previous book, *Builders of the Dawn*.)

EMPOWERMENT AND PARTICIPATION

Never doubt that a small group of thoughtful citizens can change the world. Indeed, it's the only thing that ever has.
—MARGARET MEAD

The new political paradigm focuses on individual empowerment—helping people feel confident in themselves and their ability to affect the world, and giving them training and tools to be effective in achieving social goals. It helps people overcome victim consciousness—feeling sorry for them-selves and their problems and blaming other people or "the system." It honors the special gifts and abilities, the potential, in all people while mo-tivating them to do something to improve not only their own lives, but those of others.

Abraham Lincoln once remarked, "A lot of people can withstand adver-sity. If you really want to test someone's character, give him power." The new approaches to empowerment help people overcome their fear of power or fear of misusing it. Instead people are helped to learn to use power wisely, seeing it as an opportunity for growth and a chance to learn from mistakes.

There are several types of empowerment: psychological—relating to feel-ings and attitudes; social—relating to ability; and political—relating to ac-tivism. True empowerment, according to political scientist Ed Schwerin, must be based on self-esteem, capability, knowledge, skills, political aware-ness, participation, and the fulfillment of our basic human rights and needs.[26]

Most of the interest in the issue of empowerment today is found among feminists, blacks, Native Americans, and other minorities and also in the fields of education and public health. Empowerment has also become a key word for the 1990s in corporate circles. The emphasis here is on how to empower employees to be more creative so as to make more money for the company, but in some cases the employees themselves are given incentives such as profit-sharing programs. Recently, however, empowerment has found its way into the federal government. Former secretary of housing Jack Kemp established the HOPE Project with "empowerment" initiatives for resident management and eventual ownership of public housing, with skills development, job training, and literacy programs, and President Clinton often emphasizes empowerment programs instead of direct subsidy.

There is a reciprocal relationship between the psychological emancipation of the individual and the political emancipation of humanity. As we grow personally, we naturally turn toward service for others. Serving the world in some way helps us feel more personally fulfilled.

There are many encouraging signs today that citizens are empowering themselves to solve their own social problems. The growing size and effectiveness of the many NGOs (nongovernmental organizations) at the UN is encouraging, as is the preventive, self-help, wellness movement.

The Sarvodaya movement in Sri Lanka is a very successful voluntary movement that empowers people to build a new society from the ground up. Founded by A. T. Ariyaratne in 1958, it now includes 10 percent of the total population. "Sarvodaya" means "the awakening of all in society"— awakening to the understanding that people can make and carry out their own "development plans" to meet their own needs, that they don't have to be mentally or physically dependent on government handouts. Sarvodaya believes that change in the world begins with change in local communities, and that change in local communities begins with change in individual people. The four cornerstones of their movement are respect for all life, compassionate action, dispassionate joy, and equanimity. The three million members of the movement all do a loving-kindness meditation twice a day.

When requested, the Sarvodaya staff organizes a big *shramadana* to show local villages that at least some of the solutions to their problems lie in their own hands. Sarvodayans don't come in with blueprints for change, but just listen to the villagers and model good listening skills for them, so they can really hear each other for the first time and overcome conflicts.

The goal of the Sarvodaya movement is, first, to produce goods for people to support themselves; second, to conserve resources; third, to produce by cooperative methods; and last, to consume only what is "appropriate." They address not just what psychologist Abraham Maslow identified as the lower needs—food, shelter, clothing—but also the higher, spiritual needs.[27]

The Door, a large drop-in center for inner-city youth started by good friends of ours in New York in 1972, is an excellent model of empowerment for young people, helping them stay away from drugs and violence. It was created to help disadvantaged teenagers take charge of their lives, with many human-oriented support services in a comprehensive, single facility. The Door provides an integrated approach with support groups, mental health, pregnancy, legal and nutritional counseling, job training, crafts instruction, martial arts training, and community musical sharings. The professionals who serve The Door meet daily to share perspectives on each young person, dealing with the whole person—body, mind, and spirit. Funded by corporate and local government grants, The Door has been so successful that it has become a model for similar projects in Canada, Australia, Guatemala, Mexico, and other countries.

Children of War is a national organization that empowers teenagers from international war zones as well as from "domestic war zones" in the inner city by creating emotional support in a peer group setting. A core group of youth leaders from different geographical areas of the United States and other countries travel throughout the United States, sharing their life stories and their techniques for healing and empowerment. This simple process uses personal suffering as a teacher. "If you can deeply allow yourself to share it, to feel it, to receive support around it and not be alone in it," says director Judith Thompson, "what happens is that the contradiction of breaking through isolation is so powerful that it transforms itself into a joyful experience." On the other side of despair is a deep empowerment that creates leaders, healers, and teachers for the future as the teenagers return to their own country. Children of War tours have reached more than one hundred thousand students in sixty cities over the last seven years.

The Center for Living Democracy in Vermont, started by Frances Moore Lappé and Paul Martin DuBois, promotes a new concept called "living democracy" (in contrast with "formal democracy" or the "moral community" of protest) in order to overcome the myths that control our lives. The institute empowers people to become effective citizens by "learning the arts of democracy—active listening, dialogue, negotiation, reflection, and creative controversy." They work to educate people in methods for making government accountable to citizens' real concerns. They teach people how to develop "relational power"—power that grows with others by becoming partners in problem solving.

ISAR (formerly **The Institute for Soviet-American Relations**), founded by our friend Harriett Crosby in Washington, D.C., is one of many successful "citizen diplomacy" groups around the country that empower citizen efforts for building good relationships with counterparts in "adversary" nations. Observing that the arms race was based on the lack of relationship between the people of adversary nations, the institute started to really listen to people. They hoped to uncover and build on common ground between liberal and conservative views of the former Soviet Union and to create a field of interaction—a climate of goodwill. The institute doesn't confront differences or judge which program is best. It simply supports others in their good work and reports on them in its large quarterly publication, *Surviving Together*. The institute also brings U.S. environmentalists to Russia and vice-versa to share information and skills and form working partnerships with their Russian counterparts.

Teledemocracy is another type of citizen empowerment. The "teledemocratic movement" is developing an intricate mix of electronic technologies and communications techniques to empower a massive number of citizens in a contemporary form of direct democracy. Starting in the 1970s with "anticipatory democracy" experiments to anticipate the future, such as that written about by Clement Bezold of the Institute for Alternative Futures of Alexandria, Virginia, in his book, *Anticipatory Democracy*,[28] a number of projects and experiments have been developed in the United States, Europe, and New Zealand. These projects have linked people to relevant data and expert opinions, as well as to one another, in order to involve them as an informed, deliberative, and representative "citizen legislature." Through the use of television, telephones, and computers, they discuss and vote on current issues of our time. However, one problem is that progressive groups using teledemocracy act like advocacy groups and don't want to air opposite views. Another is that the established media power structure feels threatened by teledemocracy, seeing it as a reduction in their own power.[29]

Another effective means of empowerment is using public opinion polling that is bipartisan and in-depth that helps educate the public on issues, such as the work done by Alan F. Kay with his Americans Talk Issues Foundation. He and partner Hazel Henderson have proposed legislation for a bipartisan Congressional Office of Public Opinion and Research to allow Congress to fully utilize public opinion in policymaking.

SPIRITUALITY: ETHICS, VALUES, AND MEANING

> *There must be a spirituality to what we in politics do. There's a certain spirituality in the articulation of platforms, positions, and policies, and the movement toward those goals is more than a political exercise.*
>
> —PAUL TSONGAS[30]

Mainstream politics in the United States (with a few exceptions such as the fundamentalist Right) has mostly avoided any mention of spirituality. Wealth, physical health, beauty, professional accreditation, and political power are seen as the only reliable measures of a person's worth. Only physical phenomena that can be measured and have economic value are considered to be real. Yet recently some people who have climbed to the top in all these areas but then dramatically realized the spiritual vacuum in their hearts—and within the heart of our society—have sounded the alarm bell.

Lee Atwater, former chairman of the Republican National Committee, who was known for his negative campaigning during the Bush campaign, said his sudden brain tumor helped him see that what was missing in society was missing in him: "a little heart, a lot of brotherhood." He said, "I don't know who will lead us through the 90s, but they must be made to speak to this spiritual vacuum at the heart of American society, this tumor of the Soul." Significantly, it was in the middle of telling an audience a mean joke about Michael Dukakis's riding in a tank that the whole left side of Atwater's body first started to shake and he collapsed. On the way to the hospital, he saw a message flash before his eyes: "This is the test."[31]

Former President George Bush said in early 1993: "I've concluded after having been President of the United States that it's family, friends and faith that mean everything."[32]

President Vaclav Havel of the Czech Republic in his address to the U.S. Congress in 1990, declared: "We must put morality ahead of politics . . . actions before words." Havel, who considers ethical values more important than remaining in office, is "the embodiment of moral rectitude to his nation. . . . His true passion is not for possessions or power, but for giving life a purpose," according to *Time* magazine.[33] Havel says, "It still is my profound conviction that the very essence of politics is not dirty; dirt is brought in only by wicked people. It is not true that people of high principle are ill-suited to politics. . . . [A politician] must trust not only an objective interpretation of reality, but also his own soul."[34]

John Quanjer, publisher of Britain's *New Humanity Journal* and candi-

date for The European Parliament, called this spiritually based politics
pneumatocracy. The word is derived from the Greek, *pneuma* meaning
"spirit" and *kratos* meaning "the rule of": in other words, a Spirit-infused
politics in which our souls are the guiding force. As Socrates said, "True
politics is first of all a state of soul."

Some people, such as spiritual leader Donald Walters, call a value-
oriented approach "dharmacracy" from the Hindu word *dharma* meaning
"doing what's right, what's for the greatest good." The setting of a society's
standards is what politics is all about, in the final analysis.

The Faith and Politics Institute in Washington, D.C., started by minister Doug Tanner, is encouraging spiritual growth, community, and conscience in political life among congresspeople, since their life generally
affords little time and few settings for conscious reflection on matters either
of the spirit or statesmanship.

The Congressional Prayer Breakfast is an encouraging sign of the
times. Forty to sixty members of Congress attend a bipartisan weekly
prayer breakfast to pray, sing, and bare their souls. Participants report it has
become a real spiritual refuge and one of the few opportunities where they
can reveal something personal about their life and faith, which aren't talked
about in public.

Ethics in Public Life. A movement is also under way to bring ethics
back into public life, as in the work of Elsa Porter, former assistant secretary for administration under President Carter. Georgetown University in
Washington, D.C., has sponsored conferences on this theme, as has the **Institute for American Values** in New York and the **Foundation for Public
Affairs** in Washington. Among the topics explored were ethical considerations for lobbyists on Capitol Hill and for campaign contributions.

The Politics of Meaning. *Tikkun* magazine, started by former Berkeley
peace activist Michael Lerner, has developed a values-oriented progressive
politics that goes beyond the narrow focus on economic entitlements and
political rights that has dominated the liberal and progressive agenda. *Tikkun's* position maintains that human needs for love, connection, and purpose have been neglected by the competitive market ethos of materialism,
selfishness, and moral relativism. Thus it is the deprivation of meaning and
values in contemporary society that has funneled people's desperation into
fundamentalist politics as well as toward Ross Perot's 1992 presidential
campaign, even when these movements don't really serve them.

Instead, Lerner and friends are working on a new approach that includes
the psychological, ethical, and spiritual dimensions of reality and seeks to
return a sense of purpose to people's lives. The approach is called the "politics of meaning," and its platform calls for educating for values, actively

promoting health, rewarding public investment, supporting families (both traditional or nontraditional) by teaching coping skills, and a mix of other innovative as well as traditional liberal ideas.[35]

Their cause was given a big boost when First Lady Hillary Clinton spoke about the need for a "new politics of meaning . . . a new ethos of individual responsibility and caring" in a speech at the University of Texas in 1993. She invited Michael Lerner to the White House and caused a huge uproar in the media with *The New York Times* calling her "St. Hillary" and *Time* magazine saying, "The politics of what? . . ."

Moral Re-Armament (MRA), a network that grew out of the Oxford Group, helps people around the world to solve personal and social problems through reliance on inner moral and spiritual motivation. Rather than a traditional leadership structure, everyone is responsible, in cooperation with others, to their own conscience and inner guidance. Decisions are made and leadership given through informal associations. There is no formal membership and few paid staff. For fifty-five years Moral Re-Armament has encouraged the development of love, purity, honesty, unselfishness, and reliance on God as the basis for social action in their teams in over fifty countries around the world. "Our greatest need," they say, "is for spiritual empowerment that transforms the heart and lifts people out of the mentality of defeat." A recent gathering at their major conference center at Caux, Switzerland, successfully brought together hundreds of Eastern Europeans and Russians to explore the theme "Democracy Begins with Me." Another conference called "Healing the Heart of America" drew people of all races in Richmond, Virginia, in 1993 to begin an honest dialogue on race, reconciliation, and responsibility.

The National Center for Neighborhood Enterprise. Founder Robert L. Woodson noted in his twenty years of work with community social programs that the successful ones are always spiritually based (not necessarily religious, but spiritual). He finds the greatest hunger in America is not for things—but for meaning.

Attunement

A number of transformational groups use a process called "attunement" to make decisions based on the inner spiritual guidance of everyone present. All participants are recognized as having the potential ability to reach a decision that is for the highest good of all concerned. The assumption is that there is a right decision that will work for everyone, and the task of the group is to discover it. Everyone in turn is asked to offer their unique perspectives and contributions to the governance of the whole.

This approach was first pioneered by the Quakers over two hundred years ago and is actively used today by many new transformational groups. At both **Findhorn Foundation** in Scotland and at our community, **Sirius**, in Massachusetts, we personally experienced how effective this attunement process can be, and we've used it for over fifteen years. Group members first discuss the facts about the relevant issue under discussion, then honestly express their own feelings about it. This is essentially like putting all the cards on the table, and it lays the groundwork for the next step. Participants then work on releasing their personal opinions and go into a quiet reflection or meditation to ask for guidance from their own inner source of highest wisdom, the Soul. For some, this source might be called the God within. For others it might be called the Universal Mind. For still others it is simply the Greatest Good.

Afterward everyone takes turns sharing what they experienced in the time of silence—words, feelings, images. Generally a clear consensus emerges from this—all the different views begin to fit together like pieces of a puzzle, forming a whole picture that comes clear to everyone. Guidance from a higher level always reflects "Divine Economy." It will serve the needs of the individual and the group at the same time and may also stretch people into new areas of growth.

If no clear consensus develops, members may feel that it isn't the right time to make the decision, as other factors or information need to come into the picture. Or perhaps one or more members of the group haven't really released their personal opinions and may be still personally and emotionally involved in the outcome rather than detached. The group then tries to directly address the emotional issues of those involved to see if they're able to work through them and so to release any blocks to consensus. On the other hand, an individual blocking consensus may not have any emotional issues to clear but instead have an important perspective that needs to be included in the decision. Learning to tell the difference requires intuitive listening.

PRINCIPLES FOR PUBLIC LIFE—"MAY THE BEST PERSON SERVE"

One of the difficulties we face in our world today is agreeing upon a standard of shared values. The immediate response is "Whose values?" This presupposes that people are so segmented by separate interests that they really have very little in common. This response by some of the negative forces controlling our society is the old "divide and conquer" technique. As long as these forces of division prevent people from recognizing shared values commonly held in the heart but often not expressed, their irresponsible use of power cannot be effectively challenged by the massed intent of people of goodwill. This division into interest groups is one of the fundamental causes of the inability of well-intentioned people to effect the changes that are so necessary.

In our experience of traveling all over the world, we have recognized the truth that humanity holds many values in common. Giving, generous people are as loved and respected in India or Africa as they are in Sweden or Russia. Peacemakers are universally honored. Defenders of the rights of the helpless are seen as noble everywhere. Planning and working for the long-term good of future generations is acknowledged as wise action the world over. Selfless service to the larger whole is always respected.

In order to draw out the highest good in our public officials and encourage recognition of this level of public service, we would like to offer the following Principles for Public Life. These principles are intended to serve as a code of ethics and conduct for public officials in local, state, and national government, similar to the corporate code of conduct, called the CERES Principles, that Gordon and others helped develop for the environment. By asking our representatives to sign the Principles for Public Life and to live by these standards, we the people whom they serve will have a basis for evaluating their conduct and service to society. When we are thinking about voting for our local school board member or state representative, congressman, or senator, we can ask ourselves whether they are honestly trying to meet these standards for public life. This will also begin to make the work of public service an inspiring calling that will draw our best people to serve our society.

PRINCIPLES FOR PUBLIC LIFE
"May the Best Person Serve"

1. Upholding the Highest Good

I pledge to uphold the highest good of all the people of my nation, as well as that of the peoples of other nations, to the mutual benefit of all. I will seek to eliminate the causes leading to destructive action and establish causes creating good for all.

2. Resolving Conflict for the Good of All

I pledge to work toward resolving conflict peacefully and justly wherever I find it, by looking for the highest good and the spark of truth in everyone's point of view, yet synthesizing them all into a higher solution.

3. Furthering Cooperation for Mutual Benefit

I pledge to further cooperation among all groups, nations, and peoples around the earth, for it is through working for each other's mutual benefit that we all prosper and find joy.

4. Sustainability for Future Generations

I pledge to design our current human activities to provide for the well-being and sustainability of future generations yet unborn.

5. Co-creative Relationship with the Natural World

I pledge to work for a nurturing, co-creative relationship between human beings and the natural world, of which we are all a part and upon which we depend for our life support.

6. Upholding Human Rights

I pledge to work to eliminate fear and to protect the basic human rights of all human beings around the world, regardless of their race, creed, nationality, or origins, and I will support only those governments or social systems that guarantee those rights.

7. Supporting Sharing and Personal Initiative

I pledge to work for a fair and just distribution of the resources of the earth to all peoples of the planet, while honoring the principle of reward for individual effort.

8. Honesty and Personal Responsibility

I pledge to tell the truth about myself and my work and to take responsibility for my actions and my mistakes.

9. Being an Example of Service

I pledge to personally demonstrate in my life and actions that joyful giving and service to others is the most fulfilling way of life for all humanity and a fundamental solution to our crises.

10. Serving the Whole and Not Oneself

I pledge to serve honestly in such a way that I expect no personal, financial, or other benefits from my public life beyond reasonable life support and knowing that I have served my fellow human beings.

MAINSTREAMING THE NEW POLITICS

This new transformational paradigm outlined in these last two chapters is beginning to make inroads into the political process as innovative political groups achieve more effectiveness and as more mainstream politicians on both the Left (such as President Clinton) and the Right (former housing secretary Jack Kemp) begin to promote some of these ideas and apply them to public policy. It is crucial that we transcend polarized thinking and stop projecting the worst onto our enemies—thinking, for example, that all Republicans are uncaring about the poor, that all pro-choicers are baby killers with no morals, or that everyone in the Pentagon is an evil warmonger.

Instead we need to see clearly the positive side and the truth in our opponent's position. We need to confront the real stumbling blocks on both sides: deception, manipulation, domination, greed, hatred. We must neutralize and overcome those who fan conflict and hatred among people holding opposing views. We must support honest dialogue based on goodwill. Our real enemies are those who would divide us and so conquer and destroy our democratic process. We must look this real darkness straight in the eye and not blink. We must instead approach those with different views with respect and acknowledge our underlying unity, seeing the conflict of ideas as an educational opportunity rather than as a threat.

Although many who are involved in creating the new politics may not think their small efforts are making much difference, President Oscar Arias of Costa Rica, as well as several other heads of state, told one of these groups that their support, coming from the outside, revitalized the entire Central American peace process, especially at a time when they were feeling isolated in their own countries. A colonel from the Pentagon told them that although they may think that government is the best institution to solve many problems, in fact its inertia is enormous and its decision-making abilities are frustratingly slow. But, he said, "you can take risks. You can try things the government cannot try."[36]

These new transformational political groups are like small seeds of a new politics. Although a seed may be tiny, it is nonetheless a potent force. If carefully tended and nurtured, ripened by the sun, watered by the rain, its potencies are unpredictable. When the new plant flowers and scatters its seed, it reproduces itself many times over.*

The following chart summarizes transformational solutions to social problems pioneered by groups featured in the last two chapters.

---

*See Resources section on page 423 for listing of organizations that are helping to shift the political paradigm.

TRANSFORMATIONAL SOLUTIONS
TO POLITICAL PROBLEMS

PROBLEM	GROUP	SOLUTION
International conflicts Labor conflicts Community conflicts	Search for Common Ground Harvard Negotiation Project	Win/Win Approaches— "Principled Negotia- tion": focuses on interests and real human needs, not positions; focuses on the people, not the problem; brain- storms options for mutual gain Finds shared con- cerns; fine tunes differences; re- frames conflict into broader view
Abortion conflict	Buffalo Project Public Conversations Project Coalition for Life and Choice	Acknowledges hu- manity of oppo- nents Clarifies perceptions Finds common con- cerns, like adop- tion, to work together on Facilitates dialogues and simulations

PROBLEM	GROUP	SOLUTION
Ethnic and racial conflict	Foundation for Global Community	Dialogue Process
Jobs vs. environmental conflict	Project Victory	Deep listening: be willing to be changed rather than to change others
Peace through disarmament vs. "peace through strength"	Tin Wis Coalition	
	The Natural Step	
	Moral Re-Armament	Humanizes opponents
	Pathways to Peace	Finds grain of truth, positive intent in opposite view
	Earthstewards	Shares feelings
		Active listening—mirroring
		Observes and analyzes workings of own mind
		Practices forgiveness
Tibetan/Chinese conflict	Institute for Multi-Track Diplomacy	Whole systems approaches involving business, scientific, education, media, funding communities
Conflict in Cyprus		
Indigenous peoples issues		
Instability in the former republics of the Soviet Union	ISAR	Citizen exchanges; training in business, environmental strategies; twelve-step recovery programs
	Center for Citizen Initiatives	
Crime	Communitarian Movement	Promotes neighborhood police and walking their beats

PROBLEM	GROUP	SOLUTION
Crime	Victim-Offender Reconciliation	Emphasizes restorative, rather than retributive justice Victim shares feelings with offender, then offers forgiveness
Health problems and rising cost of health care.	Institute for Noetic Sciences National Wellness Coalition	Emphasizes preventive methods and wellness promotion such as healthy diet, vitamins, exercise. Promotes Eastern and alternative forms of medicine such as acupuncture and homeopathy Treats mind/body/spirit as whole system
Deprivation of meaning, values, ethics, moral purpose, spirituality in political life	Institute for Faith and Politics *Tikkun* Magazine	Spiritual support for Congresspeople Promotes the return of a sense of higher purpose to the lives of citizens
Selfish decision-making based on inequities of money, power, influence	The Quakers Findhorn Community Sirius Community	"Attunement" and consensus—decision-making based on inner spiritual guidance of participants to promote the good of the whole

PROBLEM	GROUP	SOLUTION
"Shadow projection" onto enemies Dehumanizing enemies	Psychologists for Social Responsibility Living Politics Personal Disarmament	Training in reowning the "shadow"— denied negative aspects of self Role-playing enemies Inner disarmament— sees the self as a nation with boundaries, enemies, defenses
Environmental Problems	Elmwood Institute	Whole systems thinking about interconnection of life Long-term, "7th generation" approaches.
Conflict in the Middle East	Nevé Shalom Inst. for Social and Economic Policy in Mideast	Joint Arab/Israeli educational and living experiences.
Centralized, bureaucratic approach to foreign policy	Global Cities Project	Municipal diplomacy: economic and political alliances between foreign cities Sister city programs Nuclear free zones
Voter apathy Sense of powerlessness	Institute for the Arts of Democracy	Training in empowerment, self-governance and team work

PROBLEM	GROUP	SOLUTION
Ineffective, hierarchical forms of governance	Auroville Community Alpha Community Pathwork Communities	Honors current abilities and nurtures future potential Synthesizes hierarchy and democracy Matches creativity and accountability Consensus decision-making
Inner city youth problems: Drug addiction Violence Teen pregnancies Unemployment Victim consciousness Low self-esteem	The Door Children of War Urban Peace Trees California Self-Esteem Task Force D.C. Service Corps Teen Institute of New Jersey	Trains in self-esteem through developing a sense of identity, security, belonging and competence Telling life stories to break through isolation Wholistic self-help and skills training
Third World poverty	Sarvodaya Movement Institute for Cultural Affairs	Empowers people and trains in self-help methods Decentralization of power and decision-making
World hunger	RESULTS	Grassroots training in lobbying skills for legislation

PROBLEM	GROUP	SOLUTION
Welfare dependency	Communitarian Movement	Strengthens families and neighborhoods in addition to governmental solutions Matches rights with responsibilities Encourages giving back to the social whole Workforce training in job skills

Part 3

◆ ◆ ◆

THE HIDDEN CAUSES OF WORLD EVENTS

Chapter Five

◆

FORM FOLLOWS THOUGHT: THE MENTAL CAUSES OF WORLD EVENTS

Political research should not be omitted from a spiritual curriculum. When the inner esoteric and predisposing causes of war are discovered through esoteric research, then war . . . will come to an end.

—ALICE BAILEY[1]

Rather than taking a Band-Aid approach to social problems—patching things up temporarily with superficial programs—a more effective strategy deals with the psychological and metaphysical roots of the problems in human consciousness. "Energy follows thought" is a basic tenet of the Ageless Wisdom. It tells us that the mind is the builder of the form. Whatever we think about, we direct energy toward, and this focused energy gives thought the power to manifest physically. "As a man thinketh in his heart, so he is," says the Book of Proverbs in the Bible.[2] We are what we think, the Buddha said. All that we are arises with our thoughts. With our thoughts we make the world.

Thoughts could be compared to concentrated images held on a piece of movie film. Once we shine the light of our consciousness through them, these images are projected out onto the screen of our lives.

The physical forms we have created—our bodies, our architecture, our social institutions—can also in turn affect our consciousness positively or negatively, so it is worthwhile for us to create better and more beautiful forms. However, for most of us, the influence of physical forms on our consciousness is less powerful than the reverse, as consciousness and thought have a power greater than the environment.

The mind is a powerful creator, but it often creates negative realities for us. In the East the rational mind is referred to as "the slayer of the real." Our minds often deceive us into thinking that we have discovered truth. But, in fact, when the rational mind is disconnected from the clear knowledge that comes from the heart and intuition, it often misses the subtler spiritual realities. This is why the mind is often called "a poor master, but a good servant." But if the mind is the servant of the higher intuition, it can clothe subtle and abstract understandings in concrete mental forms and be of great service in creating a new world.

Thoughts and images have a profound creative and motivating power within human consciousness, which still remains largely unexplored. And, in fact, the ability to think involves great personal responsibility. The beliefs and feelings that we hold deeply influence who we are. "Thoughts are things" is a wise saying of the ancients. Every thought and image created by the human mind remains with us, creating either illusions and distortions—or inspiration and truth—depending on the nature of the thought. Thoughts then activate our feelings and become more potent. Hateful thoughts act like a boomerang and return to us with greater velocity and intensity, and so wreak havoc in our lives. Positive thoughts likewise boomerang, returning great blessings in our lives.

Great teachers speak about the pollution of space from the negative thoughts of violence, hatred, and selfishness that have been generated by humanity through the ages. Often people who believe they are "thinking" something are only picking up thoughts floating in the mental atmosphere of the planet. Thus weak-minded people, or those with little self-control, can be influenced or even obsessed by thought-forms and images that can drive them to acts of violence against others.

For example, we don't always get the results we expect when we simply change a law. This is because we haven't first changed the thought patterns needed to catalyze that change. A materialistic worldview is not just morally vacuous—it simply doesn't work. The material world is an effect, not a cause. Take the Prohibition Amendment (the Volstead Act) of 1920, which made the manufacture and the consumption of alcohol illegal. Rather than national sobriety, the result was bootlegging, gin mills, and the lawless Roaring Twenties. It wasn't until people's thinking changed and we collectively came to realize the personal health costs of alcohol in the 1980s that we've seen a drop in alcohol consumption.

Another case in point is the civil rights efforts over the past twenty-five years that have concentrated on reforming policy, not reshaping attitudes. A recent study by the National Opinion Research Center at the University of Chicago found that racial stereotypes die hard. A majority of white

Americans still believe that blacks are more likely to be lazy, violence-prone, and less intelligent than whites. However, these negative images are in decline among younger, better-educated Americans, suggesting that changing thinking through education is the most effective route to real change.[3] This is not to say that laws are not needed or useful, but that we need to examine the collective consciousness if they are not being effective.

It is a step in the right direction to learn how to use our mind and begin to think rather than just react to the world through our emotions, which are constantly changing from moment to moment. Alice Bailey, a respected teacher of the Ageless Wisdom, wrote in *The Destiny of Nations*:

> The fact that so many millions of people are beginning to think is one of the conditions which is inducing the present stress and strain. The united will of humanity will be the determining factor in world affairs, and this will be due to the unfoldment of the mind through the success of the evolutionary process.[4]

At the end of World War II, Bailey predicted that the next major world war would be waged in the area of world religions, but without all the carnage and blood. Instead it would be fought largely with mental weapons in the world of thought, involving fanatical idealism.[5] It is interesting to note that in the Middle East, the Arab world has been skirting the edge of a Moslem *jihad*, or religious war, against the West for some time. So far, much of this conflict has remained a war of words and media images. Likewise, some Christian fundamentalists in the West are calling for a religious war for America's Soul. Dogmatic religious fanatics around the world have been a major factor in many of the world's crises. Not only fundamentalist Moslems in Iran and Sudan, but also Hindus in India, Jews in Israel, Catholics and Protestants in Ireland, and Christians and Muslims in Bosnia and Azerbaijan.

Bailey also warned that people "should remember that through the power of their thoughts and their spoken words they definitely produce effects upon other human beings . . . and upon the entire animal kingdom. The separative and maleficent thoughts of man are largely responsible for the savage nature of wild beasts, and the destructive quality of some of nature's processes, including certain phenomena, such as plague and famine."[6]

THE POWER OF THOUGHT

Thoughts can actually create an event. They form on the mental plane and work their way down vibrationally to the emotional, etheric, and then the physical planes. Through the collective thoughts of humanity, conflicting or harmonious forces are slowly made into patterns by new or existing thought-forms and projected onto the astral (emotional) plane. The astral forces then surround the thought-form and charge it with any existing emotions or confusions. These mental-astral forms then descend to the etheric plane, where they are formed into a framework that creates a future event. This inner structure of electromagnetic force orchestrates the future event by attracting all actors and elements necessary for the fulfillment of the event. Given this process, learning to see the causes in our human thinking and emotions allows us to disentangle some of the conflicting forces at the center of an event and work more from the casual level in creating solutions. We then learn how to synthesize the opposing forces, thoughts, and emotions for constructive outcomes.

Another factor influencing current events is the buildup of a massive accumulated thought-form of all the negative thoughts, terror, greed, and media images of crime around the planet. This forms a dark cloud in the electromagnetic aura of planet Earth. Sometimes when energy strikes this thought-form, it is absorbed into this field and feeds these negative factors, causing more destruction and crime in the world. This makes it difficult for beneficial energies and ideas from the Enlightened Ones to reach humanity from the subtle dimensions. However, at the same time there is also a powerful field of positive, light energy growing stronger every day. This radiant energy is created by the aspirations and visions of the compassionate and clear-thinking people who are working to build a better world for all life on earth. This thought-form influences and nourishes the minds of people of goodwill everywhere, sustaining and strengthening them. Much of the conflict we see in the world today is the result of the inner clashing between these two massive thought-forms. Whichever of these two great energy fields an individual or group is attuned to will determine whether most of their activities are negative and destructive or positive and constructive.

So although the wrong use of the mind has been a major contributor to world problems, fortunately there has been enough positive thinking in the world to balance it out and prevent us from totally destroying ourselves. There are a number of ways that we can all contribute to a positive mental energy field:

• Every time we hold a positive, hopeful image of a national leader or a major world event, we help make it easier for that person or event to express the highest good.
• Every time we insist on seeing a problem from a broader perspective, not-

ing how it is interconnected with many other factors and understanding its deeper causes, we make a positive contribution toward finding a lasting solution.

• Every time we refuse to become entrenched in a polarizing position on a controversial issue, and clearly and objectively affirm the positive in each perspective to create a higher synthesis, we help to bring greater healing and unity into our world.

• Every time we refuse to separate questions of ethics or universal spiritual values from public life, we are helping to restore a sense of wholeness and spiritual strength to our national life.

We will begin by exploring human thoughts, both positive and negative, in this chapter, as major causes of world events, and then in later chapters explore causes generated on the emotional, etheric and Soul levels. We offer the following examples of negative and positive, old and new, forms of thinking, to help stimulate further discussion of additional causes.

SEPARATIVE THINKING/COMMUNITY THINKING

Seeing ourselves as separate is the central problem in our political thinking.

VICE PRESIDENT AL GORE[7]

According to the Ageless Wisdom, there really is only one sin—separateness. In the early years of World War II, Alice Bailey noted that we will achieve peace in the world only after we first create unity. And we will experience plenty only after we first have peace.[8] Creating a true sense of unity should be our first objective as human beings if we want true peace, rather than just trying to prevent outbreaks of hostilities or limit weapons.

Research by the International Society for the Study of Aggression shows that there is no evolutionary or genetic basis to violence.[9] Thus, the persistence of war is more likely to spring from rampant nationalism, ethnocentrism, and intolerant religious fundamentalism—all extreme and separative attitudes that tend to dehumanize "outgroups."

From an inner perspective, we see that a primary cause of the earth's suffering is that humanity is caught in the illusion of separation—the idea that we're all separate, individual units bouncing around like billiard balls, ricocheting off each other in the drama of life. The belief that we're all separate gives us the justification for our prejudices, for our lack of compassion for those less fortunate, and for our wars against "enemies," both political and religious. What is needed as a cure for separateness is a deep sense of community—that we're all in this together. As Andrew Young, former mayor of Atlanta, noted in a talk at Cornell University in 1984:

> Our ability to cope with problems of the differences between us and our national enemies . . . may well be dependent on our ability to cope with differences that exist on a day-to-day basis—the differences we have with our parents, with our children, with the opposite sex, etc. It's no accident that the countries that are doing extremely well economically right now are the countries that have solved the problems of their human differences. . . .

The Root of All Fears

The apparent reality of separateness—especially saddening when it is based on religious beliefs—is caused by our consciousness becoming identified with our limited ego—with matter, with our physical body, with thoughts and feelings, rather than with our unlimited Soul/Spirit Self, which is unified with the whole, with God and the Universe. When consciousness identifies with the part, the ego personality, we begin to believe that our being, our self-awareness, can die and be extinguished. This false sense of separateness is the root of all our fears, especially the mortal fear of death. Our ego-based identity rushes to pacify this great fear of annihilation through aggressiveness and competition to establish dominance. We do this by banding together with those of similar class, race, or ethnic background for security and out of fear of "the other." We violently defend our prerogatives out of fear of losing material security and resist all change because it leads us to contemplate the ultimate change—death.

Based on our perception of separateness, we try to create islands of peace and security in our homes or neighborhoods, but we never truly experience peace, because subconsciously and psychically we constantly pick up the anguish of those in pain whether they be across town or across the world. We can't shut others out even if we try to—because we're all interconnected. Just as "No man is an Island, entire of it self," as poet John Donne reminded us, so no nation is an island. Border issues between nations are symbolic of this deeper issue of separateness. The illusion of isolation and self-protection is being rapidly shattered in our modern age, which includes both international communications and economics, as well as global crises of energy, pollution, and diseases such as AIDS, which do not respect national borders. Politically correct debates between the overly self-righteous on opposite sides of an issue only increase separateness and create deadlock.

Unity in Diversity

By observing the diversity of the natural biosphere, we can learn an important lesson. The many different species, and the different genetic makeup of individual organisms within a species, are a source of great strength. When environmental stress threatens such a diverse system, it has many ways to respond and adapt to the change. This increases flexibility and the chances for survival. Monoculture crops that are genetically identical and carefully bred for high yield have no genetic diversity. Thus they are extremely vulnerable to pests, diseases, and climatic changes. The same principle applies to the human social dimension. Differences in race, culture, and religion are currently viewed as threatening and divisive when, in fact, they are essential to our developing a more accurate picture of reality, as well as more options for creative solutions to our problems.

In a recent speech the Dalai Lama said the following:

> Whether it is under the guise of survival and self-defense or directly expressed through dominion and greed, the failure to recognize the common humanity shared by us all lies at the heart of our difficulties. To overcome it, we should begin to develop, from the level of the individual through that of society to the world at large, what I call a sense of universal responsibility; a deep respect for every living being who lives on this one small planet and calls it home.

The esoteric spiritual traditions—whether Christian mystics, Hebrew Kabbalists, Zen Buddhists, Islamic Sufis, or Hindu yogis—all have specific practices to help individuals overcome this great "illusion of separation" and to experience the One True Self, which is in us all. For example, we can meditate on the heart, seeing it expand to include more and more of the abundance and creativity of all types of people in an outpouring of love, forgiveness, and acceptance.

LINEAR THINKING/WHOLISTIC THINKING

> *May God us keep*
> *From single vision and Newton's sleep*
> —WILLIAM BLAKE[10]

Although beginning to show signs of change, the reigning paradigm in our society today is still based on nonsystemic, linear thinking. Linear thinking moves in a straight line: a single cause produces a single effect; A causes B causes C. It assumes that everything is separate from everything else and that one part of a system can thrive while another part suffers—for example, a belief that there can be a large number of poor people without affecting consumption and therefore profit. Many of the crises we face in our world today and the inability of our public policies to deal with them stem from this limited way of thinking about problems.

The Limits to Growth Report by the prestigious Club of Rome, as well as studies by the Stanford Research Institute, concluded that the many problems constituting the planetary crisis today are in fact one vast interrelated systemic problem, and that economic and social collapse can be avoided only through a transformative "change of values."[11]

A classic example of lack of wholistic or systems thinking was a World Health Organization policy to eliminate deadly malaria in Borneo in the early 1950s by spraying DDT all over the island. At first the mosquito population and the incidence of malaria declined and the program was declared successful. However, very shortly they discovered that the thatched roofs of people's houses were falling in on their heads. It turned out that the DDT had also killed the wasps that ate thatch-eating caterpillars. What's more, the DDT built up in the food chain, killing the lizards that ate the insects and the cats that in turn ate the lizards. When the cats died, the rat population flourished. The island was then faced with an outbreak of sylvatic plague and typhus from the rats. Apparently no one had carefully studied the whole system—the interdependence of life forms on the island. As a solution, the World Health Organization finally had to parachute live cats into Borneo.[12]

Another example of a lack of wholistic thinking noted by author John Adams is that highways are often built in urban areas to relieve congestion and improve access to the city. But no one looks at the large picture and explores the deeper causes of the problem. This means that within a few years developers take advantage of the new highways, creating office and apartment towers near the interchanges, with the result that congestion becomes worse than ever.

Seeing Whole Patterns

Now that we have computers that can think linearly better than humans, it's time for us to make the next leap in consciousness to wholistic thinking—to seeing whole patterns. In contrast with the prevailing linear paradigm, the New Paradigm sees everything as interconnected and interdependent through complex patterns of relationships, flows, and feedback loops. Wholistic thinking shows that attempts to repair a problem in one area often create problems in another area and there are often unintended consequences to any action taken to solve a problem. Thus it is critical to keep the large picture—the whole system—in mind in order to create any kind of lasting solution and to avoid undue focus on effects, rather than dealing with causes that may be part of another system altogether.

This is not really "new" thinking. Many traditions of the Ageless Wisdom have taught wholistic thinking for centuries. For example, in the Native American teaching of the medicine wheel, each person begins life starting at a certain direction on the wheel. In the East we learn to see the world through direct illumination and inspiration; in the West we learn to understand the world through introspection; in the North we learn wisdom through dreams and communications with Spirit; and in the South we learn about growth through the heart and innocence. To achieve wholeness, we have to move around the wheel, to see life from other perspectives, in order to understand the interconnection of all the parts. Native Americans resolved conflicts by sitting in council, in a circle of wholeness, where each voice could be heard in turn. Similarly, the Hindus and Buddhists have long used circular mandalas to teach about wholeness.

Today, because of the environmental crisis, we are beginning to see how all of life is interconnected—how a little bit of toxic dumping in one place causes pollution in the water supplies in another place, endangering the entire chain of life, and down the line, resulting in birth defects or cancer in humans. Wholistic thinking or ecological thinking—seeing how everything affects everything else—is finally beginning to influence other national policies, such as economics, where piecemeal solutions never work, since all sectors of a nation's economy are interrelated and interdependent with the world economy. The systems view sees the world in terms of relationships and integrated wholes whose properties cannot be reduced to those of smaller units.

POLARIZED THINKING/UNITIVE THINKING

I am not an advocate for frequent changes in laws and constitutions, but laws and institutions must go hand in hand with the progress of the human mind.

—THOMAS JEFFERSON[13]

Modern political thinking, our legal system, and the media are all oriented along adversarial lines, in an overly polarized and competitive manner. Even those who consider themselves peaceful and harmonious tend to become rapidly polarized when the subject of politics arises. Psychologically this tends to emphasize differences and overlook areas of common interest—labor vs. management, pro-abortion vs. anti-abortion. All these issues are framed by idealists in such a way that it becomes very difficult to discover common ground and mutual benefit.

The Ageless Wisdom warns against sacrificing the spirit of love to the form of an ideal, no matter how lofty. Ideals as held by many people feed pride and stubbornness and engender a separation and impracticality. What is needed instead is a deep Soul love for all humanity which pursues the greatest good for the greatest number.

To understand how polarity works is to understand the deeper causes at work in the world. When we put forth an idea that is in opposition to another idea, we may unintentionally invoke or pull out the full expression of the opposite polarity. Then the opposing idea takes on a power of its own, propelled by the emotional and mental energy it begins to pull in. It's as if we unleash a powerful force that sets into motion the equilibrium of forces that is basic in the universe. When we disagree with something and begin opposing it, a momentum builds up that draws in the life and energy of the other polarity as well. The more we feed the differences with our thoughts and feelings, the more real they become. Before we even realize what is happening, we become more and more polarized and see no way to bridge the gap.

For example, those of us who started opposing the Vietnam War in the 1960s began to swing farther and farther away from the mainstream culture. Every aspect of our lives changed—political beliefs, behavior, clothing, food, music, language, drugs. Anger and rebellion against authority that was still unresolved from early childhood experiences added fuel to the fire. In response, many in the pro-Vietnam mainstream became more polarized and rigid in their life-style and beliefs. We were left with two angry camps facing off against each other. Only when each side began to realize there was something missing in their position, and slowly began to see some truth in the other's position, did the beginnings of a bridging and healing take place and a healthy cross-pollination occur.

As Einstein is said to have warned: "Two sides disagree because they are both wrong!"[14] (Or, from another perspective, because they are both right, and truth is a paradox.) He noted that no problem can be solved on its own level but must be taken to a higher level of consciousness. Unitive thinking requires us to broaden our consciousness so that we can appreciate the need for both polarities and hold them in our consciousness at the same time. Often we can appreciate one polarity only by experiencing the contrast of its opposite—for example, that great beauty is more powerful when experienced after ugliness, or that the color red is more vibrant when seen next to blue. The alternation between opposites is what creates consciousness. It is also what creates electricity. The great poets knew the secret of polarity, often putting two words with opposite meanings side by side, as Shakespeare did in his sonnets.

CONTAINING THE OPPOSITES

The most profound truths always contain the opposites in a higher unity. Just as each atom requires both positive and negative particles to be complete and to build any physical object, to construct a whole picture of reality we need to include both (or many) competing sides of a political issue. We can learn this very powerfully from observing the wisdom of our own body:

With two arms, we can embrace and hold,
With two feet we can move forward,
With two eyes we can experience depth,
With two hemispheres of the brain we incorporate both details of content and the context of the whole.

Thus by holding two points of view simultaneously we embrace and hold a higher truth, we move forward on our path, and we experience depth and wholeness. We can synthesize opposites as we learn from the deep wisdom of our physical bodies, which have already done so.

Eastern healing modalities such as polarity therapy, acupuncture, etc., all work to maintain a balance of yin and yang, the two etheric polar energy currents that guarantee optimal health. Likewise, maintaining a balance of opposites will help us maintain our collective political health.

We see in modern politics how the alternation of political parties in and out of power compensates for the negative side effects of the opposing party's previous policies. When conservatives come into power they cut excess government spending of liberals, and when liberals take over they expand social services previously cut off by conservatives. As Tony Judge of the Union of International Associations in Brussels points out, this is just like farmers rotating their crops to remedy defects to the soil caused by previous plantings. Thus over time, both crop rotation and political party rotation create balance. But unitive thinking collapses time and holds opposing ideas simultaneously, creating policies that reflect a higher synthesis of both.

Two-valued logic reinforces polarization—one side is right and the other wrong, as Jerome Glenn points out in *Future Mind: Artificial Intelligence*: "But strategic thinking puts the two views in a relationship such that together they can know how to act. . . . The stereotypical view of the industrialist and the environmentalist holds that each believes he or she is correct and the other is wrong. But actually the environmentalist can point out energy-efficient ways to create products, and the industrialist can point out the cost effectiveness of production techniques. The two could work together to plan better approaches, if each accepts the validity of the other's basic principles—the value of environmental health and the values of economic health."[15]

Another example is the issue of national defense where there is a split between liberal demands for greater arms reductions and conservative demands for maintaining military strength. A third way would focus more on reducing the economic and political roots of the conflict, finding better conflict resolution mechanisms, and encouraging more grass-roots "citizen diplomats" to visit "enemy" nations and local municipalities to involve themselves in foreign affairs.

An interesting lesson in the necessity for synthesizing polarities occurred at the final plenary session of the Planetary Initiative for the World We Choose held in Toronto, Canada, in 1983. The majority of participants were presenting positive contributions summarized from smaller discussion groups held earlier and a tightly controlled consensus semed to be building, when suddenly a group in the back of the assembly burst in with a lot of angry criticism. The moderator wisely allowed the group to express its concerns and held them in a positive, loving space. Rather than becoming defensive, the rest of the assembly listened carefully and then found a way to include the feedback, which ultimately was quite helpful and enriched the whole.

In ancient alchemical rituals, the role of the "random element" was always given to someone, who would then consciously play the fool by acting chaotically and not following the orderly ritual enacted by the rest of the group. The ancients knew the important catalyzing quality of this opposite, chaotic element in creating a pattern of wholeness and an openness to change in order to prevent crystallization. If not consciously acknowledged, this role will nonetheless always be played out unconsciously by one or more individuals and may be expressed as resistance or anger.

Seeing things from a higher perspective of unity was powerfully demonstrated when American astronauts and Soviet cosmonauts looked back at planet Earth from outer space and couldn't see their national boundaries, only the whole planet that unites us. Symbolically this might be seen as the eagle, symbolizing Spirit and vision, transcending the hawk (war) vs. the dove (peace) polarity. Or instead of pro–Star Wars and anti–Star Wars—*Star Trek:* new joint projects in space technology.

CRYSTALLIZED THINKING/EXPANDED THINKING

> *The fundamental causes of nonpeace on the planet are to be found mainly in the collective beliefs of the various societies—beliefs that are partly consciously held but are in greater measure unconscious.*
>
> —WILLIS HARMAN[16]

In order to truly create a more harmonious world, our minds have to be freed of their bonds of old programming and conditioning. When we were in Egypt, for example, listening to Middle Eastern music, we often commented, like most Westerners, that every song sounds the same. But we listened with our Western ears and focused only on the singer and the melody in the foreground. Rhythm is always background for Westerners, it's hardly noticed. But to Middle Eastern ears, the rhythm is foreground and very creative, while the background melody is usually similar and less noticed—the opposite of Western music. To perceive the world in new ways, there must be a willingness to expand beyond our cherished limitations—like being able to hear and appreciate both parts of Middle Eastern music—melody and rhythm—at the same time.

When the mind gets enmeshed in repetitive, negative patterns of thought, it limits the reality that can be perceived or created, and a sense of hopelessness sets in. Continual worst-case legalistic thinking creates worst-case scenarios. Lasting solutions to conflicts and problems are never found, because of narrow ways of perceiving reality. If we believe that our enemies are incurably evil, that government is by nature always corrupt, that the world's resources are limited and thus there will always be starving people—then we will always be stuck in these realities and ineffective. The negative and narrow views of government held by much of the electorate and fanned by the media only adds to the problem.

To revolt against something, such as an institution, is only to attack effects rather than causes. As long as the attack is upon effects only, no true change is possible. The real problem is the construction of thought that created and maintains the institution. The institution may be torn down, but unless the mind-set that produced it changes in some fundamental way, the thinking behind it will simply create another similar institution.

Our limiting rationalizations and resistance to change have to be dissipated. We can create more fundamental change and new solutions to problems by expanded intuitive thinking. The context in which problems are seen has to be broadened if effective social solutions are to be found.

The unemployment and jobs issue can be transformed by worrying less about preserving jobs and more about empowering people to do socially useful and personally meaningful work. With this new expanded focus, the jobs economy would be seen as only one part of the whole economy, which also includes unpaid labor such as mothering and child care. Expanding thinking would also include exploration of new ways of voluntarily simplifying living to require less cash income.

To address development problems in the Third World, the Institute for Cultural Affairs in New York transforms the question from "How much should we spend?" to "How can we pay more attention to what the poor themselves want in order to enable them to help themselves?" Instead of seeing development as something we buy with money, we see it as a product of people—a people-intensive process.

Rather than trying to define who is a "terrorist" and who is a "freedom fighter"—since that depends on one's political viewpoint—a 1989 joint conference on terrorism with Americans and Soviets organized by Search for Common Ground focused instead on specific acts of terrorism (kidnappings, hijackings, attacks on children) that both sides opposed. For the first time, terrorism became a shared problem, with substantial agreements resulting, such as direct cooperation to free hostages, stop narcoterrorism, and assist front-line countries in the drug war. Search for Common Ground's Task Force to Prevent Terrorism has now expanded to bring in Western Europeans as well, and a book, *Common Ground on Terrorism*, was published as a joint Soviet-American effort.[17]

MISUNDERSTANDING OF TIMING/RIGHT TIMING

> *To everything there is a season and a time to every purpose under heaven ... A time to sow, a time to reap.*
> —ECCLESIASTES 3:1–8

Some visionaries see a Utopian future as something that is just around the corner. Very often they will attempt to impose it on the present, which in turn creates fear, resentment, and rebellion in people. In the long run, a vision out of its appropriate time frame only adds to the problems in the world. As Alice Bailey noted:

*All nations are imposing some idea on their people, but most feel
force is necessary. This is because they misunderstand the time
factor and feel that the immediate good is more important than
the long-term education of people so they will voluntarily accept
these ideas.*[18]

For example, the communist ideal of sharing all resources was admirable,
one that humanity may someday achieve, but most people at our current
level of evolution aren't ready to do so voluntarily. Thus the leaders of the
former communist nations used force to impose a system, which they then
abused to their own advantage. An appreciation of the timing principle
would allow a gradual education into ever greater degrees of voluntary
sharing among peoples everywhere.

Wiser visionaries keep presenting only the next step—one that is realistically achievable—and when it comes to pass, they present the next one.
The ideal of a one-world government is very inspiring, for example, but
unlikely to manifest for many decades. However, the European Community is an ideal that is an appropriate and realistic next step. By taking each
successive step in its own proper time, we eventually reach the goal.

There is great patience that comes with knowing there is a right timing
for everything. The *I Ching,* the ancient Chinese oracle, also counsels that
there is a time for waiting and a time for action, and the wise person
knows the difference. There are seasons and cycles in political life as
well—as, for example, the alternation between conservative and progressive
ideas coming into power and providing a needed balance. Progressives
bring the change and new ideas needed to break up the crystallized patterns of the past that are no longer useful. Conservatives preserve the best
of the past and ensure that change is not too rapid and thus unnecessarily
destructive. By cultivating a sensitivity to the cyclical nature of time and
events, we develop a greater capacity to cooperate with the opportunities
presented by each cycle.

Most of the time our attention is fragmented. We tend to dwell on the
past or worry about the future. Rarely are we fully attentive to the present.
Yet it is only by being fully present in the moment that we have power. It
is in the present that we know ourselves as the creator of our experience,
and so can change our past, not on form levels—but in how it is integrated
into our present awareness.

This can free us from bondage to the past. Time is more than a measure
of linear cause and effect sequences, like links on a chain. Time is spherical,
and our true Divine identity occupies the causal center, radiating out energy in a spherical fashion, in all directions.

Time, which is the awareness of form, dissolves into the timelessness of the Eternal Now when the barriers of form are removed. On the Soul or spiritual level, there is no linear time, so cause and effect can be experienced simultaneously, as can a range of possible futures. In manifestation, however, they seem to be separated by time, with cause coming before effect. Everything we see manifested in the physical world is already in the past and is an effect. All opposites are the products of cutting up time into sequences, which prevents us from seeing the wholeness of the process. Good eventually proceeds out of evil, if we see the uncut whole.

In the Ageless Wisdom it is said that when our attention is in the present moment, we are in the Presence of God, and so bring together Spirit and matter. This is the experience of the Soul, which is essentially timeless. The question is how much of our life we can bring into the present—and thus into the Presence of God. Our efforts toward social change are more effective when we can be more fully present in the moment and intuitively know the right course of action to take at that time—rather than base decisions only on past experiences or future projections.

EXPANDING OUR TIME SENSE

However, being very present in the moment is quite different from short-term thinking—and this confusion is the cause of many of today's problems. Our sense of timing is not expansive enough. We do not pay attention to long-term causes, either in the past or the future. Native Americans, however, wisely created policies that took into account their impact upon "the seventh generation." The "wisest men in recorded history," wrote Henry Steele Commager, "couldn't give a speech or write a letter without talking about posterity." Commager noted that George Washington used the word *posterity* nine times in one speech, and Thomas Jefferson talked about the "thousandth and thousandth generation" in his first inaugural address. Given this more expanded perspective of time, our public policy on debt or nuclear waste, for example, would be considerably different. The Japanese don't seem to suffer as much from our limited time sense, however, and are already at work with other nations on a one-hundred-year plan called Earth 21 to combat global warming.[19]

If we ponder more deeply the meaning of time, great mysteries are unveiled for us. Our perceptions determine our experience of time, and unfortunately much of our thinking is conditioned by a sequential and separatist worldview. Yet we ourselves create our own experience of time. This is why we can experience time that passes slowly or time that seems to fly, depending on our psychological state. We say "Time flies when you're having fun" or "A watched pot never boils." When we have the experience of "time standing still" it is always a very profound moment that touches the core of our being, our true Self. How can we fill our time with meaning and magic rather than measurement?

Our sense of past, present, and future is subjective to our culture. Rudolf Steiner, one of the great initiates of our century, noted that humanity used to have the power of cosmic memory and only in classical times began writing down what had happened. Before then it would have been laughable to the students of the mysteries to write down in history books the events that took place. They only needed to ponder and meditate deeply enough, and events would rise up from out of the depths of their consciousness.[20]

Many primitive peoples live in the present tense and do not have our concepts of past and future. We had an experience of this when we spent several days in Arizona with the Hopi Indians in their ancient villages on the mesas. After just one day there—talking to them, watching them shell corn the same way they have for thousands of years, and opening to their state of consciousness—our subjective experience of time was that we had been there for a week or more!

Alice Bailey wrote that "time is a sequence of events and of states of consciousness registered by the brain."[21] Later she noted that "time and energy are interchangeable terms upon the inner planes. Time is an event, and an event is a focused expression of force of some type or kind."[22]

The Ageless Wisdom teaches that Spirit is matter at its highest rate of vibration and matter is Spirit at its lowest rate of vibration. The difference is in the rate of vibration or speed—which relates to time. Mastering the energy of time and timing is one of the secrets of initiation. The *Kybalion*, which contains the hermetic teachings of Hermes Trismegistus that have been passed down from ancient Egypt and Greece, states that time affects energy output. The *Kybalion* teaches that the energy inherent in matter is released when the vibration of an object is speeded up, and its form varies with the speed of the vibrations. First, sound is emitted from low notes to high. Next come increasing degrees of heat. Then color appears, beginning with dull red and going up the spectrum to violet. Next come X rays; then electrical energy; and then magnetism. Finally, if the object vibrates too fast, it disintegrates.[23]

As we move towards Soul consciousness, our vibration speeds up, energy is released, and time is experienced differently. We become more detached from events and begin to see "the big picture." As we think more clearly and make better decisions, more is accomplished in less time. We work *with* time rather than *against* time, being flexible in adapting to changing circumstances, and waiting for the right time to make a decision. When in a higher state of consciousness our timing is perfect. We begin to recognize how the flow of all events is coordinated from a higher level by the one Soul of all.

Synchronicity is an alignment of energy streams or events in time, indicating an important relationship. Many people are making conscious use of synchronicity as guidance in decision making. For example, at the Findhorn Community in Scotland, when a department focalizer, or coordinator, was looking for the right person to do a specific task, she or he would see the first person who happened to appear as inwardly guided there for that purpose. This was a totally intuitive choice guided by synchronicity, not rationality, and it was highly effective.

Barbara Honegger, who did her graduate work at Stanford University on synchronicity, told us that she used a synchronistic approach in making decisions on women's issues while she was a policy analyst in the Reagan White House. When she had to recommend a specific policy decision, she would be guided by the opinion expressed in whichever letter from a constituent happened to cross her desk at that exact moment. (But we doubt that she shared this intuitive process with her superiors in the White House!)

REJECTION OF GOD IMMANENT/ ACKNOWLEDGING THE INNER DIVINITY

> *What the scientist calls energy, the religious person calls God, and yet the two are one, being but the manifested purpose, in physical matter of a great extra-systemic Identity. . . . The Eastern faiths have ever emphasized God Immanent, deep within the human heart, "nearer than hands and feet," the Self, the One . . . The Western faiths have presented God Transcendent, outside His universe, an Onlooker. . . The Life of God, His energy and vitality, are found in every manifested atom; His essence indwells in all forms . . . God Transcendent eternally exists, but can only be seen and known and correctly approached, by God Immanent—immanent in individual man . . . Both schools of thought are right, and in no way contradict each other. In their synthesis and in their blending, the truth as it really is can begin dimly to appear.*
>
> —ALICE BAILEY[24]

Another cause of world problems is the overemphasis on God Transcendent (beyond everyday life) and the rejection of God Immanent (present within each person and all life). This is one of the deeper reasons why democracy is not functioning as well as had been hoped. If the inner Divinity were seen as a reality in ourselves and others, this act of perception would draw forth the best in each of us and empower us to take more responsibility for ourselves and our social problems. Instead, because people don't know who they are, they experience apathy and dependence on government as an outer authority, like a distant God protecting them from themselves, regulating and punishing them. Views about God that keep Divinity aloof from creation usually see humans as "miserable sinners" seeking to placate a fierce father-Deity or to win the approval of a loving Deity (depending on the era or culture).

When God is theologically removed from humanity, it is as though Divinity has been placed in a jar of materialistic formaldehyde on some distant heavenly shelf. The natural world then becomes a dead, soulless machine—raw materials vulnerable to limitless exploitation by humanity under the biblical injunction of exercising "dominion over" our world. Many of us feel that a distant and uninvolved God, not really within His creation, cannot call us to account for our actions during this life and then only possibly in a vague, heavenly hereafter.

Yet we are being called to account by the increasing signals from our planetary environment that many of our ecosystems are in dire condition, and this is threatening human life on the planet. By not recognizing Divinity Immanent within nature and the world, many good, spiritually oriented people have refused to get involved in the nitty-gritty of politics and business. As a result they have left these fields wide open to those who have fewer scruples about exploiting the world for their personal benefit and have wreaked human and environmental devastation.

Our acceptance of this concept of God removed from creation, particularly in Christianity, has also left some people vulnerable to manipulation by those who claim to be able to mediate between God and humanity. Some of these so-called mediators, such as Jim and Tammy Bakker, create more spiritual confusion and despair when they become embroiled in scandal.

The lack of recognition of the Divine within us, and identification only with our material selves, has led to a sense of sinfulness and guilt that has permeated the human psyche. Lacking self-esteem based on a recognition of innate Divinity, we obsessively seek self-worth through our roles in society, personal accomplishments, amassing great wealth, or receiving approval from others.

Humanity suffers deeply from a lack of identity with its spiritual source, and we often substitute knowing our spiritual essence with an overdependence on the mind—the "Slayer of the Real," as it is known in spiritual traditions. Although the development of the mind has been a necessary step in human evolution, when the mind becomes the focus of identity, the split between the mind and the body/earth becomes intensified. Without the inner gyroscope of the Soul, the individual caught in the mind can easily "rationalize" almost any behavior prompted by social influences. Yet even within such an outerdirected world, conscience still blooms in some individuals, testifying to the power of an eternal Essence within each human being that provides guidance and direction.

God is indeed hidden, yet present within creation. This truth is apparent in the laws and principles that govern nature and can be experienced directly by those who, according to the Bible, have "eyes to see and ears to hear."[25]

God Immanent, the Divinity within all life, is today becoming more widely recognized in the new spiritual, ecological, and feminist movements that are working to empower the individual, support human rights, and honor the sacredness of the earth as Gaia, the ancient Mother Goddess. The Christian Creation Spirituality movement led by Matthew Fox and Thomas Berry, two Catholic priests, also emphasizes God Immanent, as does the New Age movement, the New Thought movement, and others. Jungian Thomas Moore's best-selling book, *The Care of the Soul,* has helped many people see the sacredness of daily life—God present within the world.

MATERIALISTIC EVOLUTION/ THE EVOLUTION OF CONSCIOUSNESS

I shop; therefore, I am.
—BARBARA KRUGER[26]

Charles Darwin's theory of the evolution of forms—whether of plants, animals, humans, or societies—through the processes of "natural selection" and "survival of the fittest" is widely accepted. However, this is disputed by many new biologists, such as our friend Elisabeth Sahtouris writing in *Gaia: The Human Journey from Chaos to Cosmos,*[27] whose research has found cooperative behavior among all species as essential to survival. While natural selection may describe the physical development of the mineral, plant, and animal kingdoms, including the human physical form, this theory does not adequately describe the inner development of humans, especially since it has been interpreted so materially. Yet evolution is not just a scientific theory of the development of life forms, but a great cosmic principle describing the development of consciousness. Many researchers now espouse the Ageless Wisdom teaching that consciousness precedes matter and that the material universe is the outer, dense expression of Divine consciousness, the outer embodiment of a Divine Idea.

The development of consciousness—the spiritual as well as material evolution—of each atom of substance, each individual, each planet, each solar system, and each galaxy is part of the great drama being unfolded throughout the universe. All these different entities are growing in their consciousness and understanding, just as an individual grows from being a child of limited awareness to an adult with a much broader range of awareness and abilities. Our spiritual development includes purifying our desires and motivations, developing the mind, integrating the personality, and opening ourselves to higher spiritual awareness and compassion for all creation. The great men and women—saints, philosophers, statesmen, philanthropists, scientists, healers, artists, and others—who have contributed to human welfare in major ways are generally the most evolved in consciousness.

Seeing evolution as relating only to material forms, and not to consciousness as well, has had many limiting consequences. These include the economic adaptation of "survival of the fittest" as one of the major tenets of Western capitalism; the idea of growth or development interpreted primarily in terms of material success; and the validation of competition as the matrix for social relations. Competition, combined with natural selection, offers a rationale, even if unconscious, to dominant individuals or societies to assert their right to whatever they can take with little concern for the less able. This projection of what has come to be called "social Darwinism" can be seen in history as the action of nations establishing empires or of individuals creating personal fiefdoms. Thus the materialistic interpretation of evolution derived only from the study of the physical side of nature has provided some of the intellectual/scientific rationale for the organizing structures of modern industrial society.

When we accept only a form level or material version of evolution, then the goal of life seems to be about accumulating vast sums of wealth and resources rather than helping others. Life soon becomes empty and full of angst. We starve for things of the Spirit, and long for sacredness, heroism, and conscience.

Scientific studies of near death experiences are now beginning to challenge purely materialistic interpretations of life. These studies have shown that people close to death often have very similar experiences—perceiving a very powerful, bright white light, sometimes seen at the end of a tunnel, accompanied by a feeling of leaving the body and floating above it.[28] Many people seem to receive greater insights about their life from these experiences, often pledging to become more loving and helpful to others. As a result of such experiences, individuals seem to go through an expansion of their consciousness, often becoming more serene and more committed to helping the world. Many also develop psychic abilities and have difficulty with social boundaries, rules, and time, as they live more fully in the now.

According to a 1977 Harris poll, 63 percent of Americans believed it is more important to learn to appreciate human values—as opposed to material values—than to find ways to create more jobs for producing more goods. And 68 percent said that economic growth produces a false sense of security—making people want to acquire more possessions rather than to enjoy nonmaterial experiences. Pollster Lou Harris says that this means that "the age of materialism as we have known it is going to be radically altered."

One of our greatest illusions about prosperity was to think that great doses of it would solve almost any problem, and that spiritual needs could be satisfied with material goods. This bred irresponsibility in government and in corporate America. Journalist Bill Moyers remarked that America's spiritual quest will be "*the* story of the next fifty years . . . the biggest story of the millennium."[29] Historian Garry Wills noted that 90 percent of Americans say they pray sometime in each week: "More people go to church, in any one week, than to all sports events combined," he says.[30]

Since 94 percent of Americans believe in God, and 56 percent say religious beliefs are very important to them, according to a recent Gallup poll, then the problem seems to be one of truly integrating beliefs with daily life and not living as if the goal were accumulation of possessions.

THE SECULARIZATION OF PUBLIC LIFE/ HONORING THE SACRED IN ALL LIFE

> *Men since the beginning of time have sought peace. Military alliances, balances of power, leagues of nations, all in turn have failed. . . . The problem is basically theological and involves a spiritual recrudescence and improvement of human character. . . It must be of the spirit to save the flesh.*
> —GENERAL DOUGLAS MACARTHUR

Historically, great abuses occurred when Christianity became a state religion. This is why in the early days of our nation, our Founding Fathers legislated freedom of religion and no establishment of a state religion. But was it their intention to relegate spiritual values solely to the religious sphere and exclude spiritual and moral considerations—and the sacred dimension of life—from public affairs? This seems unlikely since many of them evidenced a profound belief and faith in a Higher Power.

Conservative fundamentalists have attempted to fill this void by injecting specific religious values into politics and by evaluating candidates on the basis of their religious beliefs or their stands on such crucial issues as abortion or prayer in public schools. In this approach, however, patriotism becomes equated with acceptance of specific, dogmatic beliefs—a religious straitjacket that most Americans do not accept. Yet the mass response to the appeal of the fundamentalists, despite the excesses and corruption of TV evangelists, indicates a public hunger for spiritual principles and values and a deepening sense that something is missing in our public life.

The liberal, secular, rational humanist approach to public life has also created a gap in the nation's psyche. The unwillingness or discomfort many liberals have in talking publicly about their spiritual beliefs, or in admitting faith in a Higher Power, leaves many spiritually oriented people feeling that something is lacking in those public figures. And although rejecting the dogmatism and emotional demagoguery of the religious Right, the majority of people are unclear about how to bring ethical, moral, and spiritual values into public life. This is especially difficult as we emerge from a cycle of extreme materialism, with little reinforcement of ethics and morals in political and business life. Most honest people try to be a living example of their values. Yet the assaults on this intent by a ruthlessly competitive, greed-filled, selfish social order are insistent, often pressuring individuals into severely compromising their values.

Without a national consensus on spiritual values beyond specific religious identification, our public policies often reflect the lowest common denominator rather than the highest. Similarly, what psychologists call "the suppression of the sublime" prevents us from being open to the joy of transcendent spiritual experience in national life.

As *Washington Post* columnist William Raspberry notes: "We don't want ecclesiastics running the government. But we would, I think, welcome a return to government policies that, however secular, proceed from a belief that we are spiritual beings, not merely bundles of appetites."[31]

However, there may be more grounds for a consensus on spiritual values than we realize. Former Harvard University president Derek Bok states that, "If you look at virtually all the civilization we have had over the past few centuries, one does find disagreements on details, but a remarkable consensus on certain basic ethical precepts which form the basis for a serious ethical code."[32] This consensus could become a foundation to restore universal ethics to our political life.

According to Werner Jaeger, one of the foremost scholars on ancient Greece, the highest and most central theme of the model society created by the Greeks was called *paideia,* the individual's search for the Divine center within the self.[33]

Today many people, such as Jungian psychologist Thomas Moore in *Care of the Soul* and mystic David Spangler in *Emergence: The Rebirth of the Sacred,* are promoting the idea of resacralizing everyday life—rather than just experiencing sacredness in special religious services—and pointing out the urgent need for a new politics infused with the sacred. Yale law professor Stephen Carter's book, *The Culture of Disbelief,* makes a compelling argument that liberals and moderates should also speak about their spiritual convictions and not allow conservatives to monopolize the religious debate. President Clinton has widely recommended the book.

Noting that secular humanists have failed to end the "ecocide" of the earth, and voters have defeated the "Big Green" environmental initiative in California, state assemblyman Tom Hayden is trying instead to emphasize the spiritual side of nature, urging people to revere its sacredness.[34] Prince Charles of England is encouraging Westerners to see the spiritual side of medicine: "I believe that the most urgent need for Western man is to rediscover that Divine element in his being, without which there can never be any possible hope or meaning to our existence in this earthly realm."[35]

Another hopeful sign is that several U.S. states (California, Oregon, Arkansas, Indiana, and West Virginia) are bringing the study of religion back into public education as units in the social studies curriculum, while trying not to promote or unfairly criticize various faiths. The aim is to instill religious tolerance and reduce prejudice and to raise issues of truth and individual responsibility. "For some kids, this may be the first time and place these issues are raised," notes California schools superintendent Bill Honig.[36]

Recently *The New York Times* reported that psychology has been changing the way it regards religion, as growing numbers of psychologists are finding that religious beliefs are entering more often into their therapeutic work. Although Freud dismissed religion as little more than a neurotic illusion, recent research confirms that spiritual beliefs can improve mental health and are often of psychological benefit. Significantly, it seems not to matter so much what particular faith people hold, but rather how they hold it. Studies show that psychological health is not improved nearly as much when religion is seen as a means to a social or emotional end—

praying to God to help you—as it is when the motive is communion with God.[37]

NEGATIVE MEDIA IMAGES/ POSITIVE, INSPIRATIONAL IMAGES

Television and movies depict rising levels of violence to provide ever more intense emotional stimulation to increasingly jaded audiences. Even when confronted with case after case of violent killers who have been stimulated in their crimes by what they've seen on television or at the movies, or studies that link youth violence to television, some media spokespeople continue to insist there is no connection between the media and people's actions. Yet this is totally belied by the fact that these same people make millions in profits each year convincing advertisers of exactly the opposite! If people can be stimulated to buy a new soap or a fancier car through advertising, why wouldn't they be influenced by watching violent programs, images, and action on TV and in films?

A study by Brandon S. Centerwall, an epidemiologist at the University of Washington, cites evidence from several U.S. and Canadian studies stating that without television, violent crime would be half of what it is today. In another study, children living in remote villages in Canada were studied before and after television was introduced. Five years after they began watching television, the rate of physical aggression among children increased 160 percent. The National Coalition on Television Violence estimates that by the age of eighteen the average young person has witnessed 200,000 acts of violence on television including 40,000 murders.[38] Some psychologists say that the subconscious mind of children and most adults cannot distinguish between what it experiences in a film and in reality. In late 1993, after a series of mass murders and Congressional hearings on the effects of television violence, 79 percent of the American public said they thought violence on television contributes to real life violence, according to a *Los Angeles Times* poll. This awakening helped contribute to passage of the Brady gun-control law.

There have been numerous instances where the focusing of many people's consciousness on an image in a movie has quickly resulted in real-life events mirroring that fictional image—often in striking similarity of detail. In the two months following the February 1993 release of the film *Falling Down*, which showed a Los Angeles man taking revenge on anyone who irritated him, including a Korean shopkeeper who wouldn't give him change, eight Korean-American merchants were shot in Los Angeles County, five fatally. Shortly after the 1974 New York premiere of *The Towering Inferno* showed a hotel fire that killed many people, a very similar fire broke out in a New York hotel, with people being lifted off the rooftops by helicopter exactly as it was shown in the movie.

The film *The China Syndrome*, which opened in New York on March 17, 1979, was about a nuclear accident. Only eleven days later this was nearly re-enacted at Three Mile Island in Pennsylvania. In fact, there was even a line in the movie about "fearing the nuclear fallout would spread to an area as large as the state of Pennsylvania." This movie sparked an interesting debate about whether it helped create the real thing—or whether it was prophetic.

A person's responses to images of violence is deeply related to his/her level of evolution. For example, someone who is undisciplined and con-trolled primarily by his or her emotions could be triggered into committing violence by viewing constant images of violent acts. A major problem with portraying violence in film or on TV (often without showing any negative consequences) is that it establishes violent behavior as an accepted norm of human relations, and as a way of dealing with frustration and anger. It cre-ates a climate of fear and defensiveness, adds to the negative, separative thought-forms and emotional atmosphere that can poison human relations in a society. It behooves us all to work together to create a climate of con-sciousness where violence and horror in films and television would become repulsive to most people because of the refinement of their heart qualities.

Alongside all the negative images of violence and degradation in movies and television, there have been also been many inspiring images portraying positive values, heroic action, selfless love, supportive families, self-reflection, and positive images of the future. Films such as *Gandhi*, *Cry Freedom*, *Dead Poets Society*, and *Field of Dreams*, and TV shows such as "Joseph Campbell and the Power of Myth," "Star Trek," "The Wonder Years," and "Quantum Leap," have provided inspiration and dealt with current social issues from a more conscious perspective.

Behaviorists often argue that humans have always been a violent, aggres-sive species. Yet the history of our evolution shows a slow but gradual les-sening of these tendencies as we become more aware of our interrelatedness with one another and the benefits of cooperation rather than mutual de-struction. It is likely that someday in the future we will view the current level of violence in the way we view slavery today—totally "delegitimiz-ing" it.

SELF-FULFILLING PROPHECY/
PROPHECY AS WARNING

The true spiritual role of prophets is to warn humanity about negative thoughts and behavior that will create certain outcomes if continued. Prophets tune in psychically to a possible future based on the direction that certain currents of energy are following—if they are not interrupted or changed by human free will.

Some popular psychics, such as Edgar Cayce, have high ratings for predictions. Cayce accurately predicted the stock market crash of 1929, the end of World War II, and the race riots of the early 1960s.[39] He also predicted that the Mississippi River would widely overflow its banks, which seems to have been born out with the floods of 1993. Internationally known psychic Jeanne Dixon predicted John Kennedy's assassination but couldn't reach him to warn him. Bella Karish and Wayne Guthrie of the Fellowship of Universal Guidance in Los Angeles also contacted Kennedy in spirit to warn him, but to no avail.

However, no one seems to approach 100 percent accuracy in prediction because human free will often intervenes to change events. As Nostradamus, the famous prophet of the mid–sixteenth century who is credited with accurately predicting many events centuries into the future, remarked to his son, "The future is not fixed."[40]

Nostradamus wrote a number of fascinating quatrains that seem to pertain to the great events of our century. For example, he accurately predicted the October 1917 communist revolution as well as the end of communism: "There shall be in the month of October a great revolution made . . . and this shall last only 73 years and 7 months."[41] Other Nostradamus prophecies may have related to Hitler, to the war with Saddam Hussein in Iraq, to the depletion of the ozone layer, to the comet Kohoutek, and to the famine in Ethiopia.

Nostradamus's Quatrain #37, "Century VI," as translated by French-Provençal-language scholar Erika Cheetham, clearly seems to predict John F. Kennedy's assassination:

> The ancient work will be accomplished
> And from the roof(top) evil ruin will fall onto the great man.
> Being dead, they will accuse an innocent man of the deed,
> The guilty one(s) hidden in the misty wood(s).[42]

Since as many as seven quatrains may refer to Kennedy's assassination as a conspiracy, with the real perpetrators escaping, it was clearly seen even in the sixteenth century as a major historical event with repercussions still echoing thirty years after the event.

Thousands of years ago, the builders of the Great Pyramid in Giza in Egypt left prophecies in the stonework of that structure that many have interpreted as predicting modern events such as World Wars I and II. According to interpreters of the symbolism in the pyramid, we are at this time in the "Room of the Judgment of the Nations."

The Hopi Indians are custodians of sacred carved stones that have accurately predicted events such as the explosion of nuclear bombs—which they called "a gourd of ashes poured from the sky." And they warn of future disasters if humanity doesn't return to a deeper respect for nature and to harmony among the races. The current world is out of balance, say the Hopi prophecies. It is passing through a state of chaos and purification, with weapons destructive to all humanity. The Hopi elders were instructed to make four attempts to address the leaders of the world in what the prophecies called the "house of mica on the eastern shore of this land where the nations gather"—the distinctive glass building of the United Nations—to help people realign with the original instructions of the Creator. The Hopi prophecy says that if there is no response from world leaders, then the Great Purification of the world through natural disasters would be hastened. The last of the four attempts was made on December 10, 1992. Hopi elder Thomas Banyaca and other indigenous peoples were admitted to the UN and addressed the General Assembly, although the U.S. representative wasn't present.

THE ROLE OF PROPHECY

Prophets can bring human-created negative thought-forms to public consciousness so they can be confronted and transmuted. Philosopher David Spangler says that we are currently in a period of history similar to the last days of Atlantis. Many thought-forms and fears of destruction and cataclysm remain in our racial memory from that period, and they are influencing the thoughts and emotions of people today. The danger comes when these resurrected memories create a fatalistic acceptance, for they can be self-fulfilling if work is not done to avert the doom foretold.

The best prophets, Spangler says, are those whose prophecies don't come true. This means they've helped people heed the warning and make the changes needed to avert the predicted crisis, rather than enhancing their own egos by amassing a record of successful predictions. The wrong use of prophecy is to allow it to become self-fulfilling by becoming obsessed with fear of the future. This actually feeds energy to these fears and allows them to become unconsciously manifested in the world.[43]

Prophets not only predict the future, they also help create it, as their widely publicized predictions produce strong thought-forms in the human psyche. For example, in World War II the Nazis dropped leaflets over France revealing Nostradamus's prophecy about their triumph there, while Churchill promoted Nostradamus's prediction of Hitler's ultimate defeat.

Cult leader David Koresh prophesied Armageddon at his Waco, Texas, compound in 1993 and raved that everyone was against him. His powerful, fear-driven thought-form, energized by his ninety-five followers, created a self-fulfilling prophesy when the compound was attacked by the Bureau of Alcohol, Tobacco and Firearms, and later by the FBI's tear-gas assault, and the compound burned to the ground, killing most residents.

Many psychics today are prophesying catastrophic earth changes and creating a great deal of fear and frantic preparation. On a spiritual level, people will probably draw to themselves as much catastrophe as they need to wake up and make needed changes in their lives. However, positive predictions about the future can be much more useful, for they help to create a more positive reality. Unfortunately we don't see enough of these. Nevertheless, Nostradamus's prophecy of a coming golden age and peace for one thousand years is one we might all want to keep in mind.

PSYCHIC WARFARE/PSYCHIC HEALING

We will not have peace on the planet until we have a spiritual renaissance.
—U THANT, FORMER SECRETARY GENERAL OF THE UN

Many researchers have claimed that several countries, including the United States and the former Soviet Union, are developing psychic warfare techniques called "psychotronics"—the power of the mind put to both defensive and offensive uses—although officials deny it publicly. There have been claims that psychic warfare is responsible for causing illness and confusion in world leaders, destroying computers and weapons, and creating earthquakes and erratic weather.

In their book *The Mind Race: Understanding and Using Psychic Abilities*,[44] parapsychologists Russell Targ and Keith Harary assert that the U.S. Defense Department has funded an ongoing, multimillion-dollar program of psychic research (especially remote viewing) at SRI International in Stanford, California.

Ronald McRae, an associate of columnist Jack Anderson, reports in his book, *Mind Wars: The True Story of Government Research into the Military Potential of Psychic Weapons*,[45] that the U.S. government has a thirty-year history of psychic research and that President Carter was concerned enough to have a private meeting with Uri Geller, a famous psychic, before he was inaugurated.

The power of the mind to bend metal and other materials, and to cause computers and weapons to malfunction, is being studied. Some claim the strange telephone failures that hit major cities such as Washington, D.C., New York, and Los Angeles in late 1991 and early 1992 were the result of psychic warfare. Some governments are exploring "remote viewing"—the ability to see objects at a distance, such as secret documents or technology, in order to learn about the thoughts and plans of perceived enemies, according to John White in *Psychic Warfare: Fact or Fiction?*[46]

It is also thought that irritation and disorientation that seem to have no apparent source could be induced in people by powerfully trained minds. Thought control and inducing nervous breakdowns are also possible. Although psychic activity may seem justified for truly defensive purposes, such as psychic protection, there seems to be a thin line between this and more aggressive purposes, such as harming other people or their technology, or forcing others to do your will. It is understood by most psychics that if they misuse their gifts, they will lose them or suffer damaging karmic consequences.

As frightening and farfetched as this may all sound—like something out of science fiction—it might be important to remember that a majority of Americans report having experienced ESP (extrasensory perception or thought transmission). Many people are also learning how to send telepathic messages in times of need, when there is no access to a phone. A number of our national leaders were reported to have been clairvoyant at times—George Washington saw a vision of three great crises of the Republic,[47] and Abraham Lincoln had a premonition of his own assassination, as did Martin Luther King.

But psychic abilities can also be used for positive purposes, such as the use of. psychics by police departments for finding missing persons and criminals. And most significantly, there is the use of psychic energy for healing. Thousands of Americans are now developing their abilities to heal psychically, using the inner power potential in all of us, with remarkable results. There is considerable documentation of cases that couldn't be helped by traditional medicine but were later cured miraculously through the "laying on of hands"—the transmission of healing energy through the hands. In 1991 a *Time* magazine/CNN survey found that 2 percent of the population had been to a faith healer, and over 30 percent had tried some other form of alternative healing.[48]

The potential of the mind is tremendous. Since most of us only use about 10 percent of our brain power, there must be so much more we can contribute to the betterment of the world if we develop our consciousness more fully. By transcending separative thinking and by using our heart and intuition to see the greater good, we can safely use these greater powers of the mind without creating more karmic effects for ourselves or others. This in turn will help us offset some of the emotional causes of events created by humanity, which we will explore in the next chapter.

Chapter Six

◆

THE WORLD IS OUR MIRROR: THE EMOTIONAL AND ETHERIC CAUSES OF WORLD EVENTS

*During the 1969 Revolution in Libya, I had an awakening re-
alization. I was going through the pain and separation of a failing marriage, when I realized that I was allowing the anger and
mistrust that I was experiencing in my marriage to dictate my
negotiation attitude toward the Libyans. Just as I had adopted
a win/lose approach in my marital life, I was adopting a win/
lose approach with the Libyans. The inability of my wife and
me to act with love and trust in our personal lives was a critical
factor in my role during these political interactions of the United
States Government and Libya.*

—JOHN GRAHAM[1]

Causes in the Emotional Realm

The importance of personal psychological work is clearly dramatized in this
honest statement by a former U.S. diplomat and assistant to UN ambassador Andrew Young. The anger, fear, jealousy, and power trips of our political leaders—as well as our own—affect public policy more than we
realize. At antiwar rallies in the 1960s, state assemblyman John
Vasconcellos (D-CA) would talk about "the Vietnam War in myself and in
all of us," as well as the "inner Pentagon" and our own "internal Nixon."
According to interviewer Jeff Fishel, he told people that dealing with these
issues was just as important as protesting the war.[2]

Reformers and those who bring major changes to society often have had
a personal problem themselves that was similar or related to one in the
larger society. In working through their own problem, they discovered a

useful resolution to the social problem. (This insight might inspire each of us to clean up our own act, for by so doing we might make an important contribution to society in this same area.)

Many who are working closely with business and political leaders have now learned to include the psychophysical health of the leader in their strategy. An emotional atmosphere of trust and goodwill can do much to improve intergroup and international relations.

Psychologists David Feinstein and Stanley Krippner suggest the following:

> Ideally, political leaders should be those who have undergone a substantial exploration of their own unconscious motivations and have reached an advanced level of emotional maturity. . . . The real problem is to raise the consciousness of the general public so that it is capable of recognizing public figures whose policies mask their own inner conflicts. Policy makers could be educated to find both sides of an ideological conflict within themselves. Even if the process did not change their ideology, it would increase the likelihood of empathy and respect for opponent's position, thus enhancing their capacity for creative collaboration.[3]

Significantly, the ancient Greek philosopher Pythagoras, and later Plato, introduced the principle of examination and spiritual initiation into the government of the state. They thus reconciled the elective or democratic principle with a government formed on the basis of intelligence and virtue in this higher synthesis.

In the Iroquois League, created to maintain peace among the eastern Native American tribes long before white men arrived, each representative could vote only on issues not involving his own tribe. He could not vote for any special advantage or modify the common good for the needs of his own people. After all the corruption and scandals exposed in the U.S. government, we could perhaps learn something from the wisdom of these indigenous people.

We also need to recognize how our emotional state affects not only our own work and activities, but the general emotional climate in the world. Political consultants who design campaigns have demonstrated the effectiveness of appealing to the worst in us—to our fear, anger, and greed. When we're feeling depressed or angry about our own personal life, we're not likely to vote with wisdom or clarity. But as we clarify our own emotions, we contribute to the general healing of the whole, for we all affect each other on an inner level. We then can vote with more wisdom and elect those who live by higher principles.

Becoming Aware

To begin this process, the first step is an awareness of our own negative emotional patterns. The second step is to look for the positive intent behind the negative pattern. To ask ourselves, How is this emotion trying to serve me? What is it trying to accomplish? Once this is done, we can then look for more positive and effective ways to achieve the same results.

Fortunately, in the last decade more people than ever have been seeking psychological help with their problems, and this is helping to clarify their political views. It has been estimated that over twenty million Americans are in therapy today, and many more would be if they could afford it. Millions more are in 12 Step recovery groups in the United States and around the world.

On the evening news we generally see only the problems and crises in the world, many of which are related to personal psychological problems such as greed, dishonesty, violence, or hatred. The millions of people who have overcome more of their personal problems and who are relating to each other and their world in a loving or constructive way are rarely featured. Fortunately there is much goodwill and positive emotional energy in each of us and in the world, and this helps build trust among people so conflicts can be settled justly, new solutions found, and new projects undertaken. Below we discuss some key examples of the emotional states that contribute to world problems and to solutions.

SHADOW PROJECTION/PERSONAL RESPONSIBILITY

> *What the West has tolerated, but secretly and with a slight sense of shame (the diplomatic lie, systematic deception, veiled threats), comes back into the open and in full measure from the East and ties us up in neurotic knots. It is the face of his own evil shadow that grinned at Western Man from the other side of the Iron Curtain.*
>
> —CARL JUNG[4]

The "shadow" represents our emotions and behaviors that are incompatible with our own self-image, so they are repressed into our subconscious. The substitution of someone else's guilt for our own unacknowledged guilt is often referred to as "shadow projection." Just as individuals often deny their own faults and project them onto others, so groups and nations project their collective shadow. This is the basic dynamic underlying group hatred and violence.

Swiss psychotherapist Carl Jung used the term "shadow" for this unconscious part of the personality because it often appears in dreams in a personified form. When an individual or group feels an overwhelming rage coming up if criticized about a fault, this is often a good indication of a shadow fault that is still in the unconscious. When we become obsessed with the faults of another, we are very likely noticing our own unconscious tendencies that are overt in the actions of the other.

"[N]o one can become conscious of the shadow without considerable moral effort," Jung wrote, "because exploring the dark aspects of one's personality generally meets with considerable resistance. The effect of projection is to isolate the subject from his environment, since instead of a real relation to it there is now only an illusionary one. Projections change the world into the replica of one's own unknown face."[5] The shadow usually contains values that we need, but they exist in a form that makes it difficult to integrate them into our life.

Classic examples of shadow projection were the illegal acts of former FBI chief J. Edgar Hoover, who was tough on crime committed by others but was himself involved in many high crimes and misdemeanors, as it was later learned, including patronizing Mafia-run racetracks and committing character assassinations (and some say physical assassinations) of his political enemies. He was publicly a gay basher yet was himself a closet gay and occasional drag queen. Likewise, sexual scandals surrounded Jim and Tammy Bakker, the TV evangelists who preached a rigid moral code.[6]

A classic case of shadow projection is found in the recent history of U.S.-Soviet relations. Americans used to believe that it was the former Soviets who were aggressive, expansive, and deceptive—never ourselves. Clearly they were the "bad guys." Conversely, the Soviets believed that we were the "bad guys" and that they did nothing wrong. But, in fact, both countries are mirrors for each other in certain ways. Both countries saw the other as aggressive and deceitful and themselves as innocent. Both aggressively promoted their ideology around the world, often supporting foreign leaders with little popular support.

This projection began lessening when President Reagan, who had referred to the Soviet Union as the "evil empire," actually went into "the heart of the beast" at Red Square and embraced his "shadow"—projected onto Gorbachev—thereby helping to transform the collective projection. The so-called Iron Curtain separating East and West, which Carl Jung called "a symbol of our neurotically disassociated world"—was lifted with the destruction of the Berlin Wall. This was a major step towards restoring wholeness to our world.

However, if the psychological roots of shadow projection aren't dealt

with, then the transformation of a former enemy into a friend will only ne-
cessitate the creation of a new enemy. This has happened in the United States,
with the Japanese who have been overwhelming us economically. With their
products flooding our markets, as they buy up huge chunks of symbolic U.S.
real estate such as Hollywood movie studios and Rockefeller Center, they have
become the new "bad guys." Yet their activities simply reflect practices of
wealthy Americans, who have bought real estate and even stolen national art
treasures at bargain prices around the world for decades.

Since we haven't been willing to fully confront our vast abuse and neglect of the environment, we've become obsessed with the destruction of
the rain forest in Brazil. But, in reality, we've destroyed far more of our
own rain forests in the Pacific Northwest and Alaska than Brazil has, as actual aerial photos have shown.

Another interesting example of how our projections change is the reaction
of Americans to President Saddam Hussein of Iraq. Until he invaded Kuwait
in August of 1990, Saddam had been perceived as the lesser of two evils in
the Iran-Iraq war, and we helped build up his war machine. For us, the Aya-
tollah Khomeini was the real villain. But after his invasion of Kuwait,
Saddam was denounced as a "bloodthirsty madman" and compared to Hitler.
Popular radio stations in the United States began getting thousands of requests for anti-Saddam songs. As *Newsweek* noted, "Washington has operated
in the Middle East as if the only objective of its policy is to identify Public
Enemy No. 1." As successive American administrations played this erratic
game over the last twenty-five years, the Egyptians, Saudis, Syrians, Libyans,
Jordanians, Palestinians, Iraqis, and, of course, the non-Arab Iranians have all
been both vilified and courted at one time or another. The defining issues
were Israel, terrorism, and cheap oil. Questions like democracy and human
rights, cornerstones of U.S. policy elsewhere, seldom surfaced.[7]

Each nation tends to project its shadow on other people who are different. As metaphysician Rudolf Steiner noted, the Italians see others as
"aliens," the French see others as "barbarians," the British see them as "rivals," and the Russians see them as "evil heretics."[8]

The fighting in Northern Ireland between the Catholics and the Protestants, and the endless battles between the Israelis and the Palestinians, despite the peace agreements, are other classic examples of shadow projection.
Each side sees itself as victim and the other side as persecutor and is unwilling to admit any of its own faults. As shadow projections build up between enemies, tensions mount, and neither side believes its enemy can do
anything good or can be trusted. As each side becomes more self-righteous
and angry, it attracts more negativity and begins behaving like its op-
pressor.

Similarly, the United States mined harbors in Nicaragua, which violated international law, just as it accused the former Soviets and Saddam Hussein of doing. Winnie Mandela, former wife of Nelson Mandela, the long imprisoned South African black leader, was accused of being oppressive and violent to people around her, just as she experienced oppression and violence from whites. Many sixties activists were unwilling to face their own shadow—aggressiveness, power trips, anger, and divisiveness—when they were morally crusading against injustice in the ghettos and Vietnam, and this contributed to their own decline. Today, as political scientist Walt Anderson notes, "some of the people who are most strident in their declarations of nonviolence toward nature think a little violence toward other people—environmental bad guys, of course—is justified."[9] It's clear that it's easier to point fingers than to face one's own shadow.

Joanna Macy, social activist and author of *Despair and Personal Power in the Nuclear Age*, addresses the issue of nuclear waste in her Guardianship Project and encourages people to find their own "inner toxic waste." Like nuclear waste, people's inner toxic waste—their own fears, anger, hatred—cannot be buried and then ignored as if it weren't there: it will contaminate everything. Macy encourages people to confront this inner waste and then to "bow to it, breathe with it, watch it"—for this allows it to change. And this transformation liberates people.[10] Awareness of how each nation projects its shadow is not meant to replace clear, objective analysis of actual aggressive behavior and the necessity for taking appropriate action to combat it, however. The important thing is to separate personal and collective emotional issues from reality.

Each time we are willing to confront our personal shadow, we help transmute some of the collective shadow. As each nation and each political group becomes more willing to examine and take responsibility for its own faults rather than accusing its enemy, it can strengthen itself inwardly and achieve its higher purpose, contributing its gifts for the highest good of all. As each side in a conflict develops the capacity to do this, a basis for a win/win (rather than win/lose) solution can be found.

VICTIM CONSCIOUSNESS/ PERSONAL EMPOWERMENT

[T]he mysteries of political behavior have their origin in the mysteries of the human mind, and yet an examination of the human mind in order to understand our political behavior has heretofore not appealed to either the public or to political leaders.

It may be we are frightened by the possibilities that might be revealed by some self-examination.
—SENATOR J. WILLIAM FULBRIGHT[11]

The victim syndrome and a sense of powerlessness is actually one of the root causes of many of the problems we see in the world today. It leaves the door open for exploiters to have a field day, playing on the potential victim's fears. When we feel victimized we're often too preoccupied feeling sorry for ourselves to do anything to stop the exploitation. As victims, we expect others to rescue us. Yet our very attitudes and mind-set make it nearly impossible for us to recognize and accept true help when it is offered. As a result, we slide deeper and deeper into our victimization.

Although it is true that some people grow up in very difficult environments and so have more challenges to overcome than other people, those who succeed are the ones who have let go of a victim consciousness and blaming others. For instance, when women feel they're being discriminated against simply because they're women, they need to investigate this objectively and take action. But women also need to look more deeply within to examine how their own feelings of low self-worth might be contributing to others' seeing them that way. Studies have shown that the way the majority of people respond to someone they are meeting for the first time exactly reflects that person's self-image. People who think they are stupid will be perceived that way by others, even though they may in fact be quite above average in intelligence.

We witnessed a clear example of victimization recently in a class on communities we taught. During an experiential session where class members were to cooperate to put together puzzle pieces, one young woman ignored the rules and just did her own thing, playing with the pieces instead. Another woman got particularly upset with her and told her she should play by the rules. The first woman then also became angry and withdrawn and later told us she was attacked by the woman (who was German) because she was Jewish. The German woman, not knowing anything of this, said she became angry because the first woman was acting just like her father always did and making fun of her. We were stunned: the first woman was reenacting the Holocaust, the second woman was reenacting her childhood, and both slipped unconsciously into victimhood and refused to communicate.

Victims can turn into oppressors if the deep psychological pattern isn't dealt with. For example, the South African Boers, who were victims of British concentration camps, later put black people in similar camps when they came to power. We see Israelis oppressing and killing Palestinians, repeating in some ways their persecution by the Nazis. For example, according to *Newsweek*, 366 Palestinians were killed by Jews in 1988, as opposed to 14 Israelis killed by Palestinians.[12] And we see Serbs massacring Muslims just as it had been done to them years before, beginning with invading Muslim Turks in 1389 and continuing through post–World War II atrocities. Serb president Milosevic, a psychologist by profession, knows the popularity of appealing to the age-old feelings of victimization in Serbs, and stimulating them to fight old battles again. And some blacks in Washington, D.C., who've become successful have now started discriminating against Hispanics, saying they've taken away jobs. "It's always amazing that every group that's been discriminated against [can do] the same thing toward someone else," noted black mayor Sharon Pratt Kelly of Washington, D.C.[13]

There is a widespread "victim consciousness" in society. We tend to see ourselves as victims of circumstances we can't control. We believe we "can't change City Hall," because one person can't make a difference. In the collective sphere we see this as obsessive blaming—especially of government and corporations—and a self-righteous feeling about what "they did to me." Although on one level there may be truth in this, as monied interests do have disproportionate power, it can also be a cop-out and merely a rationale for laziness and lack of responsibility. Since thousands of Americans don't vote—believing that voting doesn't make a difference—we ourselves continue to create more of the problems we're feeling victimized by. We need to break this cycle of circular causes.

Examples of Empowerment

This belief that we are victims is a false one, as proven over and over again by individuals whose courage in standing up against prejudice and whose sense of personal empowerment catalyzed the beginning of major changes—blacks such as Martin Luther King and women such as Gloria Steinem. In late 1989 the example of the Romanian priest who refused to be cowed by government threats to his ministry galvanized hundreds of thousands of his fellow citizens to pour into the streets in defiance, eventually toppling the oppressive Ceausescu government. And millions of viewers all over the world were deeply moved by the sight of Russian mothers and children overcoming passive obedience and defying Soviet tanks during the attempted coup of August 1991.

As an activist in Berkeley in the 1960s, Corinne experienced a dramatic event that reflects the shift that is needed from victim consciousness into strength and empowerment. In one of their demonstrations and strikes in support of creating a Third World curriculum on the University of California campus, students marched into Sproul Plaza and were met with the usual line of police with guns and tear gas trying to break up the march. When the police advanced the students retreated, feeling themselves as victims of the immense firepower the police had to force them back. This was a dance that happened so many times, they all knew their choreographed parts. But one day, for some unknown reason, the demonstrators suddenly charged the police instead of retreating. This threw the police off guard so quickly that they actually retreated from the demonstrators, even though they had the guns and the students had nothing. This psychological reversal was an amazingly exhilarating experience, which will never be forgotten—overcoming victimization and reclaiming power.

Native American warriors would never say that their enemy defeated them. Rather, they would try to find their own fault or weakness that created the psychological chink in their armor to make them vulnerable to their enemy. From inner perspective there are no victims, only learners in the school of life, where everything is unfolding in Divine Order.

It requires only a small percentage of empowered people to move mountains. As a writer for *The Washington Post* noted about the 1991 Soviet coup attempt, "People Power was something of a myth; out of 291 million Soviets, at first only a few thousand courageously put themselves on the line for democracy. The vast majority stayed on the fence until the outcome was clear. But it hardly mattered. The perception of a democratic triumph quickly became the reality. People thought they had the power, and therefore they did."[14]

FEAR/COURAGE

[T]he ill success . . . of all efforts made during the last decade to reach this goal [world peace] leaves us no room to doubt that strong psychological factors are at work which paralyze these efforts.

—ALBERT EINSTEIN[15]

Fear is a major motivator in many areas of our public life. We have an obsession with locks, security systems, insurance, laws, and lawsuits—to protect us from our fear of others who are different, our fear of losing material possessions that give us our identity, and our fear of change. Beneath the aggressive stances of nations lies the psychological root cause—fear and insecurity. Although this is seldom admitted by posturing political and military leaders, fear is only fed and increased when it is hidden and not addressed.

The 1973 Israeli-Egyptian war transformed the psychological configuration of the conflict, according to psychiatrist William Davidson. The Arabs' successful attacks constituted an assault on fear itself, causing an upsurge in Arab self-esteem. The Israeli sense of humiliation from the assault brought about a rapid emotional shift from a certain arrogance and over-confidence to grief, protectiveness, and insecurity. President Anwar Sadat of Egypt, in his historic visit to Jerusalem in 1977, was the first major political leader to publicly suggest that "psychological factors" constituted the greater part of the barrier between political and military enemies. He pointed out the suspicion, rejection, fear, deception, and hallucination in the Arab-Israeli enmity. By openly acknowledging the fear on both sides and realizing neither is secure if the other feels insecure, each nation can find new ways to create true mutual security.[16]

The psychological basis of the former Soviet Union's aggressiveness and expansionism was a tremendous fear of being invaded again, as she had been many times over the course of history, most recently in World War II. Never having experienced a major invasion, the United States didn't feel the same deep insecurity in her psyche about foreign invasion and thus misunderstood the Soviets, perceiving their fear as pure aggressiveness.

But the tremendous fear in the Soviet people was changed dramatically with Gorbachev's new *glasnost* policy—even he didn't realize the power of the forces he had unleashed. The new openness broke the centuries-old bonds of passivity and fear in the Soviet people, and there was no turning back to the old repressive order when hard-liners tried to intimidate people during the 1991 coup attempt. As a *Washington Post* editorial noted, "Above all, what destroyed the junta was also the main achievement of Gorbachev's reforms: the end of fear. The journalists at the Echo of Moscow radio station showed no fear when they defied troops and stayed on the air. The miners of Siberia showed no fear in declaring a general strike. Children showed no fear climbing on the tanks ... Moscow's deputy mayor, Yuri Luzhkov, showed no fear when the local Communist party boss, Yuri Prokofiev, told him to 'report in' [and he] refused. . . . Above all, Yeltsin set the tone of fearlessness."[17] Gorbachev himself showed no fear in facing his own death and the death of his family rather than surrendering to the coup.

Fundamentalist Christians have great fear of any movement toward a world government, such as the United Nations, or toward "oneness," such as the New Age movement. They see this as the work of the devil. But this fear of "oneness" and unity may be due to the fact that many who are drawn to simplistic fundamentalist perspectives are "pre-individualized" and haven't as yet discovered their own identity as individuals. For them, anything transcending individuality is not yet appropriate. A helpful way for fundamentalists to overcome their fear is to remember the "unity in diversity" theme, which forms the basis of the work of both the United Nations and the New Age movement—respecting diversity and uniqueness while focusing on the underlying unity.

The wide availability of inexpensive transportation and international tourism that provides a genuine experience of other cultures is also helping to heal some of the fear born of ignorance between peoples. To get to know so-called enemies, many "citizen diplomats" have been developing the courage in recent years to visit countries like the former Soviet Union, Nicaragua, and the Arab nations to experience these cultures firsthand. Witness for Peace and Earthstewards have both organized many ordinary civilians to travel to crisis spots in Central America and witness what is actually occurring to help deter greater aggression.

Many have overcome fear by developing greater love and a true faith in God or the benevolence of the universe in order to experience an inner peace and security, which nothing can threaten. As President Franklin Roosevelt proclaimed on the eve of World War II, "We have nothing to fear but fear itself." A helpful prayer to overcome fear is, "Let reality govern my every thought, and truth be the master of my life."

ADDICTION AND DENIAL/ ACKNOWLEDGING PROBLEMS

Dr. David Musto, a medical historian, calls addiction "the American disease" caused by our "fast lane" affluence that denies itself no thrill and by the vast social alienation felt by the poor.[18] As much as half of the population may be either addicted to alcohol or drugs, an adult child of addicts, or "co-dependent" (living with addicts and developing destructive denial patterns in order to cope).

An enormously high percentage of the rest of the population are addicted to work, food, shopping, sex, or TV. Seventy-eight percent of respondents in a national survey done by Hallmark Cards said they are, have been, or know someone in a recovery program, and fifteen million are estimated to attend support groups for alcohol, drug abuse, or other dependencies. All these are common patterns that are used to compensate for inner feelings of emptiness. Truths too uncomfortable to admit are unconsciously altered or postponed by addicts, and then this altered truth becomes subjectively true.

In recent years this classic psychological problem of denial has moved from the personal to the political world with alarming results. Denial has become a major national dysfunction. As a way of coping with the intensity of national and world crises, people often deny that there are any problems. Nowhere was this more evident than in the presidency of Ronald Reagan. According to popular author Gail Sheehy, Reagan, as the son of an alcoholic, clearly embodied the alcoholic "co-dependent" syndrome of those who live with alcoholics and deny there is any problem. Reagan admitted that he "lived in a pretend world as a kid." Sheehy and others feel he built his whole life as a Hollywood actor, and later as a politician, on fantasy and denial. One symptom of this behavior was that President Reagan often fell asleep during important meetings, and he "forgot" facts that interfered with his perception of himself as pure in motive and true to his word. This was particularly obvious in the many times he told the Iran-contra jury that he couldn't remember something that happened. As president he told the public exactly what they wanted to hear, painting a rosy picture as the numbers of poor and homeless grew, the environment deteriorated, and the nation slipped farther and farther into debt, thus mortgaging its future.[19]

Americans chose an actor for president—the embodiment of pretending that is so prevalent in society today—the image of a strong leader rather than the reality. Americans elected Reagan twice by electoral landslides, reflecting a similar pattern of denial in the national character—ignoring aspects of life that don't fit an optimistic view or a particular self-image. Although over one hundred members of Reagan's administration were indicted on ethical or legal charges, people still refused to believe how deep the corruption had gone in American public life. They were usually satisfied with finding a single culprit (or a "lone assassin") or blaming it all on a "temporary lapse" in good judgment.

However, a positive sign is that all across America the fastest-growing self-help movement today is the 12 Step program—Alcoholics Anonymous, Adult Children of Alcoholics, Co-Dependents Anonymous, Narcotics Anonymous, Overeaters Anonymous, Workaholics Anonymous, Shoppers Anonymous, Fundamentalists Anonymous, and so forth. These programs not only help people overcome their addictions, they also help them work on the psychological root causes of their problems and empower them to develop the courage to face reality. When we become willing to publicly acknowledge our personal problems and our inability to overcome them without help, the stage is set for true healing. The 12 Step healing process happens in a group context with peer support.

On a national political level, it may well be time for Americans to go through a similar process. We are beginning to acknowledge our collective addictions and denial reflected not only by our growing national debt, but also by our urban racial violence and decay and the breakdown of the family and our public educational system.

GREED/DETACHMENT

Greed is all right, by the way. I want you to know that. I think greed is healthy. You can be greedy and still feel good about yourself.

—Ivan Boesky[20]

Greed is the driving force behind much of the excess in our society. In fact, it can be seen as the cause of much of our economic downturn—the failure of so many banks and savings and loan associations, as well as corporate bankruptcies. Greed is the result of insatiable desire, trying to fill a deep emptiness inside—usually a lack of self-love and faith in any Higher Power—with an obsessive accumulation of money and material things. Top CEO salaries have gone off the scale in relation to staff salaries—a far bigger differential in the United States than in any other industrialized nation, including Germany and Japan. And this has become an important factor in our lack of economic competitiveness. It is also significant that when times get hard—as during the Great Depression as well as in 1992—the poor give more in both time and money to charity than the wealthy.

Greed was particularly fashionable in the 1980s under President Reagan, when idealism was out of favor. This era was epitomized by Ivan Boesky, a living archetype of the cynicism and rampant materialism so prevalent during this time, who played out the role of the greedy magnate who gets away with it—for a while.

The notorious rapaciousness of the 1980s on Wall Street finally became discredited with the bankruptcy of Drexel Burnham, layoffs and cutbacks throughout the financial industry, and Boesky's downfall in history's biggest insider-trading scandal on Wall Street. This was hailed by *Newsweek* as "a landmark of the 1980s—Wall Street's Watergate."[21] *Time* magazine called the insider-trading scandal "a grotesque perversion of the Reagan free-market ethos . . . perhaps the inevitable consequence of the gospel of wealth run amuck."[22] The downfall of greedy hotel owner Leona Helmsley, who had said, "Only the little people pay taxes," and was also convicted of tax evasion, was also a public morality play.

Michael Milken, another greedy manipulator called the "junk bond king," finally pleaded guilty to felonies of cheating customers, aiding others in violating securities law, and manipulating a corporate takeover. As one columnist wrote, "Milken has hurt more companies, more people, more pension plans . . . more banks and S&Ls than any other person I can ever remember."[23]

Greed wasn't limited only to businesspeople. Former FBI chief William Sessions was caught misusing thousands of dollars of government funds for personal luxuries.

The remedy for obsessive greed is detachment from material desires—taking only what is sufficient to meet one's true needs. A voluntary simplicity movement, with people simplifying their life-style, is growing around the country today. Rather than being a sacrifice, true detachment is actually liberating. Material things often possess the person rather than vice versa, in that one's whole sense of identity and self-worth is based on them, with the accompanying fear of loss. Only those who are free of desire seem truly happy. This includes not only those who seem to have little materially and don't miss it, but also some of very comfortable means who are not attached or obsessed by all of their possessions and share them wisely. As Mahatma Gandhi said, "There is enough for everyone's need, but not enough for everyone's greed."

ASTRAL INVERSION/EMOTIONAL CLARITY

The astral or emotional plane is the subtle dimension where humanity directs its desires. However, this focus creates an inversion of values, leading to much tension and conflict in the world. Everything material that excites the senses, provides pleasure, or fulfills desires seems to be the most important, while all spiritual or nonmaterial values and attitudes seem irrelevant. This overemphasizes the gratification of our material, emotional, or intellectual desires, while the question of values and the methods used in attaining these desires is diminished or ignored.

This is called an inversion because it's as if we're wearing reverse glasses that turn reality upside down. The "real world" becomes the one of money, competition, strife, and self-aggrandizement, while the world of spiritual understanding, compassion, and the joy of helping others is seen as "airy-fairy" or "unrealistic." Yet most of the progress humanity has gained is a result of spiritual impulses, visions, and ideals being implemented in the world.

This inversion is reflected in the inversion of language as well, where words often disguise reality. There are "adult" bookstores and films, for example, which are limited to adults but actually geared to the intelligence and adolescent fantasies of a twelve-year-old. There are ads for "the Spirit of Newport cigarettes"—yet this is not true spirit. It's a commercial for addiction, instead of the original sacred use of tobacco by Native Americans, where the smoke carried prayers to heaven. Ads for Philip Morris cigarettes carry a picture of Lech Walesa and a quote on freedom and the Bill of Rights. Thus a product that creates a deadly addiction is being linked to the "freedom" to poison oneself.

An ad for a shopping mall in Virginia is headlined, "Think Globally, Act Locally"—as if buying clothes from around the world truly constituted global vision. This is another astral inversion, as our overconsumption habits are depriving other countries economically and polluting the planet. Astral inversion is also noticeable in advertising that uses what's called "subliminal seduction"—subconsciously playing on our fears, greed, and sexual desires to sell a product.

Wildly popular rock star Madonna uses the name of the Virgin Mother but actually seems to enjoy playing out more of the seductress rather than the virgin archetype. "Be all that you can be" is an ad for the U.S. Army. But in the armed forces you're hardly free to be totally yourself—although you might learn to develop courage and obedience.

During the war in Vietnam, the U.S. military napalmed Vietnamese villages with the strange explanation that "we had to destroy the village in order to save it." This has carried over to the napalming of American forests to clear them for industrial-style monocropping, described as a way to "protect the environment." Of course the opposite occurs, as poisonous chemical residues remain. And since many species of trees are eliminated, serious erosion results.

Astral "Glamour"

This emotional inversion and attachment to the gratification of desires, largely conditioned by our consumer society, can be extended indefinitely—as desire can never be totally satiated on its own level. On the deepest level we yearn to satisfy our inner longings for fulfillment. We yearn to know who we really are and how we fit into the scheme of life. This aspiration for something transcendent to material existence, for spiritual inspiration and experience, creates a conflict with our materially oriented focus. This duality or conflict generates what the Ageless Wisdom teaching calls "glamour"—the astral emotional fog and confusion that surrounds many people and most of the planet today. This glamour or emotional distortion makes it difficult to see anything clearly and simply for what it is, as everything is viewed through emotionally colored glasses.

The glamour or miasma of desire, pain, self-pity, greed, guilt, and hatred forms the emotional sea that much of humanity moves through every day. It is created and fed by the thoughts and feelings of people throughout history, amplified by images projected by the media, and held in suspension on the astral plane, where it continues to exert tremendous influence on nearly everyone. The presence of this energy field explains why humanity seems to remain trapped by its endless desires, despite the teachings of the Buddha on desirelessness and Jesus on unselfishness.

Seeing Clearly Again

Two public figures recently hit bottom physically or financially and got a good look at how inverted their values were. Interestingly, both were major political consultants—Lee Atwater, former chairman of the Republican National Committee, and John F. King, a leader in the West Virginia Republican party. Both went public with their experiences and what they learned.

Lee Atwater had become famous and successful for exploiting the dark side of American politics—creating a political ad about a black murderer that helped crush the presidential bid of Michael Dukakis through a crude appeal to racism, for example. Before he died of cancer at age forty, Atwater expressed a revised view of his career, saying, "You can acquire all you want and still feel empty. . . . It took a deadly illness to put me eye to eye with that truth, but it is a truth that the country, caught up in its ruthless ambitions and moral decay, can learn on my dime. Forget money and power. I had no idea how wonderful people are. I wish I had known that before. What a way to have to find out."[24] Atwater also rediscovered God, publicly proclaiming the importance of faith in his life and seeking forgiveness and reconciliation with his enemies before he died. He said, "[M]y illness has taught me something about the nature of humanity, love, brotherhood, and relationships that I never understood and probably never would have."

John King was arrogant and proud of his "slash and burn" negative campaigning against opponents, becoming a close friend of many senators and lunching at the White House. But when he moved from West Virginia to Washington, D.C., everything went wrong. He ended up bankrupt and homeless, living in shelters, too proud to go to friends or family for help. King now says he regrets his past arrogance and his treatment of people as things to be manipulated in order to win. "I was involved in politics," he said regretfully. "I was in a position to help change things, and I just used things."[25]

It takes a conscious effort of the will, and a focused use of the mind, for us to lift ourselves out of this emotional soup that affects the motivations and activities of a large part of humanity. But more and more people are doing so today, which means they are seeing clearly what needs to be done to help the world. Their detachment from the fog of desire makes their work far more effective. The many thousands of people around the country involved in service projects to help the poor, the sick, and the disabled, or those who support various reform movements, are proof that it is possible to develop emotional clarity about true values.

DESPAIR/HOPE FOR THE FUTURE

Hope is a state of mind, not of the world. . . . [It] is a dimension of the soul, and it's not essentially dependent on some particular observation of the world or estimate of the situation. . . . [It is the] ability to work for something because it is good, not just because it stands a chance to succeed.

—VACLAV HAVEL[26]

Three-fourths or more of the world is engaged in a continual struggle to surmount immense physical and psychological difficulties and simply survive. Their struggle is filled with hopelessness and sees little beyond the certain arrival of death. Metaphysician David Spangler says that "their struggle permeates the unconscious of [our] race with a similar vibration. In this way, no matter where [we] live, the vibrations of struggle permeate [our] environment. . . . [It] fills our world with an inertia of fatalism and depression, which impinges upon and affects even those who are not directly confronted with the problem of physical survival . . . creating a vulnerability to images of destruction. . . . Fear of both a definite and a vague nature moves through the hearts and minds of people, challenging [our] powers of creativity and erecting a fog or veil. . . ."[27]

The imbalance between the Northern and the Southern hemispheres' countries is today creating more tension on an inner, subconscious level than any remaining East/West issues. The disparity between the tremendous wealth and power in the Northern Hemisphere and the poverty and oppression in the Southern Hemisphere is now widely visible to all through television and film. This tension is the result of massive energy imbalances in the body of our planetary energy field.

In the wealthy Northern Hemisphere of the planet there is a concentration of all types of energy, resources, education, information, consumer goods, money, and the like. In contrast, in the poor Southern countries little energy is available in the form of food, shelter, and clothing, and millions are starving, homeless, and full of hopelessness. It's as if in our own body we had an oversupply of blood to the head and not enough to the heart or limbs.

According to the Brandt Report, chaired by former chancellor of West Germany Willy Brandt, the North has a moral responsibility to alleviate the South's suffering because "morally it makes no difference whether a human being is killed in war or is condemned to starve to death because of the indifference of others."[28] However, even in the North there are places of poverty and despair as deep as anything in the Southern nations, as was dramatically illustrated in the riots of 1992 in the midst of wealthy Los Angeles following the acquittal of the policemen who beat Rodney King.

In the integrated planetary energy field, these imbalances and blockages in circulation of energies cause human suffering and generate anger, despair, and a sense of injustice that ultimately explode into riots, revolution, or terrorism. From an inner level, the sense of hopelessness is far worse spiritually than the death of physical bodies. The Souls will reincarnate in new bodies, according to the Ageless Wisdom. It is the sense of hopelessness that causes the greatest harm, as it creates an atmosphere that stifles the possibilities for growth of the Soul.

Throughout history, those who have had hope and a positive attitude have been able to overcome immense obstacles. An old friend of ours, who as a child survived a Nazi concentration camp, told us that the adult survivors were those who held to a positive image of the future and who shared whatever meager resources they were given.

Some groups, such as RESULTS in Washington, D.C., are dealing directly with world hopelessness through effective grass-roots lobbying on issues like hunger. Other groups have developed strategies to counteract the psychological effects of this wide sense of despair among humanity. The International Center for Integrative Studies in New York, for example, began a Center for a Science of Hope with international conferences, newsletters, and a computer data base to document how hope is understood across generations, cultures, and disciplines and to describe examples of constructive applications of hope in the lives of individuals and groups.

Joanna Macy, peace activist and author of *Despair and Personal Power in the Nuclear Age*, argues, "Like grief, despair must be worked through. It must be named and validated as a healthy, normal, human response to the planetary situation." From her studies of Buddhism and general systems theory, Macy observes that this psychic distress is actually heartening evidence of our fundamental interconnection with a larger web of life. She offers seminars that help participants get in touch with their feelings of despair and helplessness and then shift the energy by breathing through the pain, letting it move through the heart, and then releasing it back to the healing resources of the web of life. Macy feels that if you don't let yourself experience your fear, you get stuck in it. But if you acknowledge it and release it, there's room for other feelings.

According to spiritual teacher Torkom Saradarian, people relate to evil and hope in different ways. Some people always expect the worst, spreading fear of doom and destruction, and often use fear to exploit others. Some people are rosy optimists and never acknowledge evil if it doesn't affect them. Others see the corruption and evil in the world and bravely act with great hope and optimism to oppose its spread. Those individuals who change crisis into opportunities for transformation and achievement are the hope of the world. Hope acts like a spiritual magnet which draws inspiration from Higher sources. Hope is not an emotional attitude, but a clear intuitive knowing that recognizes good can triumph when charged with courage and unshakable determination.

EFFECTS OF EMOTIONS ON WEATHER/ ENVIRONMENTAL HEALING

> *The human kingdom . . . if constantly indulging in negative and destructive emotions, eventually affects the astral, the etheric, and the physical bodies of the planet. In synchronization with the emotional states of humanity, and the crises that may come because of this, there are also upheavals in nature in the physical body of the planet—earthquakes, volcanic eruptions, cyclones, winds, violent heat and cold.*
> —VIOLA NEAL AND SHAFICA KARAGULLA[29]

Science tells us that the atmosphere is a giant heat engine, and that the interactions of sunlight, atmospheric gases, and land and sea masses produce the complex system we call weather. But science is often very wrong in predicting the weather, according to scientist Malvin Artley, because the planet Earth is a living being, and the atmosphere is thus a reflection of the mental body of this being, which is influenced by the thoughts and feelings of humanity.[30]

When there is a crisis in the human kingdom, there may be great upheavals in nature. Anger and fiery passions may create heat spells and fires. Coldness of heart and crystallized states of mind may create freezing spells. Drought can be caused by the imposition of thought that prevents an adequate flow of energy to the emotions. Collective lies may catalyze typhoons or earthquakes. The accumulation of negative thoughts or emotions in one area may pollute it, creating the necessity for a tornado or hurricane to sweep it clean. In the inner realms, an "accident" is viewed as "an explosion of force" where emotional energies such as hatred, jealousy, or vindictiveness find a physical outlet. Spiritually dedicated people are sometimes guided to certain areas to act as human shock absorbers. Some have been sent to locations to inwardly balance the earth and lessen earthquakes, for example.

The Ageless Wisdom tradition has long taught about humanity's negative effect on nature. Alice Bailey notes, "The separative and maleficent thoughts of man are largely responsible for the savage nature of wild beasts, and the destructive quality of some of nature's processes, including certain phenomena, such as plague and famine."[31]

The causal relationship between human thoughts and emotions and weather patterns is not normally visible, unless confirmed by the timing of a physical event. The inner causes are often complex, including long-term cumulative effects, human karma from the past and causes in the nonhuman kingdoms, which are more difficult for humans to assess. However, there are some rather dramatic relationships that can be seen when studying the timing of events and weather patterns, as synchronicity does indicate a significant relationship. This can be seen for example, in the synchronicity of timing with the right wing coup in the former Soviet Union of August 18, 1991, and the major storm Hurricane Bob, which hit the East Coast of the United States. As Americans woke up on that Monday morning, they simultaneously heard news of the coup and the hurricane, and panic evacuations began all along the East Coast from North Carolina to Maine. The center of the hurricane passed through Kennebunkport, Maine, severely damaging former President Bush's home where he was vacationing and monitoring the Soviet coup. Nature seemed to be outwardly reflecting the inner turmoil and anxiety brought on by news of the coup—American fears about a return to hard-line communism and nuclear brinkmanship. People "battened down the hatches" of their homes and their minds, fearing the worst from both nature and global politics.[32]

In the midst of very heated discussions between the American and Philippine governments over the continued presence of U.S. military bases there, the Mt. Pinatubo volcano erupted near the base in question in July 1991, and again the following year, causing extensive damage and forcing the United States to abandon the base immediately. The Filipino people wanted Clark Air Force Base to close, and the volcano complied. A general worldwide cooling seems to be the result of the volcanic eruption. Significantly, after the base closings, one hundred new factories were created there.

A record-breaking blizzard with eighteen inches of snow fell on Jerusalem in late February 1992. It occurred the day after the Israelis deported twelve Palestinians and decided to continue settling new Jewish immigrants on territory with conflicting claims by Israelis and Palestinians, despite desperate pleas from the Palestinians living there. The blizzard effectively paralyzed work in the settlement for several days—but the Israelis didn't get the message.[33]

On November 1985 eleven Supreme Court justices were murdered in Colombia and the Palace of Justice burned to the ground by drug-trafficking forces, after the court declared it would extradite top drug dealers to the United States. Several days later a massive earthquake hit the country.

In the midst of massive demonstrations and upheavals in Soviet Armenia, where more than one hundred thousand Armenians had fled from racial riots in Azerbaijan, a massive earthquake struck on December 7, 1988. Over a thousand people were killed by an earthquake of 6.8 magnitude in Turkey on March 14, 1992, in an area where Turks had been attacking the Kurdish population.

The massive earthquake that hit San Francisco in October of 1989 occurred just minutes before the World Series game was about to be played between the San Francisco and Oakland teams, with intense emotional rivalry between the two. Oakland is just across the Bay Bridge from San Francisco, and it was this bridge that dramatically collapsed and killed several people.

Just after former Prime Minister Margaret Thatcher of Great Britain decided not to forgive a Third World debt, a massive storm tore through southern England, damaging many mansions in a wealthy area and uprooting trees hundreds of years old that had never experienced such a storm. A tornado hit Metarie, Louisiana, in February 1989, the exact area where a few days earlier the former head of the Ku Klux Klan, David Duke, had been elected as Republican representative to the Louisiana State Legislature, causing a national scandal.

After the strange and sudden death on September 29, 1978, of Pope John Paul, who had been installed only a month earlier, it rained for seven days straight in Rome. This storm broke all records and created a great deal of speculation about the real cause of the pope's death—or murder, as some claimed. Since no investigation or autopsy was performed, and no one saw the body before it was embalmed, there was much suspicion about the cause of death, as the pope had been creating rapid reforms, removing corrupt members of Church hierarchy, and calling for a redistribution of wealth.

In the United States, 1988 saw one of the worst droughts in decades, just as speculative and corporate takeover fever, seen spiritually as an over-heated desire for possession and control, reached its peak. The fever of greed raging through the American body politic found its correlation in the climate of the country. At the same time, massive forest fires throughout the West reflected back to us the blistering effects of our collective atti-tudes. The drought symbolized the lack of the waters of compassion, when self-centered acquisition and the fires of the mind dominated by the will to power burned away any heart-centered feeling and concern for the com-mon good.

The Chinese have always seen the link between nature and politics, see-ing natural disasters as a sure sign that the mandate of heaven is passing, and that it is time for a new ruler. Chairman Mao died in September 1976, just six weeks after the most devastating earthquake in Chinese history—in Tangshan—killed at least 242,000 people. The major floods that hit China in 1991 were seen by many Chinese as a sign that the Communists were losing the mandate of heaven after the Tiananmen Square massacre. This was reinforced when 10,000 crabs suddenly came ashore on Hainan Island in the south. The Chinese feel that a miracle or tumult in the natural world reflects one to come in the political world.[34]

Were all these events simply "coincidences," or did the thoughts and emotions stirred up by these events create vortices of negative energy that triggered reactions in the natural world? Perhaps people need a dramatic and uncanny act of nature to give them pause to reflect on themselves and the rightness of their actions. We need to read the "Book of Life" more carefully to see what our weather patterns are telling us about the causes we are creating.

In the Ageless Wisdom, humanity is said to be the bridging kingdom between the mineral, plant, and animal kingdoms and the higher spiritual kingdoms because we contain elements of all the kingdoms within us. Our true role is to channel love and blessing energies to these kingdoms—rather than create imbalances in them through our negative emotions. A large number of people are doing this today in their love and caring for nature and animals through the ecology and animal rights movements. Animals, in turn, absorb human emotions and help heal them. Studies have shown that plants are also affected by human emotions.[35] This is important be-cause any progress made in creating more humane conditions in the area of humanity's relationship to nature and animals affects all areas of relation-ship, because we are cultivating our heart. Our tenderness and compassion for animals and plants will create a more gentle and loving environment, with fewer natural upheavals.

Many people are sending positive, loving energy in their prayers and meditations to places of ecological devastation to help create healing. Psychics have even noted that earthquakes have been prevented in certain areas where people meditated together to visualize light protecting and sealing the fault lines. All the positive energy directed to nature to honor the planet on Earth Day April 22, 1990, very likely helped create the unusually beautiful sunny weather all along the East Coast on that day. As we give our blessings to nature, nature will bless humanity.

Causes in the Etheric Realm

Energy Bodies

The human body is surrounded and interpenetrated by subtle energy bodies that connect us to the deeper, slower frequencies of the earth and to the higher, finer frequencies of the Soul and the angelic realms. The functioning of each body is directed by the one next highest in frequency. Our various subtle bodies are listed in order of increasingly finer vibrations:

• The dense physical body.
• The etheric body, which is the life force frequency that forms the energy blueprint for the physical, and carries the energy of all the other bodies. It sustains the whole system and provides the patterning for the physical body, whether of an individual, a planet, or a solar system. It is organized into flows, or meridians, of energy that can be accessed by practitioners of acupuncture or acupressure to restore health.
• The emotional or "astral" desire body.
• The lower mental body—the rational mind.
• The "rainbow bridge," or *antahkarana*, which is the connection between these lower four bodies and the higher three:
  —The higher mental body, which is called the manasic body in the Eastern teachings and the abstract or philosophical mind in the Western. This mental body is universally inclusive and transcends duality.
  —The intuitive, or Buddhic, body of love wisdom.
  —The will, or atmic body, which ultimately aligns us with the Divine Will.

THE CHAKRAS

Each of us has seven energy centers in our etheric body. These are often called "chakras," which means "wheel" in Sanskrit. These wheels of energy step down the energy from each higher body—emotional, mental, or Soul—and channel it through the physical body. The chakras correspond to, and control, the functioning of the glandular systems, which in turn affect all the processes of the physical body. These seven energy centers, in ascending order, are as follows:

1. *The root or base-of-spine chakra* (adrenal glands).
2. *The sexual chakra* (the reproductive glands) located halfway between the navel and the root chakra.
3. *The solar plexus chakra*, just below the rib cage (pancreas gland).
4. *The heart chakra* (the thymus gland) in the center of the chest.
5. *The throat chakra* (thyroid gland) in the dip at the base of the throat.
6. *The brow or ajna (third eye) chakra* (pituitary gland), located between the eyebrows.
7. *The crown chakra* (pineal gland), located at the top of the head.

The strengths and weaknesses of our personalities that we bring with us from previous lives, as well as from the current one, are reflected in the condition of our chakras. As we begin to develop spiritually, the chakra energy centers are gradually purified, opened, and brought into alignment with our Higher Selves.

THE SOCIAL EFFECTS OF CHAKRA IMBALANCES

Each chakra's degree of openness, blockage, or imbalance determines the level of consciousness that individuals or groups operate from and the particular issues they are grappling with that affect society.

The Root Chakra at the base of the spine (relating to the adrenal glands) represents the dimension of physical survival. This chakra allows the Soul to be grounded and secure in the body and take responsibility for honoring the conditions necessary to secure life. When there is a blockage or imbalance in this chakra, there would be little contact with the earth or a physically supportive environment. We see this illustrated in the disembodied way of life of many people today who are out of touch with their bodies and nature, such as some government and corporate executives and intellectuals. This type of imbalance results in the capacity to remain disconnected from the results our actions may have on our survival as a species, illustrated in the ability of financial elites to ignore the effects of their actions on the natural world and the survival of humanity.

With too much energy focused here, there would be an excessive emphasis on physical survival and security to the exclusion of other types of awareness. We can see examples of this in the obsessive need for security and possessions demonstrated in the consumer societies of the developed countries.

The Sexual Chakra (relating to the gonads) rules sexual activity, money, physical strength, reproduction, and the drive to perpetuate ourselves. When there is overstimulation in this chakra, there is an overemphasis on sexual expression, without the balancing of the higher chakras with their emotional, love, and intellectual energies. This imbalance is also evident in the segments of society that are fixated on sexual pursuit and expression, leading to the many problems of excess sexual energy, including AIDS, teen pregnancy, abortion, pornography, and rape. Excessive energy in this chakra also contributes to the exaggerated pursuit of money so prevalent in the world today. When there is little energy in this center, we find people in society who have little strength or sexual drive and who may have difficulty acquiring the money they need to survive, depending on the energy from other chakras flowing through them.

The Solar Plexus Chakra (relating to the pancreas gland) is the focus for our emotions and desires, our creative drive, as well as maintaining harmony with the environment and maintaining ourselves. When this center is overstimulated, there can be excessive emotionalism, lack of emotional self-control, or the consumer addictions of alcohol or drugs, which we see in those whose primary goal is emotional satisfaction. When there is little energy here, there is emotional deadness, a lack of enthusiasm, vitality, and the transforming capacity, with a tendency to fixate in the rigidity of the past. We see this in the emotional adherence to religious dogma found in fundamentalism of all types. We also see a deadness in the solar plexus center in bureaucratic types, overly obsessed with details.

The Heart Chakra (relating to the thymus gland) is the focal point for the synthesis of the higher and lower chakras as it binds the rhythms of the spiritual planes to the electromagnetic currents of the physical. The heart center maintains the higher purpose for life and helps us identify kindred Souls. When active, it results in a wise group consciousness that preserves and enhances all life, such as found in the great humanitarian groups. When the heart center is closed, we have a lack of respect for human life and little concern for our neighbor—an absence of compassion. We see this closed heart center in groups of bigots and racists. When there is excessive heart energy, we become do-gooders—naive, overly emotional people who love but don't always think clearly, and so do more harm than good. These are the social helpers who are not always aware of how their help disempowers and creates dependence in those they try to help.

The Throat Chakra (relating to the thyroid gland) is the point in the energy circulation system from which the Soul and the personality energize the spiritual will for the life's purpose, allowing the choices for living we make to align us either with our Soul (or higher purpose blueprint) or with our personal self-interest. When functioning well, it enhances the capability to manage, balance, and maintain our dual spiritual/physical natures in creative living. The throat center is also the focal point for speech and creativity. When there is an excess of energy, we will be overly controlling, making wrong choices and limiting the freedom of others. We see this in overcontrolling government and corporate bureaucracies that strangle the life out of individuals with their control and lack of freedom. If there is too little energy here, we will see the inability to balance, regulate, and control one's life or the life of a society. The thyroid imbalances of former President and Mrs. Bush, for example, made it impossible for them to regulate the American society or economy in a balanced way.

The Brow or Ajna Chakra (relating to the pituitary gland) is the chakra that gives us the knowledge of the Soul—who we are and have been, why we are here, and our purpose on earth. It also energizes our higher intelligence, long-range vision, and higher insight. When we have a balanced brow center, we have an understanding of our place in the scheme of things. When we have an imbalance of too much energy, we have an excess of escapist, visionary ideas and images, but not enough practical organizing to bring them to earth. Many social reformers whose ideas are never grounded or adopted fall into this category—the utopian idealists of many different stripes. When there is little energy here, there is no higher sight, with a lack of vision and direction, as we see in so much of the short-term planning and thinking in American business.

The Crown Chakra (relating to the pineal gland) on the top of the head is the center where Universal Spirit and all the energies of the personality come together in cosmic fusion. It is the experience of Being and knowing oneself as the I Am (Divine) Presence, through balancing the lower self and then aligning our human experience to our higher blueprint to realize the enlightened state. When this is accomplished we have the truly great visionary leaders and liberators of humanity, like Buddha and Christ, who knew themselves as macrocosm and microcosm simultaneously. All the great creative ideas, designs, and potentiality come from this center. When there is no opening in this center, there is no connection to who we are and to the creative purposes of humanity. It's as if part of our intelligence is missing until this center is opened.[36]

THE TEARING OF THE ETHERIC VEIL

Like an individual, the earth too has an "etheric" or "life force" body. Nuclear explosions have added to world tension by creating a rent in the earth's etheric body—the protective veil around the planet. According to some metaphysical teachings, the tearing of this veil at the appropriate time is part of the evolutionary plan for humanity, helping us to take our next step in handling more powerful energies. This opening has brought an inflow of energy and light from the "astral" (or emotional) plane of desire. Alice Bailey writes, "This produces oversensitivity . . . and will exact its toll from the race until the human mechanism has adjusted itself to light—an occult effect with far-reaching consequences."[37] The outer reflection of this can be seen in the thinning of the ozone layer over the poles of the earth.

The thinning or removing of this protective veil between the unseen fields or dimensions of energy has also weakened the barrier between discarnate entities and the physical plane. One result of this opening is an increasing perception of Angels and Devas. (See "Devas, Angels, and the Inner Side of Nature" in chapter 9.) This phenomenon also accounts for the increased frequency of the discarnate astral entities (spirits of people who were formerly alive on the earth) that psychics "channel" in a trance state. While these discarnate entities can occasionally be helpful guides, many can be quite harmful, giving false information and creating a state of dependency or even possession. The tearing of the veil has also exacerbated the growth of crime and the spread of disease and neurosis.

Psychics with inner vision have seen that many people in prisons and mental institutions appear to have negative astral entities attached to them. Dr. Edith Fiore, a California psychologist, having seen many of her patients suffering from seemingly incurable psychological and psychosomatic problems, discovered that a significant number of them were suffering from possessions by various entities. In her case studies she has documented how depression, phobias, addiction, and other disorders can be caused by the spirits of humans who have died but still hover around people. They attach themselves to those who dabble in psychic endeavors, abuse drugs and alcohol, and even sometimes those who go through surgery or hospitalization. She recommends surrounding oneself with white light and clearing one's residence through meditation on a regular basis.[38]

THE SUBTLE ENERGY EFFECTS OF POLLUTION

Polluted air not only makes our eyes water and our throat hurt, it also weakens our etheric body. This, in turn, affects our immune system. Constant exposure to polluted air, water, and food grown in pesticide-ridden soil depletes our vitality, creates a sense of fatigue, inertia, irritation and aggression and makes us vulnerable to a host of diseases, including immune-deficiency diseases such as AIDS and Epstein-Barr syndrome. This general low-level malaise makes it more difficult for us to take on new challenges or to make changes in the social and political environment, as our sense of personal physical and psychological strength is weakened. As a result of this pollution, and the even more prevalent mental and emotional pollution, a great many of us have little energy for anything more than trying to fulfill our own basic survival needs and family commitments. Active concern and involvement in political life thus suffers. This can be remedied by supporting efforts to clean up our food, air, and water, and by personally consuming purer foods and products.

THE EFFECTS OF SOUND

The Ageless Wisdom teaches that certain sounds create and heal while others destroy. In the book of Genesis the Word of God created our world: "In the beginning was the word." We have long noticed how the spoken words of the great orators have moved nations—in positive directions, as did Plato, and in negative ones, as did Hitler.

The noise from battlefields as well as the great and constant noise of machinery in our major cities since the Industrial Revolution is one of the inner causes of the tension people bear, for sound affects us very powerfully on etheric levels, either energizing or depleting our life force. Dr. Austin Henschel of the U.S. National Center for Urban and Industrial Health has stated that "the health hazard of noise is as serious as that posed by polluted air or water." Automobiles, jet airplanes, and heavy industry with high levels of infrasound (below 20 Hertz, which is beneath the threshold of human hearing) have caused internal hemorrhaging, loss of balance, and nausea. Studies of the emotional effects of environmental pollution show that urban dwellers become uncooperative, unwilling to help others and hostile when subjected to excessive pollution.[39]

Science has shown that certain frequencies of sound (such as a high C) can shatter glass or create geometric patterns in grains of sand on a drumhead. And certain rhythms—such as the marching of feet over a bridge—

can also shatter physical objects. Recently scientists discovered that under the right circumstances, the same kinds of sound waves can make a bottle of ordinary water glow like a light bulb.[40]

In *The Republic*, Plato noted that "styles of music are never disturbed without affecting the most important political institutions."[41] Some observers say the emotional range of Beethoven's music prepared the way for the study of psychology, as it made people more aware of their feelings. The work of Dr. S. K. Bose in India, reported in *The Secret Life of Plants*, showed that certain types of music, such as classical, have been shown to accelerate the growth of plants and animals, while others, such as many types of rock and roll, retard such growth.[42]

Rhythms that reflect the human heartbeat are very life enhancing, while the opposite rhythms create irritation and ill health. Dr. John Diamond, author of *The Body Doesn't Lie*, for example, found that 90 percent of the people he tested using applied kinesiology showed a sudden loss of more than two-thirds of their normal muscle strength while listening to typical popular music with a "stopped anapestic" rhythm (two short beats followed by a long one). Rock music has been credited with helping to break up old patterns of thought and behavior in the 1960s, but also with causing nervousness and an inability to focus. Doctors at Kaiser-Permanente Medical Center in Los Angeles and elsewhere often prescribe soothing music tapes instead of painkillers and tranquilizers for their patients or play such music before surgery, during chemotherapy, or for back injuries.[43]

Ancient cultures such as the Hindu, Egyptian, and Greek used music and sound for healing purposes, and this lost art is beginning to be rediscovered today. Some researchers have found that the key of C-sharp is resonant with the vibration of the earth and with the energy flowing through the hands of healers.[44]

Research by music professor R. Murray Schafer showed that Americans and Canadians find that the easiest pitch to retain and recall spontaneously when in a relaxed state is B-natural. But in Germany and other parts of Europe, the note most easily recalled is G-sharp. Schafer found that this related to the different electrical vibrations predominant in each area. In America and Canada, we are literally surrounded by the vibrations of 60 cycles per second, which correlates with the B-natural tone, while in Europe the alternating current is 50 cycles per second, relating to G-sharp.[45]

When science focuses more attention on the impact of sound, much will be learned about the inevitable social structures that result from certain sound patterns. Perhaps research could even have shown that the extraordinary impromptu concert given by Mstislav Rostropovich, conductor of the Soviet National Symphony, inside the besieged Russian parliament building during the darkest hours of the coup in August of 1991 helped create a positive energy field that protected the building from attack. Research might also show that all the bells ringing at the same time across the nation at President Clinton's inauguration helped shatter and disperse old energies and create the right vibration to open a new era.

From all the examples in this chapter, we can see that the emotions, etheric energies, and sounds that humanity is generating are having greater effects on our world than many of the causes we usually focus on. We need to examine political dynamics from a psychological perspective, seeing the effects of human emotions. This lens may provide important clues for the future. But human thoughts and emotions are not the only causes of events—we need to explore an even greater causal level: the realm of the Soul.

Chapter Seven

MANY LIVES, ONE SOUL: THE INFLUENCE OF THE ETERNAL SELF

The soul is neither spirit nor matter but is the relation between them; it is the mediator between this duality; it is the middle principle, the link between God and his form.

—ALICE BAILEY[1]

THE NATURE OF THE SOUL

Throughout the ages there have been great leaders and geniuses who have made major contributions to human evolution through their love, wisdom, and sacrifice and who, like Gandhi, may be called "Mahatmas," or "Great Souls." These individuals who have achieved Soul consciousness—an inner experience which results in the expanded identification with all of Life—are those who truly uplift humanity. Most of the great steps forward in human evolution—the liberation of nations, the winning of freedom and human rights, peace agreements, the discovery of new inventions and medicines to help humanity—have come from courageous political or religious leaders, writers, artists, or scientists expressing some aspect of Soul consciousness, often in response to inner guidance. Those who can make wise decisions, solve social problems effectively, bring a healing energy to conflict situations, and draw forth the highest in others are expressing the Soul in daily life—even though they themselves may not as yet be perfect in every area of their lives.

There are numerous examples of Soul-infused personalities throughout history. Among them would be statesmen such as Akhenaton, Pericles, and Abraham Lincoln; great religious leaders such as Moses, Confucius, Buddha, Jesus, and Muhammad; great philosophers such as Pythagoras, Aesculapius, Socrates, and Plato; humanitarians such as Florence Nightingale, Albert Schweitzer, Clara Barton, Eleanor Roosevelt, Wangari Matthai, and Mother Theresa; scientists such as Louis Pasteur, Madame Curie, George Washington Carver, Thomas Edison, and Albert Einstein; artists such as Michelangelo, Leonardo da Vinci, and Nicholas Roerich; and many other unknown individuals who served long and well in places their karma and destiny placed them.

Advanced Souls help human evolution by incarnating together on earth at certain times, often to initiate major social changes. This was the case with the Souls who created the Golden Age of Greece and the Renaissance and worked together to found the United States.

SOUL CONSCIOUSNESS

Current psychology explores the development and integration of the human personality, primarily from the influence of heredity, environment, and conditioning. The goal of traditional psychology is to have a well-developed, integrated personality and a healthy ego. What psychology does not usually include (except for psychosynthesis and transpersonal psychology) is an awareness of the innate, inner self or Soul that is influencing and overseeing the development of the personality. Most of the world's religions have recognized that human beings have an unlimited Essence within, often called the Soul, Higher Self, or Eternal Self, that is the complete realization of everything we are and that continues after death. Abraham Lincoln called this the "Angel of our Higher Nature."

The Ageless Wisdom teaches that the world of the Soul is the Fifth Kingdom in nature, beyond the mineral, vegetable, animal, and human kingdoms. Christians call this Fifth Kingdom "the Kingdom of Heaven." Christ taught that "the Kingdom of Heaven is within" (a state of consciousness), and that "in order for a man to find his life he must lose it" (lose attachment to personality life). The Buddhists teach Soul consciousness by learning detachment from the personal self and its desires and embracing the principle of compassion for all beings and service to relieve their suffering.

From the perspective of the Ageless Wisdom, the goal of developing the personality self is to integrate the body, emotions, and mind into a functioning whole, which can then freely seek self-transcendence by invoking union with the Soul, or Higher Self. If the human personality becomes highly integrated and effective, but does not flower into expanded Soul awareness and love, it will inflate into excessive egoism, such as we have seen in a Napoleon or a Donald Trump and eventually bring about its own downfall and potential transformation. The Soul is innately inclusive, group conscious, and oriented toward compassionate service to humanity. The sense of responsibility is said to be the first expression of Soul in one's life. When individuals attain Soul consciousness, they can clearly see the highest good for the greatest number of Souls and make the wisest decisions politically, taking all views into account. Those in Soul consciousness are the inspired leaders and creative thinkers who seem untouched by ego or obsession with fame, power, and money. They are clear about their true identity.

Indwelling in all human beings is the desire for perfection and the urge to express the good, the beautiful, and the true—the attributes of the Soul. No one, however distorted in action, is without this innate desire for betterment. The Soul within us is the cause of all our restlessness, the motivator towards becoming the Divine Self. Through repeated incarnations, the evolutionary process gradually achieves this aim of perfecting the instrument, until the quality and radiation of the personality coincides with the Soul and Spirit.

The Soul of each individual is inwardly united with the One Soul of all humanity, and once we make contact with this Soul, the reality of the oneness of all humanity and, indeed, of all Life is never a question for us again. This is the inner reality behind the concept of brother/sisterhood and political movements for world unity. The experience of this Soul contact is often called a "peak experience," or a "unitive" or "mystical experience." This contact opens us up to inspiring revelations. It is intermittent at first, then gradually becomes more stabilized as we continue to follow the promptings of the Soul, providing our lives with purpose and direction and helping us purify our desires and motives.

Once we have had these transformative experiences, we are never the same again and will always hunger to return to that greater state of enhanced clarity, love, and energy. We become aware of the duality between that higher state of Being and the state of consciousness that is the world of personality-centered life. We become acutely aware of all that holds us back from being in this higher state—the habits, behavioral patterns, and conditioning that prevent us from living continuously in the upraised consciousness of the Soul.

SOUL AND PERSONALITY DIFFERENCES

The differences between these two levels of consciousness and being can be seen as follows:

Personality Consciousness

Identifying with roles
(Ego-inflated professionals who mask deeper insecurity)

Competing
(Corporate and political groups obsessed with winning)

Being separate
(Antagonistic and divisive religious, racial and political groups)

Acquiring
(Massive individual, corporate, and national indebtedness; attachment to materialistic life-style)

Feeling lack
(Dependent individuals who primarily take, regardless of outer circumstances, yet feel dissatisfied)

Needing to take in
(Obsessive consumers)

Resisting, feeling inertia and fear
(Bureaucrats with obsessive need for rigid structures, law and order, conformity)

Soul Consciousness

Identifying with the true, inner self working through the roles
(True leaders who courageously follow their inner inspiration and give vision to others)

Cooperating
(Groups working together for mutual enhancement, for world security and justice through the United Nations, and so forth)

Being inclusive
(Ecumenical and international groups of bridge builders, and unifiers, and healers of divisions between people)

Sharing
(Local and global initiatives to help the poor and disadvantaged become self-supporting)

Feeling of fullness
(Volunteers and philanthropists who primarily give and feel confident and content)

Being able to create and give out
(Creative individuals who bring ideas, inventions, art, to the world)

Opening, feeling courageous, and joyful
(Reformers who stand for spiritual principles despite the established order)

Furthering one's self-interest (Amoral financial systems leading to exploitation)	*Working for the good of the whole* (Service organizations that aid and empower others)
Following one's self-will (Egotists who selfishly strive for power over others)	*Following the Higher Will (God's will)* (Individuals who follow their inner guidance and respect others' freedom to do so)
Seeking for the personal self (Special-interest groups seeking privileges)	*Knowing the larger self* (Groups focused on meditating, studying, and embodying spiritual principles)

Each of these comparisons contrasts two vastly different states of energy and being. Focusing exclusively on personality-centered values eventually brings contraction, suffering, and pain. Focusing on the values of the Soul brings new ideas, energies, and relationships—an expanded experience of Life. While we personally feel more love and inner peacefulness while in Soul consciousness, at the same time we become more aware of the pain and suffering of others and so feel a greater sense of compassion and responsibility for helping.

Most of us identify with our personality traits and habits and think this is who we are. While living in India as a Peace Corps volunteer, Gordon had the experience of seeing exactly how this happens. After being in India for eight months, he had learned to speak the local Tamil language reasonably well, wore traditional Indian clothes, and had the walk, gestures, and mannerisms of an Indian. As he was walking down the street of his village one day, greeting all his friends there and talking with them, he realized he had become a perfect Indian, yet he knew that this identity was nothing more than a collection of learned behaviors. I am an American, he thought, yet having grown up there, my identity as an American is also merely a complex of unconsciously adopted behaviors and attitudes. If these two identities are only learned patterns, then who am I? This recognition propelled him into the spiritual quest that has led him increasingly to experience his identity as the immortal, eternal Soul/Spirit being he is. He later had an inner experience in which he recalled being a Brahmin in India in a previous life, but he had little compassion for the poor people there. This helped him understand why he so easily "became" an Indian and why his karma was to go there to serve the people of that land.

Sometimes it is only after individuals have achieved every success on a personality level—wealth and fame—and have still not felt peace or happiness that they will begin the search for something deeper. As a result of their spiritual aspiration and often unconscious invocation, eventually they come in contact with the Soul. This transformative inner experience inspires many to dedicate themselves to a life of service to others. Thus we see some of the great corporate moguls such as Andrew Carnegie and Henry Ford, having achieved the pinnacle of financial and social success, turning to spiritual studies and becoming great philanthropists. Some individuals are born with a greater degree of Soul consciousness, the result of efforts made in previous lives, which are carried into each new incarnation.

THE SHADOW—"THE DWELLER ON THE THRESHOLD"

Often, after the first brief contact with the Soul, there follows a sense of having fallen from a great peak of higher consciousness into a valley of darkness, and we are plunged into despair at the loss of such a state of grace. All the flaws and problems of the personality are revealed with painful clarity, and we may feel an acute sense of hopelessness. Yet this experience is the result of the higher contact. For it is only within this greater light and increased energy that what Carl Jung called "the shadow"—the previously unseen or unacknowledged parts of the personality—is revealed. Our work then becomes the redemption and purification of these areas of denseness to provide a more fit instrument for the expression of the Soul in everyday life. It is at this point that we may change our diet, give up smoking and/or alcohol, make changes in our employment or relationships, and begin to closely examine our thoughts and feelings toward others and the motives underlying our actions in daily life.

As our spiritual development unfolds—as both individuals and nations—we must eventually confront the accumulated negativity we have created over many lifetimes. This negativity is often personified as "the Dweller on the Threshold," which contains all the memories of mistakes, failures, fears, and illusions that have held the Soul prisoner over many lifetimes. This frightening image guards the threshold leading to greater spiritual understanding, until the time comes when we can embrace and redeem it, removing the last shreds of doubt and fear. Carl Jung called The Dweller our "shadow," and for generations it has provided rich material for horror films and books. Projections of our disowned shadow onto others is the basis for creating many of our political enemies. Humanity as a whole is confronting this projection today, and every time we confront and reown a part of our shadow we also help erase a little more of the collective shadow, and bring more light consciousness to the world.

This individual process of transformation is one of the major causes of change within the human family. Each of us who experiences contact with the Soul ultimately struggles to live up to this higher self. This gradual transformation of our personality-centered lives is helping to create a major change in the way humanity views itself, while also boosting the energy available to others to make the same changes. Since human consciousness is all part of the One, any change in a single aspect of that consciousness affects the "morphogenetic field" and thus repatterns the whole of human consciousness. This is because each Soul-conscious person who is helping to build a pathway to the realm of the Soul makes it easier for those who follow after to take the same evolutionary steps.

Yet these changes are quite subtle, and people who have not made the transition into Soul consciousness may be completely unaware of the inner changes that others have undergone.

This process of Soul recognition is being stimulated by spiritual energies bathing the planet that are producing an acceleration of human evolution. This spiritual stimulation provides opportunities to live many Earth lives in one incarnation and eliminate much past karma. Hence we see a big rise in divorces, relationship changes, and career changes in the last thirty to forty years, as people recapitulate many former experiences.

Everywhere people are steadily and surely overcoming their sense of separateness and learning to share the hard-won wisdom of the Soul with those who are ready to benefit from each other's experiences. Gradually a human body of collective wisdom, fed by the Soul, is emerging— enlightening us, teaching us what brings true joy and an expanded sense of Being. This increasing Soul awareness is aiding human evolution and more universal recognition of human rights, justice, and peace. Eventually humanity will function as a unified, coordinated consciousness, guided by the One Soul. An evolutionary system designed with such patterned, intricate beauty of function leads us to a sense of awe in beholding the lineaments of the face of God in the principles of our world.

THE LAW OF KARMA AND ITS POLITICAL EFFECTS

As you sow, so shall you reap.

—Proverb

Karma, or the Law of Cause and Effect, is one of the primary means of Soul growth: "Sow a thought to reap an act, sow an act and reap a habit, sow a habit and reap a character, sow a character and reap a destiny." The Ageless Wisdom teaches that whatever causes an individual, group, or nation sets into motion through thoughts, words, or actions will, sooner or later, come back home to roost. In the East, it is said that the wheels of karma grind slowly but grind exceedingly fine. To us, this provides major insights into events of the world both present and past.

Positive, loving thoughts and actions create positive results. Angry, hateful, or fearful thoughts and actions return negative results to those who create them. Karma is also called the Law of Balances as we are responsible for balancing out the results of all causes we have generated that are out of harmony with the Law of Love, a fundamental principle of the universe. The purpose of karma is not to punish, but rather to educate and to help us evolve our consciousness. Through these experiences we learn that love is the "measure of all things," and that we will have lives of joy, beauty, and balance if we adhere to the Law of Love.

We have seen in our personal lives that karma can be instantaneous, if we are open to seeing the connections. For example, whenever we stub our toe or break a plate, if we reflect on what we were just thinking, we realize it was probably a negative or critical thought. So we get a little reminder that we are out of harmony with the flow of the universe, because our physical world isn't flowing smoothly.

Karma is often referred to as "poetic justice." A *Newsweek* article, for example, noted the conventional wisdom that it would be "poetic justice" if Jesse Helms (a conservative unsympathetic to minority issues) actually lost the next congressional election to a black man, Harvey Gantt.[2] An African tribe has a colorful saying about karma: "He who shits in the road, meets flies on his return." People here often say, "What goes around, comes around."

The United States experienced the karmic consequences of its arming and training religious zealots to defeat the communists in Afghanistan in the 1980s, when several of those it trained were reportedly involved in the World Trade Center bombing in the United States in 1993. Depleted uranium used in U.S. shells to kill Iraqis in the 1991 Gulf war karmically returned months later as soldiers who handled these shells developed strange illnesses from their exposure to them. And *The Washington Post* noted that fundamentalist broadcaster Pat Robertson was noticeably silent about a big fire that knocked his radio station off the air—perhaps because earlier he had publicly related a fire at Universal Studios to a possible punishment from God for producing what he called a "blasphemous" movie, *The Last Temptation of Christ*.[3]

Sooner or later, often after many painful experiences, individuals and nations begin to realize that each and every one of us is responsible for the consequences of our actions. In truth no one is ever really a victim of anything. Rather it means that we have drawn a difficult situation to ourselves because of past karma in order to learn why what we initiated previously was harmful. This is true even if past causes are not consciously remembered, as all learning is stored in the subconscious and is ultimately integrated into our character, our essential being. Thus, for example, if as individuals or as members of a group we have suffered great injustice at the hands of others, we often become highly sensitized to issues of injustice in relationships and between groups and nations in the world. This arena will then be where our Soul moves us to take action to right injustices and improve fairness.

From this perspective, life's experiences can be seen as lessons to be learned from, rather than as something to react against, creating more problems and karma for ourselves in the future. We then begin to see the deeper truth of the statement "We create our own reality." The Law of Karma is also a Law of Empowerment, for once we begin to understand how we are creating our own lives through our thoughts, words, and actions, we have the power to change our circumstances by changing the causes we are setting into motion. Eventually humanity will realize that we are each microcosmic creators, and that every day we are creating our future.

As we learn how the universe works, we inevitably begin to take responsibility for our inner and outer actions. Forgiveness and desire for change is the key to releasing negative karma—forgiving others for past hurts and forgiving ourselves for anything done to others. When we truly feel remorse for past actions, we receive an inflow of spiritual energy that transmutes the energies of past mistakes, dissolving and neutralizing them. We therefore can change the past by how we think about it. Time is not linear—it is spherical, with our true, eternal self in the center of the sphere, causing change in the future and the past. In a sense, we are just as influenced by our future as by our past. Once a lesson is learned through karma and through forgiveness of ourselves and others, we often no longer have to continue suffering from its negative effects. This is the true meaning of the Law of Grace.

There is actually more positive karma in the world today than negative, although most people tend to think of karma as something bad that they have to be punished for. Good karma is accumulated through our many thoughts and acts of kindness, courage, patience, unselfishness, and giving to Life.

The interacting forces of karma are vast and complex. Since everything is interconnected, assigning specific causes to specific events can be an oversimplification. Each action causes a ripple effect. Even the smallest action can have far-ranging effects, as was illustrated dramatically in the film *Back to the Future, Part II*, where a time traveler changes a small event in the past and so changes the whole course of history for his town.

Just as individuals create karma, so do groups and nations. Choegyal Rinpoche, a Tibetan monk oppressed and driven out of his country by the Chinese, recognized this with great compassion. He shed tears as he told his story to author Joanna Macy—not for his own people or the destruction of his monastery and the murder of the monks, but for his oppressors, saying, "Poor Chinese, they make such bad karma for themselves."

Collective karma sometimes overrides individual karma, for our lives are deeply affected by the larger karmic lessons of our race, nation, religion, or ethnic group. The Civil War, and the continuing struggle over race relations in the United States, for example, are America's negative karma for not having the political courage to abolish slavery at its founding.

The collective guilt and responsibility of colonizing nations sooner or later comes back to haunt them. Britain as a major colonial power exploited the resources and populations of many nations and later had people from many of those nations emigrate to the United Kingdom. As a result, Britain must now integrate, educate, and support many people from these former colonies. This is also true for the United States, where a tide of immigrants from Mexico is trying to reclaim land in Southern California and Texas that their ancestors once controlled. Former President Bush met his karma for invading Panama when he was later confronted with a protest rally and suffered from tear gas blown by the wind at a scheduled speech in Panama in June 1992. His speech was meant to remind voters at home that he was the world leader who brought democracy there, but it backfired as he was driven from the stage to shouts of "*Yanqui,* go home!"

There is also a certain reality to the idea of vicarious atonement. While no one can dissolve the karma of another, there are more advanced Souls who can cut across time and space and become aware of blockages in the whole, taking them on for transmutation as a form of service.

It is difficult to evaluate with certainty the karma of another person or group. Nonetheless, there seem to be some connections we can speculate about in exploring the causes of events. We'd like to offer some examples and encourage further exploration of possible karmic aspects of other events.

The Marshall Plan → *Peace and Abundance*

Proposed by U.S. general George C. Marshall and developed altruistically by the United States after World War II to rebuild war-torn Europe, the Marshall Plan created positive karma for America, along with over forty years of relative peace and abundance. By affirming forgiveness and offering help instead of holding on to vindictiveness, the United States aided the recovery of West Germany and Japan with great generosity. Even though Germany and Japan are now two of the United States's greatest economic competitors, their economic strength and gratitude for our help has generally made them our allies and thus added to our economic well-being. However, karma can be multi-layered, as our post-war abundance was also partly due to our economic exploitation of other nations, the effects of which are now beginning to appear as shrinking markets and world financial upheaval.

The Welcoming of Immigrants → *A Stronger Citizenry*

"Give me your tired, your poor, your huddled masses yearning to breathe free," reads the poem by Emma Lazarus on the base of the Statue of Liberty. America's historic willingness to open her heart to millions of refugees and accord them rights has created good karma and a strong, diverse citizenry. Each ethnic group brings its particular gifts and skills and the combined impact has resulted in greater strength and creativity as a nation, increasing the labor supply and demands for goods and services, thus strengthening the economy. Except for a backlash from the late 1920s until 1965 where immigration was highly restricted, the U.S. accepts more immigrants than all other nations combined, accounting for ⅓ of its population growth today.

But America's generosity is being greatly tested today and an anti-immigrant backlash has arisen, as thousands of illegal Latin Americans and Asians pour in over her borders, putting a strain on welfare programs and competition for jobs. Americans are further challenged by those claiming political asylum, like the Haitian boat people, when it's unclear whether their oppression is truly political or economic. Immigration raises the issue of how willing we are to share our abundance with the less fortunate of other nations. Immigration policy has always been a mixture of idealism and self-interest, yet the more we are willing to "open ourselves" to sharing, the better the long-term karmic results will be.

Vietnam → Inflation and Suicide

A negative example of karma was U.S. interference in Vietnam and Southeast Asia. The United States borrowed a vast amount of money to pay for the Vietnam War, and it came back karmically as inflation in the 1970s.

In addition, the United States has had to deal with the massive psychological damage to tens of thousands of Vietnam veterans who experienced the trauma of war and death then were reviled and ignored for a decade when they returned home. This is reflected in the fact that more Vietnam veterans have committed suicide since returning home than were killed in the war. Since most Americans had a belief that our side was always right, Vietnam was a perfect setup to deflate our ego and erode confidence in the one thing of which we were proudest—our military prowess.

Third World Toxic Dumping → Poisoned Food in the United States

Dumping toxic wastes in the Third World, an increasingly lucrative business, and the selling of carcinogenic pesticides, drugs, cigarettes, cosmetics, and baby food banned in the United States to the peoples of underdeveloped countries is harming the food we buy from those same countries. For example, many of the vegetables consumed in the United States are coming back to us from Mexico heavily laden with pesticides banned in the United States. Some U.S. companies banned from polluting in this country moved to Mexico, yet their factory pollution drifted over the border and caused babies in the United States to be born without brains. This is very symbolic of our "brainless" policy and the reality that borders are arbitrary and we are not separate from others.

Economic Exploitation → The Drug Problem

Another karmic result of unjust treatment of Third World peoples is the drug problem and its accompanying violence. Cocaine, marijuana, and heroin are produced by poor Third World farmers as their main cash crop, then sold to crime syndicates that ship them to wealthy countries to poison a population that needs to deaden its pain and guilt. If the tremendous wealth, knowledge, and skills developed in the West were truly shared and circulated globally, we would not have people so desperate that they produce and sell drugs to survive, or people so out of touch with Spirit that they need drugs to exist.

It seems especially appropriate karmically that one of the cities hardest hit by drug-related crime in the early 1990s was Washington, D.C. This is where many of the policies that have encouraged the drug trade have originated, including cutting education, food, housing, and other support for the poor, which has stimulated the hopelessness that leads to drug deal-ing and addiction.

Single-Minded Profit → Pollution

Big business assumed it could focus only on profit and ignore pollution and environmental destruction. But, karmically, this has now returned to affect even corporate executives. No one could swim in some of the exclu-sive beaches off New York, New Jersey, or Boston for much of the summer of 1988, for example, as sewage and hospital waste were polluting the wa-ter. Acid rain caused by pollutants released into the air from factories is killing trees thousands of miles away and affecting everyone, rich and poor. In addition, air pollution and global warming are beginning to cause trau-matic climatic and planetary changes.

Another example of karma is that the nations of the Northern Hemi-sphere, which have contributed most of the industrial gases creating the greenhouse effect on the planet, are going to be the ones suffering the most from the rise in temperatures. *Newsweek* cited a computer forecast showing that temperatures in the Northern Hemisphere would rise 3.6 degrees Fahrenheit after thirty-five years, but it would take twice as long to rise that much in the Southern Hemisphere.[4]

Economic Injustice → Loans Not Repaid

The fact that wealthy Western banks are losing money on loans to poor Third World countries seems karmically appropriate, as it helps balance out the economic injustice between the "haves" and the "have nots." Western banks are owed over $218 billion by Latin American countries alone. In 1988 major U.S. banks "forgave" a large part of the Mexican debt, which could indicate the beginning of a trend. A positive resolution of this karma is seen in forgiveness of loans in exchange for placing areas of nature into preservation zones and upgrading environmental practices.

The Great Mississippi Flood of 1993 → Sewage Returns

Towns that had dumped sewage in their river for years experienced instant karma when the sewage flowed back to them from the Mississippi over-flowing its banks, causing tributary rivers to flow in the opposite direction, bringing sewage with it. The flooding was also karmic for some because wetlands that previously absorbed river overflow had been overdeveloped for profit. Lessons in human interdependence became very graphic as res-idents noted that "One man's levy was another man's flood." Channeling the forces of the river by the levees in one town increased flooding in the next town.

REINCARNATION AND WORLD EVENTS

Our birth is but a sleep and a forgetting:
The soul that rises within us, our life's Star
Hath had elsewhere its setting,
And cometh from afar . . .
—WILLIAM WORDSWORTH
"ODE: INTIMATIONS OF IMMORTALITY"

The realm of nature has a cyclical, seasonal order. The human body has cycles of rest and activity, of inbreath and outbreath, and pulses. Historians have traced cyclical patterns in world events. So, too, the immortal self, the Soul, has alternating periods of rest and action that continue after the death of the body. After each experience of physical existence, the Soul needs to rest and reflect on experiences and lessons learned. This cycle of reincarnation enables the Soul to develop its full potential and achieve perfection through a series of different lives. What is commonly referred to as character is actually the sum total of experiences from many lives. Our "natural" skills and talents were often developed in previous lives.

The need to understand the question of justice in the universe—why a child is born handicapped or why a political leader seems to get away with a terrible crime—led us to explore and finally embrace the concept of reincarnation. For us personally, it was the major missing piece that suddenly helped life make sense and answered many political questions about what is going on in the world. Reincarnation, combined with the Law of Karma, is the only philosophical and ethical system that proposes a rational explanation for differences in birth and station in life, explains genius and child prodigies such as Mozart, as well as birth defects and gifts, and fulfills the innate sense of justice that is found in every human heart.

People often wonder why bad things sometimes happen to "good" people and good things happen to "bad" people. But in the larger time scale of many lifetimes, good people today may not have always been good, and bad people are not all bad, nor have they always been. We are seeing only a slice of someone's personal history in one lifetime. All of us, whatever our stage of evolution, have a great deal yet to learn, and all experience contributes to the resolution of karma. However, the farther along the evolutionary path we may be, the greater are the consequences for relatively minor strayings from the path of Soul development.

According to a reincarnational perspective, individuals and groups reap the karmic results of past actions either in this life or in future lives. The present condition of our life is a direct product of past thoughts and actions, just as present thoughts and actions are determining our future right now. We as Souls have chosen our parents and the situations we incarnate into in order to learn needed karmic lessons and/or prepare ourselves for a particular service to the world. From this perspective there are ultimately no victims. Rather, there are brave souls who have chosen very intensive, difficult courses in the school of Life.

The real reason many people do not accept the idea of karma and reincarnation is that they have to accept complete personal responsibility for their life, and most people are not willing to do so. They prefer instead to "project," as psychologists call it—placing the source of their difficulties outside themselves, blaming others. It's harder to be self-righteous when we remember our own mistakes in past lives. In embracing reincarnation, people also have to accept that they must atone for the harm they may have created, which is a frightening prospect for those who have led irresponsible lives. Yet karma and reincarnation simply show how it is actually in our enlightened self-interest to live a life of love and giving to others.

The idea of the transmigration of Souls into animal bodies is a distortion created by those of evil intent to confuse humanity. Our bodies have already evolved from the mineral, plant, and animal kingdoms, and once individualized with the spark of Divinity called the Soul, we never fall back into earlier states. Animals do not have individual Souls as do humans; rather, they possess a group Soul for all members of each species. Thus humans cannot individually incarnate into an animal form.

BELIEF IN REINCARNATION

Two-thirds of the world's population embrace religions in which reincarnation is a major tenet. In the East, Buddhists and Hindus have long accepted the concept of reincarnation. So did the ancient Egyptians and Greek philosophers such as Pythagoras, Socrates, and Plato. Plato maintained that the Soul existed before the body and brought with it from antecedent incarnations many memories that, when awakened by new life, are mistaken for new knowledge. All mathematical truths, for example, are innate in this way, Plato said. Teaching merely arouses the recollection of things known by the Soul many lives ago.[5] The Socratic method of teaching was founded on this premise.

Many scholars believe that Christ taught about reincarnation. However, the Church felt these teachings lessened its power, so all references to reincarnation were eliminated from the Bible at the Council of Nicea in A.D. 325. However, some say it is still evident in certain passages, as when Christ asked His followers, "Who do men say that I am?" And they answered, "Elijah, returned to life." Perhaps the positive result is that since Christians think they have only one life to lead, they try to make the most of it. In India, however, a belief in reincarnation sometimes leads to passivity, as people think they have many lives to improve and thus become less motivated in this life.

Many well-respected Western thinkers also believed in reincarnation, among them Johann Wolfgang von Goethe, Honoré de Balzac, William Butler Yeats, Leo Tolstoy, Benjamin Franklin, Thomas Edison, Walt Whitman, Henry Thoreau, Ralph Waldo Emerson, William James, Henry Ford, Prime Minister Lloyd George, Paul Gauguin, Wassily Kandinsky, Carl Rogers, General Patton, and many others.[6]

In the last twenty years, an acceptance of reincarnation has been rapidly growing in the West. A recent *Newsweek* poll, for example, showed that at least 24 percent of Americans now believe in reincarnation,[7] and recent Gallup polls have consistently shown the same thing.[8]

The Lessons of a Lifetime

The Ageless Wisdom holds that there are definite lessons to be learned in each lifetime—both as an individual and as a member of racial and national groups. In each new lifetime the Soul arranges the perfect environment to learn whatever lessons were not understood in previous lives. Current strengths, abilities, and talents have actually been carried over from previous lives, and new avenues of creative expression are developed for future lives. As automobile inventor Henry Ford said, "Genius is experience. Some seem to think that it is a gift or talent, but it is the fruit of long experience in many lives. Some are older Souls than others, and so they know more."[9]

Reincarnation gives a spiritual foundation to democracy: although we may not all seem to be equal in any given moment or given lifetime, reincarnation assures us that eventually we will all evolve and develop the same intelligence, skills, and qualities of character—though some will always get there faster than others. Reincarnation thus makes the concept of hierarchy more palpable. Superior abilities can be acknowledged, realizing they may have been developed over many lifetimes, while a lack of abilities may only indicate a Soul new to earth, with fewer lifetimes. One of the best cases for reincarnation is its explanation of the scientifically unsolvable mystery about why children with the same heredity and environment grow up to be so different from each other.

Weaknesses and problems are the cutting edge of growth in one's current life—where something new needs to be learned. If, for example, a person hates and mistreats someone because he or she is of a different race, then that person may have to return in the next life as a member of that race, not as a punishment, but rather as an education, to experience the receiving end of the same mistreatment and understand the need for tolerance and compassion. However, sometimes very advanced Souls will incarnate into an oppressed race or culture, not out of personal karma, but to help liberate the people of that race. If someone has selfishly mishandled money in one life, he or she may be poor in the next life. Or if that person was poor and envied the rich, he or she may now be rich, unhappily trapped by the delusions wealth can create.

Death is the creative shattering of habits. From a reincarnational point of view, death isn't such a great tragedy, since the body is only a form and the real consciousness behind it will return again in another form. From the spiritual perspective, the only real tragedy occurs when lines of separation are drawn and love is shut out or when fear, hostility, or neglect determine our actions.

Some people are skeptical about reincarnation, noting that since most of us don't remember our past lives, they can't be real. On the other hand, few of us remember our births or early childhoods, and we often forget events that happened years, or even months, earlier, even though others remember them, illustrating that memory cannot be the only proof of reality in other areas of our life. It may be seen as an act of mercy that we rarely remember our past lives, as this saves us from being burdened by thousands of memories and guilts. Rather than having specific memories of each life, we are given a summary in our character, talents, strengths, and weaknesses. Reincarnation may also help explain why some people have recently remembered childhood abuse that is denied by the accused—they may have remembered a past life instead.

In a famous study, Dr. Ian Stevenson of the University of Virginia Medical School researched and substantiated over a thousand cases of children who had spontaneous detailed memories of former lives.[10] Young people seem to remember their past lives most easily, but then forget them when adults keep telling them not to tell stories. Corinne remembers, for example, that when her sister was very young she often said that her "real parents were a king and queen"—and now she realizes this was probably the truth from her previous life.

Roger Woolger, a Ph.D. and Oxford-trained psychologist, in his revolutionary book, *Other Lives, Other Selves,* documents how even the circumstances of our birth process reflect issues with which we are grappling from a previous life. Woolger's past-life approach to therapy has helped many people caught in bitter relationships understand the past-life origins of their patterns and change them through love and forgiveness. Individual problems such as chronic neck pain or fear of heights are often related to past-life deaths and traumas such as being hanged or pushed from a tall building. He has chronicled hundreds of cases of people who have been able to recall these experiences, without hypnosis, simply by giving the psyche permission to allow them to surface. Interestingly, he found his clients didn't need to believe in reincarnation for the therapy to work. They needed only to be open to it as a good story or an archetype. Through reliving the experiences and releasing the trauma, and forgiving themselves and others, the current symptoms often disappear immediately.[11]

Dr. Johannes Stein, a confidential adviser to Sir Winston Churchill during World War II, felt that history was something the living themselves had helped to create in their former lives on earth. He felt they bore the whole responsibility for what the world was, what it is, and what it will become.[12] General George Patton, a World War II hero, had conscious recall of participation in ancient battles, including the memory of being on the same battlefield in Italy in a previous life. He also had memories of being an ancient Greek soldier, a Scottish highlander with the House of Stuart, and a French trooper with Napoleon.[13]

Rather than seeing past lives as a string of pearls, the Agni Yoga teachings say it is more accurate to see one large pearl, which changes with each lifetime. These larger memories alter our perspective of things—the more we remember from our past lives, the more we understand our life today.

GROUP KARMA

Reincarnation provides deeper insight into the question of whether there is justice in the world. Whenever there seem to be "victims" and "injustice" occurring, for example, we have to look deeper to see that karma from past lives is being balanced out in this life. This relates as much to groups as to individuals, since wars, genocide, and mass suffering are often the result of group karma.

Souls incarnate in groups, either to balance out some negative karma and learn an important spiritual lesson or, if highly evolved, to carry out a specific purpose for humanity, or to bring in some new idea or energy. Such was the case with the Renaissance, when fewer than a hundred souls incarnating in the same period brought tremendous new inspiration and beauty to the world, transforming it radically. According to Alice Bailey, a decision was made on the inner planes in 1725 to hasten the entry of groups of souls into incarnation who would have a major impact on civilization for centuries, initiating the movements for freedom, economic justice, sexual equality, and scientific inventions.[14] Great leaders often bring with them other Souls who have worked together or who have been supporters in past lives to help them carry out their task. This was most likely the situation with Mikhail Gorbachev, Boris Yeltsin, and other reformers in the former Soviet Union, and with Nelson Mandela, and other crucial leadership around the planet.

Reborn as Our Enemies

Some Souls incarnate into certain races over and over again; others incarnate into a particular race to either acquire certain valuable qualities, or as a way to break out of bonds of attachment to that race and free themselves to identify with all humanity.

As the inspired metaphysical teacher Rudolph Steiner noted, nationalistic chauvinists who hate other countries are actually having premonitions that they will be born into that nationality in their next life. The Higher Self knows, but the personality resists.[15]

The Dalai Lama, in an interview with *The New York Times*, said he believed the present violence of the Chinese against the Tibetans was determined by intricate sets of causes stretching back into the previous lives of those who are affected by them. It was only an "outward appearance" that the Tibetans were suffering today because of the Chinese aggression. "The aggression must have come because we did, something bad." Similarly, he went on, the chain of causes that will eventually undermine Chinese rule in Tibet must already be lengthening, even if it cannot yet be seen. The positive side of the Chinese destruction of Tibetan monasteries has been the spread of the Buddhist Dharma to the West and its growing popularity here, which would not have happened if all the monks had stayed in Tibet.[16]

A century ago, when the Hopi Indians were being killed off by white men, they had a legend that their "children would return in white robes." In our travels around the United States we observed that many young white people, who dress in Indian clothing and beads, play drums, and participate in native-style sweat lodges, may well be reincarnated Native Americans who link into their earlier experiences by living on the land and rediscovering their sensitivity to the earth. We have also met many of these people who are now working for the environment in a variety of settings.

And as would be karmically just, those whites who brutally killed Indians or forced them onto reservations might be some of those now in Indian bodies having to live in degraded conditions on those same reservations— noticeably the ones uninterested in their spiritual traditions, who dress like cowboys, get drunk, and race around in big trucks. Many Native Americans dress like cowboys more than anyone else, and many are occupational cowboys as well, working on ranches or following the rodeo circuit.

ALTERNATING LIVES AS MALE AND FEMALE

From the perspective of reincarnation, we all experience life in both male and female bodies, so the entire male-female conflict has to be seen in group terms and in historical emphasis. Each of us is an androgynous Soul, choosing a male or female body in any given lifetime based on needed growth lessons, karmic balancing, or because of a specific mission. For example, women today who feel angry and self-righteous toward men who oppress women may themselves have been oppressors in the past—which may be one of the reasons such oppression evokes very strong feelings. In fact, some women's militant, aggressive insistence on their rights today, while necessary for gaining political attention, may be a strong indication of several past lives spent as male warriors, with the same tendencies now being expressed in a female body. These former warriors provide a needed front-line action to establish female equality. Souls are not being punished by being in a particular sex, but rather are learning lessons about tolerance and respect for the opposite sex. Gay men who seem effeminate may have had several recent lives as a female and find feminine expression more comfortable. But as Souls, each chose the sex of their body in this life for certain lessons and experiences leading to rounding out the development of all attributes, both male and female.

Now what is needed is a deeper respect for true feminine nurturing, receptive energy, in women and men. The political issue that is evolving today is tolerance of diversity and the expansion of the roles women can play—or, rather, the role of those Souls who are occupying female bodies in this particular incarnation.

REINCARNATION AND ACTIVISM

Reincarnation also may help explain some values and activities of some of the 1960s generation, as we discovered through our own personal experiences. A number of those of our generation we've spoken to have memories of fighting against Hitler in World War II in their last life, dying at an early age, and immediately coming back into incarnation. They brought with them an extremely painful memory of the horror of war and fascism in any form, with an intense commitment to work for peace. Thus they defiantly opposed the Vietnam War and have been overly fearful of "fascistic" tendencies and oppression in the United States. Some spiritual teachers say that many "old [highly evolved] souls" came back into incarnation just as World War II was ending to help the planet through this difficult time of transition.

A major rationale for war—the fear of death—encourages us to defend ourselves against our enemies by stockpiling thousands of weapons. But from the perspective of reincarnation, we cannot destroy our enemies; they will only reincarnate and be our enemies again. Thus the only way out of this endless cycle of violence—the course advocated by Christ—is to "forgive our enemies."

It is very important, however, not to use a belief in karma and reincarnation as a way to avoid compassion and activism—for we are each responsible for helping to restore justice wherever it is needed. In the Hebrew *Talmud* there is a verse that translates as follows: "It is not your duty to complete the work. Neither are you free to refrain from it." Blaming and shaming victims for karmically drawing to themselves violence, ill health, or other misfortunes is not an appropriate spiritual response. "Holier than thou" judgments about another person come only from ego.

It is important instead to respond with compassion and attempt to relieve suffering wherever we find it. Love expressed has the power to offset karma, for love is the creative energy of Deity.

Although people may become very concerned about past lives, preparation for future lives is much more important, as we are continually creating karma for ourselves, and should focus on purifying ourselves and training for service in future lives.

REINCARNATION GIVES US HOPE

In *My Land and My People,* the Dalai Lama noted that a deep-seated conviction in rebirth "should engender a universal love, because all living beings in the course of their numberless lives and our own, have probably been our friends, or may have been our beloved parents, children, brothers, or sisters. This should encourage tolerance, forbearance, charity, compassion. If there is no peace in one's mind, there can be no peace in one's approach to others, and thus no peaceful relations between individuals or between nations."[17]

Mahatma Gandhi said, "I cannot think of permanent enmity between man and man, and believing as I do in the theory of rebirth, I live in the hope that if not in this birth, in some other birth I shall be able to hug all humanity in friendly embrace."[18] Strong Souls can reduce the conflict and pain between people and hasten the transition to a better world.

The next time we watch the evening news, instead of criticizing people we disagree with and cheering ones we do, it might help us develop greater compassion and detachment by asking ourselves what karma is being played out in the latest world conflict or to speculate about what previous lives our president or congressman might have lived. And take heart. We're not left here on earth alone—help is always available beyond the human sphere from the Invisible Government.

Part 4

◆ ◆ ◆

THE DIVINE HAND BEHIND HUMAN AFFAIRS

Chapter Eight

♦

THE INVISIBLE GOVERNMENT

We study what happens in history as the reflection of an event enacted behind the scenes of history in the supersensible world ... where impulses of supersensible Beings play in upon the Earth and come to expression in the actions of humanity.
—RUDOLF STEINER[1]

In the first seven chapters of *Spiritual Politics*, we looked behind the scenes of current events to examine human causes—symbolic, mental, emotional, etheric, and karmic. In this chapter and the next, we will examine transhuman causes. Many events in our world can't always be fully explained from the ordinary human perspective. Those who reflect deeply may find that rational approaches only take them so far and thus may well be interested in considering the more unusual perspective offered in this chapter. For those for whom this worldview is new, we suggest reading initially with an open mind and reserving judgment until an intuitive consideration can be made. For us personally, exploring this perspective bridged some very important gaps in our understanding of what is really going on in the world.

Scientists are discovering that all of Life participates in a vast universal chain of being. In the field of General Systems theory, this is called the "systems hierarchy." Subatomic particles combine to form atoms, which combine to form molecules, which combine to form complex proteins, which combine to form cells, which combine to form multicellular organisms, and so on and on, into ever-increasing complexity. Each new higher system in turn becomes a part of yet another new, more complex whole. Systems theory indicates that evolution continues in humanity, but with a new focus. When the cell developed, nature shifted its developmental thrust from chemical to biological evolution. So with the human being, nature has shifted from biological to social and psychological evolution. Through the human being, evolution has become aware of itself, for the human mind extends the responsiveness of nature into a new dimension of self-awareness.

THE MASTERS OF WISDOM

The human body is the endpoint of the evolution of form—from mineral to plant to animal on this planet. Within that form, however, consciousness keeps evolving into greater intelligence, love, and will as we learn to master our physical body, then our emotions, and next our minds. Finally we begin to allow a higher wisdom or indwelling Divinity—the Soul—to take charge of our lives. Those ahead of us on the evolutionary ladder of consciousness, called "the Great Chain of Being" in the Ageless Wisdom, the ones who more fully express this indwelling Divinity, are seen as teachers and guides, just as we become guides to those who follow after us. Those ahead represent our future—the guarantee that evolution is real. "Each expansion of consciousness that a man (or woman) undergoes fits him (or her) to be a master to those who have not taken a similar expansion," writes Alice Bailey. "Therefore, mastery being achieved, there is nothing except masters, who are likewise disciples. All are learners and all are teachers, differing only in degree of realization."[2]

In most of the world's religions, there are teachings about wiser and more compassionate beings who have achieved perfection and transcended the physical dimension. Their purpose then becomes to serve as protectors and guides of humanity. Honored in every religious tradition, they are known by a wide variety of names: the Christian "Communion of Saints," "the Kingdom of God," "the just men [and women] made perfect" referred to by St. Paul in the Bible (Heb. 12:23), the Jewish "Just Ones," the Buddhist "Bodhisattvas," the Chinese "Lohans," the Native American "Spirit Guides," the Vedic "Rishis," the "Arhats," "Avatars," "Adepts," "Enlightened Ones," "Masters of Wisdom," "the Society of Illumined Minds," "the Invisible College," "the Inner Government of the Planet." Even a brief touch of their presence can be the most powerful experience of a lifetime—changing a person's entire worldview.

The earth is our schoolhouse, a place for us to learn and grow. The Adepts, or Enlightened Ones, are those who have taken the course and "graduated" from the lessons of human evolution and are now available to be our guides. They are wise, compassionate beings who are no longer required to incarnate yet are active in human affairs from inner dimensions, providing a source of strength and guidance to humanity down through the ages, and directly aiding whenever it has been requested. They are said to constitute a fifth kingdom in nature, just as humanity is the fourth and animals the third. These Enlightened Ones were humans, unlike most of the Angels or Devas (described in the next chapter), which are a parallel but distinct evolution.

We need to realize that these Enlightened Ones—male and female—have lived, suffered, failed, and attained success through the purificatory fires of daily life as farmers, businesspeople, artists, teachers, healers, scientists, and leaders of countries. They have mastered all states of consciousness as humans, thus guaranteeing to us the same ultimate achievement. A Master is a representative of the future of humanity. To study the Enlightened Ones is to study our future.

These Masters of Wisdom form an "Invisible Government"—an inner, subjective government that guides humanity's evolution. They are the true intuitives of the race who have seen the end from the beginning. And because they fully embody compassion for a suffering humanity, they are known as the Heart Center of the planet. The life cycles of entire civilizations and cultural and political expressions are said to be guided by these Wise Ones working on the inner, subjective levels to aid human evolution. They allow humanity to unfold its own karmic pattern, yet they provide enlightened direction for us all, and most especially for all progressive, evolutionary movements. (The idea of the "Illuminati conspiracy" is a distortion of the true Invisible Government, as deception and manipulation are never hallmarks of the truly enlightened.)

Great Enlightened Ones or Adepts, such as the Buddha or Christ, anchor a dynamic truth, a potent thought-form on earth, which then over the centuries steadily conditions human thinking, producing a new civilization, with its cultures, religions, governments, and educational processes. On one level history can be seen as the record of humanity's cyclical reaction to some inflowing Divine energy, a response to the teaching of a particular Adept or Enlightened One.

The Enlightened Ones work ceaselessly at the task of expanding consciousness in all forms, so that it is awakened and employed intelligently. They influence world events, without abridging humanity's free will, by the inflow of ideas and revelations to those humans who are receptive to them. This allows the unfolding consciousness of humanity to express itself through adequate social, political, religious, and economic forms. The Enlightened Ones have forecasting capabilities, within the constraints of human free will. They can sometimes head off a problem by working with certain evolved Souls who incarnate to do a specific piece of work to aid humanity, as Abraham Lincoln did in preserving the Union. As Helena Blavatsky explains in *The Secret Doctrine:*

> The Universe is worked and guided from within outwards. As above, so it is below; as in heaven, so on earth; and [humanity]—the microcosm and miniature copy of the macrocosm—is the living witness to the Universal Law and to the mode of its action. We see that every external motion, act, gesture, whether voluntary or mechanical, organic or mental, is produced and preceded by internal feeling or emotion, will or volition, and thought or mind. As no outward motion or change, when normal, in [the] external body can take place unless provoked by an inward impulse . . . so with the external or manifested Universe. The whole Cosmos is guided, controlled and animated by [an] almost endless series of Hierarchies of sentient Beings, each having a mission to perform . . . as agents of Karmic and Cosmic Laws.[3]

THE INFLUENCE OF THE ENLIGHTENED ONES

The Enlightened Ones are said to meet regularly in council to evaluate humanity's spiritual progress over the preceding decades and to transmit energies and ideas needed to further evolution. These ideas are then picked up on inner levels (even though they may not consciously recognize the source of these ideas) by those who are developed spiritually and intellectually, in touch with their Souls, and dedicated to serving humanity in some way. These individuals in turn are the ones who make the great scientific, social, artistic, and spiritual discoveries, stimulating human progress. They and their ideas produce stirring times of change such as the Renaissance, the Age of Enlightenment, the Industrial Revolution, the American, French, and Russian revolutions, and such institutions as the League of Nations and the United Nations, as well as moral-ethical revelations leading to new spiritual paths or religions.

Sometimes there may be several people in different places who receive similar "impressions" or ideas from an Adept or Enlightened One on the higher mental plane. This can account for scientific discoveries or theories emerging at nearly the same time at different places around the world, such as the discovery of steam power simultaneously in the United States and in France. The ideas of liberty, equality, and fraternity were presented to humanity by the Masters of Wisdom prior to the French Revolution but were not fully understood or embodied. The idea of democracy was also given but is as yet a philosophy largely of wishful thinking and an unachieved ideal, as the so-called democratic countries are often at the mercy of large corporations and financial elites. A true democracy will evolve at some future date when people are told the truth and can judge matters freely for themselves, and when democratic processes are extended to all spheres of society, including the economic.

A new idea given to humanity in the middle of this century as a next step was the vision of group consciousness—humans transcending self-centeredness to participate consciously in groups working for the salvation of humanity. The embryonic beginnings of this awakening can be seen in the best aspects of the movement the "New Age," in the emergence of nonseparative consensus-based groups, and in the many groups with a service orientation that empower each member. The Adepts or Enlightened Ones are working to inspire humanity today with new evolutionary ideas, such as systems thinking and the synthesis of opposites.

The emphasis of the Adepts is always on the next step for humanity, not on a Utopian vision far in the future, since vast time gaps between today's reality and a distant vision can create frustration and disempowerment. At the end of each century, there is a "push" by the Adepts, moving humanity toward a new dispensation, with much rapid change. This is what the world is experiencing today, with the dismantling of the Soviet Union, the development of the European Community, the new priority being given to the environment, and the globalization of business.

Generally, at the end of each cycle of culture or civilization, as a last chance, a high "initiate"—a very evolved Soul—incarnates to embody the best of that culture and to present a choice between decadence or a movement to the next phase of the vision. However, humanity often doesn't rise to the challenge, and the culture then degenerates and destroys itself. Mahatma Gandhi was one such example of an initiate challenging India to take a next step to freedom and tolerance of diversity.

The true spiritual hierarchy of Enlightened Ones is one of compassion and responsibility, not one of dominance—unlike human hierarchies, which can often be oppressive. The Adepts respect human free will and cannot interfere in human affairs unless their aid is requested or agreed to and can be creatively utilized in a cooperative rather than a dependent way. They generally work only with world leaders or those who are instruments of large group activities that are having a major impact on the world. The disciples or messengers of these Enlightened Ones on the inner planes may at times contact those who are not major leaders but who are dedicated to serving the world with pure motives. For example, we were told by a friend who is a U.S. senator's aide that while researching the budget proposal for a major bill, he received guidance about what action to recommend to the senator from a source on the inner planes.

CONTACTING OUR SOUL FOR GUIDANCE

For most people, the next step is learning to contact their own Soul for guidance, rather than trying to contact the Enlightened Ones directly. Those whose motive is selfish or materialistic, yet who claim to receive guidance from a Master or Adept, are probably only contacting a less evolved entity on what is called the "astral plane," the plane of illusion, where many entities masquerade as wise guides. Just because people have died and passed over into the inner planes of spirit doesn't necessarily make them any wiser than they were while alive. At times, a dark or harmful spirit will call itself a "Master" in order to try to discredit the good work of others. The media have rightly exposed many cults that wrongly claim to be in touch with the Enlightened Ones and yet do outrageous things, but this exposure has also had the effect of frightening the public away from more legitimate groups.

Inspiration or guidance from a true Adept is usually offered as brief, precise information needed to serve the good of the whole—not the long, flowery ego-inflating type of guidance from less evolved "spirit guides." The person on the receiving end is free to accept or reject the guidance— absolute obedience is never demanded from a higher source. The Adepts aid and protect, as well as provide help in a crisis. Help from the highest levels usually arrives at what seems to be the darkest hour, after everything humanly possible has already been done. Help may arrive unexpectedly through an unknown letter, a book found seemingly by chance, or perhaps a sudden, intuitive sensing of the right course of action.

Gordon had an experience of the rare intervention of the Enlightened Ones in world events when he was in New York City during the nuclear accident and disaster at Three Mile Island. During the meltdown, a giant radioactive hydrogen bubble built up in the reactor, and there was great fear in New York that it would explode and contaminate the city and much of the East Coast. Many people were fleeing the city in fear. When he turned within to ask for guidance about what he should do, he was told, "There is nothing to worry about, it is being taken care of by the Spiritual Masters." Very shortly afterward, the hydrogen bubble deflated. To this day, scientists have been unable to explain the causes for this unexpected development. Some years later, Mirtala Bentov, wife of the late Itzak Bentov, the physicist and initiate of the Ageless Wisdom, told us he was guided to go to the Three Mile Island area during the crisis to act as the grounding point for the work of the Masters in dealing with the crisis. He told his wife it was his understanding that this was the first time the Enlightened Ones had actively intervened in human affairs since World War II.

The Appearance of the Adepts in the World

At times the Adepts will appear in the physical world as very ordinary people who happen to present the information or help needed at a crucial time, and their true identity is recognized only by those who have eyes to see. For example, we were told by a retired naval officer whom we met at Findhorn about an experience he had while on a U.S. command ship directing nuclear testing in the Pacific. Another naval officer came into his cabin as he was doing the final calculations on the effects of the nuclear tests and indicated to him a major error he had made, which would have resulted in a nuclear disaster. Later, when he went to thank the officer for his help, he discovered there was no such person on the ship.

The Enlightened Ones do not usually work openly or give public lectures. Since the earliest times of human history, they have worked quietly behind the scenes—in government, business, science, religion, the arts. It is part of the Divine Plan that they or their senior disciples are not directly in control of governments or major institutions, so that governments are based upon the demand and the current point in the evolution of the mass of humanity working through their representatives. This avoids creating too great a gap between the public consciousness and that of the Enlightened Ones. This is why the Adepts at this time work to influence world opinion leaders, if they are open to it, rather than leading directly.

However, according to some metaphysical traditions, advanced initiates who work closely with the Enlightened Ones are now beginning a process of "externalization"—working more publicly in all walks of human life from business to politics. Rather than announcing themselves, they will be recognized by their wisdom, compassion, and clear vision and their universal and inclusive approach to all humanity. In some ways they may appear to be such ordinary people that recognition of what they truly are may escape the notice of most. They will work with people in every religion and in every political party who have love in their hearts and who work for the good of the whole.

Their task will be to "sweetening and clarification the political situation and the presentation of those ideas which will eventually lead to a fusion of those principles which govern a democracy and which also condition the hierarchical method," as Alice Bailey writes.[4] They will also help end the long divorce between religion and politics, a reconciliation that can now come about because of the high level of human mass intelligence.

These advanced initiates will assume leadership in all departments of human life, elected by the free choice of the people because of their proven merit as wise servants of the public and their inclusive spirit. In the area of religion they will restore the Mysteries—the public mystery dramas and initiations that have been part of so many ancient cultures such as the Egyptian, and the Greek and others through the ages.

Many traditions, from orthodox religious groups to metaphysical ones, East and West, have been expecting the imminent reappearance of a World Teacher—called the Christ by the Christians, the Messiah by the Jews, the Imam Mahdi by the Muslims, and the Maitreya Buddha in the Orient. Many see this reappearance occurring in the not too distant future, and point to the huge upheavals around the earth as signs of the final struggle with the forces of materialism (variously called the "Anti-Christ" or "Ahriman") which seek to block this return. According to Alice Bailey, before this World Teacher appears, several things will first occur: the Enlightened Ones will be more fully involved in public life; religious institutions will have begun to "clean house"; Africa and Arabia will be brought into the twentieth century; there will be a greater measure of peace and sharing evident in the world; and a great many of us will be experiencing our inner Divinity—the God within, the Soul. The World Teacher will come as a recognition of potency in leadership, through dynamic but logical changes in world affairs and through action taken by the masses of people from the depths of their own consciousness.[5]

THE DIVINE PLAN

It is often difficult for humanity to understand the reality that God, the Great Architect, would create an overall structure (the earth), a game plan (evolution of consciousness), and rules (karma, or cause and effect, and reincarnation) and then leave human beings free to choose to carry out this Divine Plan or not! This is like a baseball game with invisible umpires, players who have to figure out what the rules of the game are as they play the game, and confusion about what constitutes "winning." Yet spiritual umpires enforce the rules through karma and reincarnation, while the players figure out the rules through painful trial and error, and Enlightened Teachers come to humanity to demonstrate what true achievement really is. All this has been designed by the Divine Intelligence to allow us the full play of free will, so that all gains in consciousness, all adherence to higher principles, will be chosen freely and thus ingrained in each individual's consciousness and character. This is why the free will of humankind—the power of choice—is scrupulously guarded by spiritual law.

The main outlines of the Divine Plan have been revealed in many of the world's inspired writings, such as the New Testament gospels of Christ, the Noble Truths of the Buddha, the Hindu Bhagavad Gita of Krishna, and the Jewish Kabbalah, as a way of being for humanity today and into the future. The Enlightened Ones, the Adepts, are said to be the custodians of the Divine Plan for human evolution, which can be translated as the manifestation of God's will on earth within the appropriate timing. The underlying objective of the Divine Plan is to unify humanity into a subjective whole, whose beauty and effectiveness, as an instrument of the Divine Will and Purpose, lies in its diversity and differentiated capacities. This is a vision of the synthesis of all nations and races and life on earth into one mutually cooperative, planetary being.

This requires a unifying spirit of loving understanding and mutual tolerance, which will eventually develop into telepathic communication and the interplay of thought life. The Divine Purpose provides a regular and rhythmic progression toward unity and synthesis in all areas of life—subjective unity in consciousness with diversity in method and form. All that creates love, unity, cooperation, and the freedom and empowerment of the individual, is therefore supported by the Enlightened Ones. Separateness, fear, and hatred are seen to be the result of unenlightened human attitudes and activities.

UNITY, PEACE, AND PLENTY

According to the Ageless Wisdom, the current goal of the Divine Plan can be summarized in three words—"unity, peace, plenty"—significantly in that order. Unity in consciousness must first be achieved before there will be true and lasting peace, and peace is a necessary prerequisite for plenty or economic abundance. The first step needs to be the ending of separatism and the development of unity through ecumenical, interracial, and international movements and understanding. This will be fulfilled through the cultivation of goodwill and right human relationships, with education and enlightened public opinion as the major tools for change. From such a base, conflicts can be resolved through nonviolent means, such as mediated settlements. When there is a greater degree of peace in the world, it will enable the free circulation of food and resources to those who are most in need, ensuring abundance for all and an end to the fear and hopelessness in which a large part of humanity still lives today.

Peace should not be seen as a goal in itself, however, as it often becomes materialistic in purpose, an excuse to accumulate more consumer items. Peace is simply a temporary state of dynamic equilibrium between opposing forces, always evolving toward an ever-higher synthesis. For example, the tearing down of the Berlin Wall led to greater peace between East and West for a short time, but it was then followed by conflict about foreigners within a unified Germany. Peace at any price often becomes a deadening soporific, leading to complacency and stagnation. Change is essential for human growth.

In the political field, the Divine Plan is emerging as an international consciousness, making individuals aware that they are each part of One Humanity while still affirming their diversity. The spirit of international interdependence and cooperation will someday lead to a commonwealth of nations based on mutual need, support, tolerance, goodwill, and sharing.

In religion, the Plan will manifest as a worldwide understanding of the nature of the subjective realms, the dual spiritual and material nature of human existence, the immortality of the Soul, and the active presence, on higher levels of consciousness, of the Enlightened Ones. Eventually this will lead to the fellowship of religions and coordinated planetwide modes of worship and invocation, led by those who are wise and compassionate enough to avoid the potential abuses of power.

In science, the Plan is expressed as a collaboration between the physical sciences and the subjective sciences, such as psychology leading scientists to awareness of the etheric world. Scientific research will eventually be able to document the existence of the Soul and the effect of thoughts and feelings on the physical world.

Another facet of the Plan is to encourage the development of the mind in order to stabilize the emotions, thus helping to raise the consciousness of the masses to the mental level. At the same time, people already focused in their minds are being encouraged to develop their intuition and the faculty of spiritual insight and higher vision. The next step is listening to the wisdom of our inner Divinity—the Soul—and following its guidance in daily life. This leads to unconditional love and group consciousness, which will break the stranglehold of materialism and separative individualism on humanity.

HUMANITY'S ROLE

It is the role of humanity to serve as a bridge among the various higher kingdoms—the spiritual realms of the Soul—and the kingdoms of nature—the animal, plant, and mineral worlds. As more and more of us come into contact with our Soul, our capacity to transmit positive stimulation and the energy of love to the natural kingdoms increases, greatly aiding their evolution. This is already being demonstrated through the changing attitudes of many people toward the environment. We are beginning to view the life of all beings on the earth as a human responsibility to be loved and cared for, rather than as a resource to be exploited solely for our own use.

The energy that flows from this attitude toward nature is profoundly healing and stimulating to the growth of both the human and the nature kingdoms. Animals—both the wild creatures and those who live with humans—are stimulated in their evolutionary development by human emotions. The animal and plant kingdoms benefit tremendously when there is loving contact with human beings, which has been demonstrated in the interspecies communication between humans and whales or dolphins and through experiments with human and plant communications. (See "Devas, Angels, and the Inner Side of Nature" in chapter 9 for more on Devas; also *The Secret Life of Plants* and *Kinship with All Life* in the bibliography.)

The Plan does not focus primarily on each individual's material ease, comfort, and happiness. Rather, its purpose is to allow each of us to gain every possible experience in all phases of existence. This enables us to discover for ourselves the values of the spiritual life and to use our free will to choose greater cooperation, loving understanding, right relationships, freedom, and empowerment.

Knowing this larger Plan helps us transcend our attachment to physical and mental forms, so that we can see how the destruction of old forms frees consciousness to evolve in new and better ways. This is true of both the destruction of a physical body, which frees consciousness to evolve in another setting through reincarnation, and the forms of a civilization, which may need to be cleared away to make way for a new civilization based on greater spiritual principles.

The details of the Divine Plan are worked out by humanity itself, after understanding the broad outlines. Each of us is responsible for carrying out ideas we receive, the fraction of the Plan related to our unique capabilities. The Plan is never revealed in its totality. Rather, it unfolds slowly, according to local need and based on the overall progress of humanity. A part of the Plan is presented first as a new idea or revelation to those who are more consciously aware. Then it is revealed to specific groups and nations and, finally, to everyone. In a sense, history is the manifestation of Divinely inspired ideas working to "expand the Light" or overcome some great impediment in human evolution, such as slavery or racism. Those who consciously or unconsciously work along the lines of the Divine Plan receive help from the Enlightened Ones and their disciples; thus their united impact is exponentially greater than their numbers.

As the Plan passes from one group to another, many distortions occur that may have disastrous consequences. Those who are not inwardly receptive to a renewal of their original vision, or who are threatened by the coming changes and resist making adjustments, can often cause more separateness in the name of an ideal. Part of the Plan can also become obsolete as time progresses. Thus it is important to keep in touch intuitively with the changes required to avoid crystallization and ineffectiveness.

This is the main reason for conflict between idealists—those going forward with the evolving Plan and those idealists trapped in an outmoded, irrelevant part of it. The current conflict between religious fundamentalists and those practicing a spirituality based on the immanent Presence of God in all things is an example of this type of conflict. At some time in the future, when our understanding of the effects of ideas is more complete, we will study history as the unfolding of ideas from higher levels.[6]

THE EARTH'S ROLE

Our planet is a living being. It is also going through a process of spiritual growth and initiation into higher states of consciousness. All life on earth is now going through a time of great purification and testing to align with the planet's collective Soul. The earth is seeking to purify its physical body (as can be seen in recent erratic weather patterns) to shake off all the pollution and poisons that humanity has dumped on it, and to reorient itself toward Spirit. Humanity is particularly sensitive to such changes, and this results in increased stress (and sometimes disease) experienced by many people because greater amounts of spiritual life force energy are attempting to express through often resistant human bodies and institutional systems.

The long-term goal is for planet Earth to become "sacred," radiating light as do other planets that are known as sacred in the Ageless Wisdom teaching, such as Jupiter and Venus. According to David Spangler in *Links with Space,* in the past Earth served as a purifier for the solar system, attracting denser energies that needed to be cleansed and reunited with the whole. For ages, the Earth functioned like a kidney in the body of the solar system. But the Earth is now releasing its purification function in order to become a sacred planet.[7]

GUIDANCE FROM THE ENLIGHTENED ONES THROUGHOUT HISTORY

Help from that Source which, since time immemorial stands on constant vigil observing and directing the march of world events into the saving channels . . . [but] concealed from public notoriety, is usually extended at the turning point in the history of countries.

—HELENA ROERICH[8]

The secret history of nations, some of which is known only to initiates of the Ageless Wisdom, contains many examples of help received from the Adepts or Enlightened Ones, or their human envoys, either directly in person or inwardly through guidance in meditation. As we began exploring this, we found some fascinating and inspirational information from both historical and metaphysical sources. Although from our limited human perspective we may not agree politically with some particular guidance received from higher sources, and therefore question its authenticity, it is nonetheless instructive to observe the many historical examples where following guidance led to achieving desired goals.

For example, the ancient Greek historian, Herodotus, and the biographer Plutarch both recorded that a "divine host, a procession of spirits" arose from the temple where the yearly Mysteries of Eleusis were to have been celebrated that day and joined the battling Greeks to defeat the Persian army at Salamis in 480 B.C.[9] Again in about 300 B.C., a Gallic invasion of Greece was repelled, as a storm gathered, lightning fell, and the earth trembled under the invaders' feet. Supernatural appearances were seen, and the priests saved the temple of Apollo through "the science of fire and electricity."[10]

Many historians credit the political and artistic heights reached by the ancient Greek civilization with the high esteem its major philosophers, such as Pythagoras, Socrates, and Plato, and its statesmen, such as Pericles, placed on the Divine guidance they received from the Oracle of Apollo at Delphi. No city-state dared to embark upon any large-scale enterprise without first seeking advice from the Oracle. Even foreign kings and statesmen consulted it. The Oracle provided both ethical and practical information, as well as laws to establish new governments, and created "some degree of international conscience and moral unity."[11] The Delphic Oracle was credited with foretelling many major events in the history of nations, including the eruption of the volcano Vesuvius in A.D. 79.

At the same time as Pythagoras, great reformers in various parts of the world were making similar doctrines more generally known. In China, Lao-tzu departed from the esotericism of Fo-Ti; the Buddha, Sakyamuni, was preaching on the banks of the Ganges; in Italy the Etruscan priesthood sent an initiate, King Numa, to Rome to restrain the threatening ambition of the Roman Senate by setting up wise institutions. It is not by coincidence that these reformers appear at the same time among such different peoples. Their various missions are united in a common goal. They prove that at certain times a single spiritual current mysteriously passes through all humanity. It comes from that Divine but invisible world, whose seers and prophets are its ambassadors and witnesses.[12]

In A.D. 312, the Emperor Constantine saw a sign of Christ's cross in the sky and heard a voice saying, "In this sign you shall conquer." He then put the cross on the shields of his army and defeated the army of Maxentius in a miraculous battle. Maxentius had followed a dream he had, and the advice of the Sibylline Oracle, both of which told him to join the battle outside the city, where he lost.[13] Thus, from the inner side, influences were brought to bear and guidance was followed that changed the course of history.

Some Crusaders believed they were supported by a heavenly army led by St. George and others who helped disintegrate the army of the Moslem, Kerbogha.[14] The Russian people hold sacred a miraculous event that occurred in Yelets in 1395 when the Mongul conquerer Tamerlaine was on the march north to Moscow, destroying everything in his path. The people of Yelets prayed to the Mother of Jesus to protect their town, and marched around the town carrying icons of her, holding crosses to their hearts and ringing bells. Tamerlaine, a Muslim, later reported he saw a vision of a beautiful woman who told him to turn back, and he obeyed. Yelets still celebrates this remarkable event today. There is also the famous story of Joan of Arc, who in 1425 heard the voices of the Angels urging her to lead the French troops. She obeyed and led her troops to victory against the English during the Hundred Years' War. She was to be burned as a heretic by the Church, but was later made a saint.

Plato, Spinoza, Abraham Lincoln, and Florence Nightingale, among others, are said to have been guided by the Enlightened Ones or Adepts. Many heads of nations throughout history have received guidance from these Adepts, according to Helena Roerich, founder of the Agni Yoga Society:

The International (Invisible) Government has never denied its existence. It has proclaimed itself, not in manifestoes but in actions which are not even recorded in official history. One may cite cases from the French and Russian

Revolutions, as well as from the history of Anglo-Russian and Anglo-Indian relations, when an independent outside Hand altered the course of events. The Government did not hide the existence of its envoys in various countries. On the contrary, they showed themselves openly, visited various governments, and were known to many. Literature preserves their names and adorns them with the fancies of their contemporaries. . . . The fact of this Government's existence under varied names has penetrated the consciousness of humanity repeatedly. . . . Each nation is warned but once. Envoys are dispatched but once in a century—this is the law. The acts of the Invisible Government conform with world evolution. Hence their conclusions are premised on exact mathematical laws.[15]

Napoleon was following the guidance of the Adepts as he successfully began to unify Europe, but they warned him not to invade Russia. His own ego and lust for power overcame him, and he refused to listen. His obsession with power was dramatically expressed by demanding a coronation as emperor and then suddenly seizing the crown and placing it on his own head, rather than allowing the pope to crown him, as was the custom. This symbolized his supreme arrogance in setting himself above even the pope as God's representative on Earth. By not following the spiritual guidance he was given, Napoleon cut himself off from further help and eventually brought disaster upon himself and his armies.

King Charles XII of Sweden was also warned through guidance not to attack Russia. He, too, ignored this advice and so harmed the development of his country. Marie Antoinette was advised about the danger threatening the royal family and nobles of France. Likewise, Queen Victoria was warned not to let England become politically involved with China or it would bring a disaster to the empire.[16] In 1926 the leaders of the Soviet Union were warned about avoiding authoritarian excesses but also did not listen, with disastrous results.

Many writers have suggested that the Comte de Saint-Germain, a mysterious character in European courts and diplomatic circles in the eighteenth century, was in fact one of the Adepts who assumed many identities, including Prince Ragoczy of Hungary, when needed for work furthering human evolution in both Europe and America.[17]

THE DIVINE GUIDANCE BEHIND AMERICA'S FOUNDING

While researching the secret metaphysical side of America's founding for over fifteen years, we made discoveries that had a major impact on our work and inspired us tremendously. We discovered links between the Ageless Wisdom and our Founding Fathers that are never reported in traditional history books. We discovered that the seeds for America's founding were planted much earlier by the wise initiates of many cultures, from ancient Egypt and Greece to latter-day England and France. Many see Francis Bacon as being guided by the Enlightened Ones in his work with the court of England and the founding of America. He wrote of America before its founding as "the new Atlantis" in his book by that name. He was also a member of the company that founded colonies in Virginia and the Carolinas.

Bacon, known as the "Father of Modern Science," is thought by many metaphysical researchers to be the founder of modern Freemasonry and the head of the Rosicrucian Order (a secret metaphysical society), as well as an earlier incarnation of the Comte de Saint-Germain at the French court of Louis XV. Bacon is also thought by many researchers to be the secret author of the Shakespeare plays, as he was uniquely well educated in political, literary and metaphysical ideas, while the actual William Shakespeare was illiterate.

Many spiritual teachers say that the founding of America was aided by the Enlightened Ones. Several sources, for example, report the story of an unknown person who gave an inspiring speech to the delegates as they were hesitating to sign the Declaration of Independence, saying, "God has given America to be free. . . . Sign, and not only for yourselves, for that parchment will be the textbook of freedom, the bible of the rights of man forever!" None of those present knew him, or at least did not acknowledge it, but somehow he managed to enter and leave a locked and guarded room unnoticed.[18]

Some say this man might have been the mysterious one who was simply called "the Professor." He appeared to be on close personal terms with George Washington, Benjamin Franklin, and Thomas Paine, and he helped to design the American flag. He was a vegetarian, drank no liquor, and spent most of his time perusing rare books and ancient manuscripts. He was over seventy years old but apparently in the prime of his life, referring to events of the previous century as if he'd been a living witness to them.[19]

The role of Divine guidance in America's founding was acknowledged by many, including George Washington in his first inaugural address: "No people can be bound to acknowledge and adore the Invisible Hand which conducts the affairs of men more than the people of the United States. Every step by which they advanced to the character of an independent nation seems to have been distinguished by some token of Providential agency."[20]

Washington believed he was constantly guided by higher sources in directing his troops to outsmart the British. He was often called clairvoyant because it seemed he could look into the future and predict troop movements with amazing accuracy. According to a report by Anthony Sherman, who was with Washington at Valley Forge where the incident occurred, Washington had a vision of an Angelic presence. He was shown the birth, progress, and destiny of the United States in three great crises where enemies within and without challenged the Union, but it persevered. He was told that "while the stars remain and the heavens send down dew upon the earth, so long shall the Republic last. The whole world united shall never be able to prevail against her. Let every child of the Republic learn to live for his God, his land, and the Union."[21]

THE METAPHYSICAL SOCIETIES

In our research, we have found reports that many of America's Founding Fathers were members of ancient secret societies that studied the metaphysical sciences and were guided by the Enlightened Ones. This is difficult to prove beyond all doubt, as these societies remained secret to avoid persecution. Many famous philosophers, scientists, artists, and political leaders down through the ages are said to have been members of these societies, such as Roger Bacon, Francis Bacon, Giordano Bruno, René Descartes, Paracelsus, and William Blake. We have found many intriguing hints that Thomas Jefferson was a Rosicrucian (the Brotherhood of the Rosy Cross),[22] as evidenced by a secret code he used that was known only to high initiates of the order and the fact that he designed the building of the University of Virginia in a pattern relating to a Kabbalistic metaphysical design.[23] Helena Blavatsky, founder of the Theosophical Society and author of The Secret Doctrine, stated the following in 1883: "[S]everal Brothers of the Rosy Cross . . . did take a prominent part in the American struggle for independence. We have documents to that effect, and the proofs of it are in our possession."[24]

John Adams's forebears in England were said to belong to a sect of English Druids called the Dragons, which also included Sir Walter Raleigh and John Dee, Queen Elizabeth's astrologer. The Dragons sought to renew the ancient wisdom of earth energies and studied the astrological procession of the equinoxes.[25]

Benjamin Franklin published an astrological ephemeris in his *Poor Richard's Almanac* and wrote an epitaph that seems to suggest he believed in reincarnation: "The Body of B. Franklin, Printer . . . lies here, food for worms, but the work shall not be lost; for it will appear once more, in a new and more elegant Edition, Revised and corrected by the author." Franklin also published the books of Johann Conrad Biessel, who founded Ephrata in Pennsylvania, the first Rosicrucian community in the New World. Franklin visited there frequently and brought gifts.[26] This community was a focus for the spreading of the Ageless Wisdom in America, and after its disbanding, most of its metaphysical library passed into Franklin's keeping.[27] George Washington was also a friend of the community and released a prisoner at the request of one of its leaders, Peter Miller.[28]

In addition, Franklin spoke of the "Father of Lights," as the Rosicrucians do, and his speech to the Continental Congress reflects other Rosicrucian themes: "God governs in the affairs of men. If a sparrow cannot fall to the ground without His notice, is it probable that an empire can rise without His aid?"[29] Some believe that Franklin himself was secretly a Rosicrucian.[30]

At least fifty out of the fifty-six signers of the Declaration of Independence, including John Hancock, Benjamin Franklin, and Thomas Jefferson, were Freemasons.[31] At the time of America's founding, the Masonic lodges had a strong metaphysical orientation, which developed deep bonds of loyalty, as well as common values and purposes, among members. The traditional secrecy preserved in Masonic lodges allowed members to communicate and organize the American Revolution with little fear of exposure. Several significant contributors to the revolution, including the Marquis de Lafayette of France were also Masons, and Franklin and Jefferson had both been initiated into a French Masonic lodge.[32]

The cornerstone of the U.S. Capitol Building was laid in a Masonic ceremony, with George Washington presiding as Grand Master. The Boston Tea Party was the work of the Masons of the St. Andrews Lodge while taking a "recess."[33] Through the lodges of the Freemasons, the ideas of such Age of Enlightenment thinkers as John Locke, David Hume, François Marie Arouet, Voltaire, and Jean Jacques Rousseau became widely disseminated in the new colonies.[34] The structure of the U.S. Constitution was based on Masonic ideals, and the federalism created by the Constitution is identical to the federalism of the Grand Lodge system of Masonic government created in 1723,[35] as well as to that of the Iroquois Confederacy.

Masonic architects also laid out the city of Washington, D.C., in a metaphysical design to make the best use of the earth energies—called "ley lines," or "dragon lines," for creating healing or harmony. The original design of Pierre-Charles L'Enfant was later modified by Washington and Jefferson to produce the specifically octagonal patterns incorporating the particular cross used by the Masonic Templars.[36] Just as ancient sites such as Stonehenge are aligned to the positions of the sun and moon, the same is true of the Washington Monument. For example, a line of sight for the winter solstice can be established from the top of the monument to the southeast, down Virginia Avenue.

Little of the Masonic influence on the founding of America is discussed in most history books, as the Masons are very controversial in certain conservative and Christian circles, where they are feared as part of an evil world conspiracy. From our review of current Masonic literature and historical documents, as well as observing something of the spiritual life and service of high degree Masons, these fears are unfounded. Many people automatically suspect anything secret. At various times, however, a few Masonic lodges (such as the P-2 Lodge in Italy) have become subverted to serve personal power and manipulation, as is true of any human institution.

The esoteric link between Masonry and Rosicrucianism is very close, as a study of Albert Pike's Masonic *Morals and Dogma* and Max Heindel's Rosicrucian *Cosmo-Conception* will reveal. According to some historians, in the late 1660s and early 1770s Rosicrucianism and Freemasonry not only overlapped, but their teachings became virtually indistinguishable from one another, although Rosicrucianism was more selective and secretive.[37]

OTHER EXAMPLES OF SPIRITUAL GUIDANCE

The Civil War
During the U.S. Civil War, General George McClellan of the Union Army had a vision of George Washington, who told him about the coming crisis facing the nation, and then indicated where to move his troops to defeat the Confederate Army and preserve the Union. McClellan was convinced the information given him in a dream was reliable when he woke up and saw that it had actually been written on his maps. Using this information, he was able to prevent the capture of the city of Washington by Confederate troops, which were very close at the time.[38]

Abraham Lincoln was shown his own death by assassination in a dream and knew it was the price he had to pay for saving the Union, through the blood of thousands of soldiers on both sides who fought in the Civil War. After the dream he looked to the Bible for guidance, and every passage he opened to referred to the importance of dreams, visions, and supernatural visitations.[39] Lincoln was also guided by psychic Nettie Colburn, whom he felt had a "gift from God," to act immediately on the Emancipation Proclamation and to go to the front lines at Fredericksburg to raise the flagging morale of soldiers during that battle.[40]

Lincoln once said to a friend, "That the Almighty does make use of human agencies and directly intervenes in human affairs is one of the Bible's plainest statements. I have had so many evidences of this direction, so many instances when I have been controlled by some other power than my own will, that I cannot doubt that this power comes from above." Among his intimates, Lincoln continually referred to an invisible "Upper Cabinet" with which he was in communication and from which he received instructions.[41]

Sojourner Truth, a former slave, was guided by an inner voice to preach both the emancipation of slaves and women's rights all over the American North around the time of the Civil War. Although illiterate, she was a powerful orator and traveled everywhere on foot, lecturing about the abuses and indignities of slavery and finding jobs for freed slaves.[42]

In 1851 Harriet Beecher Stowe, in contemplating the mysteries of Christ's sacrifice, saw a vision of an old black slave being flogged to death by two younger slaves while a cruel white master looked on. The dying slave, his body bathed in blood, prayed for forgiveness for his oppressors. This became the basis of her famous book *Uncle Tom's Cabin,* which probably did more for the struggle against slavery than all the antislavery societies combined and helped catalyze the Civil War.[43]

WORLD WARS I AND II

Colonel Edward Mandell House, a close aide of President Wilson's—who was called a "man of mystery"[44]—was guided inwardly to bring the idea of a League of Nations to the world. Colonel House was a quiet, self-effacing adviser with tremendous dedication, practical intelligence, and skill. "By his idealism he touched those belonging to the Inner Government of the world, and by his mastery of practical politics he was able to influence those who governed the outer," noted metaphysician Theodore Heline.[45] Colonel House was also called by some "the Hidden Master of the New Deal."

Nicholas Roerich, the Russian painter and scientist who cofounded the Agni Yoga Society with his wife, Helena, and was nominated for the Nobel Peace Prize, was in direct contact with the Enlightened Ones. He was guided to design the "Banner of Peace," which was to fly over the great monuments, cathedrals, and museums to protect them during times of war. This Peace Pact was signed by President Roosevelt in 1935 and eventually by the heads of thirty-nine other countries.

Helena Roerich wrote a series of letters to President Roosevelt from the Himalayas beginning in 1934, offering him guidance from the Enlightened Ones on the conduct of world affairs. These letters seem to indicate that Roosevelt accepted the guidance the messengers sent him—and history records the resulting success.[46]

Henry Wallace, secretary of agriculture and later vice president during Franklin Roosevelt's third term, was a close disciple of Nicholas Roerich's for some time, before he severed the relationship. After correspondence with the Roerichs, Wallace persuaded Treasury Secretary Henry Morgenthau, Jr., to print the reverse of the Great Seal on the dollar bill, as it had not been used since it was designed in 1789. Used this way, the Great Seal is a powerful spiritual talisman. (See chapter 10 on the spiritual destiny of the United States for more information.) Wallace's later campaign for the presidency was greatly harmed in the public's mind by publication of his so-called guru letters to Roerich many years earlier, although Wallace denied he had written them.[47]

A British officer, Major Tudor Pole, was inwardly guided during the dark days of the bombing of Britain during World War II to create a national moment of silence each day at noon when the BBC radio played the tolling of Big Ben. All over Britain people stopped whatever they were doing and joined in a moment of silent prayer to defeat Hitler. This was an extremely effective metaphysical technique for creating a united national will and was later credited as one of the reasons Britain was able to hold out and ultimately triumph over the terrible onslaught by Hitler and the German air force. A memorandum from one of Hitler's aides said that the führer couldn't defeat Britain because the English had some sort of "secret weapon" associated with the striking of Big Ben.

During the early part of the Battle of Britain in 1940, the Germans launched a massive air strike against the fledgling Royal Air Force. However, as they approached England, German pilots reported seeing an overwhelming armada of RAF fighter planes headed toward them, and so they retreated. The British planes were an illusion, as the RAF was in no position to launch such a strike at that time. According to some, this inexplicable event might have been another example of the intervention of the Enlightened Ones on behalf of humanity during one of its darkest hours.[48]

Sir Winston Churchill was conscious of being guided by higher forces, as he said in 1942: "I sometimes have a feeling—in fact, I have it very strongly—a feeling of interference. I want to stress that I have a feeling sometimes that a guiding hand has interfered. I have a feeling that we have a guardian because we serve a great cause, and that we shall have that guardian as long as we serve that cause faithfully."[49]

In August 1914 during World War I there were also many reports of help arriving from a mysterious "comrade in white," whom the French and British saw as Archangel Michael or St. George on a white horse. The Germans reported seeing an army of thousands suddenly appearing when they were invading France and crossing French lines. Seeing this army, the Germans turned and fled.[50] Former British military officer Sir George Trevelyan told us that in the British military paper the *Guard's Gazette*, the Germans claimed to have been defeated by "the white cavalry" in a battle in World War I, which they had previously been confident of winning. Yet they suddenly threw down their arms and fled when they saw a big man on a white horse trotting as if in a parade and followed by an army that was advancing steadily.[51]

On file in the Pentagon is a report about an Italian monk named Padre Pio, known widely as a great holy man. When the Germans were about to invade his town, San Giovanna Rotunda, the villagers asked him to do something. No one knows what he did, but the Germans did not invade the town. The Americans, however, didn't know this and sent a squadron of bombers over the village. Suddenly the entire squadron of B-52 bombers saw a monk standing in the sky motioning them back, so they turned their planes around and dropped their bombs over an empty field.[52]

Former President Anwar Sadat of Egypt told Julliet Hollister, founder of the Temple of Understanding in the United States, that he had an experience, before he became president of Egypt, of an angel offering him guidance.

These examples of the guidance provided by the Enlightened Ones throughout history give us a sense of hope that all is not totally dependent on human strengths and weaknesses. Help is available from higher dimensions if we request it.

But the work of the Enlightened Ones is not the only transhuman cause of events. We will now explore additional cosmic causes.

Chapter Nine

◆

THE COSMIC CAUSES
OF WORLD EVENTS

*That which is a mystery shall no longer be so, and that which
has been veiled will now be revealed; that which has been withdrawn will emerge in light and all men and women shall see
and together they shall rejoice.*

—THE OLD COMMENTARY
ALICE BAILEY[1]

The purpose of Divinity is outworking in human events today through the
agency of great Beings and cycles of time which we call "cosmic causes,"
as they originate beyond our planetary system. The Masters of Wisdom on
our planet work with them and transform and step down their energy for
humanity. Though formerly incomprehensible to most of humanity, many
people, as their own mental and intuitive faculties evolve, are beginning to
recognize the influence of these cosmic causes and their impact on our
world.

As we have discussed, the Enlightened Ones are those humans who have
graduated from the lessons of Earth and now serve as guides for humanity's
evolution. But according to the Ageless Wisdom, there are other great beings and causal energies beyond these, both good and evil, that affect our
world. They are described in some Buddhist and Hindu texts in great detail, and the teachings of the Ageless Wisdom offer many insights into how
they affect human events.

Today many people are aligning their personal will with God's will and
are sensing the battle of Light and Darkness in the struggles of our planet
to progress beyond war, injustice, and separation. Many others are having
experiences of Angels guiding them or of nature Spirits in their gardens.
The use of astrology as a celestial mirror reflecting to us the right timing
for earthly action is becoming increasingly popular even with political lead-

ers. Many people are noticing a shift in energy today, as the old ways of organizing our civilization are no longer working and a new inflow of energy is vitalizing a reinvention of the social order.

We would like to attempt a description of some of these cosmic causes and explore their effect on world events in order to encourage our readers to think in broader spheres about current world changes. It is hoped that this understanding will make our individual contributions to the world more effective.

INFLOW OF ENERGY FROM SHAMBALLA

The Masters of Wisdom act as direct links to the spiritual realm where God's will is known—called "Shamballa" in the teachings of the East or the "Abode of the Father" in the Christian teachings. This is a center of consciousness and energy where very advanced beings receive and hold the energy of Divine Will for planet Earth.

Shamballa is said to be the mystical city of enlightenment sometimes referred to as "Shangri-la" in the world's literature, but it is actually located on the inner planes. The Enlightened Ones mediate the powerful energy released from Shamballa, "stepping down" its power by translating it, through compassion, into a plan for earth's evolution in progressive steps that humanity can accomplish. The full impact of this energy was, until recently, too stimulating of the will aspect and humanity was not yet prepared for its right use. The Lord's Prayer, which Jesus first gave to the world, was an example of a prayer that invoked the will of God and anchored it on earth.

The Synthesizing Force

The Shamballa force is an energy that works downward into form, bending form consciously to Divine Purpose to establish right human relations and circulate the energies of greater Life to all people throughout the planet. It destroys those material forms that have outlived their usefulness and that hinder the free expression of the Light of God. It contains within it the recognition of the unconquerable nature of goodness and the inevitability of the ultimate triumph of good. Its release to humanity is determined by the Enlightened Ones' evaluation of the collective Light within humanity and the inner unexpressed reactions of people—not by outer happenings in the physical world.

Once the obstacles to its free expression have been removed, the unifying force released by Shamballa will bring events and great ideas together in a new synthesis. The motivating urge of Divinity is to synthesize, to create union and interdependence in religious, social, political, and economic fields. The influence of Shamballa, through those who have been its representatives on earth, can be seen in the great declarations of freedom and unity in human history: the Magna Carta, the Declaration of Independence, and the Charter of the United Nations, for example.

Release of Shamballa Energies

Some spiritual teachings indicate that in 1925 and again in 1975 there was a direct release of the Shamballa energy to Earth for the first time without the mediation of the Enlightened Ones, who had previously protected humanity from the potency of its full impact. Like all spiritual energies, the the results of the Shamballa inflow depend upon level of consciousness that expresses it. The first release in 1925 eventually resulted in the destruction of crystallized attitudes and forms of civilization that were preventing growth of human consciousness. But the distortion and wrong use of this will energy by Hitler and others in World War II created immense suffering.

The 1975 inflow stimulated both the destruction of thought-forms about materialistic living and crystallized, authoritarian forms of government and stimulated a demand for unity and a spirit of internationalism in world affairs. This change in consciousness took place just after the Vietnam War, as the United States was healing its wounds and reassessing its role as a military power in the world. By the end of the following year over twenty governments had been toppled around the world, in order to make way for less restrictive, more participatory forms of democratic government.

The inflow of Shamballa energy has stimulated movements for peace, philanthropy, the recognition of our common humanity, and the principle of relationship. This has manifested in increased communication through telecommunications and travel, as well as through a greater emphasis on good human interpersonal communication. The Shamballa principle of synthesis—bringing together people, groups, and nations around essential identification with one another—is evidenced in the ecumenical movement in religion, the urge toward greater international cooperation through the United Nations, the European Community, citizen diplomacy, cooperation among public service organizations, and the development of transnational corporations, free trade and the global economy. However, economic structures need a change of motive and realignment with Shamballa to express the true higher synthesis.

THE HUMAN EXPRESSION OF SHAMBALLA ENERGY

The Shamballa force is expressed in two ways in the world. The first way is through dominating First Ray (power-oriented) personalities active in the world, who, if they fail to observe the Law of Love, have a powerful but passing influence. When these willful personalities meet human emergency and need, their actions may bring destruction in the early stages, but fusion and blending of diverse elements may occur in the later and final results. An example of the first type of willful personality is Augusto Pinochet, general and former president of Chile, who was powerful in his time but had no influence once removed. The second type of personality is represented by Kemal Atatürk of Turkey, who unified his nation, freed it from Greek control after great struggle, and established political and cultural reforms providing legal codes, rights for women, and progressive education.

The second way the will of God from Shamballa is expressed is through the voice of the masses of people throughout the world. The sound of the nations has been heard as a mass sound for the first time in recent years, demanding human betterment, peace, and understanding among people. This voice of the people is, for the first time, being determined by the will of God.

Francis Bacon anticipated this in his book *Bacon's Remains*: "God will use a voice, which sometimes He useth, that is: Vox populi—the Speech of the people." There have been powerful recent examples of the will of God being expressed through the voice of the people. One example was when great masses of people chanted, "Down with communism" and "We want freedom" in Poland, Czechoslovakia, Hungary, Romania, and East Germany, creating breathtaking changes in their Communist-led governments and tearing down the hated Berlin Wall. In Prague, Czechoslovakia, nearly a third of the city's population gathered to chant to their unpopular leader, "Jakes, Jakes, Jakes, your time is up!"[2] And after their general strike in 1989, nearly a million Czechs chanted, "The bells toll—the day has come!" These chants were the cry of the oppressed against dictatorships, demanding the basic human right to speak and express themselves freely. No force on earth can prevent the ultimate triumph of the human Spirit claiming this right, as it is a demand for a higher principle to be expressed— freedom—which creates an alignment with Higher Will. It results in principled destruction rather than random destruction without principle or reason. And it always leads to the release of greater life and creative expression.

Understanding the potency of the Shamballa force behind these chants answers the question of why the communist leaders relinquished power in such an unprecedented manner without major violence. Even Romanian dictator Ceausescu's final defeat was triggered when large crowds began chanting against him to his face. These leaders were overwhelmed by the power of the voice of the people, which carried the will of God through the Shamballa energies, ensuring that humanity be permitted to use its free will to solve its own problems, and which ultimately destroys all forms that hinder the expression of that freedom.

These expressions of the will of God created an accelerating wave of spiritual power that telescoped the time required for the liberation of the peoples of Eastern Europe. It took Poland eight years to win freedom, East Germany eight months, and Czechoslovakia eight weeks—illustrating the accelerating wave of the Shamballa energy as it set off a nuclear chain reaction in consciousness, galvanizing free will and the demand for its expression throughout the world. It has since rippled into Namibia, Somalia, Ethiopia, South Africa, Israel, China, Chile, Myanmar (Burma), Cambodia, and many other nations.

SHAMBALLA 2000

The next release of the Shamballa energy into human consciousness is planned for the year 2000, according to some metaphysical teachings, which will bring another cycle of major upheaval and change as we move into the next millennium. This high-voltage energy of synthesis will test every individual and institution to determine if they are aligned with the Higher Will. The Shamballa energy can most safely be handled by groups of people dedicated to the service and uplifting of humanity. If groups are aligned with the Higher Will when this energy is released through them, they will expand and become more creative, alive, and powerful. If they are out of alignment, they will degenerate emotionally, physically, and mentally.

This process has already begun, as we can see through the downfall of groups that are opposing evolution and synthesis, and will only accelerate in the years ahead. Our task is to purify our motives and purposes and prepare ourselves to channel this energy, as part of the regenerative, creative worldwide group that is building a positive and uplifting future for humanity.

FORCES OF LIGHT/FORCES OF DARKNESS

The only thing needed for evil to triumph is for good men to do nothing.

—CHIEF JUSTICE
OLIVER WENDELL HOLMES

One of the unique features of our Earth is that it is a planet of polarity. Everything on the physical, emotional, and mental level has its opposite. Physically there are males and females; emotionally there is love and hate; intellectually there is conservatism and liberalism. We learn and grow into consciousness through experiencing these contrasts and swings in polarity throughout this lifetime and others. Eventually we learn how to be detached from, and finally control, the swings of these polarities.

Personally, we have found that one of the major learning opportunities in our spiritual growth process has been dealing with the polarities of Good and Evil, Light and Darkness, and with the organized forces on each side. We have learned that each has an important purpose within the Divine scheme of things, and we must understand both of them to freely choose the Light, as we progress to each new level of understanding. From the perspective of the Ageless Wisdom, God can be defined as a Being who knows good without needing evil as a reference point. The leaders of the Forces of Light are the Enlightened Ones, the Saints and Masters known in every religion, as well as many who are unknown. They are aided on earth by evolved humans called initiates, who work with great love and intelligence for human evolution.

EVIL AS MISPLACED ENERGY

Evil can be defined metaphysically as an energy that is out of place, misdirected, or out of timing. For example, an emphasis on individual selfishness can be appropriate at an early stage of personality development. However, it can crystallize into a type of evil when the person should be ready to move on to self-transcendence and transpersonal love. Evil can thus be interpreted as persisting in something we should have outgrown. Humanity is responsible for growing into maturity and taking responsibility for dealing with the effects of the evil it has created. Yet there is a distinction between the evil generated by human thought, feelings, and actions and the major evil organized by the Dark Forces, which seeks to control humanity through the opening provided by human negativity.

From our personal experience, we found that it is essential to recognize clearly and come to terms with the real power of evil in the world today—with what the Ageless Wisdom calls "the Forces of Darkness." To deny their existence, we learned, leaves us more vulnerable to their attacks and leads us to take too much blame personally for good works that don't succeed, as often happens when we won't recognize what we are up against. Many good people thus feel overwhelmed and discouraged when their work of a lifetime leads to minimal apparent results. However, it is also important that we not blame all our own problems on evil forces outside ourselves—and wise intuition helps us to know the difference.

THE BATTLE OF LIGHT AND DARK

The Forces of Darkness are the organized forces of materialism and selfish power on the inner planes that strive to hold back the evolution of humanity toward greater cooperation, unity, and spiritual growth by driving us deeper into materialism and separateness. Often, the Dark Forces are able to destroy the good work and progressive efforts of humanity. But not all destruction is evil and the work of the Dark Forces. Some destruction is necessary and good, to break down old, crystallized forms—physical, emotional, or mental—that hold back life and growth in consciousness. New growth is often made possible by destruction of the old.

According to the Ageless Wisdom, during the time of Atlantis there was a tremendous battle on the astral (emotional) level between the Forces of Light, who wanted to lift human evolution out of materialism and separateness, and the involutionary Forces of Darkness, who wanted to enslave human will and more deeply immerse humanity in matter. This resulted in the sinking of that ancient continent—the origin of the nearly universal myth of the Flood, which is found in the Bible and in the legends of many cultures around the world. World War II was a recent expression of this battle manifested outwardly in the world, in which a major thrust of the Dark Forces was defeated in the physical world. The battle still rages today on the inner planes—the Forces of Light against the Forces of Darkness, who will fight to the bitter end in an effort to destroy humanity and the Earth. In *The Destiny of the Nations*, Alice Bailey offers this explanation:

> These two directing energies of Light and Darkness . . . work in opposition on the mental plane and the plane of desire. One group, under the Divine Plan, works with the form aspect entirely, and in this group the light of love and of selflessness is absent; the other group is working directly with the Soul or consciousness aspect, and in this group the doctrine of the heart and the Law of Love control. The margin of difference . . . is to be found

solely in intention, in the underlying purpose and the concrete objectives. The major instrument of the Dark Forces is the organizing power of the mind and not the coherent influence of love, as is the case with the Masters of the Wisdom.[3]

THE ENSLAVEMENT OF MATTER

The Dark Forces originate beyond human control. But the "shadow" aspects of a personality—such as unacknowledged fear, hatred, anger, jealousy, ambition, and greed—can draw them in, thus providing a human tool for them to influence events. These forces represent involutionary energy—movement into matter and enslavement to it—at a time when humanity should be moving in an evolutionary direction, away from overattachment to material things and toward Spirit. An example of this would be focusing the attention of humanity on endless consumerism, when the evolutionary goal in this cycle is right human relationships.

Humanity is receiving help today, however, from an incoming energy called the Seventh Ray (see later section of this chapter), which assists us in creating a balance between Spirit and matter. This energy helps us to focus on the Divine Presence within the form and honor the sacredness of the body as a temple of the Spirit rather than as an end in itself, as the Dark Forces encourage. The Dark Forces work to prevent the understanding of applied spiritual principles and to hold back the forces of progress for their own ends. They work to preserve that which is familiar and old by increasing fear, separateness, and inertia among people. Dion Fortune, a British metaphysician, referred to evil as "the principle of inertia that binds the good."[4]

Divide and Conquer

Through violence, drugs, manipulative advertising, and other tools, the Dark Forces create hatred, disruption, and lack of established security. They are very clever and use the potent forces of psychology to achieve their ends. They work by distorting human thinking, presenting half-truths, imputing false motives, raking up past grievances, fostering ancient prejudices, clouding issues, and feeding the existing fires of hate, criticism, and cruelty. They often work through character assassination—creating false charges and thus making headlines is their strategy, knowing that most of the public don't read the contents of articles to see the lack of substantiation. They are behind much of the escalating and senseless violence in our culture. The Dark Forces are actually like vampires, living off the suffering and pain of humanity. Human ignorance of their existence only contributes to their power.

While some of the Dark Forces exist solely on the inner levels and seek to influence people from there, others work outwardly in the world. Generally, those who are very evil don't work publicly, as many would recognize their negative vibration. Rather, they work through others who fall into the "gray" zone and are not recognized as easily. Weak, greedy, selfish, or destructive men and women who "sell their Souls" for personal gain can be used as the puppets and instruments of the Dark Forces. The famous story of Dr. Faust by Goethe is a daily occurrence.

Possessions by evil "astral entities" are also real but never happen by accident. A person in some way opens the door to possession by being obsessed with obtaining power at any cost, or by abusing drugs, or by practicing black magic rituals (even as a parlor game). Often, such human beings have no idea of the vastness of the evil for which they are tools. Obsession or possession by these astral entities is often the cause of the murderous rampages of mass killers who follow these "inner voices" or urges. When humanity understands more about the necessity for spiritual hygiene through positive thought and emotion, tragedies like the Long Island Railroad commuter train shootings may be prevented.

These forces have been very successful at creating moral ambiguity and clouding the issues in politics, business, and entertainment, so it is often difficult to tell good from bad, right from wrong. This results when people do not understand that the fundamental choice in every decision is between separateness or love, material or spiritual values guiding their lives. They also work through the principle of "divide and conquer"—fanning differences and suspicions among friends and co-workers in groups working to create a better world. This can be seen, for example, in the necessary struggle for full and equal rights for women, as the Agni Yoga teachings note: "[T]he servants of darkness will expel women from many fields of activity, precisely where they bring the most benefit. . . . [T]he renewed struggle between the two elements, male and female, will be the most tragic one. It is hard to imagine how disastrous is such a struggle. It is a struggle against evolution itself."[5]

THE DARK LODGES

According to Alice Bailey, the Dark Forces are ruled by six Oriental leaders and six Occidental leaders and their followers who are to attack those who are doing significant work in the world to benefit humanity.[6] Viola Neal, Ph.D., and Shafica Karagulla, M.D., describe several Dark Lodges or evil groups on the inner planes. The first works with dark witchcraft to disturb the elemental fires of the earth and cause earthquakes. Another lodge works with narcotics to damage the life force (or etheric) bodies of victims and hold back their evolution. A third sabotages the education of young people, and a fourth works to sabotage the world economy and create debilitating debt. A fifth lodge works in the political field to confuse and weaken world leaders and to control them through blackmail, bribery, and assassination.[7] This lodge has been very active in recent years, and much could be learned from studying the effect of these Dark Forces on the assassinations of Abraham Lincoln, Mahatma Gandhi, John and Robert Kennedy, Martin Luther King, Lord Mountbatten, Anwar Sadat, Olaf Palme, and perhaps Pope John Paul I, among others.

ADOLF HITLER

Adolf Hitler and his Nazi inner circle consciously invoked, and were possessed by, the Dark Forces through black magic rituals that involved torture and cruelty, probably using the suffering of thousands in the gas chambers as part of their dark rituals. The passivity of the German people, and their inability to take decisive action to stop it, allowed the inflow of this ancient evil from the astral plane. The Nazi swastika distorted a sacred symbol— one that had been used by many ancient peoples, such as the Native Americans and others—representing the sun and the four directions. They reversed its direction to symbolize the antievolutionary Dark Forces of materialism.

Hitler himself was possessed by a Dark Spirit whom he called the "Superman"—the pure will to power, unmediated by love. According to some accounts, he also used drugs to alter his consciousness. Trevor Ravenscroft, in *The Spear of Destiny,* reports Hitler told his friend Hermann Rauschning that "our Party must be . . . the Order of a Secular Priesthood."[8] The forty original members of Hitler's New German Workers party were all drawn from the most powerful occult society in Germany, the Thule Gesellschaft, whose inner core was involved with seances and black magic rituals. As is the pattern with those working on the dark side, Hitler misused and distorted medieval magic for his own purposes, particularly some of the occult aspects of sound, using his voice to mesmerize. At the end of the Third Reich, many of Hitler's inner circle of Nazi leaders died of strange brain ailments, reflecting the fact that evil eventually turns back on and destroys those who use it.

Winston Churchill reportedly insisted that the black magic of the Nazi party not be revealed to the general public after the war, and the Allied prosecution and judges at Nuremberg consciously ignored the occult aspects of the Nazis' tremendous power and cruelty.[9] Churchill may have been concerned that the public would not have been able to integrate this knowledge well, resulting in increased fear. Although Hitler criticized and persecuted occultists, Freemasons, and astrologers, he spoke of his own belief in the occult and misused it, according to historians Dr. Jackson Spielvogel and David Redles.[10]

Hitler can also be seen as embodying the collective shadow of humanity, acting out an extreme scenario of separateness, racial superiority, and cruelty that most nations are guilty of to some degree. He demonstrated the dire consequences, writ large, of this approach to life. Out of this darkness, however, a positive result has emerged in a new sensitivity to anti-Semitism around the world and to racial or genocidal attacks, which are again on the rise in Germany, Bosnia, and elsewhere.

MOBILIZING THE GOOD

> "... As through a magnifying glass behold the good and belittle tenfold the signs of evil, lest thou remain as before."
> —AGNI YOGA SOCIETY[11]

While being aware of the existence of the Dark Forces, it is important not to become overly fearful or angry in our response to them or to focus too much attention on them. We are susceptible to them only through our own negative emotions, such as fear and anger, and we have a built-in protection whenever we invoke the love of our Soul or Higher Self or great Masters such as Christ or Buddha. Rather than resisting evil, we need to organize and mobilize the good and thus strengthen the hands of those working for love and the good of the whole so that evil will find less opportunity. We need always remember that love burns the Dark Forces—they cannot stand its radiation.

The role of the Forces of Light—the Enlightened Ones, or Masters of Compassion—is to stand as a wall between humanity and cosmic evil so that humanity is not overwhelmed, but still sufficiently challenged to understand the karmic results of its own choices. The Forces of Light are prepared to help humanity with organized methods and procedures for a highly constructive and creative society when we are ready. Until human beings have suffered enough and seen drastic enough results of their harmful choices, they often do not cooperate consciously with the efforts of the Forces of Light. But that time is now approaching, and it is necessary that large groups of thinking people understand clearly how the Dark

Forces contribute to the problems of humanity, so that right choices can be made.

The Forces of Light have an advantage in that they are able to forecast coming events and so can initiate moves to counter the Dark Forces. While the latter are more powerful in the material world—the physical, emotional, and lower mental (rational) levels, the Forces of Light are more powerful on the higher mental, intuitive, and spiritual planes, which insures that ultimately Light will triumph. Their work is continually to turn the effects of evil to good purposes, so humanity can learn from past mistakes. The Forces of Light are always present where there is universal love, support for human free will, and encouragement for people to learn from their choices and stand in the power of their own Spiritual Being, the Soul. As free will is a major spiritual principle for humanity, wherever there is conscious coercion or manipulation of human free choice, you will find behind it those influenced by the Dark Forces.

THE POWER OF THE LIGHT

The power wielded by those who are seeking to live as Souls in touch with the world of spiritual realities is out of all proportion to their awareness of their power and usefulness. Those who endeavor to wield spiritual force constructively and selflessly are far more potent than they realize. Wishful thinking, hoping, and praying are not as powerful as the mental intention of focused mind and will, motivated by love of humanity. It is essential to identify constructively with human pain. Sympathy that does not produce some positive action becomes a festering sore. Sending love energy to truly evil people is not helpful, as love is an impersonal power, dependent for its effect on the consciousness of those receiving it, and only irritates and intensifies their lower nature. It is more effective to send thoughts of love to strengthen those of good character who can receive it and use it for human betterment. For those leaders who possess a mixture of good and evil, like many today, it is best to focus on their Soul or Higher Self, to help draw it forth.

There are cycles in world events where Light and Darkness seem to alternate. After there is progress on the side of Light, there is often a corresponding blow from the other side. In late 1989 and early 1990, for example, the world seemed to respond to greater Light and higher impulses of freedom and human love. The Berlin Wall came down, democracy triumphed in Eastern Europe with the people's overthrow of communist dictators, Nelson Mandela and F. W. de Klerk were negotiating to end the violence in South Africa, and a new environmental awareness spread glob-

ally with Earth Day 1990. It was as if things were suddenly coming together on the earth and humanity was being given an opportunity to make
a major shift in consciousness, releasing the need for enemies and embodying a new healing Spirit.

But most people weren't ready for such a sudden major shift in their values
and perceptions of the world, and they clung to old, familiar dysfunctional
attitudes. On an inner level, many retreated spiritually, missing an opportunity. Barely six months later the world felt the influence of the dark side
again as new enemies conveniently emerged in the Middle East, resulting in
the Persian Gulf war and increased military spending and budget deficits.
Once again, violence between black groups escalated in South Africa, as did
ethnic violence in New York City, Los Angeles and Germany. And there were
increased cutbacks in environmental protection, education, and aid to the
disadvantaged because of the economic crunch. It may be that in electing
President Clinton, people seemed to say they are ready for another cycle of
Light, as his campaign emphasized healing and reconciliation, but this depends on Americans' willingness to assume what he called "shared sacrifice."

The successful resolution of the problems presented by the Forces of
Darkness allows humanity to take another step forward into the Light. The
Dark Forces play a necessary part in the Divine Plan. By overcoming the
resistance and opposition they provide, human beings grow in strength,
will, clarity, and love.

From a larger perspective, good and evil are relevant only in our limited
space and time-bound perceptions. According to Alice Bailey, "Evil per se
is nonexistent, as is good. Only in time and space are there varying states
of consciousness, producing differing outer effects."[12] In other words, in
the Mind of God, all is One, but on our human level, where duality exists,
we need to learn to choose good over evil, evolution over involution, and
spirituality over materialism. Although the Forces of Darkness can delay
the outworking of the Divine Plan because of human weakness, in the end
they cannot stop the inevitable triumph of good and the fulfillment of the
Divine plan.

DEVAS, ANGELS, AND THE INNER SIDE OF NATURE

The planetary environmental crisis looks hopeless when viewed only from
the physical, or form, level. But when seen from the inner side, things look
quite different. Nature is not a blind force, but a conscious one that works
through inner essences and energy fields. The inner forces of nature play
a key role and can be of major assistance if we can learn to cooperate with

them consciously. Pollution can be transformed, deserts can bloom, and enough food can be grown to feed the world, with the cooperation of these inner forces.

In the East, these forces of nature are referred to as "Devas," which means "Shining Ones" in Sanskrit. The Christians call these forces "Angels," and the Hopi Indians call them "Kachinas." The Ageless Wisdom teaches that they are the great builders of all that we see in the world, part of the body of Divine Mother, producing form out of energy flowing through their beings.[13] They are like beings of dancing energy that hold the blueprints or matrix for the perfect pattern of minerals, plants, and animals.

The sudden surge in popular interest in Angels reflects a growing sensitivity to these subtle realms by many people. According to *Time* magazine, 69 percent of the population now believe in Angels.

There are many different levels of evolution of Devic beings: great Archangels who rule vast dimensions of space, those who are the embodiment of qualities such as courage or wisdom, Divine messenger Angels, guardian Angels who guide humans, regional nature Angels, and nature Spirits and elementals in a forest or garden. The great Devas function like architects of physical forms, carrying within them the blueprint for each species of plant, animal, or mineral, while the nature Spirits and elementals are like builders. They include the elements of fire, air, earth, and water. Devas work in mantras and movements that produce sound, ultimately creating patterns. They sound a multidimensional note around which a life-form will grow. Every species of plant is overlighted by a particular Deva or Angel that directs the energy needed to materialize the forms of a plant, making sure that a rose turns out looking like a rose and not a daisy.

Under a high-powered electron microscope, all dense objects are seen to be made up of various particles in constant movement. And yet modern science cannot explain how these protons and electrons actually arrange themselves to produce the solid matter that we can see and touch. According to the Ageless Wisdom, the energies that create form out of subatomic particles are the Devas or Angels. Technically the electrically positive or solar (Father) aspect of electrical phenomena are the greater builders or Devas (evolutionary forces), and the electrically negative or lunar (Mother) aspect are the lesser builders or elementals (involutionary forces). From the union of Father and Mother comes the Son, or material form with its unique level of consciousness. The Devas provide the matrix for manifestation. The Ageless Wisdom offers some profound insights into electricity and the mysteries of matter through understanding of the role of the Devas.[14]

THE HEALING POWER OF NATURE DEVAS

It is beneficial for humans to spend time in nature, as we are fed by the energy fields of the Devas, and in turn our energy fields give the Devas and Angels more building blocks to work with. Consciousness of beauty in any part of the universe brings us into oneness with the whole. Our natural environment is full of forces that correspond to—and can therefore draw out—some part of our own makeup. We are influenced by our environment in many subtle ways. For example, trees not only affect the rainfall and the air, but they are essential for our mental stability, since they act as a protective skin for the earth and also convert higher forces of sunlight and cosmic radiation through the ground into energies that balance and sustain us.

It is possible to tune in to the inner life-giving state of the Devas and so link up with God's perfection. The Devas teach us that by thinking in terms of Light, we add more light to that which already exists and thus speed up the growth and enhance the beauty of all aspects of nature.

Devas work in the formless worlds and are not bound or rigid in form as humans are. They have no form themselves but are dancing whirls of energy, more like a double spiral or vortex, open at the top to the cosmos, and forming an energy cape downwards to enfold the life with which they are working. When humans attempt to communicate with them, Devas sometimes make themselves visible in a form with wings recognizable to humans from fairy tales or religious literature—such as an Angel, a fairy or gnome, as this is what most humans expect. Some may see them merely as sparks of light out of the corner of the eye.[15]

Humanity developed in part from the womb of nature and is thus a product of the Devic or Angelic kingdom, so communication is possible when we become peaceful and turn within. Individuals throughout the ages have testified to this communion and to the joy and upliftment it brings.

Connecting With the Devas

Several groups, such as communities we lived in—Findhorn in Scotland and Sirius in Massachusetts, as well as Perelandra in Virginia, started by Michelle Small Wright—have demonstrated that by cooperating with the Devic forces, healthy vegetables can be grown on sandy soil in harsh climates, insects can be minimalized, and animals can be kept out of gardens. Findhorn became world famous for its forty-two-pound cabbages and roses that grew in the snow. Experts from the British Soil Association, such as Elizabeth Murray and UN agricultural expert Professor Lindsay Robb, did research in the garden at Findhorn in its early days and concluded there must be a mysterious "factor X" (which was actually attunement with the Devas) that made this unusual garden more beautiful and productive than any in the surrounding area.

Dorothy Maclean, a co-founder of the Findhorn Foundation, dedicated herself entirely to this work in the early days of the community. Her perseverance in learning to work with the Devas and Angels helped create the famous Findhorn garden. She received many inspiring inner messages from the Devas while at Findhorn and elsewhere, messages like the following:

> You can connect with the Deva world by tuning into nature until you feel the love flow. . . . When you are lifted out of yourselves, looking into the beauty of a flower, or a sunset, or a wonderful shape of a seashell, this is an experience of the Devic world. . . . As your consciousness expands into new insights and deeper communion with your own nature, you can come into communication with the forces of nature, and work together to transform our planet.[16]

Our experiments with the Devas at Sirius Community resulted in some deep lessons. We always have a quiet time of "attunement" (at-one-ment) with the Devas in our garden before working there. We attune to the Devas of trees before we cut them and we have successfully attuned to the Devas of insects to have them leave plants. But when we tried to attune to the Deva or Spirit of the deer to ask them to stop eating our garden, we found that it took many days of meditation to get into rapport with that Deva. The deer had been hunted by the former owners of the land and trust needed to be reestablished. We also found that we could not attune to nature if we were not attuned to each other. So any conflicts had to be cleared up first. We then discovered that we could not think of nature as just the small plot of garden created by humans, but also must include the surrounding landscape and forest in our attunement.

After several months of in-depth meditation and inner work on ourselves, we were finally successful at keeping the deer fully out of the garden the next summer. We in turn offered the deer a sanctuary on our land during hunting season, and we have been delighted to see hundreds of their tracks on our land at that time. The key to successful work with the Devas is recognizing the oneness of all life, opening to it in love, and being willing to go more deeply into our own growth process.

Many people believe that the late biologist Luther Burbank of Santa Rosa, California, communicated with the forces of nature in order to achieve the amazing results and new species he developed, but he had to be very quiet about it in those days. At his former home there is a huge cactus Burbank had worked with that is very famous because it shed all of its prickly spines. While visiting there, Gordon became inwardly aware of the powerful, overlighting presence of the Deva of that cactus and asked it how long it would take for humanity to establish a cooperative relationship with the Devic kingdoms. Inwardly he heard it respond, "It will happen when humanity drops its spines toward nature." Gordon replied, "That could take quite a long time." The Deva responded, "That's all right; we can wait."

THE OVERLIGHTING DEVAS

Devas are present not only in gardens and forests, but also in cities, working with groups of people. Some of these Devas embody the energy of the landscape and the folksoul of the people, holding the blueprint for the ideals that are in the psyche of the people. An English friend of ours, Dr. William Bloom, author of *Devas, Fairies and Elves* and former professor of international politics at London School of Economics, told us about his profound experience of the great Deva who overlights London and is related to the Goddess Athena, a great Deva who was the protectress of classical Athens.

His experience came as a result of many years of disciplined meditation practice and a ten-day fast, camping out overnight near the Parliament buildings by special permission. He found that the large Deva overlighting London works with another Deva whose job is to protect Parliament and Westminster Abbey from outside thought-forms and emotions, so Parliament members can focus on just their own concerns. William sensed that this Deva contained the matrix for the democratic ideal of social justice, which allows competing ideas and interests. The Deva's purpose is to hold the perfect note for events to grow into, so that the highest good is served.

He sensed a smaller Deva, resonating to the purpose of the larger Deva, is present in the personal aura of each member of Parliament, so that the energy of democracy is held and radiated by each member. He also experienced similar Devas overlighting and protecting other democracies, such as the United States and India. We have noticed that on top of the U.S. Capitol Building is a Goddess-like statue of Freedom, which may be a representation of a similar Deva.

There are national Devas, as well as international Devas, who are working with the Enlightened Ones to bring about cooperation between nations. They work through music, art, and literature and also through politics. They help to initiate important international conferences and then overlight them to try to preserve harmony and achieve the desired result.

Devas and Human Evolution

It is important to understand that the human and Devic evolutions are separate but parallel. While our own physical, emotional, and mental bodies are composed of lower Devic or elemental substance, our Soul body is made up of higher Devic (Solar Angel) substance. Thus, the Christian teaching about guardian Angels is true, in a sense, from a metaphysical perspective as well. We are guided and protected by our Soul, which is related to what's called "The Angel of the Presence," and which many see in the form of a guardian Angel.

The difference between the lesser Devas or elementals and the greater building Devas is that the former are on the path of involution and the greater Devas are on the evolutionary path (including guardian Angels and Archangels). All life forms, including the Devas, either have been or will become human in their evolutionary history, and many of the great Devas have passed through the human stage long ages ago, according to the Ageless Wisdom, while the elementals have yet to do so.

There are many contrasts between humans and Devas, which are intended to maintain their distinct but parallel evolutions.

Humans evolve through developing conscious thought; Devas evolve through feeling. Humans seek to know; Devas seek to feel. Humans grow by developing self-control; Devas develop by being controlled. Humans evolve through shattering limiting forms that cause pain and discontent; Devas evolve through building forms. The Devas's work is with form; the Enlightened Ones work with the development of the consciousness within the form.[17]

ENVIRONMENTAL HEALING

The crises that humanity has created in the natural or human worlds can be transformed and healed through our love and cooperation with the Devas. The pollution and devastation of large areas of the planet can be restored to health if enough people consciously cooperate with these powerful forces. The Devas are overjoyed when they find members of the human race who are eager for their help. However, it is important not to try to summon or evoke the lower Devas, elementals, or nature Spirits, as this can be very dangerous. Rather we should work only with the higher Devas, from the intuitive or Soul level.

The communication from the Devas at Findhorn even holds out the promise that someday humanity could create new species of plants and animals, such as inexpensive sources of protein or drought-resistant grain. Simply by humans holding in mind the desired qualities, and asking for cooperation, the Devas could create the form desired, as long as it is aligned with the Divine Will and for the highest good of all.

THE TRANSITION IN RAY ENERGIES

In the Ageless Wisdom tradition, all of life can be seen as expressions of different cosmic energy frequencies, called "ray" energies. Each cycle of development on earth is governed by the influence of one or more of seven basic ray energies, much like the seven colors of the spectrum and seven notes on the musical scale. These rays represent seven different aspects or frequencies (or the seven Spirits before the "Throne of God," as the Christian tradition describes it) that in their totality make up all of the Divine aspects of God—the one basic energy of the universe. The various rays cycle in and out of influence on the planet over specific periods of time:

- *The First Ray of Will and Power*   governs synthesis and politics
- *The Second Ray of Love/Wisdom*   governs education and psychology
- *The Third Ray of Active Intelligence*   governs philosophy and administration
- *The Fourth Ray of Harmony through Conflict*   governs creativity, art, and beauty
- *The Fifth Ray of Concrete Science*   governs science and the rational mind
- *The Sixth Ray of Devotion and Idealism*   governs religion, healing, and devotion to causes
- *The Seventh Ray of Ceremonial Order and Rhythm*   governs creative manifestations, ritual, and business[18]

These ray influences also condition each individual's personality and Soul energies. For example, one might have a First Ray personality that is concerned with will and power and a Second Ray Soul that expresses a compassionate, inclusive wisdom. Each nation also has a soul and personality expression, as for example the United States and Russia both have Sixth Ray personalities—both idealistic and fanatical about their values. (See the next chapter for the rays of other nations.)

In addition, every type of human activity and institution expresses various ray qualities. For example, the Founding Fathers of the United States designed our three branches of government to wisely represent the first three rays (even if they may not have understood this consciously), which is why the branches provide a triangular balance for each other. At his best, the president expresses a First Ray quality of sounding a particular keynote of vision and purpose to which the country vibrates, and he then uses his will to mobilize people, synthesizing divergent interests to move in the indicated direction. At their best, the two Houses of Congress reflect a Second Ray inclusive quality of love and compassion, listening to the voice of all the people and wisely balancing special interests and the good of all. The Supreme Court, at its most enlightened, expresses a Third Ray quality of abstract thought, impersonally upholding the rule of law and striving to align human laws with higher cosmic law. At their worst, each branch of government reflects the negative, distorted aspect of each ray, such as the Congress listening to only some interests, and losing sight of what is good for the whole.

THE OUTGOING SIXTH RAY

Long cycles of activity and whole civilizations are governed by incoming and outgoing rays, which condition human life. As a ray cycles into expression on earth, new ideas, impulses, and life forces are available for changes in human life-styles and institutions. As a ray leaves expression, the underlying energy that has supported the forms of a social order is withdrawn and the structures begin their inevitable decline. Such is the situation we have in the world today.

The Sixth Ray of devotion and idealism has been a primary influence in human affairs for the past two thousand years of the Piscean era. Christ came to earth to inaugurate this cycle by providing an example of a perfected human being. The Sixth Ray energy has helped humanity develop the capacity to imagine this higher ideal and the devotion to strive to live up to Christ's ideal and other ideals. The various religious, political, and scientific ideologies that struggle for supremacy in the world today have developed through this energy of idealism and devotion to particular ideas. The Sixth Ray also contains tendencies toward fanaticism, personality worship, and the desire to impose beliefs on others—a tendency that manifests most powerfully when a ray energy reaches the end of its cycle of expression.

Significantly, all people and nations are being required to adjust to a great transition that is taking place upon the planet. At this time, the energy of devotion and idealism is waning in influence, and the Seventh Ray of ceremonial order and rhythm is entering with the emerging Aquarian era. The Seventh Ray, which links together Spirit and matter, recognizes the sacred within the physical world and provides energy for the building of new forms for civilization.

During this shift, the clashing of these two energies is producing chaos and turmoil in the world. The Sixth Ray of idealism and devotion, which is potent due to its two-thousand-year influence, is today being expressed mostly by political and religious conservatives, some of whom may be reactionaries or fanatics, although there also have been some Sixth Ray fanatical liberals or radicals, such as the Chinese Red Guards of the '60s. The Sixth Ray rules emotionalism in religion and ideologies and is thus woven into most institutions in the world. These institutions, although often resistant to change, provide a stabilizing influence in the current turbulent period. This can be seen in the emotional, ideological adherence to chauvinistic patriotism or to a dogmatic scientific ideology that may refuse to admit new data or hypotheses that contradict current theories.

THE INCOMING SEVENTH RAY

The change-over from the Sixth Ray to the Seventh Ray is occurring gradually over a long period of time, as its general radiation increases, and more and more Souls who embody this new, incoming energy are entering incarnation. The Seventh Ray energy helps human beings contact and recognize God within themselves and all humanity—God Immanent—which is the focus of today's new spirituality. It brings together Spirit and matter. The purpose of the Seventh Ray is to provide the impetus for manifesting spiritual principles here on earth, in our daily lives, in contrast with the earlier Sixth Ray, which was an otherworldly spirituality trying to reach a transcendent God beyond the sinful world.

The Seventh Ray sees all life—the planet and all peoples and species—as sacred. It is one of the hidden, inner causes underlying the global environmental movement and the efforts to beautify and purify the earth. The Seventh Ray helps energize the idea that our bodies are the temples of the Spirit and should be treated with care and reverence. This underlies the health and fitness movements to detoxify human beings of pollutants, chemical poisons in food, stress, and fatigue. Those under the influence of the Seventh Ray work with steady practicality to create new cultural forms such as worker-owned businesses and international communication systems. They work to bring forth beauty in the physical world by restoring and beautifying neighborhoods, cities, and devastated natural environments.

As the ray of ceremonial order and rhythm, the Seventh Ray brings an increased emphasis on rhythm and ritual as essential to balanced, spiritual living. It is behind the growing interest in creating new ceremonies and rituals that express the awareness that Spirit is present, immanent, in all life. An example is Joanna Macy's work with the Council of All Beings, which creates a council ritual where participants take on the role of various minerals, plants, and animals to identify with them and speak for them. The growing participation in rituals at sacred sites around the world, highlighted by the Harmonic Convergence of 1987, is another example of the Seventh Ray influence. The popularity of drumming, particularly in men's and women's groups, also reflects the incoming influence of rhythm. The Seventh Ray controls the sexual chakra, and its influence underlies the strong focus today on sexual issues of abortion, rape, sexual harassment, birth control, excessive sexual expression, and pornography.

TRANSITION CAUSING CONFLICT

The energies of the First Ray of Divine Will from Shamballa which create destruction of old forms and the Seventh Ray building energies of ceremonial order and rhythm have begun to have a major impact on the former Soviet Union and Eastern Europe. These energies are now challenging many other nations, especially in Africa and South America, through indigenous freedom and environmental movements. Their influence will continue to grow, while the Sixth Ray force of fanatical devotion to an ideology or leader spends itself—as seen in the gradual receding of Islamic fundamentalism in Iran and the discrediting of some Christian fundamentalists in the United States. The fall of dictators such as Ferdinand Marcos in the Philippines, the Duvaliers in Haiti, and Nicolae Ceausescu in Romania under the pressure of people's demands is also indicative of this changeover.

Today there are three distinct groups in each nation. One group, by far the most widespread and currently in control, is aligned with the Sixth Ray conservative element that is resisting change, but which provides stability. In some cases this group is crystallizing further into entrenched patterns of ideology, belief, and privilege—as, for example, the wealthy elites who refuse to accept responsibility to the larger whole.

A second group is composed of organizations and individuals who, although small in number, are working with the impulse of the incoming Seventh Ray manifesting energy behind them and thus have potency out of proportion to their numbers. These are the creative builders, innovators, and problem solvers of goodwill in every field of endeavor who are not fanatical but, rather, inclusive in their consciousness.

The third group are people who respond to neither the Sixth Ray nor Seventh Ray energies. Some of these people feel lost and bewildered and that life holds no desirable future for them. This group is composed of many who destroy themselves through drugs or other addictions or who live lives of hopelessness and despair, including the vast masses of poor around the world.

Conflicts today within and between nations are usually based on clashes between those who think things are fine the way they are and those who feel things are "out of order" and need to be put right. The justice and equity movements around the world are demanding a new ordering of priorities for allocating global resources, to be sure that opportunities exist for everyone to meet their basic needs. Those involved in the environmental movement see the Divine within nature and are attempting to reorganize and purify the physical world. Their work is summed up by the Seventh Ray idea of "a place for everything, and everything in its place," which is being made manifest with the rapid growth of the recycling movement. There are also some valuable syntheses of the best of the Sixth Ray Christian values of stewardship and responsibility, and the Seventh Ray emphasis on Spirit in all creation, in the growth of the Christian ecology movement.

Ultimately the way ahead for nations is to combine the best of traditional values with the energy and impetus of the new, incoming life energies. This will create a synthesis that will continue to open and expand consciousness, while maintaining enough stability to allow us to adjust to the increasingly rapid changes.

ASTROLOGICAL CORRELATIONS

Just as the sun and sunspots have been correlated with certain activities on Earth and the full moon with the tides and the crime rate, so the movements of larger heavenly bodies, the planets of our solar system, have been correlated with various changes on Earth. Astrology is the study of cosmic timing, celestial alignments and radiations from various stars and planets. The movement of Saturn, for example, is related to limitations and crystallizations, Uranus to the unexpected, Mercury to communication, and Mars to aggressive behavior. These correlations don't, of course, prove sole causation, as there are always complex, interrelated causes to any event. Human free will is a powerful determining parameter, and major events come about through the energy interaction among the spiritual realm, the planets, and human free will—as well as past causes, or karma. Thus, the wise person keeps abreast of the current influences and works with them, rather than trying to swim against the stellar currents. Understanding these currents or cycles is helpful in understanding the past and present and for preparing the future.

Like any other discipline, astrology can be practiced on many different levels, from popular newspaper forecasts to intuitive and deeply esoteric perspectives on individual and world situations. Although astrological charts can be cast precisely and mathematically, interpretation is an art. The spiritual development, intelligence, and intuition of the astrologer greatly influence the quality of the results. Although it has always been widely practiced in the East, for centuries in the West the validity of astrology has been disputed hotly by its supporters and detractors. Only in recent years is it again gaining popularity. According to a Gallup poll, 80 percent of Americans believe in astrology.[19] A 1988 survey for the National Science Foundation found that 38 percent believed astrology to be "very scientific" or "sort of scientific."[20]

Astrologers are doing a booming business on Wall Street today, with sophisticated new astrological computer software that does calculations for every trading bent from gold to T-bills. Wall Street astrologer Arch Crawford predicted a "tremendous crash" after a market top around August 24, 1987, when five planets formed a "grand trine" with Jupiter. The actual top was August 25, followed by the crash in October.[21] In the former Soviet Union, the Soviet Academy of Sciences conducted serious studies into astrology and all areas of parapsychology. A famous healer and astrologer, Dzhuna, was called to the bedside of ailing Premier Leonid Brezhnev and had an honored place on the Soviet Peace Committee.

TIMING IS ALL

Everything has its own timing and its cycle of manifestation, as we continually leave behind old values and forms and move into new expressions. Due to the precession of the equinoxes—the apparent movement of the grouping of stars we call a "sign" of the zodiac, caused by the wobble of the axis as the Earth rotates—we move astrologically from one age to another. We are leaving the age of Pisces—the watery sign of emotion, mysticism, idealism, and devotion to authority—and entering the age of Aquarius—the airy sign of the intuitive mind, electronics, group consciousness, pouring out the waters of new life through planetary service. Each age has a cycle of approximately 2,120 years. The alternation in cycles is not merely a rhythmic repetition, but rather a significant change that has direction and ultimate meaning. Each change is on a higher turn of a spiral, leading to an expanded awareness for humanity and greater depth of understanding of the Divine Purpose in evolution.

There are also shorter astrological cycles which can be correlated with world events. One configuration astrologers consider most significant is a conjunction, when two or more planets are together in the sky and their energies are concentrated and fused, becoming the seeds of a new cycle. The Uranus–Neptune conjunctions of 1993–1994, occurring once every 171 years, brought together the revolutionary change associated with Uranus with the idealism and dissolving influence of Neptune in Capricorn— the sign of material forms and institutions. This conjunction, according to astrologer Chris Hedlund, marks major breakdowns and critical developments in our intellectual, technological, and spiritual foundations, which are often transformed by major creative leaps and experimentation.

The period from 1988 to 1993, leading up to the conjunction, was characterized by a completion of the old cycle and a dissolution leading to the womb stage preparing for new development. During this period we saw the dissolution of communism under Gorbachev and completed by Yeltsin, major "restructing" in the economies of developed nations, and many social upheavals. Dissolution of empires is not uncommon during Uranus– Neptune conjunctions; between 1818 and 1825 the Spanish colonization of Latin America collapsed, and in the 1640s Cromwell overthrew Charles I in England.

In mid-January 1994 the conjunction became exact, joined by five other planets (Sun, Moon, Mars, Venus, and Mercury), which gave a major push toward creating the best future we can collectively envision. At that time, new answers and solutions were seeded that can help resolve the critical problems in our world. It was a time of birthing of new energies, with all the struggles of labor, as portrayed in the efforts of Boris Yeltsin to establish a market economy in Russia, and in the battles Clinton faced to establish a new agenda in the United States. Such a time also powerfully mobilizes the forces of resistance, as we have seen.

In the postconjunction phase, as Uranus moves away from Neptune, new frontiers are often explored, and choices are made that have resonances for the next 171 years. As a result of this conjunction, the cycle of 1994 and onward is a cycle of intense creative inspiration and opportunity for projects aimed at bettering life on the planet. Pursuits focused on creating a better quality of community, ecological health and social well-being will get a boost and breakthroughs for projects that have been incubating for years can occur.[22]

Pluto moved into Scorpio, its "home" or natural sign, in November 1984, where it will remain until 1995, as hidden negativity or corruption comes to the surface and catalyzes purification and eventual healing. We have seen things like the Iran/contragate scandal, the savings and loan scandals, Wall Street scandals, and many members of the Bush and Reagan administrations facing allegations of questionable activities.[23] Likewise, we saw exposés coming to light on supposed models of uprightness, such as former FBI chief J. Edgar Hoover.

Long denial of hidden atrocities have come to light in many countries: twelve years of murder and torture in El Salvador primarily by the government and right wing death squads; France's collaboration in the crimes of its Nazi occupiers during World War II; Japan's forcing hundreds of thousands of Korean and Asian women into prostitution for Japanese soldiers during World War II; Sicily's struggle to root out the entrenched Mafia; many high-level officials being prosecuted in Italy and Japan; and dictators such as Marcos in the Philippines, Duvalier in Haiti, and Noriega in Panama being exposed and overthrown.

On May 13, 1989, seven of the front-page stories in *The Washington Post* were about corruption of various kinds being brought to light. The John Tower, Gary Hart, Jim Wright, and Marion Barry controversies have shown that during Pluto in Scorpio very little can be kept hidden, in contrast with previous cycles. Revelations of child abuse and even sexual abuse in the clergy, as well as drug, alcohol, and food addictions (as reflected in the growing 12 Step programs), will lead ultimately to a more purified humanity. When Pluto enters Sagittarius in November of 1995, we will begin a period of exposing more light, with healing for both the earth and humanity, as Sagittarius is the sign of goals, higher mental life, religious movements, and optimism.

The surprising political changes in Russia and Eastern Europe were connected to several Saturn-Neptune conjunctions in 1989—conjunctions that occur every thirty-six-plus years. These were predicted by Mark Lerner as a "second Russian Revolution" in *Welcome to Planet Earth* magazine, as early as in 1983. The Soviet Union was born on November 8, 1917, the day of a potent Neptune station and a Saturn-Neptune conjunction. The next conjunction was in 1952–1953, during the Korean War and the death of Stalin. Saturn relates to form, structure, government, limits, and the material world. Neptune is associated with the formless, illusions, ideals, self-sacrifice, universal love, the conscious, religion, and the spiritual world. Neptune, at these times, was related to the dissolution of structures and limitations in the political world.[24]

Some astrologers have made accurate predictions of major earthquakes, and if government officials paid attention, they could be more prepared. The violent earthquake that shook San Francisco in 1989, for example, was predicted by Ann Parker three years earlier and was only three days off the exact date. The prediction was based on the completion of an eighty-four-year cycle of Uranus (which governs sudden change) and its return for a seven-year stay in the Earth sign of Capricorn. This return marked the eighty-third anniversary of the famous San Francisco earthquake of 1906.

ASTROLOGICAL CHARTS OF LEADERS AND NATIONS

There are also daily astrological cycles that can be helpful to take into account in decision making, as former President Ronald Reagan seemed to have discovered. Perhaps his use of astrology, as many claimed, was the real reason for his "Teflon image," where he seemed to sail easily through so many problems with nothing "sticking." Good timing—rather than just being a good communicator—may have been another part of his secret. His first major economic address as president, for example, was scheduled exactly on the Taurus full moon—a good time for focusing on issues of money and security. His major press conferences were often scheduled for perfect astrological timing. The signing of the INF Treaty was scheduled at exactly 1:30 P.M. on December 8, 1987, at Nancy Reagan's insistence, as Jupiter was ascending. This is commonly held by astrologers to be a good time to begin new partnerships or activities.

Former White House chief of staff Donald Regan, in his book, *For the Record: From Wall Street to Washington,* says that Nancy's astrologer friend, later identified as Joan Quigley, affected "virtually every major move and decision" made by former President Reagan during his two terms in office.[25] Joan Quigley herself says that she "briefed the President through Nancy for every meeting with Gorbachev in Geneva," advised Reagan to go to Reykjavík and "negotiate there as long and hard as possible," and was asked advice about members of Congress who had a key vote in a bill Reagan wanted passed. She claims to be responsible for the timing of all presidential conferences, State of the Union addresses, and the Reagan-Carter debate.[26]

The astrological charts of public figures need to be viewed differently from those of ordinary citizens, as the planets in their charts will be connected to events that affect the lives of many others. Their charts often symbolize a role that others have unconsciously asked them to play or a role that needs to be acted out at that time. For example, former presidential candidate Ross Perot is a triple Cancer—sun, moon, and rising sign—all in the water sign of strong, but often hidden feelings and mass

278 ◆ ◆ SPIRITUAL POLITICS

consciousness. His chart shows that he was truly in tune with and able to reach the psyche of many Americans and their desperate call for a third choice in the 1992 election.

As a Gemini, former President George Bush displayed great strengths in communication and mastery of facts, although some might argue that he lacked a clear commitment to goals or policies. Bush's sun in Gemini (twenty-one degrees plus) falls on exactly the Mars of the U.S. chart, linking him directly to the war and military aspects of the nation. He also had Mars exactly conjunct his South Node, denoting that war was the path of least resistance for him, as his military invasion of Panama and Iraq illustrated.[27]

In the chart used by most astrologers for President Clinton, Libra the sign of balance and harmony is rising and Mars, Neptune, Venus, Chiron, Jupiter, and Juno are all in the first house in Libra. Clinton represents the unifying principle and can bring us all together because he has the cosmic signature allowing this to occur, says political astrologer Mark Lerner. Clinton is a catalyst, a national agent of change, renewal, and hope. "His flaws and weaknesses may parallel and reflect our own. His pain is our pain, as he is the wounded healer who was tested in the national crucible and came out reborn, as a social healer," says Lerner. His natal Uranus (a revolutionary force bringing sudden change) at twenty-one-plus degrees Gemini is close to his North Node indicating the area of growth and destiny. His Uranus is also conjunct Mars in Gemini on the U.S. birth chart, indicating he can be a lightning rod to transform America's military—as we have already seen in the issue around gays.[28]

Vice President Gore has a North Node Ceres-Venus conjunction in Taurus, an earth sign, in his 10th house, clearly indicating his environmental commitment, according to Mark Lerner.[29]

Astrological charts can be cast for nations, cities, and organizations, using the time of their founding. If the exact time is not known, the timing of major events can be charted, and from that one can work back to determine the founding time and so cast a chart. Astrology is increasingly being used by dozens of major corporations to guide their decision making and to set the timing of start-ups and new product introductions. Chicago-based business astrologer Grace Morris, author of *Working with Businesses*, works with McDonald's, State Farm Insurance, and TCBY frozen yogurt, among many other companies. Disney companies used astrology to open their Euro Disney theme park—just as they have done with their parks in California and Florida. Financier J. P. Morgan gave his astrologer credit for his billionaire status, and President Theodore Roosevelt kept his birth chart on his desk and knew how to use it.[30]

Although there are various opinions about the exact birth chart of the United States, astrologer Dane Rudhyar says that the U.S. has Sagittarius rising, indicating self-righteousness, humanitarianism, intuition, optimism, and a religious approach. It also has Aries on the cusp of the fourth house, indicating a pioneering spirit. Libra in the midheaven of the chart indicates a proclivity for togetherness and cooperation. With Uranus in the sixth house of labor, health, service, and technology, Rudyar sees a transforming role for the United States in the evolution of humanity. The sun in the seventh house indicates the United States has a strong focus on interpersonal relationships geared to collective national enterprises.[31]

For Germany, the date of November 9, with the sun at 15–16 degrees of Scorpio, has been historically significant. On November 9, 1918, Germany became a republic. November 9, 1923, brought the first coup attempt by the Nazis—the "Beer Hall putsche." On November 9, 1938, anti-Semitic riots occurred in Germany and Austria during Kristallnacht ("Night of Broken Glass"), when 26,000 Jews were sent to concentration camps. On November 9, 1939, (at 11:20 P.M.), an assassination attempt was made on Hitler's life. And on November 9, 1989, the Berlin Wall came down.[32]

An astrological chart can also be cast for the exact time a new president is inaugurated and interpreted for the opportunities and challenges facing the new administration. For example, according to astrologer Mark Lerner, Uranus (planet of sudden, revolutionary change) was conjoined with Neptune (ideals, universal love, mass consciousness) at President Clinton's inauguration, providing awesome opportunities for spiritual growth and humanity's evolution—if Clinton doesn't get consumed with minor problems and miss the larger picture. Pluto setting in Scorpio (bringing hidden things to light) is a reminder to President Clinton and Vice President Gore to fulfill their promises about cleaning up the environment and corruption in government. Venus, ruling the inaugural chart, is sextile to the ascendant in the eleventh house, may signify inspiring input from women and an artistic revival or renaissance in the country.[33]

Inauguration day for our new presidents was changed to January 20 in 1932, just before Franklin Roosevelt was sworn in. This is the first day of Aquarius—the astrological sign of the new era we are entering and the sign of innovation and brother/sisterhood. This helps bring in a new energy that makes change easier. It's interesting that this particular date was chosen and not January 1 or 2, for instance. Could this date have been determined deliberately by those familiar with astrology?

The curious case of presidents elected every twenty years being assassinated or dying in office (as prophesied by the Indian chief Tecumseh) is the result of a Jupiter-Saturn conjunction or mutation in an Earth sign, according to astrologers. The last dates were the 1960 election (John F. Kennedy was assassinated) and 1980 (an assassination attempt on Ronald Reagan).

Major planets have been discovered by our scientists at historical times that correspond to the energy the planets represent, indicating that humanity is ready to receive that new energy and that a new stage in human evolution is to begin. For instance, Uranus, the planet representing sudden change, liberation, and new ideas, was discovered on March 13, 1781, by Sir William Herschel—in between the American and French revolutions and just twelve days after the U.S. Articles of Confederation had been signed. Not only did governments change, but major ideas about human rights and "liberty, equality, fraternity" transformed the world. Neptune, the planet of the unconscious, dreamy introspection, and mysticism, was discovered in 1846, just as psychoanalysis began and spiritualism became popular, U.S. slavery and Russian serfdom ended, and Karl Marx published the *Communist Manifesto*.[34]

Looking at world events through this cosmic lens—through seeing the effect of astrological or ray cycles, Shamballa, the battle of Light and Darkness, or the Devas—gives us a much broader framework to understand the forces at work influencing and shaping the world we know. It may also relieve some of the anxiety overly responsible, idealistic people experience when they can't change the world as easily as they would like, and it also suggests types of cosmic help that are available. Change does take place, but we need to have the very long view of the Enlightened Ones, who view the cycles of civilizations as the real timing within which to hold current events. We also need to hold the secure, inner knowing that all is working for the highest evolutionary good of all Life in the long run.

Chapter Ten

◆

THE SOUL
OF NATIONS

[E]very nation is assigned its role in a Divine scheme, has its own specific place and mission, is governed by an idea or a central meaning. [H]istory is moved by ideas in the minds of men.
—THOMAS G. MASARYK,
FIRST PRESIDENT OF CZECHOSLOVAKIA[1]

WHAT IS THE PERSONALITY OF A NATION?

The Ageless Wisdom teaches that just as each individual has both a personality and a Soul, the same can be said for nations, which results in new insights. Most nations have come into being as the result of a group or an individual who articulated in some way a tiny spark of the spiritual Soul of that nation, and who began to bring to it a sense of coherence and direction. The great Indian sage and political reformer, Sri Aurobindo, said, "The nation or society, like the individual, has a body, an organic life, a moral and aesthetic temperament, a developing mind and a Soul . . . [I]t is a group Soul that, once having attained a separate distinctness, must then become more and more self-conscious . . ."[2] Just as individuals must struggle with the process of personality integration, bringing the physical, emotional, and mental components of their personalities into a coordinated, working whole, so too must a nation become an integrated personality before it can successfully invoke its Soul.

Just as integrated, individual personalities tend to be separative, self-centered, arrogant, and materialistic, the same is true of the developed personalities of nations. Nations identified primarily with their personalities tend to be self-aggrandizing and assume their nation is superior to others. The United States, for example, is idealistic to a fault and thinks all other nations should adopt its political and economic values. England thinks it is superior to all others because of its age and long experience, while France has relied more on its brilliant intellect than on its spiritual Soul, and China has thought it could stay separate from the rest of the world to protect its authoritarian governing system.

Different social groups within a nation's population can be seen as representing the physical, emotional, and mental bodies of the national personality. For example, manual laborers, athletes, and body builders and all those who focus their consciousness primarily on physical reality represent the physical energy and body of the nation. Those who focus essentially on the emotional plane, including therapists and entertainers, represent the emotional body of a nation.

The mental body is defined by the intellectuals, scientists, corporate executives, media commentators, and political leaders—the organizing minds who direct the thought and life of the society into the directions they determine. They have the capacity to exercise control over the daily activities of emotionally focused people, which they do by establishing social institutions with which most people comply. This is analogous to a developed individual's mind generally controlling his or her emotions.

SUBPERSONALITIES

According to Donald Keys, former World Federalist representative to the UN and founder of Planetary Citizens, all the various interest, ethnic, and religious groups within a nation represent its "subpersonalities"—internal groups within the nation that correspond to the conflicting voices often found in individual personalities. Just as individuals must struggle to harmonize and integrate their many subpersonalities, such as an internal judge or a martyr subpersonality, so too must a nation integrate the divided energies in the national life represented by the many internal groups with different and conflicting values, ideas, and goals. Thus, the energy of an ethnic or minority group with urgent unmet needs will be largely lost to the nation until that group is accommodated and its reasonable needs satisfied.[3] An example of this in the United States is the loss of the labor and talents of poor minorities who cannot obtain adequate training and support. Racial violence and "ethnic cleansing" are the extreme results of suppressing subpersonalities.

The former Soviet Union was an attempt to superimpose a national structure on a collection of cultural and ethnic groups that were never integrated into national life. The suppression of these ethnic identities made it difficult to maintain the country's internal balance or create stable, balanced relationships with other countries. The passionate ethnic/religious hatreds were barely contained within the fabric of that nation, showing the lack of emotional balance and mental control within the national personality.

When the authoritarian control of the Communist party ended (which could be seen as controlling superego) and the Soviet Union broke apart, fanatical tribalism and ethnic violence erupted in many of the new republics. The cleavage that existed between the party and its ideology (mental level) and the masses of the people who labor for a living (physical) pointed out a lack of integration between the mind and body of the nation. The emotional, mental, and spiritual repression of seventy years of Communist rule resulted in the need for a cathartic outpouring of anger, frustration, and demands, which was expressed in outspoken articles, strikes, public demonstrations, and republics declaring their independence. The resulting conflicts continue to devastate the former republics.

Two major subpersonalities in the United States (and in many nations) are the conservatives, who both maintain stability and resist change because they are benefiting from the system as it is, and the progressives, who are pushing for change as creative builders, innovators, and problem solvers in many fields of endeavor who sometimes push too fast.

Powerful special-interest groups can represent conflicting voices or subpersonalities in the corporate personality of national life and be laws unto themselves. Thus, economic interests with narrow, self-oriented goals often wield sufficient power to convince the leadership and citizens of a nation that their wishes and well-being represent the interest of the nation as a whole. Corporate CEOs, until recently, had convinced Americans that their inflated salaries were good economics and good for their companies. However, we have now discovered that what's good for General Motors is not necessarily good for America. Likewise, liberals have overloaded the nation with debt through well-meaning social welfare programs, while conservatives have built up debt through overkill in the defense budget and bailing out corrupt financial institutions.

The leadership of a nation can become narrowly identified with a particular group, just like an individual whose sense of self is habitually identified with only one or a few of the many elements within the personality. In both the individual and national cases, *disidentification* from specific parts is needed for the emergence of the true Soul identity—one that is capable of accepting and integrating all separate elements. Then the nation can move into expressing higher-quality ideas and energies, such as a synthesis of liberal and conservative positions, within itself and within the world community. An example of the coordinated functioning of the national personality aligned with higher Soul purpose was the joint effort of many different groups in the Unites States during World War II, which created a unified national energy that people still talk about today.

Just as there can be dysfunctional individual personalities controlled by a dominant, pathological subpersonality (an unintegrated element within the personality), so nations can be controlled by the inflated ego of a dominant individual. Ceausescu's Romania and Kim Il Sung's North Korea (representing the extreme of totalitarian egomania), Marcos's Philippines (acting out limitless greed and corruption), Khomeini's Iran (illustrating worship of a distorted personality), and Saddam Hussein's Iraq (manifesting the endless thirst for more military power), are examples of some of these potential problems.

Pathological patterns within a nation's psyche can also contribute to the emergence of pathological leaders, as many psychologists have noted. Adolf Hitler was subjected to severe beatings as a child by parents who were expressing the accepted child-rearing philosophy of their times, which advised parents to drive out the child's "animal" nature so that a "civilized" one could take its place. Joseph Stalin was also an abused child, illustrating how unexamined attitudes and practices of a nation can create dire long-term karmic results.

NATIONS SCORED ON GLOBAL VALUES SCALE

As one indication of whether a nation is usually expressing its Soul or its personality, we can look at votes at the United Nations, scored for support of world order values such as minimizing violence, maximizing social and economic well-being, realizing fundamental human rights, and maintaining environmental quality. In a study done a few years ago by Donald Keys, we see Mexico (88.7 percent), Kenya (88.2 percent), Ghana (88.1 percent), Zambia (87.2 percent), Ecuador (87.1 percent), and Singapore (87.1 percent) having the highest scores in their voting records at the United Nations.

The Nordic nations—Sweden (84.2 percent), Finland (82.4 percent), Norway (76.5 percent), Iceland (74.8 percent), and Denmark (73.5 percent)—have very high scores as well, probably because they have relatively small and homogeneous populations, long periods of stable government, freedom from internal strife, and relative success in meeting the basic needs of the populace.

Thus, the lack of divided energies and a greater unity in national life has often resulted in the maturity to support the development of other nations. Third World nations tend to vote for the good of the whole because they know it is the most likely way to have their own needs met, since they are at the bottom of the international pecking order.

In contrast, the larger, developed nations tend to have more internal diversity and express more self-interest in the international arena, often believing that their views should be given more weight than those of other nations. They suffer from an attitude of superiority, fearing that they will lose their greatness and uniqueness if they become a subordinate part of a greater whole. According to Keys's study, the United States has one of the lowest scores at the UN (35.5 percent), followed by the fairly low scores of other Security Council members: United Kingdom (49.3 percent), France (54.4 percent), USSR (60.1 percent), and China (61.4 percent)— voting patterns that reflect strong self-interest.[4]

This pattern illustrates the challenge that developed and integrated individuals or nations face when they have greater power than those around them. Will they use their power only for their self-interest or grow into the Soul awareness that knows one's own good proceeds from the growth of all? The greater, systemic truth is that when each nation in the whole is strengthened and balanced, the stronger nations are also enhanced by greater peace, stability, increased trade, and cultural exchanges.

Nations are not going to disappear in the near future. But they can become the building blocks of a true new world order, if we learn how to invoke their Souls and a greater Soul consciousness within their populations. Citizens will have to demand that their countries start realizing that the survival of our planet depends on nations' considering their own interest within the context of larger planetary needs.

Some aspects of national sovereignty have already eroded in recent years—especially in economics and defense. "The last time Germany's Bundesbank raised interest rates, the Bank of England followed suit within an hour," *The Washington Post* reported. "The nervous systems of the major national economies have become linked like Siamese twins. If one country raises taxes or fails to provide adequate schools or infrastructure, firms are likely to move elsewhere. Similarly, defense has become a collective concern."[5] Indeed, the United States and the former Soviet Union at one point seemed to be disarming with the same speed and competitiveness they used in building up the arms race. As this process of planetization proceeds, the importance of national boundaries will gradually be diminished, as exchanges of information, capital, resources, and technology become more important than lines on a map.

INVOKING THE SOUL OF A NATION

Whenever we emerged victorious, it was primarily because of spiritual superiority rather than physical power, and whenever we were defeated, the fault always lay in a lack of our spiritual strength, moral courage, and stamina.

—FRANTISEK PALACKY,
CZECH HISTORIAN AND STATESMAN

Once a nation has become integrated, successful, and powerful, its evolution does not stop there, as most people think. Just as with the individual, once the personality of a nation is fully developed, the fulfillment and apotheosis of its existence is to invoke, contact, and express the nation's Soul, its inner, spiritual potential.

Georg Hegel, one of the West's great philosophers, saw pure Spirit incarnating into the world, not just as one great beam of Light, but as refracted Light of many different rays. He described these rays as incarnating into particular geographical regions that have an ecological integrity or clear boundaries. The local ecology—fauna, flora, and humanity—interacts with the incoming ray of Spirit, and the result of that interaction eventually becomes a nation. Thus, each geographical community has its own ray of Spirit, which, as it incarnates, creates the emergence of the *volkgeist*, or folksoul. The folksoul, which also has been described as an overlighting Angel or Deva, carries the unique energy of its people and can be seen manifesting in the culture, songs, and myths of its people. This loose-knit grouping of peoples eventually unifies as the Spirit of the nascent nation incarnates more fully. Eventually the Soul of the nation begins to express through the sophisticated form of the state, with all its social forms and laws of great complexity, which embody the ever-growing collective learning and wisdom of its people.

The Soul of each nation holds the inner pattern for the nation's development. This includes its historical unfoldment; integration of major ethnic and racial constituencies; understanding of national karmic issues that need to be lived through and resolved; fulfillment of its higher purpose; and, ultimately, self-transcendence and identification with the whole. This Soul dimension or synthesized, collective identity inwardly knows the purpose and goals not only of that nation, but of the whole community of nations. This Soul of the nation, if invoked, helps inspire national leaders to make decisions for their nation that will further the evolution of the planet. It recognizes unity of consciousness and multiplicity of form. It leads to compassion for, and ultimately identification with, all the nations and peoples of the world. This continuing national evolution ultimately leads to national self-transcendence, a higher level of energy, and a greater, more inclusive national purpose. Eventually, in the more advanced stages, a nation even makes national sacrifices for the good of other nations.

The role that Great Britain, led by Sir Winston Churchill, played during World War II is an example of an individual focusing a nation's Soul purpose. His famous quote promising people of England only "blood, sweat, and tears" in their ultimate struggle to resist Hitler's Third Reich was an invocation of Soul sacrifice for the common good. The voluntary relinquishing of outer worldly power in response to the inner promptings of the Soul asks a nation to do what is right regardless of the national cost. This was demonstrated to a certain degree by Great Britain in a wise and relatively bloodless withdrawal from her colonies during the waning of her personality power, as she began the long process of integrating her personality with her Soul. This process continues today with Britain finally realizing, after twenty years of violence in Northern Ireland, that it must allow the people to decide their future.

An invocation of the Soul is made when the personality of the nation asks for spiritual help, which happens when the collective cry for change or help arises from the people of a nation. This invocative cry then meets with a response from spiritual sources, as it must under spiritual law. This spiritual aid can be in the form of new ideas, new vision, a fresh infusion of energy to achieve a higher purpose, the emergence of new leaders, or protection from enemies. The process of invocation, whether by an individual or a nation, needs to be preceded by integrating, purifying, and controlling the personality as a fit instrument for higher impulses. If not, shadow elements can distort any higher energies invoked.

As the shadow elements in the national psyche are gradually cleansed through painful experience, national "soul-searching," and ultimately corrective action, the nation's Soul, its higher values and impulses, can manifest more fully. The Soul itself expressing through Soul-infused personalities, when invoked, will do its work of destroying limited aspects of the personality, attracting new energy, and rebuilding the national personality. The effort made to eliminate institutionalized racism in the United States as a result of the 1960s civil rights movement is one example of this type of cleansing process. It was part of the country's cleansing of the karma of participating in slavery.

The efforts of individuals and groups who are truly working for inclusive solutions to problems help invoke the Soul of their nation, such as the Institute for the Arts of Democracy in California. Whatever draws out the highest impulses, brings forward progressive ideas, helps win a victory over fear, inspires to self-sacrificing efforts, or promotes beauty and nobility in national life helps to invoke the Soul of the nation. Individuals and groups can invoke the Soul of a nation by consciously calling for its influence, meditating on its qualities, and praying for assistance. (See "Meditation for the Soul of a Nation" in chapter 13.)

EXAMPLES OF SOUL-INFLUENCED NATIONS

The Soul of America responds to every form of idealism and humanitarianism and to compassion for all suffering. The Soul of Russia responds to comradeship, to sharing, and to linking the cultural gifts of East and West. Great experiments in fusing many racial types are going on in both the United States and the republics of the former Soviet Union, both very different and yet equally important experiments in government by the people.[6]

The Soul of Great Britain has been a great champion of liberty against autocracies, such as Philip II of Spain, Louis XIV of France, and Kaiser Wilhelm and Adolf Hitler in Germany. The Soul of Japan expresses a great degree of loyalty, sacrifice, hard work, reverence for moral codes, and orderly organization. (A more complete exploration of the Soul of various nations follows later in this chapter.)

An example of this invocatory process of the Soul is the resolution of the war in El Salvador in Central America, which cost the country twelve years of bloodshed and 75,000 lives. All sides to the conflict ultimately invoked peace, a Soul quality, and created a "negotiated revolution," according to Alvaro de Soto, UN special mediator. After twenty-one months of U.S.–sponsored negotiations, both sides—the revolutionaries and the government elites—compromised instead of battling until one side triumphed. The negotiated agreements include human rights and judicial guarantees; reform and reduction of armed forces; and economic, land, and social reform. Although the grinding poverty of this country remains, efforts to resolve disputes have moved from the military battlefield to the political arena and dialogue of all kinds is under way. Here we see an example of the Soul of a people beginning to come through after enough suffering has proved the futility of divisive conflict and purified the country of some of its hatred.

Argentina, through the suffering and oppression of a military dictatorship under General Leopoldro Galtieri and the humiliation of the Falklands war with Britain, had an opportunity to purify itself of some of its darker tendencies. After the defeat it was revealed that certain strains of Nazi-like anti-Semitism existed in the military. After the generals were discredited by the war, debt, and inflation, there was a popular election and a democratically elected president, Raul Alfonsin, emerged. Although some former military junta leaders were put on trial and their kidnapping and murder of many citizens was exposed, Alfonsin chose to avoid major retribution for military excesses. This allowed some cleansing of the evil of the past, forgiveness, and the possibility of a further step in Soul development for the people of Argentina.

As with individuals, the Soul of a nation is often called upon only in times of great need or emergency, such as during war, famine, or oppression. A good example of this was the great French contribution to world evolution that emerged during their revolution of 1789—the Declaration of the Rights of Man. This document enunciated the principles of freedom, equality, and brotherhood as rights for all peoples, during a period of upheaval and bloodshed in that nation's life. This document was part of the planetary evolution of human rights that included the signing of the Magna Carta during the reign of England's King John in 1215; the Declaration of Independence in the United States in 1776; and the Atlantic Charter and the Four Freedoms signed in 1941 by Franklin D. Roosevelt and the Allies, which later became the United Nations' Universal Declaration of Human Rights. These documents have codified, strengthened, and steadily expanded the rights and responsibilities of all people throughout the world and are examples of the touch of the Soul influencing the personalities of various nations, resulting in evolutionary progress for all humanity.

Another way the Soul of a nation is invoked is when either a sufficient number of citizens become more Soul-infused or when an inspired leader, along with his or her accompanying Soul group, emerges as a true or partial expression of the Soul of the nation and is willing to take difficult action for the greatest good of all people in that nation. Mikhail Gorbachev is an example of a Soul-inspired leader who offered a clear choice between the imposed values of the past based upon separation, fear, and selfish isolation and the new Soul values of sharing, cooperation, and goodwill emerging from a recognition of the underlying oneness of humanity.

Gorbachev, and the people working with him at the time (who were likely a group of Souls who incarnated to carry out the work of transforming the former Soviet Union's government), realized that for the good of the people of his nation and of the world, he had to stop the repressive totalitarianism and the endless arms race and its accompanying economic and moral ruin. He was able to transform a climate of repression and fear into one of open dialogue and debate—at the cost of his own political future.

PERSONALITY AND SOUL EXPRESSION IN NATIONS

To sum up the difference between a nation's personality and its Soul, we might see Soul expression in the following paraphrase of John F. Kennedy's famous statement: "Ask not what the world can do for your country, but what your country can do for the world." When a nation is governed primarily by its personality, it will be materialistic and self-seeking and see itself as the center of the world. There will be an attempt to manipulate relations with other nations solely for its own advantage, and there will be little likelihood of cooperative group effort. The world will be viewed through the lens of *realpolitik* (the politics of expediency), and all relations will be seen as a struggle for power and dominance. This type of expression governs most nations in the world today.

There are struggles within any national psyche between those elements representing the Soul and those representing the personality. But, ultimately, in the long sweep of evolution, the Soul will come to overlight and control the personality of a nation. To the degree that Soul impulses are not heeded and the lower desires are allowed to dominate, there will be problems and even disaster in the national life. In many countries around the world, such as the Philippines, Haiti, El Salvador, Brazil, and Mozambique, there are extreme inequities between a small number of landed, wealthy families and massive numbers of destitute people. This imbalance results in conflict and violence, the end product of control by the personality-centered values of selfishness and separativeness.

Where there is long-standing racial or ethnic antagonism that crystallizes into hatred, such as the old animosities among Serbs, Croats, and Muslims in the former nation of Yugoslavia, there will inevitably be an outer explosion of these inner destructive attitudes. This has resulted in the brutal civil war and "ethnic cleansing" of Muslims by Serbs that erupted in that country in 1992.

Crises present opportunities for a fresh look at national priorities and purpose. They often signal a conflict between the values of the Soul and those of the personality. The oil crisis of the 1970s was an opportunity for the Western industrialized nations to examine their inefficient and wasteful life-style and to develop energy-saving technologies and a simpler way of life. Although more fuel-efficient cars were an interest for a time, ultimately the people of the United States went back to costly, fuel-wasting cars, while Japan dramatically increased its energy efficiency.

In the longer sweep of the evolution of a nation, it first develops its personality through selfishness and self-expression, then it learns from experience the Laws of Life, eventually invoking higher purpose and ultimately fusing with its Soul. This is done by strengthening its national will through developing self-discipline rather than self-indulgence, looking ahead and evaluating the future results of current choices, and willingly choosing to live by higher principles. The national will then aligns with the higher Divine Will and becomes a gift to humanity rather than an obstruction to evolution. An example of this was the ancient Athenian city-state.

THE LEARNING TASKS OF NATIONS TODAY

All the nations of the world face certain shared tasks that each must successfully complete before there can be a larger worldwide synthesis of nations. From an astrological point of view, with the planets Saturn, Uranus, and Neptune currently positioned in the sign of Capricorn, where they are keeping up a relentless pressure for structural transformation, every nation will be forced to confront and restructure the shadow side of its national life. Whether it is the helpless victim attitude in underdeveloped countries or the exploitive, dominating attitude of wealthy nations, each will be offered opportunities to examine separative, limited attitudes and to make changes in these areas of consciousness.

This means that in the decade of the nineties, ethnic hatreds, corruption, economic imbalances, and exploitive power will all be challenged, as we have seen in the bloody ethnic clashes and violence in the former republics of Eastern Europe and the Soviet Union. The way through these challenges is honest self-appraisal as a nation and the willingness to forgive the past and change harmful attitudes and practices.

An outstanding example of this process is Nelson Mandela. Through his forgiveness of the South African apartheid government for his twenty-seven years of imprisonment, as well as through his steadfast adherence to his principles, Mandela raised collective human consciousness around the world. He opened the doorway for a negotiated settlement of his nation's racial problems leading to elections by all the people. Forgiveness of the past is also the key to solving the seemingly intractable problems of the Middle East, but all sides must be ready to release past grievances to build a better future together if the peace agreement is to become a reality in people's daily lives. As Helena Roerich said, "Unity is the lightwinged dream of humanity; when the dream approaches fulfillment, only a few followers remain. The transformation of intention into action drives the majority away."[7]

The learning task for nations that already have a tradition of freedom, such as the United States, is to extend the same rights we enjoy to others, by being especially scrupulous about the effects of our actions and dealings on other nations. Wealthy nations must change their practice of supporting repressive dictators who are seen as allies. Developed nations who contribute the most to global pollution must commit to reductions and provide aid to developing nations for energy-efficient, sustainable technologies. For those nations emerging from the shadows of repression, such as countries of Eastern Europe and the former Soviet Union, the Soul lesson entails learning about the individual and national self-responsibility that must accompany their new freedom.

This learning about individual freedom is gradually being accompanied by learning about each individual's responsibility to the whole—because each individual is an inherent part of humanity. From all this learning emerges a new vision of human diversity as an enrichment of the whole. The present trend of ethnic groups and nations to affirm their identity by separating from what they see as the tyranny of the larger whole will end when that larger whole, backed up by world economic and political structures, is no longer authoritarian or oppressive toward difference, or minorities, but expressive of the inclusive, centripetal force of the Soul, which holds all things within the circle of Divine love.

THE SOUL AND SPIRITUAL DESTINY OF THE UNITED STATES

Each nation has a spiritual destiny—to embody the highest ideals to which its Soul aspires. As Americans, we personally began to explore the spiritual destiny of this country fifteen years ago, after an inspiring trip across the country visiting many beautiful national parks and meeting many ordinary Americans. After much in-depth research and meditation work, we created a slide show entitled "The Spiritual Heritage and Destiny of America," which we presented to thousands of people all over the country, including some on the White House and Pentagon staffs. In discussions following the presentation, we often discovered that people had been so disillusioned with the United States that they couldn't see anything positive in the nation. The perspective we shared, exploring the nation's spiritual destiny and also its distortions, opened new doors for them, and brought a new sense of hope for the future. We'd like to offer here some sample perspectives on the spiritual destiny of the United States and of several other nations, and then encourage you to explore the spiritual destiny of other nations.

Freedom is the keynote of the United States, the very breath of her national life, and the innermost signature of her Soul. Americans were given the freedom to choose their own path of development, along with wide-ranging religious and civil liberties never before granted in the history of the world. The key to the right use of freedom is in living and applying the truth in one's own life—especially the one engraved on all our currency: "In God We Trust." Personal achievement and self-actualization—development of one's full potential—are honored, with each citizen guaranteed the right to the "pursuit of happiness" in our founding documents. Now, the country's next evolutionary step is redirecting the desire for improving our material standard of living to one of improving our character.

The personality of the United States often distorts freedom into irresponsible license and self-will, to the detriment of others. As it is said in Agni Yoga, "Only he who has gone through the discipline of the Spirit can realize how stern the reality of freedom can be."[8] The quest for individuality and self-expression needs to become the quest for universality—to become fully oneself and fully united with others. Unity in diversity is the solution: respecting individual differences but affirming the underlying commonalities.

As a "melting pot" with many diverse races and cultures, the United States is learning to live another of the profound mottos engraved on its money: E Pluribus Unum—"Out of Many, One." Living with so much diversity is helping to develop tolerance in the national psyche and pointing to the need for a spirit of unity. Since people from every nation on earth have become citizens of the United States, this has helped us create etheric energy links with all nations. The racial complexion of the American population has changed more dramatically in the past decade than at any other time, as nearly one in every four Americans now has African, Asian, Hispanic, or Native American ancestry. Some see this as the dawning of the first universal nation.

Another Soul ideal that the United States is seeking to embody is human equality—a recognition of the inherent dignity of each individual, regardless of race, sex, class, or religion. To honor this proposition, each citizen has been accorded equal rights and opportunities. On a deeper level, this is a wise recognition of the inner Divinity of us all and our equal potential, even if not yet fully actualized. Learning to express and live with this Divine principle of equality is teaching Americans the importance of right human relationships. It is the deeper spiritual reason for welcoming (until recently) refugees of every race and nationality—receiving a gift from each and in turn bestowing something of America's priceless heritage of freedom upon all. She has thus become a beacon of light and hope to the more subjugated and oppressed peoples of the world who also dream her dream of freedom.

Historically, the United States' founding principles have all encountered distortions. But we can also see their higher counterparts:

PRINCIPLE	HISTORICAL DISTORTION	HIGHER CORRESPONDENCE
EQUALITY Equality of all before the law.	SLAVERY Racial, economic, social forms of inequality and exploitation.	UNITY IN DIVERSITY Recognizing the unity of a people while respecting diversity.
LIFE Individual right to the fundamental necessities of life.	ANTI-LIFE ATTITUDES Undervaluing the lives of others who are different through unfair social, economic, military policies.	LIFE MORE ABUNDANTLY Sharing the abundance of our physical, emotional, intellectual, and spiritual life with all others.
LIBERTY Freedom of speech, press, assembly, religion.	LICENSE Irresponsible greed, selfishness, lack of self-control.	HIGHER SELF-GOVERNANCE Using free will to choose the highest good of all.
HAPPINESS Right to pursue one's individual path to happiness and personal growth.	OVERCONSUMPTION Materially defined happiness and comfort, with possessions as status symbols.	TRUE JOY Discovering and fulfilling one's life purpose in serving others, and striving towards the unknown.

In *Conversations with John*, philosopher David Spangler writes:

The United States has particular responsibility to "be about its Father's business," and to honor the spiritual sources and visions that gave it birth. It is a planetary nation, emerging not from a particular race or people, but from the efforts, hopes, and dreams of men and women of all races and nations. It is the site of a great planetary experiment, a human experiment; the United States emerged with a destiny to serve humanity in ways no other country has ever done before. [I]t was ordained to be the trustee of hope and service for humanity in this time. . . . To respond with force and power to the needs of humanity will not be successful; the lessons of this decade will be to discover that there are true limits to power. . . . If the U.S. fails to meet its challenge, there are other countries that will do so.[9]

Each nation is overlighted by a Devic or Angelic presence, which helps guide and protect its evolution. The Angel of America, however, existed long before this nation came into being, says Spangler, as it is a planetary Angel whose work is not to help this nation survive, but rather to help harvest, digest, and thus produce seeds for a whole new cycle of development for humanity. The spiritual destiny of America is to provide the initial stages for the emergence of a planetary culture, which other nations must then contribute to and fill out. America is the home of a powerful spiritual force incarnating on the planet, and its institutions of government and business are space-time constructs trying to express a new energy from the timeless realms. The Soul of America seems most tangible in the great monuments in Washington, D.C., built to honor the ideals of Washington, Jefferson, and Lincoln, the nation's secular temples that are invocative of ancient Greece. Meditating at these monuments can be of great spiritual help to the country.

When the United States does not respect the freedom of other nations, or the Divine equality of other peoples besides her own, she violates her deep Soul purpose. If freedom and equality are sacred principles, their sacredness cannot end at her own borders. The United States has to transcend her immature need to tell the world what to do and impose her particular values on others. Americans are often seen as being very idealistic and generous, but also very naive and arrogant.

The immature personality of the United States was evident in her expression of "Manifest Destiny"—a belief that all land across the continent was meant to belong to her and so could be greedily grabbed without regard for its original inhabitants, the Native Americans. The selfish personality of the U.S. shadow is also seen in her refusing to sign the international Law of the Sea treaty, as well as in her self-serving invasions of Grenada and Panama and in ignoring international law when it serves her self-interest, such as mining the harbors of Nicaragua.

Just as an individual who is wealthier and more powerful has a greater spiritual responsibility to others, so does the United States have a greater responsibility to the world. She needs to expand her identity to include the rest of the world and transcend self-interest. As President Kennedy said in Berlin, *"Ich bin ein Berliner"*—"I am a Berliner"—meaning that the fate of others who suffer injustice in the world is also our own fate; we are not separate. The United States needs to grow into the realization that her own needs can be met in honoring the needs of other nations. She can become a catalyst for a win/win rather than win/lose solution to world problems. Group consciousness is the next step for humanity, as we expand our identification from our family to our community to our nation and, finally, to the planet.

Humanity is still emerging from a long cycle of identification with the physical form, rather than with the Divine presence within each individual. This identification has caused human beings to place an overemphasis on an individual's racial, cultural, and ethnic background, rather than seeing them as Souls occupying different forms.

NATIVE AMERICAN CONTRIBUTIONS

A Hopi Indian legend says that they were to look to the East for the return of their lost white brother, for he was to bring a missing stone tablet to match the one the Hopis already had. The lost white brother had traveled to the East to develop, record, and invent things. However, when he returned, he did not recognize these Native Americans as his brothers. He killed most of them and pushed those remaining off their sacred lands and onto reservations. The white man had developed the mind, while the Native American developed the heart—and we see this symbolically as the two halves of the stone tablet that must be reunited if America is to fully express her Soul and her true spiritual destiny.

Learning to deal with these original inhabitants of the land provides a major test in right relationship for us today, according to David Spangler: "[I]lls visited upon traditional peoples, such as the Indians of North America, may result in karmic reactions from forces within the Earth to whom these people are deeply related. American culture's present relationship to these people and to the land is part of the initiation that the United States is passing through to test its worth as a leader of the world's peoples into a new age. The traditional people throughout the world are the remnant of a much older civilization . . . which has left a profound spiritual legacy for our use, not as a teaching, but as a force within the Earth. The remnants of these civilizations are like the children of that force. How you deal with its children will influence how it can deal with you."[10]

Significantly, the U.S. Articles of Confederation and the Constitution were based on Native American principles, although most Americans don't realize this. Our systems of checks and balances, popular participation in decision making, direct representation, states' rights, and bicameral legislatures were part of the Great Binding Law of the Iroquois Confederacy, dating back to 1400, which served as a source of inspiration for Ben Franklin.[11]

THE SYMBOLISM ON OUR GREAT SEAL

The United States is the only country with a two-sided national seal. The reverse of the Great Seal of the United States, which wasn't used for 150 years until FDR put it on the dollar bill, is a symbol of the spiritual destiny of America. The Eye of God on the seal is a symbol representing spiritual vision that was used in many secret societies, including the Rosicrucians and the Freemasons. The pyramid is a symbol of material power and was used by many ancient cultures as an initiation chamber. The triangular All-Seeing Eye of God is being placed above the incomplete four-sided pyramid of materialistic life—symbolizing our need to use our material abundance with spiritual vision. From the lower level of the pyramid there are many different viewpoints, depending on which of the four sides one is looking from. But at the top, all the viewpoints unite, and there we can see with the Eye of God.

On the Great Seal are several Latin phrases. *Annuit Coeptus* ("God Favors our Undertakings") and *Novus Ordo Seclorum* ("The New Order of the Ages") reflect America's esoteric motto in the metaphysical teachings, "I Light the Way." America often initiates evolutionary change in the world—illuminating the path for others to follow. *E Pluribus Unum* ("Out of Many, One") not only reflects the unity of the original thirteen states, but on a deeper level reflects the law of God—the One expressing through the many.

The eagle on the front side is the bird of Zeus, the incarnation principle of the Deity descending into the field of time, the world of opposites, as Joseph Campbell says. In one foot the eagle holds a sheaf of arrows, symbol of war, and in the other the olive branch of peace. Unlike in traditional heraldry, the bird looks to the west, to peace, rather than to war.

Numerologically, the number thirteen embodies a key quality for the United States, as it appears repeatedly in the Great Seal as well as being the number of original colonies. Throughout the seal the number 13 is used thirteen times—in the number of stars, clouds around the stars, stripes, arrows, leaves and berries in the olive branches, feathers in the tail, layers of stones in the pyramid, number of letters in *E Pluribus Unum* and in *Annuit Coeptus*, and the number of letters (three times thirteen) in the title: "The Coat of Arms of the United States of America." Thirteen is the number of transformation, as it adds the catalyzing number one to the completed cycle of the magical twelve—the twelve disciples plus Christ, the twelve signs of the zodiac plus the sun, the twelve knights of the round table plus King Arthur.[12] For better or worse, the United States has had a major transforming role in the world—sometimes positively, as with her exportation of democracy, and sometimes negatively, as with her exportation of an excessively materialistic life-style.

RAYS OF THE UNITED STATES

The United States has a Sixth Ray personality, which means that it is governed by devotion and idealism. This is why she becomes fanatical about her ideals of democracy and capitalism and tries to impose them on others. The ray of America's Soul is the Second Ray, of love and wisdom, which reflects a deep humanitarianism and compassion for the needs of others.

According to Alice Bailey, the United States, Britain, and Russia are the great fusing energies or vital centers present on the earth and have a major role to play in the destiny of the planet. Because they are in a position to fuse and blend many types of people, are far-visioned in their world purpose, are basically unselfish in their intent, and because their governments are fundamentally for the people, they will strike a keynote for human living that will greatly influence other nations.[13]

Note: Having been born in the United States, lived here most of our lives, studied U.S. history and politics, and meditated here for many years, we found it relatively easy to contact the Soul of the United States. However, we would also like to present some initial thoughts on the Souls of other, more diverse nations, to stimulate further study and meditation on the part of our readers. Since we haven't spent any time in the following countries we discuss (except Britain and India), our information is necessarily colored by having to rely on secondhand reports in the literature and U.S. media, and from friends and expatriates here.

THE SOUL AND SPIRITUAL DESTINY OF RUSSIA

Before the collapse of communism, the United States and the former Soviet Union were mirrors for each other on a deep level—symbolizing the yin and yang of world politics. While the United States emphasized the primacy of the individual, the former Soviet Union valued the collective above all and emphasized sacrifice for the whole. During the period of Communist party repression, the Soviet people have supported and relied on each other to a greater degree, valuing family more than in the United States, where affluence has often led to greater isolation and alienation.

When Mikhail Gorbachev promoted openness—*glasnost*—and restructuring—*perestroika*—he began to change the internal balance of energies in the former Soviet Union. Then Boris Yeltsin opened the door to capitalism.

A bit of Western energy began to grow in the East, although resisted by old hard-line Communists and the masses frightened by change.

In the West, some of our major accomplishments—as well as our problems—stem from the fact that we are all socialized to glorify our separateness and uniqueness, and to compete constantly with each other. In reality, however, we are not separate, but are all connected within the One Life. There may be something for the West to learn from the Communist motto "From each according to his means, to each according to his need," as it acknowledged the great spiritual principle of sharing, even though it wasn't fully embodied in the former Soviet Union. Truly meeting the basic needs of all, the beauty of mutual service, and the importance of constructive work are great expressions of the Russian Soul that may one day be realized. Russians are unusually generous to friends and guests and often make tremendous personal sacrifices for them. The Communist ideal at its highest taught the sense of connection and caring for the needs of one's brothers and sisters. But cynicism grew when the old Communist regime didn't actually embody the ideal.

Americans have, to date, only focused on what we have to teach them (capitalism and democracy). But what Americans can learn from the Russian people is their ability to think first in terms of the group, in terms of the whole. Even prior to the overlay of a Communist system, the East has always had a more group-oriented culture than the West. The Russian language doesn't even have a word for privacy. The individual simply takes second place to the collective.

As Liza Schnadt, a friend of ours from the Findhorn Foundation in Scotland and a frequent "citizen diplomat" to the former Soviet Union, noted in the late '80s that, "The lack of emphasis their society placed on things preserved a simplicity in their Souls which we in the West long for." They have had to draw more on their own human resources for relaxation and entertainment. This simplicity is now at risk with the change in their economic system, but ideally they will preserve some of the depth of human connectedness they have needed to survive in their system and bring this gift to the West.

There is great passion in the Russian Soul and a tremendous sensitivity to beauty, art, and poetry. Tears of joy and tears of pain are normally very close to the surface in many of them. Nicholas Roerich, a famous Russian painter and cofounder of the Agni Yoga Society, wrote poetically of this passion: "Beneath the sign of beauty we walk joyfully. With beauty we conquer. Through beauty we pray. In beauty we are united. And now we affirm these words, not on the snowy heights, but amidst the turmoil of the city, and realizing the path of true reality, we greet with a happy smile the future."[14]

Our friend Nancy Seifer, who was writing a book on the Soul of Russia while in Moscow during the attempted coup of August 1991, noted:

> [C]ore beliefs about life that maintain their hold on the Russian psyche [are]: first, you can't control the future, but you can make the most of the moment; second, even when circumstances appear desperate, there are higher forces at work that help to salvage things in the end; and third, there is nothing more valuable in life than one's friends, one's chosen community. [The Russians] are open people who give everything away freely, naturally. They like to give for the sake of giving. If having money becomes a goal, everything will change.[15]

While Americans have generally seen the Russian personality as overly paranoid about war and invasion, we forget that the Russians were invaded many times by other nations and lost over twenty million people during World War II. By contrast, the United States has never been invaded and lost far fewer lives during the war. This fear and insecurity are part of the Russian personality and are part of the reason for her past closedness and overprotection, which has been hard for us to understand. The great ethnic unrest within her borders, which became apparent to the rest of the world only in recent years, is another major source of her insecurity.

SPIRITUALITY IN RUSSIA

Because institutionalized religion was discouraged in the old Soviet Union, people could not rely on outer forms and symbols. Thus they have developed their own inner spirituality, all the more valued because it was suppressed, unlike in the United States, where the availability of every possible religion is taken for granted.

"Religion is what gave sense to Russian life for centuries," says Russian philosopher Aleksandr Sivak, "and we've recently realized that our people became emptied and debased when they were forbidden to express it. We're being drawn back to liturgy because it offers the reawakening of an internal culture. . . ."

Many Western visitors have noted that spiritual life seemed more deeply experiential and personal than in the United States. The deep mysticism of the Russian people is something they could, perhaps, teach us about. Recent visitors to Russia have reported that nontraditional spiritual books, such as the Agni Yoga series written by Russian Helena Roerich over fifty years ago, are now in great demand.

A Russian named Renita interviewed by Nancy Seifer noted, "Every country on this planet has a special part to play, just like the musical sections in an orchestra. Russia's part in the future is to see the relationship with the transcendent in all its various forms."[16]

The mystical side of the Russian Soul is reflected in people's deep emotional bonding with the land and the Church, despite years of suppression. Synchronistically, the August 1991 coup occurred on the Feast of the Transfiguration, at the thousand-year anniversary of the Russian Orthodox church. This feast is one of the twelve most important Russian Orthodox holidays, celebrating the transfiguration of Jesus' body into light, witnessed by the three disciples. This day symbolized the attainment of Divine grace within the world of earthly problems. Significantly, the coup occurred in the year of the Jubilee celebration of one thousand years of the Russian Orthodox church, and recently the government itself has helped heal the split between Church and State dating back to the Communist revolution of 1917.

After Yeltsin rallied the people to defeat the coup, many noted that the faces of the people were transfigured by their joy in defeating totalitarianism. Dr. Yuri Dzhibladze, a Moscow activist, noted that "[people] now realize they can make a difference, that the changes in their lives don't come from above. The people aren't afraid anymore. It's the plotters who were afraid."[17]

A deep-seated flaw in the Russian character, according to many observers, is "the slave that lives within every Russian soul," as Chekhov put it— the psychology of the victim. The centuries-old Tartar yoke of oppression was thrown off, yet the command system under which Russians had lived for so long has left a deep imprint on family as well as political life and is hard to eradicate.

Frustration with the slow pace of economic reforms and resultant hardships has led many Russians to be deceived by the false promises of demagogues such as ultranationalist Vladimir Zhirinovsky, whose party won a plurality in the Russian Parliament in 1993 promising free vodka, racial purity, and restoration of Russia's military power.

RUSSIA'S RAYS

Like that of the United States, the personality of Russia is governed by the Sixth Ray of devotion, idealism, and mysticism. This is the reason for her former fanaticism about her ideology and why the two countries were for so long locked into such intense conflict over their ideologies. Although the content of the ideologies differed, both countries express the same self-righteous and often fanatical emotional commitment to their ideology, a common characteristic of the Sixth Ray energy.

As mystic Rudolf Steiner notes, all Russian wars prior to the Communist revolution were religious wars. In a rather mystical way, Steiner says the Russians would rather "pray and wait for what is to come . . . feeling that something belonging to the future has to come toward them."[18] This illustrates another side of the Sixth Ray personality of Russia—a mystical, dreamy idealism that can at times become very passive and thus become easily dominated by powerful individuals or groups, and may flare up into righteous fanaticism.

The Soul of Russia is governed by the Seventh Ray of ceremonial order, and with highly developed rhythms leading to an idealized order and a community of interests. The Seventh Ray emphasis is on group living and coordination through order and pattern. The Russian Soul longs for creative, not repressive, order that honors right relationships between people. This ray expresses true brother/sisterhood and a more scientific rather than religious or devotional approach to life. With the increasing influence of this ray, and the withdrawal of the Sixth Ray of devotion in the current cycle, Russia is becoming motivated to reorganize itself and so express more of its Soul qualities and less of its ideological personality.

PREDICTIONS ABOUT RUSSIA

In 1944 Edgar Cayce made an uncanny prediction for the time: "In Russia there comes the hope of the world . . . that each man will live for his fellow man. . . . Guided by what? That of friendship with the nation that hath even set on its present monetary unit 'In God We Trust.' "[19] With the ending of the cold war between the United States and the former USSR, foreign policy agreements over issues like the Iraqi invasion, dismantling of nuclear weapons, and U.S. economic aid to help soften the transition to capitalism, perhaps this prophecy is beginning to be fulfilled.

"The spiritual entity that is the Soul of the Soviet Union is now asserting itself," David Spangler wrote in 1980. "The Soviet Union has a destiny to fulfill in bringing about the well-being of humanity. A spiritual light will emerge out of that country. [She] is attempting to graft a sophisticated and ultimately complex Soul purpose onto a highly diverse and unintegrated mass consciousness. . . . [It is] a field of energy and consciousness that is transplanetary . . . [and] a giant step forward in the evolution of consciousness. The Soviet Union you experience in your world is not yet the Soviet Union that was seeking to emerge or was intended to emerge by the spiritual guides of your world. Human free will altered the hoped-for outcome in this.

[But] it should be considered as a delay, not a defeat of a spiritual objective, for in time the true Russian spirit will emerge as has been prophesied, to be a force of great good upon the world."[20]

Russia is part Western and part Asian, and its esoteric motto, according to the Ageless Wisdom, is "I link two ways"—linking both East and West. Many Russians feel torn between identifying with the West and its capitalistic evils and the East with its group identification and more communal culture oriented toward sharing. Russia's spiritual destiny will be to help the world to understand the gifts inherent in both intuitive, mystical Eastern cultures (the planetary right brain), and Western rational, materialistic cultures (the planetary left brain). In the process, it will help humanity synthesize the dual aspects of its own right- and left-brain functions. When we have done this, we as a planetary species will be capable of understanding and being guided by the higher spiritual reality.

Alice Bailey predicted that the secret of true brother/sisterhood will be Russia's gift to the world. In 1949 she said that there will eventually emerge "a great and spiritual religion which will justify the crucifixion of that great nation, and which will demonstrate itself and be focused in a great spiritual Light held aloft by a vital Russian proponent of true religion. . . .[He will be] that man for whom many Russians have been looking and who will be the justification of a most ancient prophecy."[21] Many Russians are aware of these prophecies, and they help to guide the thinking and aspirations of the people toward the great future of this complex and significant nation.

THE SOUL AND SPIRITUAL DESTINY OF JAPAN

The Soul of Japan is just beginning to express itself through an awakening realization that the economic aggressiveness that Japan has pursued since its defeat in World War II is coming to the end of its usefulness. A rising tide of criticism from around the world about its economic policies threatens to damage its relations with other countries, on whom it depends for trade. There are now stirrings that Japan may need to sacrifice some of its own internal interests for the greater good of the international order. Because Japan has been isolated by water from other cultures and remained rather homogeneous, it has never had to learn how to live side by side with other cultures.

The national mania for learning English is, according to the head of one Tokyo language school, not merely for business, but also to escape the tight confines of group life in Japan—a genuine cosmopolitanism. Akio Morita, cofounder and chairman of Sony Corporation, notes that Japan needs strong leadership, which means having the right to say no to the West; it also means that they must be willing to sacrifice their interests for the good of the international order.[22] The Soul of Japan will begin to emerge as it reforms its political structures to allow more public discussion of its economic policies, moving it toward taking a more selfless role in world affairs. This has begun to happen with the emergence of the reform coalition government of Prime Minister Morihiro Hokasawa and the growing role of television helping citizens to see and listen to their political leaders directly.

Tokyo, as a major planetary energy center, is an influence throughout east Asia. Although many east Asian countries have a fear of Japan because of its invasions during the war (similar to Europe's fear of Germany), they also realize the need for cooperation with Japan. Japan's true spiritual work is to be an integrating, unifying force for all the nations of Asia, including mainland China. It is rapidly integrating all the nations of the region through trade, direct investment, aid, financial services, technology transfer, and its continuing role as a developmental model.

Yukio Matsuyama, former chief writer for the newspaper *Asahi Shimbun*, has said that Japan should become a unique "super–middle power," uninterested in world hegemony, very generous with foreign aid, and very enthusiastic about disarmament, human rights, the environment, food, and population issues. To truly fulfill this purpose, however, it will have to sacrifice more of its self-interest and work more fully for the true good of other nations. Japan is facing some clear dilemmas in that it must continue to maintain positive relations with its European and American trading partners if it wishes to continue its economic prosperity, since more than half of its trade is with these partners. Currently, European and American business and government leaders see Japan's trading practices as "adversarial and unfair," and the Japanese way of doing business is simply not accepted.

Akio Morita is a voice for the Soul of his nation. He sees the European Community as a model of the sacrifices nations are willing to make to be part of a larger whole but has warned that until Japan is ready to redefine itself, it cannot hope to be accepted on the same stage as Europe and North America.[23]

Japan's rise from the defeat and devastation of World War II, to preeminent Asian economic power and challenger to U.S. economic supremacy, has left many Western observers in puzzled confusion. But Japan's ascendancy is understandable when viewed as the careful application of the techniques of Western capitalism to a society with a strong communal and militaristic past, influenced through its capital, Tokyo, by its First Ray of will and power. A national policy based on strict financial and social control from above also expresses the First Ray energy through a strong sense of national purpose, with little ideological disagreement or even separation between the public and private sectors. By its economic success, Japan may be demonstrating to the world what is possible when a nation's resources aren't depleted by a huge defense budget, as Japan was forced to cut its military after World War II. However, Japan's economic dominance may now be challenged by structural changes in the world economy, as its economic slump of the mid-90s indicates.

Japan has a long history of adopting and adapting the ideas of other cultures, as both Confucianism and Buddhism were imported into Japan, along with the Chinese system of centralized, hierarchical government during the greatly admired Tang dynasty of the seventh through tenth centuries. In this century Japan has transformed the individualistic model of Western capitalism by using the group-oriented idealism of the Sixth Ray energy of the Soul of Tokyo to make economic success the national purpose to which every individual, institution, school, research laboratory, and human relationship is dedicated.

As a homogeneous but resource-poor island nation, Japan has learned how to build a social consensus on working together to ensure its people's survival. The Japanese have applied these skills with extraordinary dedication to the physical world, resulting in a perfection in physical detail of form epitomized by Japanese temple gardens and the art of bonsai. Through careful pruning, cutting, bending, and shaping, small young trees over many years are shaped to exquisitely perfect forms. These bonsai trees seem to symbolize the process the young Japanese person goes through as he or she is carefully constructed and shaped to fit perfectly into the economic structures that so fully determine each individual's life. This same dedication to perfection of form that creates bonsai trees also produces a steady stream of innovative and ever higher-quality products that are purchased eagerly by consumers around the world. Sensitivity to beauty is evident in the care and attention given to each family's home decor and small ornamental gardens.

COMMUNITARIAN VALUES

The extraordinary social cohesion and communitarian values of Japan have given rise to business associations, teamwork, corporate loyalty, growth-producing industries, and cooperative government strategies that have built Japan's economic powerhouse. These values emerge out of Asian group-conscious culture and include hard work, filial piety, national pride, and a fundamental focus on the importance of the society rather than on the individual, as in the West. Thus in Japan a person's existence has meaning by virtue of fulfilling a specific role within that society, not by individual expression or development. The positive side of these qualities in Japanese culture is a sensitivity to the feelings of others and a desire to listen rather than sound off, based on the assumption that anyone can voice everyone else's needs and feelings. The rigid forms and rituals of Japanese life also may provide a sense of security so that a subtler and more refined interplay of relationship is possible.

All these traits give Japanese leaders a population that can easily be directed into whatever goals the leaders determine. Because there has been little real political dialogue and discussion, until recent scandals catalyzed change, the fundamental decisions about the purpose and focus of the society have been economically determined. The administrators of the economic power structures have pursued the policy of economic expansion and the creation of enough economic power to render Japan invulnerable to outside forces with a singleness of purpose using the First Ray energies of the nation. This had been aimed at overcoming the fundamental insecurity of an island nation with limited resources.

A grouping of major corporations, known as *zaibatsu*, which would be outlawed under U.S. antitrust laws, and business federations called *keiretsu*, who supply these groups, have developed a tightly woven network of financiers, producers, and suppliers. Outsiders see a well-oiled economic machine that they find nearly impossible to penetrate and claim is unfair. The Japanese, however, see their methods as an adaptation of capitalism to their more cohesive and homogeneous society.

Japan is fundamentally a producer-oriented economy, as opposed to the consumer-focused economies of Western capitalist countries. Consumer groups focus on pollution and pesticides but have nothing to say about cartels and business relationships that protect profits and keep prices high for consumers. Japanese labor leaders have accepted the idea that wages do not have to keep pace with company profits and growth, and worker dissent is almost nonexistent.

Many of the ancient military traditions of Japanese society have been translated into modern business terms. When modern corporations were formed in the nineteenth century, they drew their first work forces from samurai warriors who had lost their jobs when their lords' fiefdoms were abolished, and their sense of lifelong loyalty was simply transferred to the corporation. These samurai who wore the crests of their *daimio* in feudal times now wear pins bearing the logos of their corporations.

The Japanese people have a different kind of freedom from Americans—one that is rooted in job security, a low crime rate, and a sense of belonging. But their particular freedom is purchased at a price—fear of deviation from the norm, a work ethic so ferocious that men often die at their desks from overwork. Women have two choices in society. They can become housewives, only seeing their husbands after midnight six days a week, managing the household and bringing up the children alone (depending only on their husbands' income). Or they can become career women who will have to work as hard as the men and still face obstacles to advancement. Nevertheless, more and more Japanese women are choosing to remain single and pursue careers.

The sense of duty and obligation of the Japanese is applied to the village, family, school, or work place, but there is little goodwill for people they don't know and little sense of the broader public interest. All foreigners in Japan are required to carry a fingerprinted ID card. Japanese citizens have little effective legal recourse against either corporate power or bureaucratic ignorance.

From the perspective of the Soul, an incarnation in Japan would provide an intensive experience of group life, a practical teaching in the fundamental interdependence of all life, and an experience of working with others for a unified purpose, even if only a materialistic one. Souls who become excessively individualistic from incarnations in the West are likely to have several Asian incarnations to help balance out their development.

Part of the lack of communication that consistently takes place between the United States and Japan is based on an assumption of similarity by Americans. However, there is little if any domestic political discussion of Japan's economic and political policies. According to Karel van Wolferen, a Dutch newspaper correspondent for east Asia, few institutions oppose an incumbent administration, and citizens effectively have had no say, until recently, in how the government is run through politicians or nongovernmental organizations.[24] Peter Drucker, America's management guru, pointed out that for over a hundred years Japan's policies have aimed at putting it in the modern world without being a part of it.

In Japanese public discourse, social conflict is taboo, especially if it pits one group against another. Japanese learn early in life that the whole point of any discussion is to achieve *wa*, or harmony. When interpreted on the personality rather than on a Soul level, it seeks to achieve harmony and consensus at all costs, discouraging dissent.

Another controversial and symbolic subject in Japan is the "rice curtain." There is a deep symbolic meaning to rice in Japan, and this sacred food source is protected by the government so that it can continue to be grown domestically and not have to be imported from other countries. As long as the "rice curtain" remained, it was a symbol of Japan's unwillingness to trust the international community to provide for its basic needs. By ending this protection as part of the GATT agreement, it enabled a more internationally minded political constituency to emerge in Japan despite difficulties created for small scale farmers. It will also tie Japan irrevocably to its Pacific trading partners, thus guaranteeing internationalism through interdependence.

THE KARMIC DANCE BETWEEN JAPAN AND THE UNITED STATES

The United States and Japan have a long karmic relationship that began when Admiral Perry arrived in Japan in the mid-1800s and forced Japan to begin trading with the rest of the world. The Japanese have always seen economic development as part of national defense, a military strategy for remaining independent and becoming powerful, which continues to this day—a materialistic application of the First Ray energy of will and power.

After the surprise attack on Pearl Harbor, the United States fought Japan throughout Asia and was instrumental in hastening the defeat of Japan with the development and use of the atomic bomb on Hiroshima and Nagasaki. From the perspective of the Ageless Wisdom, the use of the bomb twice on Japan disrupted the etheric web in these locations and let in a flood of new energy by shattering the veil between dimensions and thus allowing rebuilding to take place on somewhat new lines.

This karmic relationship with the United States has taken many interesting turns. When General Douglas MacArthur took over the administration of Japan after its defeat, he worked to completely change Japan's totalitarian society into a democracy with freedom of expression. The tradition of "administrative guidance" of the famous Ministry of International Trade and Industry (MITI) grew out of MacArthur's practice of giving verbal instructions to the Japanese leaders, while he encouraged them to be initiators. MITI, which orchestrates Japan's unified industrial and trade policies, has now become the focus of U.S. complaints about its exclusionary policies on trade.[25]

Another karmic connection is "quality circles," where employees work at upgrading production and reducing defects. This concept was imported to Japan by American Edward Deming after the war when no one in the United States would listen to his ideas. This has been one of the keys to Japan's production of high-quality goods and one of the ways it has beaten its American competitors, especially in the auto industry. Deming's success in Japan has led to the widespread adoption of his ideas by U.S. business. These are certainly examples of some interesting karmic feedback loops in international relations.

This leaves the United States and Japan struggling to work out relationships where the organizing principles of the two societies are actually polar opposites. The value of the individual, exalted in the West in opposition to Eastern communal values, which seem to make Japan a better economic competitor, are teaching something to the West about the need for a focused national purpose that transcends individual interests. The synthetic resolution to this relationship has yet to be achieved but could add to the Soul expression of each nation.

THE SOUL AND SPIRITUAL DESTINY OF THE EMERGING AFRICAN NATIONS

It has been prophesied in the Ageless Wisdom teachings that Africa will make a major contribution of spiritual assets and creative cultural expressions to the world. Currently, the emerging African nations, especially those of sub-Saharan Africa, are struggling with the challenges that youthful humans face in establishing their own identity and integrating their personalities.

Africans in many countries are showing unprecedented determination to gain the same basic freedoms people everywhere want: the right to speak their minds, the right to attend a meeting, the right to live without fear of government attack.

One example of a Soul-inspired leader is General Olusegun Obasanjo, a former leader of the federal military government of Nigeria from 1976 to 1977, who aided the peaceful transfer of leadership in the country to an elected civilian government in 1979. General Obasanjo outlined clearly what he considers to be the causes of the "dereliction and decay" of the African continent as the "failure to stimulate the spring of creativity in our people through the establishment of those social institutions that make for a humane society." His goal is to build relationships between current and future leaders in government, finance, industry, agriculture, and education, working toward integrating Africa into a web of cooperating nations.[26]

Here we see a leader emerging from the people who truly expresses the Soul of Africa and the best of the human spirit, who continues to work where he is to improve the life of his people. He correctly sees that many of the development efforts to help Africa have failed because they did not involve local people in determining what is needed, planning the solution, and implementing the projects. From the Soul's perspective, the improvement in material conditions is not as important as the learning opportunity for growth in consciousness, developing new skills, and increased self-empowerment—all of which stimulate progressive human evolution.

Kenya's Greenbelt movement is an example of a sustainable development project, initiated by African people themselves and reflecting the Soul of Kenya. This is a popular movement of over fifty thousand people who are planting trees through many of the country's most desolate areas. Well over seven million trees have been grown as seedlings, planted and cared for by villagers until they become mature, adult trees, for which the villagers receive a small fee. The project has generated a genuine popular enthusiasm for trees and is an example of an indigenous African movement organizing the goodwill of ordinary people.

The coordinator of this movement, an internationally acclaimed Soul-inspired visionary, is Professor Wangari Matthai. She has written: "There is a new consciousness emerging in parts of Africa and other parts of the world. It is the awareness that every being on this planet shares a common destiny. All of Africa should be part of this awakening, so that, unlike her recent past, Africa can participate directly in the direction of her destiny."[27]

Another leader working with a higher vision for Africans is Bernard Ledea Ouedraogo, a former civil servant in Burkina Faso, who has turned the Naam group, a traditional society for young people designed to develop moral qualities and cooperative activities, into a dynamic institution for village development.

We can see a similar process in South Africa, where the country's racially divided political system has hurt both blacks and whites, and has invoked two leaders who express the Soul of that nation—Nelson Mandela and F. W. de Klerk. Their joint effort to create resolution of their country's racial agony is helping to cleanse the nation of its divisive impulses, symbolized by apartheid. A new constitution empowers blacks by establishing majority vote to elect Parliament and dissolving the separate black homelands, yet it also protects the white minority through a bill of rights. Mandela and de Klerk were both honored as peacemakers by winning a joint Nobel Peace Prize in 1993 and being featured on *Time* magazine's "Man of The Year" cover, along with Yasir Arafat and Yitzhak Rabin.

The discipline, commitment, and courage of an inspired leader such as Nelson Mandela is an example to the world of the Soul qualities of Africans. Whites have to overcome their fear of blacks and instead see their beautiful heart qualities as a needed balance to the overly controlled white personality. Blacks have to learn to make peace among themselves, overcoming their intertribal violence to prove they can be good citizens and step into self-governance. The resolution of these national personality issues will eventually lead to greater well-being for all of South Africa. New economic relationships are growing between South Africa and other black nations in the region, who see a racially just South Africa as a partner in developing their countries.

THE SOULS OF OTHER NATIONS

Each nation has both a Soul and a personality expression, and although there isn't space to explore all of them, we can offer a few hints based on Alice Bailey's *The Destiny of Nations* and encourage readers to explore further.

Great Britain

Britain's esoteric motto, according to the Ageless Wisdom teachings, is "I serve." Her highest Soul path is service to the world. Her personality expresses the First Ray of will and power, reflected in the British art of control, the "stiff upper lip," but also in the country's remarkable will in resisting Hitler's bombing attacks. The First Ray relates to governance, and Britain has pioneered new democratic forms for the world from the signing of the Magna Carta in 1215 to the British Commonwealth of Nations. Britain's Soul expression is the Second Ray of love wisdom, like that of the United States, showing their common link on a higher level. If England's ideal of justice, the pattern of her personality ray, can be transformed by her Soul ray of love wisdom into just and intelligent world service, then she will give to the world the pattern of true government. To accomplish this England must overcome the rigid, conservative tendencies of her personality. According to metaphysical teacher David Spangler, "Britain's pattern in the world will be that of a catalyst, a way shower, and . . . a gateway through which humanity will emerge into the New Age. . . ."[28]

France

The esoteric motto of France is "I release the Light"—spreading illumination to the world. Her personality is the Third Ray of active intelligence—hence her love of philosophy, her contributions to the knowledge and thought of the world, and, as well, her love of political scheming and manipulation. France's Soul expression is the Fifth Ray of concrete science, and Bailey notes that when France ceases living in the wonder of its past and goes forth into the future, she will demonstrate the fact of illumination that is the goal of all mental effort. She may then prove to the world the fact of the Soul and give a demonstration of Soul control. The recognition of the rights of humanity as a whole was given to the world through the French Revolution, which struck a major blow for the release of humanity from bondage. The profound rallying cry of "liberty, equality, fraternity" symbolizes the goal ahead for humanity.

Germany

The esoteric motto of the newly reunited Germany is "I preserve"—saving and protecting the best of the past. Like Britain, her personality is governed by the First Ray of will and power, and the destructive side of this was apparent in its negative manifestation by the control and domination exerted by Hitler and his distortions about Germany as the home of the master race. But the Soul of Germany is governed by the Fourth Ray of harmony through conflict—the ray of the artist. Her Soul has been expressed in the music and philosophy she has given to the world and recently in moving toward a new harmony in Europe through the embracing of East Germany, with all the difficulties that entails.

India

The esoteric motto of India is "I hide the Light." Her gift to the world is the Light of the Ageless Wisdom, which she has hidden for centuries, for in that Light we will eventually see the Light of Life itself. The spiritual energy field of India has been built up by Adepts and spiritual seekers for centuries, which has a major impact on visitors. India's personality is the Fourth Ray—harmony through conflict—as seen in the ongoing struggle between her Hindu and Moslem peoples. Her Soul is the First Ray of will and power, so the energy that pours through her stimulates the will to power unless it is purified. But this Soul ray has also helped create the largest democracy in the Third World.

Brazil

The esoteric motto of this vast green land is "I hide the seed." She is the custodian of a revelation of Light far into the future. Her personality is governed by the Second Ray of love wisdom, which is apparent in the heart-centered qualities of her people. Her Soul ray is the Fourth Ray of harmony through conflict—which is seen in her hosting the first major UN conference that dealt with environment and development in 1992, and brought together so many conflicting countries into the first seeds of harmony around these issues.

THE NEW SYNTHESIS

We are accustomed to viewing changes and crises in the life of a nation as the result of external events—of pressures from other nations, shortages of vital supplies, influxes of new immigrants, or other causes. Yet from an inner perspective, change and crisis are not solely the result of external circumstances, although these may trigger a crisis. Rather, change is a response to the impact of inner impulses, ideas, and energies that are seeking to emerge onto the world scene, guided by the Enlightened Ones who work for the evolutionary good of the world. These new energies and ideas carry with them fresh vitality and the seeds of a new culture and civilization that is seeking always to be born within the body of an existing civilization.

However, we tend to be preoccupied with what is happening to our loved but slowly decaying civilizational forms, rather than seeing the emergence of new life and forms more responsive to vital spiritual energies and ideas. Yet this impulse to reach out beyond barriers of ideology or culture—made increasingly easier by modern telecommunications and the development of multinational institutions—is leading to the birthing of a planetary civilization.

Citizen diplomats, political activists, and visionary political, business, and scientific leaders are using fax machines, computers and modems, and all the electronic wonders of the modern world to link up with those of similar mind and heart around the earth. Together they express the impulse toward planetary synthesis, working to weave the world into a unified but diverse web of shared intent for a new and better world.

The most powerful example of this impulse to melt borders is the gradual emergence of the European Community (EC). It is fitting that the part of the world that first gave birth to the idea of nation-states in the fifteenth and sixteenth centuries should be the first area of the world to outgrow them. Nation-states are entities that have helped stimulate a necessary expansion of consciousness beyond the individual's identification with self, family, or tribe. They provided havens of relative security for groups of people of shared language and values to develop their unique culture and identity.

However, when a significant number of people mature to become autonomous individuals and outgrow limited group identifications, national frontiers become superfluous. They begin to develop a feeling of respect for all other individuals, no matter what their origins, and can overcome some of the fear and mutual suspicion that frontiers represent. Then the powerful economic forces driving the world toward greater integration can help eliminate trade barriers and promote the value of shared commerce. This is the present situation as the Western European nations prepare to step beyond the separateness represented by their borders to create a common economic and social community. Old patterns and thought-forms have power, however, as European nations learn as they gradually move towards more interdependence. Yet the referenda on the Maastricht Treaty has wisely given a greater voice to the concerns of average people about excessive bureaucratic and corporate control over their lives resulting from the union.

The most important aspect of the EC, however, is that it will provide, when implemented through the election of the European parliament and other common institutions, a working model of international cooperation and a voluntary fusion of identities into a greater whole, while still respecting unique national qualities and contributions. This will offer a very useful blueprint of an evolutionary step for a united states of Europe. It is also powerful training in learning to think in terms of a greater whole, a step to becoming planetary citizens.

According to Alice Bailey, Europe is the field for educating the world in the ideas of a true planetary unity and for a wise presentation of the Divine Plan. From that continent the inspiration can go forth to the East and to the West.[29] The EC should be based not purely on economic self-interest, but the ideas of brother/sisterhood, the will to good, freedom, and goodwill. The challenge is to ensure that materialistic forces do not use the new entity for increasing corporate control and dominance or for creating exclusionary immigration or refugee policies. Together these countries could rise to the challenge of ending poverty, creating a just economy, and implementing environmental reforms.

On an inner level, the idea of a united Europe has been supported in meditation work for several years by a number of groups, such as the Spirit of Europe Foundation, which has nurtured the idea of spiritual unity in diversity in Europe. Growing out of a European conference held at the Findhorn Foundation in Scotland in 1985, it strives to promote trust, harmony, and understanding among the peoples and nations of Europe through meetings, seminars, newsletters, and other initiatives. The Lucis Trust of London has also sponsored meditation groups for decades that include the unity of Europe as a long-held inner vision. John Quanjer, editor of the non-partisan New Humanity magazine, ran for the European Parliament on a similar "Spirit of Europe" platform, emphasizing what he called "the heart and soul connection" within Europe and "the spirit of politics" linked to "the needs of the future and the mentality of tomorrow."

One result of seeing the benefits of Europe's merger is that regional groupings of nations are being discussed in South America, North America, Asia, and the Pacific Rim nations. Once this pattern of synthesis becomes established in political thinking, and nations become comfortable with the idea of yielding some national sovereignty for the benefits it brings to themselves and the whole, it will eventually facilitate the fusion of these regional blocs of nations into a working, unified planetary system of governance. The first step has begun in North America with the 1993 North American Free Trade Agreement approved by the United States, Canada, and Mexico.

THE UNITED NATIONS

The Soul of the United Nations is the Soul of a nascent One Humanity. The simple fact that for the first time in history representatives of all the diversity of humanity meet together physically in the same location offers a profound experience of humanity as a whole, as an entity. Underlying all the activity of the United Nations is a deeper spiritual current—the birthing of a new ethics that originates from a central place of synthesis where all the aspirations and values of humankind converge. Despite the usual political manipulation, bureaucratic inefficiency, and lack of coordination in some military operations, the UN is a powerful force for a new human synthesis.

The United Nations is essentially a living thought-form and an evolving entity, so our perception shouldn't be limited mainly to its outer appearances, notes Jan van der Linden, director of the School for Esoteric Studies in New York. Any evidence that a nation assumes more responsibility for the global good and for the well-being of humanity, any truly inclusive thinking along international lines, serves the deeper goal of the UN, he says. It provides a living center of contacts and a network of information on global issues.

The United Nations arose out of the failure of the League of Nations and the ashes of World War II. After the suffering of the war, the leaders of all nations were ready to establish an international body that could help keep the peace. Over the years the UN has evolved into a world body with 184 member nations and has become an organizing center for humanity's difficult passage to a planetary government. Through its worldwide data collection, studies, and conferences—political, economic, social, scientific, cultural, and environmental—the United Nations has become the greatest observatory and warning system of planet Earth. Through the UN governments are beginning to make an honest effort at cooperation in many fields—although much still remains to be done.

The UN Charter itself is one of the boldest codes of ethics ever drafted for the behavior of nations. Although its agreements are often broken by its members, it progressively nurtures a better behavior, a greater understanding, and an improved moral political atmosphere. The UN's efforts at keeping peace have been only as successful as member nations have allowed them to be, based on their willingness to yield sovereignty to the international body. Votes for sanctions against aggression had been blocked in the Security Council (mostly by the former USSR) until the major breakthrough of the unanimous resolution against Iraq's aggression in Kuwait in August 1990. This represented a major step for humanity and its first demonstrated example of its strength in unity.

According to visionary Robert Muller, former assistant to three secretaries general, " . . . The UN is an incipient brain of the human species, registering global dangers . . . and fostering a better knowledge of our planet's resources and constraints. . . . [It] is an incipient world nervous system which relays global findings and warnings to governments, local collectives, and the peoples. [It] will be considered someday as the paradigm of the new millennium." Muller says that the UN has helped one billion people gain independence with a minimum of bloodshed, helped the emergence of the poorer countries into the modern age, provided a code of ethics for relations between armed nations, enhanced a planetary acceptance of the racial equality of all human beings, and been a moral force for progress toward political maturity and defusion of tensions.[30]

Because of a little-known agreement with the United States as a condition of its location in this country, the UN cannot publicize its work here. Instead it must rely on independent groups, so we hear less about it than people do in most other countries. UN peacekeeping soldiers, known as "soldiers without enemies," have bravely interposed themselves many times between warring parties, separating them and preventing or halting conflict while the dispute goes to the conference table. Since the end of the cold war in 1988, the UN supervised the withdrawal of Soviet forces from Afghanistan and of Cuban forces from Angola, established a verification mission in Angola and in Cambodia, and embarked on a massive disarmament of Iraq's nuclear arsenal. New UN operations include civilian monitoring of elections in the western Sahara, human rights verification in El Salvador and elsewhere, the protection or return of war refugees such as the Kurds following the Persian Gulf war, relief for civilians in war-torn Bosnia Herzegovina, and humanitarian work in Somalia. There are about eighty thousand personnel in the field and peacekeeping operations currently in fourteen countries.

The UN monitored the 1990 election in Nicaragua and the demobilization of twenty-two thousand contras, an operation without precedent in UN history. The UN also negotiated and agreed to monitor the cease-fire agreement in war-torn Cambodia, the largest and most complex operation ever undertaken by the UN and an election was successfully carried out there under its auspices.

The "good offices" of the secretary general of the UN have often been used behind the scenes to settle differences between nations such as Perez de Cuellar in El Salvador.[31] Because of the UN's successful role in 1991 in returning Western hostages held for years in Lebanon, and in working with the United States to stop Iraq's aggression and its nuclear capability, a Gallup poll that year reported that 86 percent of the American people supported the UN and want it to take the lead in collective security.[32]

As a result, the international community, including heads of state, special commissions, NGOs, and the secretary general supported a strengthened UN and a major increase in the power of the Security Council, including responsibility for nonmilitary threats to peace. Ironically, many nations now want to solve their problems within the UN, and with an average of ten to twelve conflicts to cope with at the same time, the demands on its resources are overwhelming. Money is a constant problem at the UN, and the United States is currently millions of dollars in arrears, although President Clinton had recently promised to pay what is owed.

The expanding role of the UN illustrates an evolution in the concept of national sovereignty. After becoming angered with the way food and medicines have been used as weapons of war, leaders are considering establishing the right of humanitarian intervention in international law. Authorities claiming sovereignty are now held more accountable for meeting the needs of their people or allowing the international community to help.

The UN is a multifaceted organization with many functions, including synthesizing information about humanity and the planet as a whole. This work of expanding and synthesizing the totality of knowledge is being carried out by eighteen specialized agencies and fourteen special programs of the UN which are active in every field of of knowledge and human endeavor such as the UN Environmental Program which recently promoted an international Environmental Sabbath Day to honor the Earth and to make environmentalists more aware of the spiritual dimensions of nature.

Many problems being grappled with at official levels at the UN and by member nations individually have already been solved by the vast network of over 1,300 NGOs based at the UN with observer status, who provide important information and resources that have a worldwide effect. Amnesty International, for example, is consulted frequently on human rights violations, as is Greenpeace on the environment. Religious groups often help with refugees, major disasters, and humanitarian causes.[33] Many observers see the NGOs as a functioning alternative world government already in place.

At the center of its work, the UN has given emphasis to the human being, attempting to clarify the proper relationship between the individual and the surrounding world and universe. The Universal Declaration of Human Rights is a statement of consecration to the sanctity of the individual. However, many nations do not yet believe that they must respect their citizens as human beings, claiming instead that citizens owe total allegiance to the state, a religion, a way of life, or a philosophical concept.

The UN can also be seen as a focus on earth for the love of God. When the United Nations moves into its full and wise use of its power, the welfare of the world will be assured. That welfare is love in action, right human relations among individuals, groups, and nations. International cooperation is in essence love on a world scale.

Someone who understood very clearly the role of love and sacrifice in the life of the United Nations was former Secretary General Dag Hammarskjöld, one of the most widely respected world leaders in modern history. He was instrumental in redesigning the UN meditation room, which had come into existence through the efforts of the Laymen's Movement for a Christian World. The room is a place of quiet stillness and has been referred to as one of the holiest of holies on the planet, yet it is accessible to the public on request from the visitors lobby. It is the focus for the energies of a unified planet and humanity, and for right relations among all kingdoms of life. When Gordon worked for the UN for four years with World Goodwill, an NGO there, he meditated daily in this room and experienced a very powerful energy helping to support the synthesis of nations and the emergence of the Soul of humanity.

From the deeper perspective of the Ageless Wisdom, there are certain vast Beings of great Love and Light on an inner level whose energy can assist humanity only when there is a group consciousness and an energy field composed of the entire human family. One such Being, which could be called an Avatar of Synthesis, is said to focus energy on the United Nations General Assembly, to assist the efforts of humanity in synthesizing the vast diversity of earth peoples and nations by strengthening a slowly growing will to unity. Delegates and staff who work in the energy field of the UN and are of goodwill speak of being profoundly changed by being there, of developing respect and compassion for all humanity by their exposure to the energies of human convergence focused there.

Now fifty years old, the UN is still very young when one considers the millions of years it took humanity to evolve to its present stage. It is the embryonic brain of the central nervous system of the family of nations. It carries the seed pattern for the Soul of the One Humanity. Thus, our role as planetary citizens is to evoke the potential of the UN, its possibility of transformation, by thinking about and meditating on the positive forces in the UN.

THE NEW WORLD ORDER

There will be no day or days then when a New World Order comes into being. Step by step and here and there it will arrive, and, even as it comes into being it will develop fresh perspectives, discover unsuspected problems, and go on to new adventures.
—H. G. WELLS

The accelerating tempo of evolutionary change in the last quarter of the twentieth century has begun to approach a climax, as the drive for human political and economic rights has transformed our old, bipolar world order and released tremendous energy for change everywhere. We now have an opportunity to reorder the world along the lines of principles derived from the collective Soul of Humanity.

What are these principles, and what would this new world order look like? Since former President Bush promoted the ideal of a "new world order" without being able to articulate exactly what it is, it might be useful to include here the principles of a new world order proposed over fifty years ago by Alice Bailey, through her work with the Tibetan teacher Djwhal Khul, based on the Ageless Wisdom:

• The new world order must meet the immediate need and not be an attempt to satisfy some distant, idealistic vision.
• The new world order will be founded on the recognition that all people are equal in origin and goal, but that all are at differing stages of evolutionary development; that personal integrity, intelligence, vision, and experience, plus a marked goodwill, should indicate leadership.
• In the new world order, the governing body in any nation should be composed of those who work for the greatest good of the greatest number and who at the same time offer opportunity to all, seeing to it that the individual is left free.
• The new world order will be founded on an active sense of responsibility. The rule will be all for one and one for all. This attitude among nations has yet to develop.
• The new world order will not impose a uniform type of government, a synthetic religion, and a system of standardization upon the nations. The sovereign rights of each nation will be recognized, and its peculiar genius, individual trends, and racial qualities will be permitted full expression. In one particular only should there be an attempt to produce unity, and that will be in the field of education.
• The new world order will recognize that the produce of the world, the

natural resources of the planet and its riches, belong to no one nation but should be shared by all. There will be no nations under the category "haves" and others under the opposite category. A fair and properly organized distribution of the wheat, oil, and mineral wealth of the world will be developed based upon the needs of each nation, upon its own internal resources, and upon the requirements of its people. All this will be worked out in relation to the whole.

In the preparatory period for the new world order, there will be a steady and regulated disarmament. It will not be optional. No nation will be permitted to produce and organize any equipment for destructive purposes or to infringe the security of any other nation. . . .[34]

People all over the world are taking responsibility for solving the problems that beset them, and humanity is beginning to recognize that its own thoughts and ideas, forming public opinion, are the determining factors in directing the tides of change. The support of public opinion is what enables inspired leaders to force through difficult proposals on disarmament, international debt, and the environment.

It is important also to note that an enlightened approach to a new world order does not demand the enforcement of a uniform religion or government, a prospect feared by fundamentalist Christians like Pat Robertson, Pat Buchanan, William Still, and others. (This fear may, in fact, be a shadow projection on their part, as they are the ones wanting to impose their religious beliefs on others around national policies like abortion or school prayer.) Rather, the different faiths of the world need to come closer together in a way that preserves their uniqueness yet enriches the contribution each can make to humanity and world betterment.

The principle of sharing, which needs to come to life in the new world order, is perhaps the most difficult and most fundamental of all. But it can begin with taking small, realistic steps in the right direction. It is essential that we begin to create structures of international relationships that will enable nations and people to begin to share the resources of the planet. There cannot be freedom, human rights, democracy, and unity unless there is a willingness to share wealth, technology, skills, and knowledge.

These principles implicitly recognize the human Soul—that at the very core of our being there is a sacred center that wants us to share, cooperate, love, and exercise our potential to live together with all life in goodwill and harmony. It is important that we recognize this universal sense of the sacred and foster it by developing an inclusive approach to humanity's spiritual life.

The process of realizing this vision of a new world order is the evolutionary story of humanity. The ethic of evolution says we are responsible to evolve ourselves as individuals and to evolve new ways of being together on the planet. The challenges of the last decade before the millennium can be successfully met once we realize the necessity to truly reorder our world based on higher principles and not just tinker with current systems.

The current disintegration of political, economic, and social structures is the process we seem to require in order to make fundamental changes in our order of living. During this transitional period national sovereignty is beginning to be redefined, both along ethnic lines as larger nations break up and move toward supranationality, as in the European Community. The United Nations is emerging as the center for international diplomacy and coordinated humanitarian activity. The 1990 Children's Summit, the 1990 Stockholm Initiative on Global Security and Governance, and the 1992 Rio Earth Summit, all have contributed principled ideas on peace, development, environment, democracy, human rights, and global governance. Despite all the chaos and upheaval, as more nations (and the conscious individuals within them) begin aligning their national personality with their Soul and their true spiritual destiny, a truly compassionate and just new world order will emerge.

Part 5

◆ ◆ ◆

CREATING A NEW PLANETARY ORDER

Chapter Eleven

◆

THE NEW PLANETARY ECONOMICS

The clue to the establishment of the world order lies hid in this symbology [the circulation of the bloodstream]—free circulation of all that is needed to all parts of the great framework of humanity. The blood is the life and free interchange; free sharing and free circulation of all that is required for right human living will characterize the world to be.

—ALICE BAILEY[1]

The word *economics* comes from the Greek *oikonomos,* meaning "household manager." On a consciousness level, our challenge as human beings is to see the entire planetary economy as our own household and to learn to care for it as if it were our own. The economy must work for all members of the earth household, or it won't work for any part of the human family in the long term. Thinking this way, we realize we wouldn't tear our house apart to make a fire to keep warm or dump garbage in our living room. And we soon become concerned with the nature of the legacy we will be passing on to future generations who will inhabit the earth.

As the old systems continue to break down, new spiritual ideas from the inner side are received by creative thinkers who then use them to restructure economic thinking and build new systems. These new ideas boost humanity's evolving understanding of how to create an economic system that is in harmony with universal laws. This new system will be sustainable when it meets the needs of all the peoples, and life forms on the earth, without compromising the ability of future generations to meet their needs.

A new definition of economic progress is emerging that includes increasing the satisfaction of the whole range of human needs: social justice; good health for all; achievement of personal aspirations; more equitable sharing of work; new emphasis on the quality of work life; greater economic self-reliance at the individual, local, regional, and national levels; regional and global conservation; and sustainable use of natural resources.

New economic values are also evolving from East-West cooperation and the emergence of the European Community. These include developing all nations in a given area for the good of the whole; cooperation between previous enemies (e.g., France and Germany); and sharing resources with countries trying to change their economies (Western European aid to Eastern Europe and the former Soviet Union).

Let us use the interpretative, symbolic thinking presented throughout this book to offer some fresh insights into the deeper causes of our current economic dilemmas.

DEBT—WHAT WE OWE TO LIFE

Today, the total U.S. public, corporate, and personal debt equals over $9 trillion, making the United States the largest debtor nation in the world. This debt is a symbol of the excessive and ever-growing desire for all types of goods and resources by people everywhere. This $9 trillion mortgage on the future represents the karma of excessive desire—a symbol of how much we have taken from life and how little we have given back to it. This pattern of endless growth and consumerism is based on taking money and life from future generations, who will find their options severely limited as they are required to pay for the credit-spending binge of the current generation.

Yet the "hidden costs" of our current growth economics to the ecological future of humanity are even greater. The magnitude of this practice of mortgaging the future has reached planetary scale. Endless revelations of ever more deadly pollution spreading into our air, water, and soil, the garbage crisis, and the carbon dioxide threat to the ozone layer are the price tag of the paradigm that sought to dominate the natural environment, with little thought for future generations of humans or other life forms on the planet. The bill is coming due, and humanity is holding a giant "accounts payable" invoice from the environment, upon which all of our economic activities are based. "Spaceship Earth" has become a unified economic system in which the actions of one individual, state, or nation affect all others. This not only changes the economic game; it changes the very board upon which the game is played.

The Polarity of Wealth and Poverty

One of the most striking symbolic messages we have ever seen were two contrasting images presented on one evening's television news: one of well-to-do, overfed, overweight Westerners parading to reducing salons or plastic surgeons to remove excess fat and another of destitute children in Brazil foraging all day through mountains of garbage, looking for something to eat, along with homeless people begging and searching for food in American cities. These images tell us a great deal about the fundamental problems with our economic system today.

Another symbolic picture of the problem in the United States was presented by the very people who should have been warning us of the danger—our representatives in Congress—but instead let the nation slide into outrageous debt. During this time, Congress also allowed major banks and savings and loan associations to go unregulated and ultimately bankrupt—all while not paying their own personal debts. Their inability to live within their means was symbolized by more than $300,000 in unpaid debts for services in the Capitol buildings owed by members of Congress, and over 8,300 bounced checks in one year at the House Bank.[2]

The poverty that exists in the world today is a symbol of the moral poverty that cannot take into consideration the needs of others. According to the UN's 1992 Human Development Report, of the world's five billion people, the top 20 percent hold 83 percent of the world's wealth and the bottom 20 percent only 1.4 percent. The same massive inequities of wealth that exist within the developed nations (in Japan and the United States, 10 percent of the population controls 72 percent of all capital, according to *The New York Times*) have many implications for the economy.

However, these inequities have even larger implications as a measurement of the willingness of human beings to share. According to 1986 U.S. tax returns, those in the lowest income brackets were thirty times more likely to make donations than those with the highest levels of income. Thus it seems that increasing wealth tends to insulate people from a sense of connection to the struggles of the rest of humanity, while those who have struggled with poverty have more sympathy for those in similar difficulties. This illustrates the spiritual learning that emerges through the experience of poverty, which is to develop a compassion and a willingness to help others less fortunate.

From the perspective of karma and reincarnation, there are many evolutionary purposes fulfilled for the Soul incarnating into conditions of poverty. There can be karmic reasons for poverty related to the misuse and abuse of excess wealth and power in the past. Souls may also be learning valuable lessons about how much is truly needed to be joyful in life or learning values of mutual support, compassion, and solidarity that are prevalent in many poor communities, or learning that the poor should be helped to develop their skills, rather than be blamed. These lessons are then carried into the next life, helping one to build a better character. This perspective should be a cautionary one for wealthy people who misuse their wealth in this life through indulgence or indifference to others' needs, as their Soul may then require them to learn some of these lessons in future incarnations.

In the 1980s, through arbitrage, greenmail, and leveraged buyouts, part of the wealth that had previously been held by corporations moved into the hands of individuals, epitomizing the essence of the capitalistic ethos "Looking out for number one." The inner purpose of this expression of unrestrained greed and egoism may well be to allow humanity to see clearly what happens when selfishness, ambition, and accumulation are unchecked by any sense of concern or compassion for other humans or the earth. However, the solutions to the world's economic problems will not be found in the realm of the ego—only in the consciousness of the Soul. The accumulation of effects from ego-centered economic activities is steadily becoming so overwhelming that egos are being driven to reach to the Soul for answers for the future.

The United States has had to deal with the humiliating experience of having Japan, its former wartime adversary, buy up many of its cultural icons, including movie studios and major New York real estate. Japan, a youthful capitalist country, is holding up a mirror to the gradually aging, tired face of corporate America. As in Oscar Wilde's *Picture of Dorian Gray*, the image shows a host of sins: forced by raiders and brokerage houses to keep stock prices high to avoid takeovers, U.S. business has been driven to make numerous short-term decisions based on quarterly profits. And although the Japanese economy also suffered a recession, Japanese companies still work with long-term planning and a more secure and thus dedicated work force. They continue to dominate whole new markets with high-quality products financed by low-interest "patient capital" provided by prodigious Japanese savers and long-term corporate investors.

REGULATION AND GREED

The deregulation philosophy of former President Reagan and the conservatives led to hundreds of savings and loan (S&L) bankruptcies due to corruption and incompetency. By refusing to acknowledge its role in maintaining a healthy financial system, the Reagan government could be likened to a nonfunctioning thyroid gland. The thyroid is called the "master gland," as it regulates all other glands in the body, maintaining a balance among them. Once its regulatory function was thwarted—through elimination or reduction of the government's role in oversight, enforcement, and accounting—all the other systems in the economic body went out of control. Without the oversight function the government provides, these systems lost a relatively more principled, ethical coordination that made certain all economic actors were playing fairly. Former President Bush continued and even accelerated this disastrous policy, and it is interesting to note that both he and Mrs. Bush have a thyroid condition, which made them incapable of properly "regulating" themselves or the government and economy.

The issue of what constitutes a fair distribution of the profits from a corporation arose anew with President Bush's ill-conceived trip to Japan in 1992 to ask the Japanese to purchase more American cars and goods. The trip was epitomized by President Bush getting sick and collapsing on the lap of the Japanese Prime Minister, who ended up holding his head, symbolic of the overfed and weakened condition of much of the U.S. populace, not to mention the U.S. economy, which needs to be supported by other nations. A huge controversy was ignited when it was revealed that the twelve American CEOs who accompanied Bush made an average of more than $2 million a year, compared with Japanese CEOs (of much more successful companies) who averaged less than $400,000 a year. What really produced an outcome far different from expected as a result of the trip, however, was the revelation that Robert Stempel, CEO of General Motors, made $2.2 million in a year when his company lost $4.5 billion and announced 74,000 layoffs of workers. A Japanese Finance Ministry official told *The Wall Street Journal* that in Japan "you'd cut executive pay before eliminating jobs."

This spotlight focused on top executives' pay (which often exceeds by 100 times that of the lowest-paid worker and can reach as much as 1,200 times, as it does at United Airlines) shows the power of bringing an issue into the light. Shortly thereafter, American boards of directors and stockholders voted out ineffective or corrupt executives in many companies and nonprofits, including American Express, United Way, and others, and gave stockholders more of a voice in determining executive pay.

DECRYSTALLIZING ECONOMICS

Many well-respected critics are seeing the limitations of capitalism and are helping to remove the collective blindness we sometimes have that prevents us from seeing its shortcomings. The rationale for capitalism owes much to the eighteenth-century British economist Adam Smith, who postulated that social good would emerge from the countless selfish individual decisions of all members of the society, regulated by the "invisible hand" of the free marketplace. Critics of capitalism have pointed out that the marketplace is often stacked against those who are disadvantaged, exploited, or lacking in resources. This simple model of the economy was developed before the emergence of the vast technological society that exists today and does not accurately account for the effects of social structures, access to media, and other advantages that accrue to those with access to privileged information.

Endless economic growth as the indicator of well-being is now being questioned. The U.S. gross national product (GNP) includes such things as hospitalization costs for cancer and mental illness and the bills for cleaning up oil spills—certainly none of which indicates well-being. And it does not deduct from the balance sheet the depletion of environmental capital resources, which is financing much of the current growth. In addition, the GNP ignores the nonmonetized "sweat equity" sector of the economy, as well as the natural environment on which the entire economy depends. This nonmonetized sector—all the work that people do on their own homes, projects, volunteer work, caring for relatives and friends, and barter exchanges—is actually of greater monetary value than the entire sector of the economy measured by money.

Economist Hazel Henderson envisions us moving from the current information age based on computer-chip technology to the dawning Solar Age, a paradigm shift she calls the "Age of Light." This will be an economic era in which we recognize that the light of the sun is what powers our planet. The Age of Light will be characterized by our growing abilities to cooperate with and learn from nature. Development will be reconceptualized as investments in people and in the restoration and maintenance of ecosystems.[3]

There are many people questioning whether basic human needs are being met by the current consumer-oriented marketing society. These include the need for permanence (or subsistence), protection, affection, understanding, participation, leisure, creativity, identity (or meaning), freedom, and being as well as having.[4] Others point out that the need for self-chosen tasks and personal challenges to stimulate human growth is not included in most sectors of the conformist, corporate model. Many thoughtful people are raising the question of the scale of economic entities, the lack of control most people feel over their economic destinies, and the terms of their work participation. Many of these criticisms apply equally to both capitalistic and more centrally controlled economies, such as China's, since both are inherently technological, resource exploiting, and focused primarily on material goals.

FREEING THE FLOW

The fall of the Berlin Wall has removed one of the blockages to circulation in the planetary economic system, which is now allowing capital, resources, technology, and information to flow into a united Germany and other Eastern European nations. In an unusual development at the economic summit of major economic nations in 1991, the leaders of the economically powerful G-7 nations (United States, Britain, Japan, Germany, France, Canada, and Italy) came together, not to take advantage of the problems of the former Soviet Union, but to decide who would help them and how it could be done.

Some in the West see the collapse of Soviet communism as a "victory" for capitalism. But any sense of victory will be short-lived, as the inequities of capitalism will continue to confront wealthy nations around the world and will lead inevitably to a crisis. According to Willis Harman, Director of the Institute for Noetic Sciences and a consultant to Fortune 500 corporations, this will happen by the end of this century as the sense of legitimacy is gradually withdrawn from certain distorted aspects of capitalism, including banking and insurance systems, health care systems, and even some large international corporations: "People will continue to demand that corporations have more of a sense of purpose, do meaningful things, and be environmentally responsible."[5] With the fall of communism, justifications for continuing as large military weapons production, an economic driver for Western capitalism, have become ever more insupportable.

BALANCING THE INDIVIDUAL AND THE WHOLE

As a result of the fall of communism, the illusory concept of the "free market" has triumphed, which says government direction of the economy is dangerous, while at the same time providing massive subsidies, tax breaks, and bailouts for those with political influence. Although models exist in the United States for a middle or "third way" taking the best of both communism and capitalism, serious discussion of these has only recently been introduced into the political dialogue. Socialism in Europe and Scandinavia has made issues of participation and fairness part of the political dialogue, with the result that those societies have moderated some of the worst abuses of "savage capitalism"—as the French call the American system—while still allowing reward for individual initiative and effort.

According to Lester Thurow, dean of MIT's Sloan School of Management, there is a very significant difference among capitalist models—between the "I" model of American and British capitalism and the "We" model of Germany and Japan. American/British capitalism champions individualistic values, resulting in the brilliant entrepreneur, Nobel Prize winners, large wage differentials, individual responsibility for skills, profit maximization, and hostile mergers and takeovers. In contrast, Germany and Japan hold communitarian values of business groups, social responsibility for skills, teamwork, company loyalty, growth-promoting industry, and government strategies. Japanese and German firms play a game of capitalism best termed "strategic conquest." Americans believe in "consumer economics"; Japanese believe in "producer economics."

In American/British capitalism the individual is expected to have a personal economic strategy for success, while the business firm must develop an economic strategy reflecting the wishes of its shareholders. Since shareholders want maximum profits, customer and employee relations are merely a means of achieving higher profits. Wages are to be beaten down where possible and employees laid off when unneeded. Workers in the American/British system are expected to change employers whenever opportunities for higher wages exist.

In Japanese business firms, however, employees are seen as the number one stakeholder, customers number two, and shareholders number three. Thus, higher employee benefits and wages are a goal in Japan, and the firms can be seen as a "value added maximizer" rather than a "profit maximizer." Profits will be sacrificed to maintain either wages or employment. Workers in the communitarian system join a company team and are then considered successful as part of that team. The key decision for the individual is to join the right team.[6]

The collapsing communist economies of Eastern Europe are struggling to become privatized, while private enterprises in the United States are finding they become most productive and profitable when workers are given increased participation in decision making, job definition, and profit sharing. Both systems are experimenting to find the best ways to stimulate economic development, while maintaining some degree of public or governmental participation in determining the goals, values, and processes of the economic system.

The world community—and each nation individually—needs this dynamic balance, the yang principle of the individual initiating spirit, balanced by the yin principle of the good of the social whole—the matrix that makes individual achievement possible. Recent developments in China, with its southern free trade zones, and introduction of the free market in the former Soviet Union indicate the growing acceptance of this balancing of principles. The record of democratic socialist welfare states in Western Europe—Scandinavia, West Germany, Austria, and Holland, with high standards of living, low unemployment, and high quality of life and sense of community (although challenged by a recession and immigration)—are proof of the benefits of capitalism and socialism coexisting peacefully within a democracy. However, without understanding the deeper, human evolutionary purpose of life as growth in consciousness, and deepening service to humanity, high suicide rates and hopelessness can occur amid material prosperity, as in Sweden.

Business as a discipline offers important spiritual lessons to the Soul who incarnates to work in this energy field. Some of the principles of business include the importance of meeting a need or the principle of service to the customer—a learning ground for the larger concept of service. The principle of individual responsibility, where the individual is responsible and accountable for his/her own performance and achievement, is also present in business. And the principle of grounding your visions, or practicality, is an essential learning that many idealists—and visionaries especially—need to develop.

MONEY, MONEY, MONEY

THE PSYCHOLOGY OF MONEY

In his book *Wealth Addiction,* Philip Slater notes that the development of civilization has seen a steady growth in the importance humanity gives to money, until today, when money has become the single standard of value to which all life is reduced. Its limitation, however, is that it can measure only quantitatively and not qualitatively. By this standard, a sunset has no value, while it costs $400 a barrel to dispose of toxic waste. In addition, money has become an end in itself, rather than a means to be used to purchase things that we need. People say, "I need money," but when they have acquired it, they often forget what they need it for and have to consult a shopping catalog to discover what to spend it on![7]

Once people see money as the key to satisfying all their needs, money is no longer a tool, but a master. It also distracts our attention from the desires that money can't satisfy toward those it does. People who have made money the master of their lives are driven by an emptiness they are trying desperately to fill with external substances or experiences that can be bought. As long as the ego controls—instead of the soul—money will rule.

In this state of consciousness, the satisfaction derived from money does not come simply from having it. It comes from having more of it than others do and having more this year than last. This distorted view can be summed up in the words of a Wall Street banker as "net worth equals self-worth."

The pursuit of money as an end in itself has become an accepted way of life, but it is actually an addiction preoccupying large numbers of people all over the world. Suprisingly, the majority of poorer people in a capitalistic society don't resent those with great wealth—they hope that they will someday "strike it rich" and be wealthy, too. This attitude is reflected in the current proliferation of lotteries—in which everyone pays so a few can win big. This pattern bears a great deal of resemblance to the capitalistic system, where the lowest-possible wages are paid so those at the top of the hierarchy can "win big." Americans spent $286 billion on lotteries and gambling in 1990, and gambling is spreading because it reflects the underlying societal money psychology. In contrast, in a society based on spiritual values, the ruling ethic would not be "May the best person win," but rather "May the best person serve."

Slater comments that the neurotic traits of extreme wealth addicts have become the official ideology of capitalistic society: greed, duplicity, ruthlessness, self-centeredness, and a narrow focus on accumulating money to the exclusion of all else.[8] Once people see all their desires being fulfilled because they have enough money, says Slater, all their goals and desires capable of satisfaction will be replaced by the desire for money itself, which has no natural limit. Since money cannot in itself satisfy anything, they can never have enough. This is true addiction, yet it has become the socially sanctioned way of relating to money for most people.

Addictive behavior is a response to a sense of lack within the personality. This usually means the personality/ego is not listening to some part of the whole Self that would provide the psychological element that is missing. There is an underlying fear, which the ego attempts to control and repress. But that serves only to cut off the individual from the inner connection to all of life and the strength of the life force within the individual. For money addicts, the inability to deal with these deficiencies, which are really imbalances, means that money and the false sense of security it provides become a substitute for inner security. But when the Soul, the inner or Higher Self, is attended to and its advice acted upon, that Self will be able to keep money in proper perspective and use it for the good of the whole.

What Is Money?

Money is a symbolic global medium of exchange among people, representing accumulated human and planetary creative energy. Money is essentially neutral—its value depends on the uses to which it is put. The highest view of money is to see it as a sacred trust to be used for the good of all humanity. Today, the idea that those who own and control money have a "social responsibility" to use it for the benefit of everyone is beginning to influence individuals and public policy around the world.

As a measure of exchanges among people—a system of collective IOUs—money has been present as an energy upon the planet since early Greek civilization. A variety of objects and symbols has been used to represent this medium of exchange, from dogs' teeth and shells to silver and gold, then paper, and now computer digits, as money becomes more and more etherealized. Today, money is credit anchored on the physical plane by a check or by symbols such as figures on a bank statement attached to an individual, group, or corporation. These evidences of symbolic credit confer the power to use money. Over time, humankind has gradually dematerialized actual valuable coinage, and today most governments issue paper promises to pay. This has allowed the devaluing of money, with no reference to what it will actually purchase, as well as increasing opportunities for speculation and manipulation by educated elites.

Money is a golden, flowing stream of concretized life energy. From the perspective of the Ageless Wisdom, money is a thought-form created from Divine energy, vitalized by human desire, and kept in existence by humanity's constant, unceasing demand. However, when the desire for money is separative and greedy, and its use runs counter to humanity's growth and development, it brings trouble and suffering.

What we call money is actually a freezing of the flow of life force energy, and accumulations of money are simply eddies in the stream of life. However, what is important is the flow—not the temporary crystallizing of it. This golden flow represents the physical, emotional, or mental energies moving through an individual or group. It becomes money only when this energy comes in contact with the collective human economic system. For example, a person's physical energy or vitality can be exchanged for money when it is marketed as physical labor. A person who has emotional charisma and charm can find many ways of turning that energy into money as an entertainer or politician. People working with ideas, such as writers or professors, can use innovative ways of conceptualizing to create wealth.

All this is the flow of energy generated by the creative capacities of human beings, expressed at different levels of vibration depending on the purity and clarity of the individual. Together, all the collective flows constitute the human economic system, within which we can each exchange the results of our flows for the results of other people's, through money. However, this golden stream is currently entrapped by man's selfishness, greed, fear, insecurity, love of power, and other ego-controlled attitudes and behaviors. Money is currently magnetically bound to selfish purposes by desire and is not free to circulate where it is needed.

Gordon had a personal experience of the energy that surrounds money when he became the Executive Director of the Social Investment Forum after living in a protected spiritual community for ten years, where money was not a major focus. As he traveled into the financial district of Boston each week and worked closely with people in the financial world, he experienced the "aura" or atmosphere that surrounds money. It is not a pleasant energy, as it is loaded with human thought-forms and emotions such as "There isn't going to be enough," "I have to accumulate," "I might lose it all," and "The more money I have, the more powerful I'll be." All these energies are floating around in the energy field surrounding money, and it is necessary to be aware of them so that our consciousness does not become caught up by or encased in one of them. The challenge for all of us today—with the global evolution in consciousness now taking place and with the spiritual regeneration that comes from listening to the inner Self—is to transform money into a magical tool to be used for the redemption of the world.

A perspective on the question "What is enough?" is that enough is simply that which is required to fulfill one's destiny. What is enough would depend on what the person's responsibilities are, the type of life she/he leads, and the circumstances in which life and his/her karma have placed him/her. It would vary greatly if someone were a president or a plumber, someone with a large family or someone with none. Each of us has a particular destiny to fulfill based on our Soul's plan, the lessons we need to learn, and the gifts we can give to the world; and what is enough will depend on what is required to fulfill our Soul destiny. Of course it is easy for our personality to have exaggerated ideas of our destiny and attempt to accumulate excess resources, but this will only bring difficulty and suffering if it is more than truly needed.

THE DIVINE CIRCULATORY FLOW

Our planet is a living organism, balancing energy flows throughout the realms of nature as well as among individuals, groups, and nations. All economic interactions, from the individual to the international, take place within this body of moving energies. The planetary economic system flourishes best when there is a maximum circulation of goods, resources, and services throughout the entire body, nourishing all life in the system, thus strengthening the whole. Given access to this basic life support, human beings will become producers as well as consumers and contribute to the overall health of the system.

ECONOMICS AS AN ENERGY SYSTEM

Using the alchemical principle "As above so below; as below so above," if our individual bodies are seen as energy systems composed of flowing lines of energy in motion, with major intersection points, or chakras, then our planetary body is also an energy system, a living organism with its flows and circulation system. Our economic system with its circulation of resources, capital, goods, education, and information is part of and dependent on the moving energies of our planet's life flows, especially the biological flow systems.

Therefore we can see that unimpeded flow is the key to economic health. In a relevant analogy from Chinese medicine, illness is defined as too much or too little energy concentrated in one place in the body. Thus in one sense, our planet and its economic system are ill. Too much energy is concentrated in certain areas of the planetary body (the wealthy nations) and too little concentrated in the underdeveloped nations. When one visits these underdeveloped countries, there is a sense of low energy, of few resources, little education, information, and, most important, sense of hope or self-empowerment in the people. Most of the diseases are diseases of deprivation—malnutrition, unsafe water, lack of adequate housing and health care.

By contrast, the United States, which has 6 percent of the world's population, consumes 30 percent of the world's resources. It suffers from a multitude of "diseases of excess" that occur in many wealthy nations—overeating and attendant diseases, high stress, addictions of all kinds, pollution, the garbage disposal crisis, the recent problem of "infoglut" (information overload), and most significant, the existential crisis of trying to find meaning in life through endless consuming and accumulating (often palliated with drugs).

Yet at the same time this wealth has given us the security and time to concern ourselves with Soul development, culture, beauty, and refinement. The real distortions come when excess accumulates and is not circulated.

One way to make this question very personal is to ask yourself, "If I weren't already born, and didn't know where I would be born, how would I like to see the resources of the world distributed?" One of the major lessons for wealthy countries in the 1990s is likely to be the realization that they cannot be islands of prosperity in a sea of deprivation. A flood of starving and homeless people will constantly threaten developed countries, as Germany, the United States, and other countries have learned.

The current complexity of our financial system often masks the simple purpose of promoting economic life and exchange. According to economist Peter F. Drucker, this is the result of "the emergence of the symbol economy—capital movements, exchange rates, and credit flows—as the flywheel of the world economy, in place of the 'real economy'—the flow of goods and services."[9] As a result, money—the symbol of exchange and circulation—has become a commodity divorced from the life-sustaining goods and services it represents.

All these problems are indications of living a life out of balance with the Law of Supply and Need, the true spiritual economic law, rather than the Law of Supply and Demand. The Law of Supply and Need says that resources should flow to help people provide for their own basic needs such as food, shelter, clothing, education, and health care—and that these needs must be met within the entire system before resources are devoted to less fundamental human needs, otherwise known as desires.

Many of the political struggles on the planet today are about balancing the right of all to share in a decent way of life with the equally important responsibility to learn how to help themselves. But it is also becoming clear that it is in the self-interest of wealthy nations to use their wealth to assist other countries in developing themselves. Richard Fremel, in a study for the Arms Control and Foreign Policy Caucus, stated that 85 percent of every dollar of foreign aid comes back to buy exports from the United States. Economic stagnation of underdeveloped countries costs us greatly—to the level of $440 billion in annual lost exports and 1.8 million lost jobs.

Highly respected Wall Street investment banker Felix G. Rohatyn stated in late 1993 that no major Western country is capable of generating sufficient economic growth to cure its structural unemployment. He noted that, for the first time in modern history, the locomotive for the West must come from growth in Asia and Latin America. He affirmed that the future of our economy is organically and permanently tied to the developing world.

ECONOMIC VALUES OF THE PERSONALITY AND THE SOUL

There is a growing realization that we do have the planetary resources and human capacity to feed, clothe, and house everyone on earth adequately with proper circulation and careful use of those resources, combined with education in sustainability and self-reliance. Our task is to transform our identities that are now based on scarcity, fear, and greed, which cause excess accumulation, into identities as limitless channels of energy, inventiveness, and abundance. We must change our self-definition from personality consumer to Soul creator.

To accomplish this, we must understand the causes of our current economic problems, and consider factors that are excluded in standard economic equations—the psychological and spiritual dimensions of human beings. Because classical economics refuses to deal with larger spiritual questions, it defines human beings as solely wage or salary earners and consumers.

Yet much of the current economic crisis is a reflection of the conflict between the values of "economic man," or the personality, and the values of the Soul. These two value systems or states of consciousness are now in great conflict, causing a global crisis of identity. The personality values are based on separation, dominance, control, and grasping for the isolated self. The personality is governed by its desires—defining itself by what it owns, controls, consumes, spends, or eats. This leads to a consciousness of scarcity and competitiveness and keeps us preoccupied with material standards set by elites, harassed by debt and so starved for time that we think we have little time for our inner spiritual lives. All this is a major triumph for the forces of materialism on our planet, yet it is also a learning process for us all. For in exhausting the possibilities of self-centered living, we finally come to realize that it doesn't really bring satisfaction or happiness.

The personal, separative state of consciousness is a kind of "black hole syndrome." All effort is bent toward bringing energy to the self—using, consuming, and accumulating to ease the inner sense of emptiness that can never be fulfilled materially. We do need to take in basic things to sustain ourselves, but if our fundamental orientation is that of taking energy into the self, a pattern is established that reinforces passivity and the habit of consumerism. There is a sense of emptiness or lack, which we then try to fill with things, and we become habituated to having to take in to feel happy or have self-esteem. Our identity becomes defined as what we consume, own, or control.

This is symbolized perfectly by a major bank credit card whose ad promises to give its possessor "more power to get what you want out of life"—as if life were a sponge to be squeezed to the last drop of selfish satisfaction. In order for us to redefine ourselves as more than just "consumers," we have to overcome the hundreds of messages we receive each day from Madison Avenue urging us to buy—something, anything. This takes real inner strength.

The transformation of identity from the personal self to the Soul is based on aligning ourselves with this inner, spiritual source, which is always present as a potential within the human being. It is available whenever the personality can break through the frantic busyness of modern life and become quiet enough to listen to the still, small voice of the Soul. The Soul will make us aware of what brings true inner happiness and provide access to the energy to develop and express creative abilities from within. Our need to consume is thus transformed into the ability to love, to create, to give to the world. We shift the energy flow from being a consuming black hole to being a radiant sun.

We can then begin to experience our own Being as an unlimited source and flow of Love, Light, and authentic power, which flows from us to others and our world. When this flow of our energies—whether our vitality, creativity, mental ideas, or emotional charisma—comes into contact with the collective human economic system, it then can be turned into money, the crystallized measurement of this flow and a medium to be exchanged for the results of other people's flow. This Soul energy flowing through us will provide what is needed for the individual Self, but not necessarily all that is desired, which in itself is a deep learning experience. The experience of this energy flow, this higher state of Being, is where true joy and fulfillment are found. It leads to the radiant, cellular health of the entire human kingdom. If there is any doubt about the truth of this, we can ask ourselves how we felt after buying the latest consumer item promising to bring instant happiness and compare this with how we felt after doing something that truly helped someone else.

Out of our experience of identity with the Soul arises the sense of abundance. We begin to realize that we have unlimited energy resources within us. We can then drop the old sense of scarcity, of "There's not going to be enough" and "I have to compete to get what I need," to a sense of infinite abundance within us and around us. Once we come in contact with these inner resources, we realize we have not only an abundance of energy that can be converted into money if we choose, but that by choosing to need less money and doing more for ourselves (voluntary simplicity), we can have more time to experience, express, and give away the gifts of our Being. Much of the pressure many of us feel to obtain money is because we are out of touch with our inner, spiritual source.

Once we develop this sense of abundance, sharing becomes a natural and spontaneous overflow from a loving heart and an intelligent mind. As we share, we gradually experience greater unity with others, with humanity as a whole, and with the planet, as the polarity of giver and receiver dissolves in the experience of unity. As this sharing circulates throughout the planetary web of life, we all experience greater abundance and joyous living.

ECONOMIC CIRCULATION—THE KARMIC BANK ACCOUNT

Money itself has provided developed individuals with the means to exploit and manipulate financial systems, people, resources, and the earth for purely selfish purposes, with the present disastrous consequences, where the starving stand in agonized accusation of the overfed. This situation is caused by holding the wrong thought about money. In addition, wrong educational methods emphasizing selfishness and competition, and the ease with which the weak and helpless can be exploited, have contributed to the problem.

However, individual, national, and group selfishness, based on a fear of lack and scarcity, has now come to a climax. It is increasingly clear that these conditions can be rebalanced only by changing human attitudes and freeing humanity from economic bondage. In the future, money must meet group and world need.

One way to change attitudes about money is for us to understand what we call our "karmic bank account." We know that if we go into the world with the clear motive to "make a bundle," it is possible to become very wealthy and build up our worldly bank accounts. What is less obvious, but nonetheless true, is that it is possible to live happily by going into the world with a different motivation: to offer something at very low cost or free to those in need, or perhaps to work for an organization whose purpose we are committed to, volunteering, or taking a much smaller salary than we know we're worth. When we choose to do this, we are building up our "karmic bank account."

It has been our observation that we each have two accounts operating at all times. One is our worldly bank account, and the other is our karmic account. When we are receiving more than we are actually contributing to life, we may build up our worldly bank account, but we're taking it out of our karmic account. When we give more than we receive, we are building up our karmic account.

We worked for years building organizations for no or little pay, without really being concerned about how much we were giving or recieving. Then, when we needed financial assistance, it was always available, either as gifts, loans, or well-paid work. Building up our karmic account is based on the motive behind the work done, and when work is sincerely given with intent to serve others, the account does grow.

Some people, of course, have exhausted their karmic account, so they always seem to lose what they try to accumulate in their worldly accounts. Even in conventional wisdom, there is a sense of this, according to *Newsweek,* as many people see charity as a way of "placating the gods" and keeping catastrophe at bay. Princeton University sociologist Robert Wuthnow noted that "for some donors, there is a sense that giving will somehow help you at a later point if you need it—like a form of insurance."[10] However, the best thing about your karmic account is that you can take it with you, as it is a factor in determining your financial circumstances in your next incarnation.

INTEREST, DEBT, AND ECONOMIC CIRCULATION

For money to be used for the good of the whole, however, major changes will have to take place in the structure of our global financial system. The practice of charging interest on the use of money was called "usury" in the Bible, the Koran, and in historical canon law. It was outlawed, with severe punishment for its practice. Yet over the centuries, this practice was renamed "interest," and today all money that is loaned or circulates through the economic system has compound interest attached to it. Compound interest means that a debt or investment will grow exponentially through the years, illustrated by the fact that if $1 is borrowed or invested at 10 percent compound interest, the interest on the interest grows to $13,780 in one hundred years.

In the United States, as a result of the Federal Reserve Act of 1913, all currency printed or put into circulation by the federal government must be borrowed at compound interest from the Federal Reserve—an agency with a deliberately misleading title, as it is really a private consortium of banks, with its chairman appointed by the president. The system works similarly in most other countries, and this means that the international banking cartel and the world's financial elite are receiving compound interest for every dollar, yen, or deutsche mark that is circulating in the global economy.

One of the outcomes of this system, says Thomas H. Greco, Jr., in *Money and Debt,* is a necessity for the money supply to expand at a rate equal to the interest rate, so that money will be available to pay the principal and ever-growing interest in the system. This does not usually happen, which creates a shortage which is worsened by the Federal Reserve's practice of taking money out of circulation when loans are repaid. Since the only way to get more money into circulation is to borrow it into the system from the Federal Reserve, new money must be constantly issued, all with compound interest attached to it, payable to the banks. The U.S. government currently serves as a "borrower of last resort" to put money into the system and keep it from collapse. If the money supply is not increased at a rate equal to the interest rate, inflation usually results, because the growth in production does not equal the interest rate.[11]

This financial system is especially devastating to poor countries, which try to drive up their rate of productivity and growth to meet the interest rate, converting their natural resources into cash—which current accounting systems do not indicate as resource depletion and consumption of a country's ecological capital. This in turn spurs ecological devastation and ultimate impoverishment of their people.

There are other important ramifications of this unbalanced system. Since the entire money supply is currency, or is issued through checking accounts and bank credit borrowed into existence from the Federal Reserve (upon which banks continuously collect interest), it is mathematically impossible for the people of the United States (or the world), in the aggregate, to ever get out of debt. The total owed requires more money than is ever in existence at one time and, if paid off, would leave the economy with no medium of exchange. Currently there is fifteen times more debt owed by individuals and institutions than there is money in the system to pay for it.

It is a bizarre fact that the creation of a medium of exchange (money) requires people to go into debt to a banking cartel, which now holds a mortgage on most of the property in the world. And because of the high cost of borrowing money—for instance, the current cost of a house, including all mortgage costs, is two-thirds interest—most people spend two-thirds of their lives working to pay interest to these institutions. In addition, debt is used as a driver for consumer spending, which is two-thirds of the U.S. GNP. This which could not be maintained at current levels without massive consumer debt, since spending so far outstrips income.

The total debt and interest that poorer nations owed to the wealthy nations meant that the net transfer of payments from the poor to the rich nations in 1988 was $43 billion! Thus the lavish life-styles of the wealthy nations are financed by the poverty of the rest of the world. This is a system that is so totally out of harmony with moral balance and karmic law that it will have to be reformed or it will eventually destroy itself. (For a fuller explanation of this issue see *Debt Virus* by Jacques Jaikaran in the bibliography.)

Proposals for reform of this distorted system are being made. William Raspberry, for example, writing in *The Washington Post* discussed an idea from Ken Bohnsack, a Midwestern businessman, who proposed that tax-supported bodies be able to borrow money interest-free, directly from the U.S. Treasury, for capital projects and for paying off existing debt. The Treasury would get the money not from the federal budget, but by Congress creating interest-free money as it is authorized to do in the U.S. Constitution. Bohnsack correctly argues that the size of the money supply does not cause inflation; the interest on the money does. He proposes taking the interest-free money out of circulation as loans are repaid.[12]

INEQUITIES OF WEALTH AND THE CIRCULATION SYSTEM

The results of the manipulation of the financial system by the banking cartel is a vast inequality in the distribution of wealth. According to Ravi Batra, in *Surviving the Great Depression of 1990*, the wealthiest 1 percent in 1987 held 36 percent of the national wealth in the United States, compared with 24 percent in 1969. The wealthiest 10 percent of the population controls 72 percent of all capital in the United States and 94 percent of all noncorporate assets. The consequences of this concentration of wealth are profound. When the wealthy have more money—as they did from the tax cuts of the 1980s—they prefer to speculate rather than invest. This resulted in a rash of corporate takeovers and the development of monopolies. Mergers grew from $11.1 billion in 1975 to $180 billion in 1986.[13]

The vast differences between the rich and poor have many detrimental effects on the functioning of the democratic system. Those who have accumulated massive wealth have much greater ability to donate to political candidates and thus to affect the political system to their advantage, as is evidenced by the current tax code. This corrodes citizens' belief in the fairness of the political system and leads to the cynicism and alienation that we see today.

The vast inequality in income distribution also affects the ability of U.S. companies to be competitive in the world marketplace, as the inflated salaries of U.S. CEOs take money away from more practical uses such as research and development, which would make companies more competitive. Also, when workers know there are such vast salary differentials, it makes it difficult to develop the atmosphere of teamwork experienced by the Germans and Japanese.

Finally, the unlimited wealth of a small, select group has a corrupting effect on average citizens, who will often compromise their moral principles at the prospect of a higher income, because it is considered the measure of one's self-worth. This inner structure is held in place by the illusionary dreams of many people who aspire to vast wealth yet are trapped in an exploitive wage system.

Throughout the 1980s, tax cuts for the wealthy increased the disparities and debt, as funding of social programs and defense spending were financed through borrowing rather than taxing. Consumer debt rose because the poor and middle class had less wealth to purchase necessities, and corporate debt increased because of the rush of mergers and takeovers. Interest rates rise as greater disparity of wealth creates greater demand for loans—especially when the poor borrow more. It also weakens the banking system, for the rich put more cash in banks, which must be lent out, but the borrowers become ever poorer credit risks, which leads to bank instability and failures, as we have witnessed.

Ravi Batra points out that this inequity of wealth has proven to be the most reliable indicator of an oncoming depression—the economic and karmic corrective for an unbalanced condition of disharmony. In an economic depression there is a leveling of wealth, a lessening of the emphasis on material values, and more mutual cooperation. Depressions also remove false images of the self, which have been defined by possessions rather than a sense of inner worth. People then discover what their true worth is—the ability of an individual or a nation to create unity and harmony with other people and the environment so that the evolution of all is enhanced.

When the Weimar republic collapsed in 1933 after the hyperinflation of the early 1920s, professionals and tradespeople were soon solvent again while speculators were ruined. The spiritual purpose of any economic upheaval is to create a convergence of situations so uncontrollable that the ego will have to reach to the Soul to survive, recognizing that life cannot ultimately be controlled by manipulations of the ego.

INDIVIDUALS CIRCULATING THEIR ABUNDANCE

There are many examples of individuals who have transcended or are in the process of transcending the fears and attachments of the personality, to living as an example of the Soul expressing its sense of infinite abundance and willingness to give. Albert Schweitzer, impelled by a deep inner conviction, left his successful life as a musical prodigy in France to serve as a doctor to the lepers of Africa—an example of the joy and wonder of living the abundance of the Soul. Dag Hammarskjöld, former secretary general of the

United Nations who was killed trying to bring peace to the Belgian Congo, saw his life of sacrifice for public service as a demanding yet joyous path.

There are also generous-spirited people like our friend Jamie Babson, a peace activist who was born to an upper-class Boston family descended from John Adams. Describing his process of identity transformation, he told us: "I felt like the Buddha growing up in a castle, never being told what was happening in the world. When I saw people in Morocco and Central and South America being joyful and living reasonably well with very little, I began to question the surplus I inherited when I turned twenty-one. I had been taught the Thirteenth Commandment, engraved on my father's cocktail glasses, which said, 'Thou shalt not invade thy principal!' "

Babson came in contact with two spiritual leaders in India. One, he said, "showed me the power of love, which money can't buy." The other leader he met advocated the voluntary redistribution of wealth. Within two years Babson had given away two-thirds of his $600,000 inheritance to social change groups and put the rest in an irrevocable trust.

"When I gave away this wealth I felt I received other, intangible things that were of greater spiritual power—more of a real connection and commitment to other people on the planet," Babson recalled. "Money creates walls of inequity and fear that keep people away. Even though I was taught to build them up, I tore my own walls down. Now I don't evaluate myself by how much I have, but on what percentage I give away of what I have."[14]

Chuck Collins, another wealthy heir who works to empower the poor to create land trusts and low-cost housing, gave away his entire $250,000 inheritance to peace, justice, and environmental groups. In an interview in the newsletter *Community Economics,* he said his basic philosophy is that "all the money that had accrued to me did not belong to me. There is a social mortgage on capital, meaning that society has a claim on all that wealth. I don't question that capital should be formed, but that it should not be controlled by a limited number of individuals. A more economically just society would have a fairer distribution of assets and more wealth owned by social institutions, not just by the state."[15]

SHARING AS CIRCULATION

The key to right circulation is sharing. By sharing, concentrations of resources become beneficial to more people than just those who hold the assets. This can be done through socially responsible investing, which is concerned with careful consideration of the social effects of our investments or philanthropic giving. As these investments circulate, they build well-being and prosperity for all. This type of sharing is based on a realization of the unity of all humanity, a unity that is often discovered by systematically taking into account the interconnectedness of all life. This leads to inclusive thinking and ultimately to the experience of our common humanity.

The idea of free circulation and sharing is emerging today with the concept of "free trade zones." In addition to the European Community, there is the North American Free Trade Agreement (NAFTA) approved by the United States, Canada, and Mexico. A leveling of the economic playing field throughout the hemisphere would in the long term benefit practically everyone except for those few who now enjoy protected monopolies.

However, the downside of free trade agreements such as the international General Agreement on Tariffs and Trade (GATT) and NAFTA is that the U.S. environmental standards on food, air, water, and endangered species could be reduced by conformity to weaker international environmental regulations. This provides an opportunity to work toward standardizing environmental regulations around the world to the highest level that currently exists. Thus, even though these free trade zones bring problems of job flight and the ability of multinational corporations to play one country off against another in a competition to see who will offer the lowest environmental standards, cheapest labor, and natural resources, in the long run the result will be beneficial. These agreements will increase the circulation of goods, resources, services, and ultimately ideas and consciousness among peoples of different nations.

Another area of sharing that promotes circulation is the issue of equitable sharing of jobs. With so many people already unemployed, and more young people seeking work for the first time every year, the economic challenge is not only to create as many jobs as possible, but also to share available work more equitably. One of the transformations that could take place is reducing the work week as a means of providing employment for more people, an idea long espoused by European trade unions.

This could help resolve the current ludicrous situation where some people are working sixty to one hundred hours a week, under great stress and pressure, often at two or even three jobs, while many others are not working at all. This shift could occur as people realize they do not need to work endless hours to possess every possible consumer item and vast sums of money in the bank to feel secure. This shift in work schedules would give us more time for our families, for doing more things for ourselves, for volunteering or working on community projects, rather than hiring people to do all the things we can't because we're too busy and rushed. This ultimately helps create a more balanced way of life, allowing the time for reflection and self-development necessary for the Soul to deeply influence the personality.

NEW MODELS OF SHARING

Many groups are beginning to demonstrate how this type of circulation and sharing can be accomplished within the existing economic structures. They are based on new ideas and values of cooperation, group solidarity, and individual empowerment. The work of several of these groups is outlined below.

The Grameen Bank

Through credit rather than outright donations, many new groups are helping to increase the flow of resources from the wealthiest part of the planetary economic system to areas where there is the greatest need. The spiritual grandfather of this movement is Dr. Mohammad Yunus, founder of the Grameen Bank in Bangladesh, who for thirteen years has been making loans averaging $67, with a 98 percent payback rate, to poor people who create their own businesses. Yunus developed the basic model of bringing together groups of five people, training them in starting small businesses, loaning money to two people in the group, and in six weeks, when that loan is repaid, loaning to the next two borrowers, and to the last members when the second loan is repaid. He sees economic development and credit as a matter of human rights, not just economic growth. "Credit is a powerful economic weapon," says Yunus, "and can equip a dispossessed person to fight the economic odds. It creates an opportunity for self-employment, in which the poor person can control his economic destiny."[16]

ACCION

ACCION International also addresses the problem of extreme poverty and unemployment throughout Latin America by providing small loans and business training to over seventeen thousand owner/operators of very small businesses each year. In 1991, working in partnership with local private organizations in fifteen different countries, including the United States and Nicaragua, ACCION loaned over $5.2 million each month to very poor people who created their own businesses out of scant resources and minimal capital. These loans average $371 each to fruit vendors in Colombia, furniture makers in Mexico, or seamstresses in the Dominican Republic. All of these people had no access to any credit and yet maintain a loan repayment rate of over 98 percent, similar to the results of other such groups.

Those receiving these loans come from a vast number of hardworking people who are self-employed or working for family, neighbors, or friends and have no legal status in their society. They often lack access to commercial loans, insurance, legal assistance, and formal education. From Gordon's work in India he learned the importance of small loans to microentrepreneurs, who often pay 20 to 50 percent interest rates to local money lenders. In 1991 ACCION lent over $64 million in loans averaging $371 to 96,600 microbusinesses, indirectly assisting 350,000 of the most needy as family members or employees. For every dollar contributed to ACCION, 87.5 cents goes directly to program services, in contrast with U.S. government foreign assistance, where 70 cents of every dollar allocated remains in the United States for administrative costs.[17]

ACCION uses a variation on the Solidarity Group program developed by Dr. Yunus for the Grameen Bank. Since five to eight individuals take responsibility for a group loan, peer support keeps defaults to a minimum and makes the group eligible for further loans. Members of the self-selecting groups are given bookkeeping and management training and technical assistance. On the rare occasion that a group defaults, a lawyer goes out to collect the money so that people understand it is a business endeavor, not welfare.

ACCION's innovative programs are now functioning in over sixty cities and towns in fifteen countries, including programs in Arizona, southern California, and Brooklyn, New York. The principles of these programs could be applied in many other countries, providing the key to meeting the needs of some of the most disadvantaged people in underdeveloped countries, by circulating resources to those who have the most difficulty obtaining them.

The Korean Kye

A variation on these models is the indigenous Korean method of self-financed businesses that is used by many Korean immigrants to the United States to set up the ubiquitous convenience stores and green grocery businesses. The typical Korean immigrant begins by working for friends or family, holding three or four low-paying jobs and saving every penny. After several years the immigrants save up enough to join a *kye*. These are usually set up by a woman, gathering together a group of relatives or friends whom she trusts. Each month every member of the *kye* contributes a set amount of money to the group. Each member in turn gets to keep one month's collections to use for whatever purpose, usually for starting a business. In a

$20,000 *kye*, each of twenty members will contribute $1,000 each month and one member will receive $20,000. After twenty months each member will have been repaid and the *kye* will dissolve.

Kyes also help to build the strong community ties that assure no one defaults on a payment, which would bring great shame on the family and make it nearly impossible to get a job among Korean-Americans. This system provides strong incentives for Korean immigrants to save, to invest in new business, and to succeed, so as not to let the group down.

SOCIALLY RESPONSIBLE USE OF MONEY

"The most important single question an investor can ask is not, 'What is the purpose of my money?'" says Paul Hawken, entrepreneur and business author, "but, 'What is the purpose of my life?'" Investments should first be assessed for what they do to the investor. "Does an investment make you feel more secure? Does it support an entity or activity that you wish to see benefit by the investment?"[18]

The idea that the owner and controller of money has a "social responsibility" to invest and use money in a way that benefits not only the individual, but the whole of society, has gradually taken hold since the 1960s. Growing numbers of individual and institutional investors now accept the idea of making investments using social as well as financial criteria. Newly awakened socially conscious investors and consumers are beginning to realize that by voting with their investing and buying dollars, they can influence the kind of economy and environment their money is creating.

When Gordon served as Executive Director of the Social Investment Forum, the national professional association for socially responsible investment professionals, he saw the total assets invested with some type of social screen grow from $40 billion in 1984 to $700 billion in 1992. The growth in this social investing movement reflects the power of an idea whose time has come. Many of the people he worked with were baby boomers who had either inherited money or had increased their incomes developing their careers. They had substantial money to invest but wanted to do so in ways that were congruent with their values of peace, economic justice, and environmental awareness.

These concerned people use three different strategies for social investing:

• Avoidance—refusing to invest in companies that make products or services they don't support.

• Positive reinvesting—supporting companies or community loan funds that are doing things they want to contribute to.
• Activism—investing in companies they want to change and exercising ownership rights through shareholder resolutions.

Today, portfolios, mutual funds, money market funds, IRAs, and insurance plans have been created to help people invest according to their ethical values. The Calvert Group of funds and the Working Assets Money Fund are two such examples. After initial resistance, social investing has been accepted by the mainstream brokerage houses, primarily because customers are asking for it. Even Lehman Brothers now has its own social investing division. The social investment movement also includes the National Association of Community Development Loan Funds, with forty-one loan fund members who provide capital to those traditionally excluded from economic benefits.

Critics of socially responsible investing (S.R.I.), claim that stockbrokers are simply offering "guilt-free" investing to wealthy individuals. They also insist that such investing has had no real effect on corporate behavior or in the larger world, as in South Africa, for example.

However, it is clear to us that the divestment of stocks by pension funds has been a major factor in U.S. companies' withdrawal from South Africa, and has proved very effective in the international effort to strangle the South African economy, thus bringing about much-needed social change. Otherwise, why would Nelson Mandela have urged Americans to keep up the embargoes on investment and trade until negotiations with the South African government were completed?

S.R.I. is having a growing impact because its very existence is creating an entirely new context for doing business. If nothing else, it now requires that a company's activities be registered, researched, and made available to the public. This has a powerful effect on a corporation's public image—which spends millions to maintain. It also deeply affects their long-term competitiveness in their ability to attract the best of the new, young talent entering the market. The most gifted young managers often refuse to work for a company—or in an industry—that exploits people and the environment.

The issues raised by socially responsible investing are gradually being incorporated into business's thinking processes, future scenario-building, and long-term planning. Socially aware companies do prosper over the long haul, which is illustrated by the fact that environmentally oriented companies are growing, while defense companies are shrinking or retooling to beat their swords into plowshares.

Critics also claim that the ethical screening of stocks should not be defined as socially responsible investing, as it doesn't funnel capital into new enterprises much needed by society, such as development funds for innercity small businesses.

Our point is that just as our current society didn't come into existence overnight, deep, fundamental changes in our way of doing things will also build slowly, step by step. Whatever leads to an integration of social and spiritual values in the marketplace, however tenuous at first, is helping to end the split between our society's spiritual and material values.

Corporations don't operate in a vacuum. Even the most rigid gradually come to reflect the values and priorities of the society at large—as with environmental issues—mostly because it's simply good business to do so. Gordon was told that one of the drives for change on corporate policy came from the children of CEOs asking their fathers over the dinner table why their companies were polluting the Earth. This generational difference is essentially the crux of the matter. One thing the critics who focus only on this one moment in material time underestimate is that, year by year, graduating class by graduating class, we are evolving into a new consciousness, a new perception of reality. It's not a question of instant transformation. It's challenging the thinking that underlies "business as usual" each and every day.

Gordon helped establish the Coalition for Environmentally Responsible Economies (CERES), a group of social investment professionals, environmentalists, pension fund investors, and labor leaders. In September 1989 they drafted a code of environmental conduct for corporations, which they call the "Valdez Principles," after the Exxon oil spill in Valdez, Alaska. The code asks companies to protect the biosphere by: minimizing pollution, making sustainable use of natural resources, reducing and eliminating waste and pollution, conserving energy, minimizing risk to employees and the public, producing safe products and services, restoring environmental damage, informing the public of environmental problems, informing the CEO and board of directors about environmental issues, conducting an annual self-evaluation, and filing a report with CERES each year.

By 1993 fifty-two companies, including Sunoco, had signed the principles (renamed CERES Principles), and environmental codes of conduct were promulgated by everyone from the Bank of America to the Chemical Manufacturers Association. This effort proves that mobilized, organized public opinion, backed by the principled use of large pools of capital, can be highly effective at leveraging change even with very large, very conservative institutions. As a result of these principles being developed, the Maquiladora Principles were also developed for companies operating in

Mexico, covering the environment, wages, safety, and community development. Business Executives for National Security (BENS) also issued the BENS Principles, calling on weapons exporters to help stop the spread of chemical, nuclear, and biological weapons.

CONSCIOUS CONSUMPTION

Another socially responsible use of money that has grown is the awareness that when we spend money for a product or service we are supporting the activities, good or bad, of a particular company. This movement grew out of the co-ops and alternative businesses of the 1960s and 1970s that used "cause-related marketing" to sell food grown without exploiting workers or the earth, products produced by village craftspeople around the world and by worker-owned, ecologically conscious companies. By purchasing products from these types of businesses, we are "thinking with our money" and supporting these socially responsible companies and helping them flourish.

Gradually this awareness has spread into the purchasing habits of a growing percentage of consumers who have begun to make these types of evaluations of major corporations. Sophisticated analyses of products on supermarket shelves, rating the companies who make the products on the social responsibility of their policies, are now available through *Rating America's Corporate Conscience* and *Shopping for a Better World* by the Council on Economic Priorities in New York. Conscious consuming is a classic example of how major social trends begin with a small segment of society with strongly held and practiced values, who gradually and increasingly influence mainstream society. The same process has occurred with the women's movement, the environmental movement, and the whole-foods movement.

Today, major corporations have realized that cause-related marketing is a growing trend and have begun to change their policies to retain their market share amid "vigilante consumers" who are paying more attention to how their companies are run. Environmental packaging by Burger King and McDonald's, Avis selling customers on its worker-owned business, Ben and Jerry's popular 1 Percent for Peace ice cream, and a host of cause-related credit cards are a few examples of this trend. American Express Co. ran a "charge against hunger" campaign in 1993, in which two cents of every credit card transaction went to a hunger relief organization, Share Our Strength. A total of $5 million was raised to provide breakfasts for hungry children in the U.S., as well as bring food from restaurants to shelters and establish nutritional clinics. Loews Hotels has a "good neighbor" policy in which each hotel is involved with community charities. Many hotels have held a series of monopoly breakfasts where celebrities, business and community leaders play a thirty minute version of Monopoly viewed by the public, which has raised over $365,000 since 1988. The Body Shop, a natural cosmetics company, takes the trend the farthest with environmental packaging, natural ingredients, no animal testing, refillable containers, and donations to activist groups such as those working to save the rain forests. Their $378 million in sales in 1990 has stimulated Estée Lauder to begin its own socially responsible product line.

Business in this new era will have more to do with building a trust relationship with a public seeking to know what's in a product, how it was tested, who produced it, and under what working conditions it was produced before they will support the company with their spending dollars. All these developments and new models of business indicate that new ideas and values are beginning to be integrated into the economic system, gradually transforming it.

South Shore Bank

One institution that is a model of social responsibility is the South Shore Bank of Chicago, a small bank that has since 1973 carried out a very large commitment to improving the economic and social conditions of nearly eighty thousand low- and moderate-income residents of its once declining 265-block neighborhood on Chicago's South Side. Cited as a "national model" for community development, South Shore Bank has loaned nearly 50 percent of its deposits back to the local community when no other bank would loan people there a cent. And through its affiliates it has helped low-income property owners to use "sweat equity" and organize housing co-ops to rehabilitate their community. By offering its parking lot for a local farmers market, and helping to develop small businesses, the bank and its affiliates have become the leading force in revitalizing the South Shore community. Gordon has personally toured the South Side neighborhoods with friends who are officials of the bank and has seen block after block of the beautiful buildings, parks, and neighborhoods that have been restored by the bank's lending.

Unlike most banks, South Shore, controlled by Shorebank Corporation, is owned by thirty-three national foundations, church organizations, corporations, and individuals whose interest is, in the words of their annual report, "to work with community residents to develop a permanent renewal process in urban neighborhoods." The bank was purchased in 1973 by a group of eleven investors in a rapidly declining neighborhood with a 95 percent black population and has helped rehabilitate ten thousand rental housing units. Nearly half of the bank's loans are invested locally, three times the average for other Chicago banks, and it has a 98 percent repayment rate on its loans. As a result, South Shore's assets have tripled to over $200 million since 1973, and it made a profit of over $1.3 million in 1991.

The Shorebank Corporation also developed The Neighborhood Institute (TNI), a nonprofit economic and social development corporation that assists low- and moderate-income people through job training and placement and by providing affordable housing. It offers remedial education and job training, generating 380 job placements in 1991, as well as helping to organize people for neighborhood planning and crime prevention.

Today, South Shore Bank has attracted over $100 million into Development Deposits, a pool of funds from which development loans are made, and where investors know their deposits are financing innovative efforts. The bank has become a national model, demonstrating how committed, socially concerned entrepreneurs can use well-managed money to achieve positive social goals and make a profit.

Shorebank Corporation has been asked to provide management expertise or direct investment in projects as diverse as administering a small business loan program in Poland, which includes training Polish managers; helping to set up a nonprofit organization to provide financial and technical assistance to emerging businesses in the fifteen counties of Michigan's upper peninsula; setting up a bank for rural small business development in Arkansas; and helping to reorganize the oldest minority-owned bank west of the Mississippi, in Kansas City, Kansas.

In this chapter we have seen how the economic values of the Soul differ from those of the personality and how flow is the key to economic health. We have explored the spiritual and psychological aspects of money and how it can be invested and used to benefit others. In the next chapter we will explore how we become ecological stewards of the planet and empower human beings to meet their needs in a sustainable fashion.

Chapter Twelve

◆

PLANETARY STEWARDSHIP AND HUMAN EMPOWERMENT

No wonder we have become disconnected from the natural world—indeed, it's remarkable we feel any connection to ourselves. And no wonder we have become resigned to the idea of a world without a future. The engines of distraction are gradually destroying the inner ecology of the human experience. Essential to that ecology is the balance between respect for the past and faith in the future, between a belief in the individual and a commitment to the community, between our love for the world and our fear of losing it—the balance, in other words, on which an environmentalism of the spirit depends.

—ALBERT GORE, VICE PRESIDENT[1]

Our interconnection with all humanity and all life is reflected very tangibly in the reality of our environmental crisis today. The Ageless Wisdom says that the appropriate relationship between humanity and the nature kingdoms is one of co-creation. Humanity's particular function is to connect with spiritual dimensions and transmit love and healing energy to the natural world—the animals, plants, and minerals, which stimulates their evolutionary development. Thus, what is most significant about the environmental crisis is that we are developing a new attitude of love, respect, and appreciation for the natural world, which is helping us to establish a co-creative relationship with the nature forces. We, as humanity, also can originate plans for working in partnership with the natural living systems of our planet, and to the degree we are in alignment with Divine Will, the results will be harmonious.

We can see this environmental wisdom beginning to be reflected in the recognition that right management of the planet's ecological resources is an urgent necessity, as today we have the capacity to destroy or nourish all life on earth. The United Nations and other development agencies have urged humanity to follow a course of "sustainable development," which is defined as meeting humanity's needs today without compromising the ability of future generations to meet their needs. This indicates a broadening of our time frame, and a willingness to look deeper into the causal cycles of the natural world. This emerging consciousness gives careful consideration to the long term effects of all proposed actions that would affect the planetary biosphere. This reflects the practices of some cultures, past and present, that have maintained their ancestral lands productively for centuries— planning for generations into the future. This can best be done when we have a sense of detachment from ownership and see ourselves instead as stewards of the planet's resources. We will know this principle is grounded in our lives when we think first of the pollution a large car causes rather than the status it gives us.

UNDERSTANDING AND REDIRECTING THE URGE FOR MORE

The principle of ecological stewardship and human development asks us to look at what will bring true inner fulfillment to all people. However, to do this, everyone has to confront the meaning of the fundamental desire for "more," which seems to be innate in human nature. Yet as basic needs are satisfied, the Divine evolutionary urge, or spiritual Soul within each of us, gradually shifts the focus of desire and aspiration from material to more spiritual goals and values—if our personality is not hypnotized by the media and consumerism.

The never-ending desire for more is in reality the urge for more life, more experience, more growth in understanding and consciousness. This evolutionary drive is the source of our Divinely inspired dissatisfaction with whatever has been achieved. However, a basic misunderstanding of this drive focuses it exclusively in the material realm. But, rightly understood, it can move human attention from the quantity of goods to the quality of life. Goods, services, and shared wealth are required for human development and are rightly perceived when seen as means to human growth. They become destructive only when they are pursued as ends in themselves, or as substitutes for inner growth, and their excessive pursuit endangers human life on the planet.

Currently, worldwide corporate advertising is marketing expectations that people all over the world can acquire the lavish Western consumer lifestyle of fast cars, two houses, and disposable everything. To achieve this the world economy would have to produce four times its current output. However, the growth of the world economy by a factor of four is problematic, as the human economy currently uses one-fourth of the global net primary product of photosynthesis—quadrupling growth would consume all of the earth's natural systems output! We have yet to fully face what will happen when rising expectations of the world's underprivileged meet this biological reality. The demand for more equitable sharing of the world's resources that we saw at the Rio Earth Summit of 1992 will only grow, and it will have to be faced honestly by the privileged.

Consumerism in the Western nations will never be changed or reduced by asking people to stop consuming. It will change only when people are inspired by a more noble, worthy, and fulfilling purpose for their lives. This purpose could be described as the spiritual growth and mutual empowerment of all people in the world.

This higher vision will also allow us to make the necessary structural adjustments to a world economy that currently requires growth in consumerism to continue functioning. By transferring resources from military and nonessential consumer goods, we could finance the production of basic necessities, environmental regeneration, and human growth—all of which would provide ample employment for people to be able to earn enough to purchase what they truly need.

The transition to a sustainable economy has been made more difficult because the forces that resist change and benefit from the current modes of production and consumption have framed the issue in terms of jobs *versus* the environment. Yet Michael Renner, writing in *World Watch* magazine, notes that industries such as those engaged in the production of solar and wind energy have demonstrated that businesses can be designed to employ large numbers of people while using less energy and generating less pollution, all without sacrificing productivity. The costs of building and operating a wind farm are far less than those of running a nuclear power plant, for example, yet the wind farm can employ 642 workers and the nuclear power plant only 100 workers to generate 1,000 gigawatt-hours of electricity per year.

In his work financing the environmental industry, Gordon has seen that recycling is another industry in which more jobs are created as pollution is decreased. These commonsense arguments will begin to have an effect on the elites when either they transform their fear of losing privileges as a result of their own inner changes or public opinion forces them to change through increasing pressure to deal with economic and environmental dislocations and crises.

BENEFITS OF "HEALTHY HELPING"

How can humanity realize that the empowerment and growth in consciousness of every human being on earth is in our mutual best interest? There is a great deal of evidence to indicate that "healthy helping" or selfless giving to others in balance with our abilities, energy level, and interests is not only more fulfilling than endless consumption, but also improves physical and psychological health and enhances feelings of spiritual well-being. In their book, *The Healing Power of Doing Good,* Allan Luks and Peggy Payne state that a national survey of volunteers and helpers revealed that 95 percent of volunteers reported that personal helping on a regular basis gives them an immediate physical feel-good sensation, including warmth, increased energy, and a sense of euphoria, called "helper's high."[2] In the Ageless Wisdom it is said that the first indication of the presence of the Soul is a sense of responsibility for others. The increased energy and well-being experienced by helpers is the inflow of Soul energy flooding through their personalities as they reach out to serve others, creating a channel for these higher energies to flow, which they always do, according to spiritual law.

People who experience healthy helping have better health and overall well-being, which improves the more they volunteer and the more personal contact they have with those they are helping—most especially when helping those they don't know.[3] When our giving is outside our family or community, our actions take on deep, symbolic power, for we are helping to break down the barriers of separateness and enhance collective human unity. There are indications from other research that such helping strengthens the immune system, decreases pain, and helps eliminate attitudes of hostility.[4] This is not surprising, since the influence of the Soul is a great transmuting power, which can uplift and change even the cells of our bodies. In his book, *Healthy Pleasures,* psychologist Robert Ornstein concluded from a study of volunteers that "the greatest surprise of human evolution may be that the highest form of selfishness is selflessness."[5]

This type of scientific research proves that spiritual living is worthwhile not only for moral reasons, but because it makes sense as a way of life for intelligent, loving people who wish to live in harmony with themselves and their world. As more and more of us reach a mature level of human evolution and this type of understanding grows, gradually the emphasis on selfish consumption will be left behind, just as we left behind the toys in our nursery when we discovered there was a much bigger, more fascinating world to explore and live in.

If this way of life is pursued by enough individuals, it will have major implications for society as a whole. The great historian Arnold Toynbee concluded after a lifetime of studying the rise and fall of the world's civilizations that the measure of a civilization's growth was not to be found in the conquest of other people or the possession of land. Rather, the essence of growth is in what he called the "Law of Progressive Simplification." True growth, he said, is the ability of a society to transfer increasing amounts of energy and attention from the material side of life to the nonmaterial side and thereby advance their culture, capacity for compassion, and the strength of democracy.

ASSISTANCE AS MUTUAL SPIRITUAL GROWTH

Sustainable development is based on the recognition that humanity does not have an infinite supply of physical resources, but that there is a vast reservoir of underutilized human resources—highly visible in the many under- and unemployed around the world. As a Peace Corps volunteer in India, Gordon saw firsthand this huge untapped human resource. As he would ride his bicycle through his village in the west of Madras state, he would see hundreds of young men and women sitting on their heels by the side of the road, simply watching people pass by, all their talents and gifts having no outlet. Yet at the same time, in that same village, many people lived joyful lives with very little of what we in developed countries consider to be necessary for a good life. Their family and social relationships, participation in the life of the village, and ability to live in simplicity and frugality often resulted in more radiant faces than are seen in New York City. And the opportunities for individual growth increased when people worked together on villagewide projects and learned that they could empower themselves to solve their own problems.

Working for human development is actually a spiritual impulse, as it shifts attention from endless economic growth and consumption that serves no real need to a focus on human spiritual growth. For this type of development to succeed, says Lester Brown in *State of the World 1990*, "those being helped must be put first, not only as intended beneficiaries, but as active participants, advisors, and leaders. True development does not simply provide for the needy, it enables them to provide for themselves. This implies a great deal of humility on the part of outsiders."[6]

When this approach is followed it brings mutual and reciprocal growth for both the giver and receiver of true assistance. For the provider it means developing a wise understanding of human nature by listening to the needs and aspirations of others. It means learning how to help people help themselves, learning how to get oneself out of the way, and experiencing joy in *their* empowerment and development. For those being helped it means learning to release victim attitudes. It means becoming self-sufficient, over-coming inertia, social conditioning, and survival competitiveness in order to work together and improve human relationships and economic circum-stances. In Gordon's work in Indian villages as an agricultural adviser, he saw the struggle that farmers had to go through to break out of old pat-terns of thought about successful farming in their area. In introducing corn, which had not been grown before in their villages, Gordon would tell them that if they planted it, they would have better yields and incomes. They would often reply with a fatalistic, "If God wills it." The struggle for these people was to believe that they could somehow have some control over their own destiny.

SHARING THE PLANET

GUIDELINES FOR STEWARDING RESOURCES

Wealth-producing resources, including the land and oceans, are the "com-mon heritage of all mankind," according to a United Nations manifesto. The financial benefits of developing productive capacity through the use of ideas, technology, land, labor, or capital need to be distributed between those who create the innovation and the social-planetary web that makes the production and wealth possible.

The control of resources either by powerful opportunistic individuals (capitalism) or by an all-powerful bureaucratic state (communism) inevita-bly creates wealthy elites and a deprived populace. Since the majority of human beings have not yet reached a state of Soul consciousness, where sharing is spontaneous and inevitable, guidelines for the stewardship of the planet's resources are necessary. These guidelines must balance the individ-ual's need for incentives to innovate and take risks, with the need of the whole to receive a portion of the wealth that it has made available to the individual by providing the political, social, and economic infrastructure.

Such guidelines were proposed in the United Nations Law of the Sea Treaty. Although rejected by the United States, this farsighted treaty saw the wealth of the seas outside a two-hundred-mile territorial limit as the "common heritage of all mankind," and negotiators struggled for ten years to devise a formula for making this wealth available to all nations. Because of the influence of powerful elites, the treaty was never approved. Yet many treaty provisions are being observed as customary international law around the world, with positive effects on fish stocks, ocean pollution, and free-dom of the seas. The treaty is a forerunner of the types of agreements that will ultimately guide humanity in stewarding and sharing its resources—the current agreement among nations for the development of Antarctica being an example. Someday our grandchildren will very likely look back at the individual, selfish control of the wealth of the world by a small elite the same way we view slavery today.

Another agreement that illustrates moving controls to a higher regulatory function is the Montreal Protocol limiting chlorofluorocarbon (CFC) emissions, passed in January 1989, which called for a reduction by half in industrial CFCs by 1998 and restrictions on purchase of CFCs from nonsignatory countries. Ninety-three nations agreed to stop using CFCs altogether by the year 2000 and extend the treaty to cover other ozone-depleting chemicals. A $240 million fund was established to help developing countries purchase CFC substitutes.

An additional international arrangement that has been made is the sharing of the communications systems of the world by all nations, to facilitate the free flow of information and ideas. Despite numerous wars and conflicts, the transoceanic communications cables have never been severed. The world's radio frequency spectrum is protected by mutual agreement through the voluntary International Telecommunications Union, under the UN umbrella. Frequency agreements keep satellites from interfering with ground microwave links, and the jamming of radio transmissions around the world has ceased. Through these common agreements, voluntarily achieved, every individual telephone in the world is able to access every other, facilitating international communication and understanding.

THE RESPONSIBILITY OF THE POWERFUL

A deeper perspective on the issue of distribution and control of wealth and resources raises the question of the responsibility of the more developed individuals to those who are less evolved in the realization of their capacities. The Ageless Wisdom recognizes that all individuals are in essence equal, in that each is equally a part of the same Divine Presence and all have the spark of Divinity within their Being. It also acknowledges that at any given time these individuals are at differing stages of an evolutionary process of integrating their personalities and fully actualizing all their Soul capacities of power, intelligence, compassion, and wisdom.

Understanding this process has profound economic implications. Today's economic difficulties have been characterized in the Ageless Wisdom as a basic problem between "equipped and unequipped" individuals. Some individuals are far more capable than others of becoming productive, self-sufficient, and even dominant in the economic arena. Through their own evolutionary development as integrated personalities—their emotional balance and mental development—they find it easy to play a leading role in major industries or to control vast flows of capital through their mental ability to understand and manipulate the financial system.

Humanity needs these powerful personalities in service. The great challenge comes when such an individual allows the personality to inflate into excessive egoism, rather than taking the next maturing step in human evolution of self-transcendence and identification with the life and well-being of all. If there is no transcendence, then the process of evolution has been frustrated—until the ego learns through experience the sorrows of selfishness. At that point it can then open to the redeeming influence of the Soul. Donald Trump is an archetypical example of the labyrinth of effects the inflated ego enters when it refuses to go beyond itself and acknowledge its responsibility to give back, with love, to life.

What is the responsibility of those strong personalities, unaware of the Soul, to those who are not so developed? Are the less equipped to be seen simply as a supply of labor to be used, paid as little as possible, and given a few grudging benefits when they complain? Is the physical planet to be viewed simply as a supply of raw materials and other nations merely as markets? And what are the karmic implications for these more developed individuals, who function as unawakened exploiters of people and the planet, with no thought of the greater good? What will be the future lives of such individuals, to balance out the pain and suffering they have caused unknown millions? Ignorance of the spiritual law will not excuse them from these karmic consequences.

At any time in our personal evolution we have the opportunity to ask for the transcendent help of the Soul to move beyond the perils of egoism and selfishness. We then enter the great community of dedicated individuals all over the planet who labor ceaselessly to help those in need to overcome their limitations and actualize more of their innate Divine potential. At this stage, our evolutionary development becomes a blessing to humanity rather than a curse, and we all move ahead in our collective evolutionary progress. Many today are actively working within the highest levels of the economic system to bring about a better life for all of humanity.

Many powerful businesspeople, upon achieving great wealth and success, have felt the transforming touch of the Soul. An excellent example is Sir James Goldsmith, entrepreneur and corporate raider who suddenly announced he was retiring to give his energies and much of his billion-dollar fortune to ecological and environmental causes. He has become an active campaigner, speaking, writing, and funding projects. It is his belief that "great wealth is of no value in a crumbling world."

There is also industrialist Eugene Lang, who adopted an entire sixth-grade class in Harlem, promising to pay college tuition for those who stayed in school. Dozens of executives followed his example to personally mentor underprivileged youth. Lang's I Have a Dream Foundation today has more than 140 projects nationwide.

When a personal friend of ours retired from a successful career as a crusading newspaper publisher in Ohio, she used her wealth to generously support transformation work all over the world. She also spends many of her weekends inside prisons, teaching prisoners alternatives to violent behavior and helping them develop self-esteem. This type of commitment on the part of powerful individuals who are willing to give their time, energy, and wealth to aid the less developed and solve human problems is leading all of humanity in a positive evolutionary direction.

MODELS FOR SHIFTING FROM THE "I" TO THE "WE"

One avenue for human development is to give workers more control over the land and resources in their communities, and ownership and creative participation in business enterprises. This is taking place in a variety of settings, including inner-city and rural areas and in industries such as airlines, steel companies, auto rental agencies, and many small businesses. Giving workers a share in the ownership and running of companies transcends the old split between management and labor, helps eliminate the fear of losing one's job, elicits more commitment and productivity, and ultimately makes companies more profitable for all who help produce the wealth.

An example of this is Weirton Steel in Pennsylvania. On the verge of bankruptcy in 1982, it was purchased by its employees. Since the takeover it has had the best profits per ton of steel in the industry. Another example is Avis, the rental car company that was bought by its workers in 1987 for $1.75 billion. The company's 24 million shares are held in a trust and gradually released to the employees as the debt is paid off. This employee stock ownership program boosted the company's performance by motivating its employees to make the company successful—and customers support employee ownership.

The trend toward giving those who create the wealth a greater share of it is fundamentally a move from the "I" to the "We" model. It makes the well-being and growth of each individual in the company important to everyone. The result is real service to the community as well as political change, as people experience their own empowerment.

• • •

Institute for Community Economics (ICE) is a community economic development organization committed to the principle that local communities should help plan and benefit from their own economic development. Because poor people do not control land, housing, employment, or the financial institutions of the communities in which they live, their incomes flow away from the community to outside interests. ICE works to provide capital and create institutions that give local communities control and enable them to build an economic base that breaks the cycle of poverty. As Greg Ramm, executive director of ICE, puts it, "We work to turn market principles on their head. Banks provide the lowest interest rate to the largest and wealthiest corporations and individuals. We believe that the priority for the lowest interest rate should be for those in greatest need, so the factor of justice is included in the market."

ICE will often help a community housing or development group set up a community land trust (CLT) as the best way of solving the problem of skyrocketing housing costs and the increasing shortage of low-income housing. A nonprofit land trust, controlled by a local community board, will buy a property in a neighborhood it wishes to preserve and then resell the house to a low- or middle-income buyer. The land is leased to the buyer under a long-term agreement, which lowers both the down payment and the monthly payments for the buyer. In return the buyer must agree to sell their house at a limited price to the next low-income buyer. "Community land trusts have provided over two thousand units of housing, which will forever be affordable to future generations in these communities," says Greg Ramm.

The ICE Loan Fund, established in 1979, brings investors who have capital for projects that are socially constructive and promote economic justice together with people with technical expertise and experience in community development. Over the life of the fund it has made over 280 loans, totaling more than $19 million, to community land trusts, limited equity housing co-ops, and businesses owned by workers or consumers.

The fund receives loans from individuals, religious organizations, and other institutions. Interest rates are set by the lender and range from no interest to money market rates. Sixteen percent of ICE's lenders opt not to receive interest, and most receive between 3 and 4 percent. The fund has lost less than $12,000, and no lender has ever lost a penny. Greg Ramm notes that "statistics show that the highest-risk loans and default rates are not from low-income people and cooperative institutions, but from those who speculate on property development."

ICE has also helped establish over a dozen other community development loan funds, and in 1986 along with other loan funds founded the National Association of Community Development Loan Funds (NACDLF), which now has forty-one funds lending over $70 million around the country, with a loan loss rate of less than 1 percent. Martin Trimble, executive director of the NACDLF, says, "We are proving that low-income people and communities are creditworthy, and we are providing the capital upon which self-development and community vitalization depend." NACDLF and its members helped draft the Clinton administration's legislation that provides federal support for this type of lending.

James Rouse, called by *Time* magazine "America's Master Builder," is one of a number of individuals who are working to give control over resources back to local communities. Rouse, who made his fortune from innovative revitalization projects like Baltimore's Inner Harbor and Boston's Faneuil Hall, has a different view of business. "Profit is not the legitimate purpose of business," he says. "Its purpose is to provide a service needed by society. If you do that well and efficiently, you earn a profit."

Rouse's current megagoal is to eliminate homelessness and substandard housing in America's inner cities by giving residents the means to turn slums into decent homes for themselves. Through his **Enterprise Foundation**, based in Columbia, Maryland, he is lending low-interest money to local community groups that will renovate and develop low-cost housing, financed by a for-profit real estate company. Chattanooga, Tennessee, is the first test market, with the goal to eliminate that city's slums by the end of the decade—without displacing current residents. If Rouse's formula is successful there, he hopes it will be used around the country.

Franklin Research and Development Company is moving toward a "We" consciousness by empowering worker–owners. A highly innovative Boston-based investment management company, Franklin is unique for two reasons: it manages only socially responsible investments, and it is an employee-owned corporation. All of Franklin's clients—individual, institutional, or corporate—establish financial and social guidelines for their investments. The company then seeks investments that support these concerns by collecting data from established research organizations and conducting their own research on socially responsible investment opportunities.

Franklin uses eight criteria to measure a company's social performance, each of which is given a numerical value and then combined to produce a company's "social assessment rating."

• *Corporate Citizenship* measures a company's participation in local communities through monitoring the sharing of corporate resources to solve community problems.

• *Employee Relations* looks at the way companies relate to their employees, including equality in employment, compensation, unionization, concern for the health and creative development of workers, and employee sharing in ownership, decision making, and profits.

• *Energy* measures a company's effort to use or produce energy in a safe, clean, and efficient manner.

• *Environmental Record* rates a company according to EPA reports and those of other monitoring bodies in relation to other companies within its industry.

• *Product* rates the impact of a company's products or services on its customers, including its affordability and safety.

• *Human Rights* looks at a company's record of ethical conduct in foreign countries where the government is repressive or permits actions deemed illegal or unethical in the United States.

• *Weapons* identifies companies that are prime defense contractors working on weapons systems.[7]

• *Animal Rights* looks at a company's policies with respect to the humane treatment of farm and other animals, including alternative forms of testing, sales of animal products, and dealings with other groups with similar or different concerns.

Franklin has been a 100 percent employee-owned corporation since its founding in 1982, with each of the twenty-one employee–owners holding shares of common stock, entitling them to vote. All employees are eligible to purchase shares of the company after their first anniversary of employment, pending approval of the board. The stock is nontransferable and can be sold back to the company only when an employee terminates employment. Dividends on common stock are voted by the board of directors. Some upper management salaries at the firm are as little as half what they are in most investing firms; Joan Bavaria, the founder and CEO of the company, could be making at least twice her current salary at a traditional Wall Street firm. "Making a bigger salary isn't what motivates me," she says. What does motivate her is making a difference in helping others.

Ownership of the company engenders a deep feeling of commitment, which leads to cooperation rather than competition among employees. In a supportive environment with high morale, ownership leads employees to the belief that change can be effected when necessary and that they have a stake in the long-term future of the company.

FACILITATING SELF-EMPOWERMENT

There are encouraging signs that it is possible to reverse the downward spiral of poverty, hopelessness, and environmental decline, as poor people organize themselves to overcome their circumstances and rebuild their environment. Self-help groups have been steadily proliferating and now probably number in the hundreds of thousands, with their collective membership in the hundreds of millions.

CETHA, an independent group in Bolivia, offers hundreds of impoverished peasants high school–level courses in the market towns where they come to sell their produce, as well as vocational courses tailored to local conditions offered during the slack agricultural season.

The Group Farm Forestry Program in the Indian state of West Bengal began distributing free tree seedlings to poor families who had been given small plots of infertile, degraded land by the government. By covering their land with the hardy trees, lower-caste villagers were able to use their earnings to purchase small irrigated fields in fertile valleys from absentee landlords. By returning control over all common lands to the local council, tribal villagers in the community of Seed in Rajasthan created an oasis in the denuded Arvalis hills that withstood the severe drought of 1987, when cattle died by the thousands.[8]

The Body Shop is one prime example of how entrepreneurs and companies within the corporate world are helping to empower the poor. Anita Roddick, founder of The Body Shop, started with a small natural cosmetics store in 1976 and by 1990 had built a global network of 370 such stores in thirty-four countries doing $387 million in sales. In the process she transformed the idea of social commitment for a corporation. It is company policy that every shop be involved in a community project, such as an AIDS program or a battered women's shelter, with employees being paid to assist in these community services. After two years all staff members become shareholders, and the company locates factories in underemployed areas around the world and puts a healthy share of the profits back into the community. Committed to "trade, not aid" with the Third World, The Body Shop created a Boys Town in central India to produce massage rollers. In the process the community also provides eighty boys with a home, security, and a trade, as well as paying First World prices for the products. In Nepal The Body Shop plans to acquire several abandoned paper plants and employ a local women's association to make paper.

Osage Resource Recovery was set up by Jack MacAllister, CEO of U.S. West, to train the unemployed and homeless to do environmental remediation and promotional mailings for other firms. Last year Osage placed ninety people in permanent jobs, made a profit, and didn't require any federal funds.

Aetna Life and Casualty in Hartford, Connecticut, trains former unemployables for entry-level positions. Community groups help screen applicants, and those accepted are guaranteed jobs and four weeks of paid training in clerical skills and literacy.

These and hundreds of other examples around the world illustrate that it is possible to facilitate the empowerment of the poor in ways that help meet basic human needs as well as ensure environmental sustainability and stewardship. The ingredients of these successes follow a common thread throughout the world. Literacy, especially for women, gives access to information and leads to higher incomes, improved health, and smaller families. Secure land rights allow the poor to increase income and economic security. Local control over common resources helps arrest the ecological downward spiral. Credit gives the poor access to productive assets such as livestock and tools. Clean drinking water and primary health care reduce the incidence of debilitating diseases that sap adults' strength and kill children—a pattern that induces parents to have larger families. Family planning allows poor women to effectively control fertility and improve their health. Grass-roots organizations enable the poor to work together to direct the development process.[9]

This type of development also helps deal with one of the underlying causes of environmental degradation—growing population. We have added 2.5 billion people to the world over the past forty years, and at current rates of growth, we will be adding 5 billion over the next sixty years. Unless this growth rate is changed, the outlook for sustainable development is limited.

In its annual *State of the World Report,* Worldwatch Institute examines the mass of data on the state of the world's biological systems, including food supplies, population, soil erosion, air and water pollution, transportation systems, and many other components of our bioeconomic system. As a result of its studies, Worldwatch has concluded that a sustainable society is the only way for humanity to have a future:

> Because of the strain on resources it creates, materialism simply cannot survive the transition to a sustainable world. As public understanding of the

need to adopt simpler and less consumptive life-styles spreads, it will become unfashionable to own fancy new cars and clothes. This shift will be among the hardest to make. Yet the potential benefits of unleashing the tremendous quantities of human energy now devoted to designing, producing, advertising, buying, consuming, and discarding material goods are enormous. Much undoubtedly would be channeled into forming richer human relationships, stronger communities, and greater outlets for cultural diversity, music, and the arts.[10]

DEVELOPING SUSTAINABLE TECHNOLOGIES

In order to develop a sustainable economic approach, humanity is beginning to find new ways of looking at technologies. We are developing ones that are "lighter" on the earth and don't take such a heavy toll in resource use and pollution. The ratio of information to material resources is shifting towards products that contain much more information in design, lighter weight parts, computerized controls, thus using fewer natural resources. Many groups and initiatives are pioneering in these areas.

Rocky Mountain Institute, headquartered 7,100 feet up in Old Snowmass, Colorado, was founded in 1982 by Hunter and Amory Lovins. Its mission is to foster the efficient and sustainable use of resources to help build global security. Each year the institute shows thousands of visitors around its energy-conserving building, pointing out the appliances and devices that keep its monthly electric bill averaging around five dollars and its heating bill zero. However, the bulk of RMI's work is with large institutions, including local and state governments and utility companies, who hire the institute as consultants on energy policy. The institute has several major programs:

1. The **Energy Program** informs individuals, corporations, and communities about state-of-the-art opportunities to use energy far more productively and how to harness appropriate renewable sources. RMI's research has documented how least-cost energy strategies can stem nuclear proliferation, abate acid rain, save wild rivers, rescue troubled utilities, cut electric rates, and forestall the carbon dioxide threat to the global climate. The institute has helped many utilities, Congress, federal agencies, and state and local governments to understand the new energy marketplace.

2. The **Water/Agriculture Program** points out that water policy today is repeating all the mistakes of energy policy in the 1960s—seeking more water rather than using efficiently the water we already have. RMI is ex-

ploring these land/water/money linkages as well as about how organic and inorganic farms compare—economically, ecologically, and socially.

3. The **Economic Renewal Project** helps communities keep money in their local economy by:

a. Plugging the unnecessary leaks of 80 to 90 percent of the money that leaves the community.

b. Strengthening existing businesses.

c. Encouraging new local entrepreneurs; and carefully recruiting outside business.

An example of how effective this can be comes from Osage, Iowa. The head of the municipal utility there decided he didn't want to pay to put up another power plant, so he worked with his customers to save over $1,000 per household per year through energy-efficient lighting, insulating, and equipment, resulting in rate cuts totaling one-third of the electrical use rate. As a result, more people are wanting to relocate in Osage, and two new factories have moved into town. When electrical demand increased, the manager got more active in getting customers to save energy and convinced them to spend the money they saved in the local town. Local grocers and car dealers are saying, "The only reason I'm in business is the energy-saving program."[11]

CYCLEAN, a Texas-based asphalt recycling company, is another company that models sustainable technology. Using a new microwave process and portable recycling plants, CYCLEAN is able to melt down asphalt pavement torn up from roads, rubble which constitutes 40 percent of landfills by weight. The reconstituted asphalt produces a recycled pavement that can be reapplied to the road surface at 25–35 percent less cost, as good as or better than the original, also eliminating the environmental and financial costs of trucking it long distances from a plant.

National Green Plans

The Dutch became a world laboratory for environmental policy when Queen Beatrix told the nation in 1988 that "the earth is slowly dying and the end of life itself is becoming conceivable." The government responded with a 233-point National Environmental Policy Plan to reduce air, water, and soil pollution by 70 to 90 percent by the year 2010 and to convert the economy to sustainable industries. The plan was implemented and the government sets the goals for reductions, then allows industries to determine how they will get there. The government supplies incentives, such as subsidizing company transportation plans, but it also requires that polluters pay for environmental damage caused by their failure to comply.[12]

President Clinton has created a twenty-five-member Council on Sustainable Development, which includes representatives of industry, labor, government, environmental, and civil rights organizations. The Council's primary goals are to develop specific policy recommendations for a national strategy of sustainable development. The Council will contribute to the U.S. plan for the UN Commission on Sustainable Development and sponsor sustainable projects that demonstrate and test the viability of the Council's recommendations.

The United States Solar Industries Association has detailed a plan of how the United States could provide at least 20 percent of its annual energy needs from solar power by the year 2000, through the use of tax credits, solar bonds, carbon dioxide taxes, and solar applications on all new federal buildings. To put such a plan into effect requires the response of farsighted political leaders willing to overcome the resistance of entrenched interests and to explain to the public why this is important and needed.

Corporate Environmental Efforts

Although corporations have been responsible for many of the environmental problems in the world, and some companies simply try to "greenwash" their activities with environmental public relations or green product advertising, other companies are beginning to face up to the problems their activities cause. These companies have recognized that environmental viability is a crucial issue for our times and have taken important first steps in solving environmental problems. In addition to McDonald's use of recycled paper containers—worked out in unprecedented cooperation with the Natural Resources Defense Council—there have been some notable corporate efforts in recent years to reduce pollution and waste. 3M's Pollution Prevention Pays program to reduce hazardous waste at its source has saved the company $400 million and proven to the chemical industry that it's smart business to cut the production of hazardous waste.

Over thirty thousand cars powered by natural gas or ethanol are being used in company fleets of Brooklyn Union Gas, Equitable Resources of Pittsburgh, and People's Energy Corporation of Chicago. Office furniture manufacturer Herman Miller has begun developing wood veneers that are alternatives to rain forest hardwoods and has begun labeling products from sustainable regions. The *Los Angeles Times* now prints on paper that is 83 percent recycled. Turner Broadcasting Systems has led the media with extensive environmental coverage, including a National Geographic Explorer series, Network Earth, and the animated Captain Planet environmental series for children. After extensive work with the Environmental Defense

Fund, Pacific Gas & Electric has decided not to build nuclear or coal power plants. Instead it will construct wind or solar power plants.

Recycling

Nature, the great economist, is highly energy- and resource-efficient. We function in harmony with universal laws when we use what we need with care and maximum recycling. In the natural world little is left unrecycled, from leaves to human bodies, and we humans harmonize with nature when we carefully reuse the material resources entrusted to us. Individuals also keep their resource channels flowing by caring for and improving what is entrusted to them and circulating what is not needed. A transformation of attitudes toward possessions occurs when, through a sense of detachment, people see themselves as caretakers and stewards of goods, rather than owners.

In nature processes are cyclic, i.e., one organism's waste becomes another's sustenance. The challenge is either to construct human systems that utilize our wastes for other productive purposes, stop creating those wastes, or have producers pay the full cost of storing them safely. By replacing the current throwaway mentality with a recycling ethic, society will become dramatically less energy-intensive and polluting. In Worldwatch Institute's *State of the World Report*, Lester Brown points out that just 5 percent as much energy is needed to recycle aluminum as to produce it from raw materials. For steel, the saving is 60 percent and for recycled paper 25–60 percent. Steel produced from scrap reduces air and water pollution by 76–85 percent and eliminates mining wastes altogether.[13] Recycling also saves municipal costs, since collecting recyclables is cheaper than collecting garbage, and processing them makes them a resalable commodity rather than something you have to pay to dispose of in landfills.

The false choice between jobs or the environment, usually manipulated for political purposes—evidenced by the U.S. position in 1992 at the Rio Earth Summit—is clearly exposed when we examine the impact of recycling on employment. Recycling is already a more important employer than metal mining in the United States. The ALCOA company estimates that at least thirty thousand people in the United States are involved in recycling aluminum alone—twice the employment rate in the primary industry. Compared with incineration and landfilling, recycling offers more employment and is cheaper, thanks to its much lower capital requirements.

Denmark has emerged as a model by banning throwaway beverage containers. By forcing a shift to refillable containers, that nation has cut the energy invested in beverage containers by two-thirds, and lowered the amount of water pollution and increased employment.

The National Polystyrene Recycling Company, founded by a consortium of chemical companies (including Amoco Chemical Company, Dow, and ARCO), is planning to build five national recycling centers for foam cups, plastic silverware, and plastic food containers, which can be made into videotape cassettes, flower pots, and plastic food trays, all of which can be recycled again.

But Germany's Environmental Protection Encouragement Agency has taken this process even further by proposing a system of classification of all manufactured goods and materials into three types:

1. *Consumables* are products that are either eaten, or when placed on the ground degrade with no negative biological results. This can include many items that could be designed to be composted such as clothing (which currently contains many toxic chemicals) and biodegradable packaging.

2. *Durables*—cars, TVs, VCRs which would not be sold but licensed, always belonging to the original manufacturer and returning to them in a closed loop. This is beginning with companies in Germany and Japan designing products for disassembly and reuse.

3. *Unsalables*—toxins, radiation, heavy metals, and chemicals which have to be stored at manufacturer's expense until ways are found to use or detoxify the substances.

As the world moves toward an economy that emphasizes reductions in the absolute amounts of materials processed, as well as substitutions in the kinds of materials consumed, profound changes in the job market are inevitable. Recycling, along with development of nonpolluting manufacturing and processing, cleaner energy and transportation and production of more benign and durable goods, opens the possibility of whole new areas of economic growth and job creation.[14]

THE INTERDEPENDENCE OF RICH AND POOR

Economic life today demonstrates that all people and nations are now part of an interdependent web of complex interactions, and that changes in one part of the web affect all participants. Thus, establishing just, cooperative, and honest relationships is the key to economic well-being for all. One of the great learning opportunities the twentieth century has offered humanity is this realization of our interdependence. This is highlighted through the world of economics, where one can see the results of actions taken in New York or Tokyo affecting events in Sri Lanka or even a small village in

Peru. But we find it difficult to take this fact into account when we plan and manage our affairs, as we do not yet have a widely developed sense of the underlying unity of humankind.

International trading relations in money, goods, and services illustrate this dilemma. All the nations of the world, rich and poor, are linked by mutual needs. The underdeveloped nations look to the industrialized countries for the capital, technology, services, and markets for their materials and products that they need in order to develop. The wealthy nations need the poorer ones to develop because the growth of the industrial economies depends upon the growth of markets in the underdeveloped nations. Yet the rules and institutions that govern trade relations and dictate the way money moves through the system are heavily weighted in favor of the wealthy nations at the expense of developing countries.

Nevertheless, the effect of running a global economy under a system controlled by a small group of the rich and powerful has been harmful to everyone. It has been the major cause of deepening global poverty, as well as a significant factor in environmental destruction. In return, the massive debt load carried by the poorer countries, and their attempts to meet International Monetary Fund conditions for further loans, has meant curtailing their imports, causing the loss of vital markets for developed countries. Still, despite these problems, some innovative solutions are emerging.

COUNTERTRADE—PROFIT TO THE WHOLE

Economic transactions require the voluntary cooperation of all parties, and only if all concerned in the transaction benefit—including producer, seller, buyer, and the earth itself—is there a true "profit" to the whole. Because of the disadvantages to poorer countries in the rigged international trading system, many developing countries are returning to the most ancient form of trade known—barter and exchange. Called "countertrade," it functions as a direct swap of goods or services of equal value between two countries. During the last two decades, countertrade has grown enormously among developing countries, as a way to avoid using global financial systems, since they extract a large percentage of any transaction in interest and fees. Estimates for the volume of global barter trade range from 8 to 30 percent of total world trade and 50 percent of all East–West trade.

These exchanges enable one country to dispose of its own products by balancing them against the imports they need. There is no cash transaction and no depletion of scarce currency. This type of economic interaction expresses the principle of mutual benefit, as these agreements are conducted through agencies under the control of the governments involved, and the exchanges can be made to work for the general economic prosperity of the countries concerned. This introduces an element of planning at both the national level and between trading nations.

Through such arrangements we see the free-for-all, competitive type of exchange, in which private companies and multinationals trade exclusively for profit, evolving into a consciously planned global economy that will ensure all nations a share in the riches of the earth and the creativity and inventiveness of mankind. In addition, skills exchanges and local currency systems are being developed in communities in Canada and the United States, as well as experiments in other ways to further encourage economic exchange without relying on the money system. During the ongoing economic crisis in the former Soviet Union, as much as half of most Russians' economic life was based on bartering with neighbors for goods and services.[15]

The LETSystem

Another approach to barter for local communities that has spread to several dozen communities around the world is the LETSystem. This community-wide program is based on a new kind of local money called the "green dollar." A group of people who live locally and want to trade get together and agree to the LETSystem rules. Each person makes out a list of what they need and what they have to offer in trade. A combined list is circulated to everyone, and members then see who has what they want and start trading. Barter becomes collective because members trade with all the people in the system, eliminating the limits of one-to-one trading.

Green dollars don't exist as tangible money, and no notes are printed. When people trade, the purchaser calls up the central office and leaves a message on an answering machine, telling the record keeper their account number and the amount of credit in hours for the person who provided the good or service, based on its current market value, and debiting their account for the same amount.[16]

The LETSystem represents a complete break with the concept of tangible money, as it enables money to remain as information about transactions. Once money is seen as "solid," it takes on a life of its own, and people begin to deal in money as a commodity. Because the green dollars in the LETSystem have no tangible existence, they cannot be forged, devalued, hoarded, stolen, or lost. They are decentralized, created only by someone creating something of real value and trading it with someone. Thus the creation of green dollars is related directly to its source—the creativity of human beings.

The LETSystem was invented by Michael Linton in Courtenay, British

Columbia, and it started trading in 1983. By 1986 it had six hundred members and had done over $350,000 worth of trading in everything from vegetables and goats' milk to dentistry, building work, and room rental. There are currently over one hundred similar start-up LETSystems world-wide. There are also over two thousand of these types of computerized barter systems in the United States, and although transactions are taxed by the IRS, they continue to grow rapidly.

Care Shares or Time Dollars—Local Service Credit Organizations

Another variation on this model is the "service credits," "care share," or "time dollars" credit organizations. Individuals earn credits by helping others and can then pay for other services with these care shares or time dollars. A teacher tutors a twelve-year old boy in English, and he mows her lawn. Or a retired secretary types poetry written by a neighbor with multiple sclerosis, and the neighbor repays her by reading the newspaper to the secretary's blind daughter. Some three thousand service credit volunteers, most of them over sixty, are already at work through programs administered by community agencies, schools, local hospitals, and community colleges. This system allows citizens to address critical needs that would otherwise be neglected. Time dollars simply reward people for helping people, and the IRS has ruled that such exchanges are tax-exempt, as they are not commercial in nature.

People are able to pay part of their medical bills or health insurance premiums in time dollars in El Paso, Texas, and Washington, D.C. Time Dollars are based on four truths of the economy:

1. The real wealth of the nation is not money, but the willingness of people to use their time in helping others.

2. The household economy, which has been supported by women, has been eroded by women joining the work force, but it can be rebuilt using the principle of helping others.

3. People respond to rewards other than money.

4. Even a lot of money cannot substitute for what the family, neighborhood, and community used to provide.[17]

Co-op America

The interdependent linking of mutual needs is addressed by Co-op America with one question: What is a fair profit for the producer and the seller that is also a fair price to the buyer? Co-op America is an international marketing cooperative of forty-five thousand people and groups concerned with building an "alternative marketplace" based on an economy of cooperation, accountability, environmental sustainability, and social responsibility. The business practices of Co-op America's consumers and producers are based on an interdependent awareness of environmental impact, work place democracy, strengthening local communities, and ensuring that money spent reaches the people who produce the goods.

This membership marketing organization brings together one thousand socially responsible businesses, co-ops, and nonprofit groups with individuals who want to have their purchases reflect their values. Through a mail-order catalog, a quarterly magazine called *Co-op America Quarterly,* and an annual directory of member organizations, Co-op America sees itself as contributing to rebuilding a "socially responsible marketplace." Alisa Gravitz, executive director, notes that "we all have relationships with the dominant institution of our time—corporations—as consumers, investors, workers, and neighbors. Are these relationships healthy? Do we have a say in the relationships—in the direction and decisions of these corporations? The idea of socially responsible marketing and business is that all of the stakeholders in a corporation—customers, investors, suppliers, workers, neighbors, and Mother Nature—are brought together into the decision-making process, which will give us very different decisions than we see today."[18]

Co-op America provides new opportunities for socially responsible businesses, including alternative trading organizations that work with Central American craft cooperatives like Pueblo to People, One World Trading, and Friends of the Third World. These groups see to it that money from customers in North America goes directly to the productive people who are contributing to their country's economic development. Through its catalog, distributed to one hundred thousand of their members and interested buyers, Co-op America offers products from groups like the Zuñi Craftsman Cooperative (fine Native American jewelry), Redwood Records (tapes and records by progressive artists), and Workers Owned Sewing Company (clothing). Of the total $1 million of income earned from the catalog in 1991, $750,000 was paid out to producers! This compares with an average 12 to 25 percent given back to producers in traditional marketing arrangements.

THE LARGER MEANING OF THESE MODELS

In developing these growing institutions, innovative leaders are gradually synthesizing the best aspects of both conservative and liberal thought. Conservative values of individual initiative, private enterprise, efficiency, productivity, and self-reliance are being synthesized with liberal values of equality of opportunity, sharing, and caring for each other and the environment. This synthesis can be seen in worker-owned and -managed cooperative businesses, innovative loan programs to make capital available to those most in need all around the world, marketing that shares profits fairly with producers, land trusts that conserve land and help keep land costs low and housing affordable, and investment that brings social as well as financial returns. The emphasis among these social innovators is not on ideology, but on finding out what works, to make changes in the economic system that will make it more economically just and environmentally benign.

It is also clear in viewing the whole picture that these new models for economic activities include many of the components, on a microscale, of a new socially responsible, sustainable global economy. This economy is concerned with human development, and right relations among all people, ecological sustainability, a co-creative relationship with nature, equitable access to the world's resources for meeting everyone's basic needs, the celebration of human creativity and unity.

Most of the traditional realms of economic activity are represented by the groups highlighted in this chapter. Together they represent micromodels of a new, socially conscious society.

- Banking—South Shore Bank
- Investment—Franklin Research and Development Co.
- Land and housing ownership and mortgages—Institute for Community Economics and the National Association of Community Development Loan Funds
- Management/labor relations, productivity and quality of work life—Franklin Research and Development Co.
- Marketing—Co-op America
- Sustainable development—Grameen Bank and ACCION
- Financial system reform—Countertrade, LETS, Care Shares
- Sustainable technologies—Rocky Mountain Institute, CYCLEAN

The models discussed in this chapter attest to the fact that a new economic system is gradually emerging. Although they are not yet joined into a larger network, there is a degree of cooperation among most of these organizations. For example, Franklin Research and Development places deposits for its cash accounts in the South Shore Bank's Development Deposits account and directs social investors to the Institute for Community Economics Loan Fund. And all five of the groups are members of the Social Investment Forum and Co-op America.

However, if these enterprises were systematically linked together and steadily expanded, they or similar local versions could offer a viable economic model for increasingly larger systems, such as a city, a bioregion, or a county. This could be done by strengthening the areas of cooperation among these and other existing groups through shared business activities, building stronger relationships among these socially responsible organizations and individuals, creating an aggressive development banking capacity to spur new products and businesses, developing a wider constituency by increased marketing to the public, and acquiring or converting mainstream businesses to fit within a socially responsible framework. This process has begun with provision by the Clinton administration of "seed capital" to banks and credit unions and other institutions lending to low-income neighborhoods.

The following chart lists major economic problems we are confronting today and the successful transformational solutions implemented by groups addressing these issues.

TRANSFORMATIONAL SOLUTIONS TO ECONOMIC PROBLEMS

PROBLEM	GROUP	SOLUTION
Capital scarcity for inner-city reconstruction.	South Shore Bank of Chicago.	Solicits social investors and targets capital to planned rehab strategy in inner-city neighborhoods.
Investment strategies that ignore all social considerations.	Social Investment Forum, Coalition for Environmentally Responsible Economies, Council on Economic Priorities, Franklin Research and Development Co.	Careful screening and rating of companies and investments based on social criteria.

PROBLEM	GROUP	SOLUTION
Disempowerment and poverty of inner-city neighborhoods.	Institute for Community Economics, National Association of Community Development Loan Funds.	Provides capital for setting up land trusts controlled by community groups and rehabbing buildings for permanent low-income housing.
Lack of educational opportunities for the poor.	I Have a Dream Foundation.	Encourages executives to mentor underprivileged youth; provides scholarships to inner-city youth who stay in high school.
Lack of educational opportunities for the poor.	CETHA.	Provides courses in Bolivia for peasants on market day.
Development assistance that benefits ruling elites and not poorest of the poor.	Grameen Bank, ACCION.	Provides capital for micro-enterprise development to tiny businesses in poorest countries.
Marketing networks that take unfair advantage of impoverished producers.	Co-op America.	Returns a high percentage of its profits to Third World producers.
Conflictual management/labor relations.	Avis, The Body Shop, Franklin Research and Development Co.	Workers share, to varying degrees, in ownership and management of company.
Exploitive manipulation of financial system.	LETSystem, Care Shares, International countertrade.	Provides systems for direct exchanges of goods and services by producers, outside financial system.

PROBLEM	GROUP	SOLUTION
Economic development that destroys and pollutes the Earth, encourages excessive consumption.	Rocky Mountain Institute, World Watch Institute, E. F. Schumacher Society, Dutch National Green Plan.	Planning that analyzes energy use, capital costs and costs to the Earth, creates sustainable development.
Lack of ethics in business world.	*Business Ethics* magazine.	Promotes examination of ethical issues in business.
	The Body Shop.	Encourages involvement in community by employees.
Lack of employment opportunities for the poor.	Osage Resource Recovery.	Trains unemployed and homeless to do environmental remediation and mailings.
	The Body Shop.	Sites factories in underemployed areas, trades with Third World.
	Aetna Life and Casualty.	Provides training for unemployed.

ECOCAPITALISTS AND ECODECENTRALISTS

Integrating these ideas and models into mainstream economics elicits different scenarios, depending on various people's points of view. Ecocapitalists see the gradual adoption of ecological and social principles and values by corporations that wish to maintain public legitimacy. Yet even carefully designed socially responsible businesses find themselves caught in the contradiction of promoting the idea that they can "do good" and make a profit by meeting environmental needs, when their very existence encourages the basic attitudes of overconsumption that are degrading the world's environment. As Paul Hawken notes, a jet flying across the country, a car rented at an airport, or an air-conditioned hotel room all cause the same amount of environmental degradation whether associated with The Body Shop, Sierra Club, or Exxon.[19] Yet even with these ambiguities, socially responsible business entrepreneurs are making an effort to change business as usual by risking their capital and expertise in the struggle to create companies that reflect deeply held spiritual values.

However, businesses will not be able to fulfill this new social contract to be socially and environmentally sound until the systems they operate within are sensitive to the natural world and guided by higher principles. For this to occur the government must assume its rightful role as the protector of the welfare of all the people and the biological systems upon which we depend. For this to happen the power of business must stop controlling the processes of government.

Another area where the public may have unrecognized leverage over large corporations is through corporate charters, which come from the citizens themselves. As Paul Hawken notes, the privileges granted by states (as representatives of the people) to corporations, such as limited liability, implies accountability of the corporation to society as a whole. When a corporation violates public trust, citizens should have the right to revoke its charter, causing a company to sell its enterprises and go out of business. This would create a degree of accountability to the public that is missing in the current power structure, but is implicit in the public–private partnership of state licensing of corporations.

When Gordon met with corporate executives to discuss their signing and implementing the CERES Principles, they admitted that they were deeply concerned that their social contract to produce chemicals at all might be rescinded if the public became alarmed enough about pollution. This fear has motivated many corporate giants like DOW and Du Pont to make major public commitments to drastically reduce emissions within the decade.

Ecodecentralists envision a radical restructuring of the economy to give local economies and groups much greater autonomy, flexibility, and self-reliance along with a waning of the power of large institutions and corporations. Trends showing the importance of small, local businesses for generating employment remain unchanged. Technologists see ever greater microcircuitry and genetic engineering leading to an ever more efficient future, with implicit centralization and control. This scenario is being increasingly questioned by many nongovernmental organizations around the world, who see the benefits of some of these developments yet question who will determine and benefit from their use.

AN ECOLOGY OF ECONOMIC MODELS

In the future we are likely to see some combination of all of these, with the economy being an ecosystem of models of different types and scales depending on the economic and cultural background of a country or region. Thus the countries of Eastern Europe and the former Soviet Union are likely to have somewhat more centrally regulated, yet private-enterprise market systems with selective managed growth, while the United States and other Western democracies might well have more entrepreneurial types of systems with less control, and corporations would be of all types and sizes, as appropriate.

According to Michael Rothschild, an economist and environmentalist, comparing the economy to a rain forest helps us see it evolving by technological innovation and market competition, just as biological life evolves by genetic mutation and natural selection. When the economic environment shifts, some industries disappear and new ones spring up. Diversity and complexity are signs of life. Yet the role of government should be as the creative regulator of the economic ecology, not as the controlling bureaucracy, which destroys life and initiative as we have seen in the former Soviet Union. Japan, instead of trying to micromanage each industry, patiently cultivated its capitalist ecosystem by fostering competition, encouraging recycling of profits into new technologies, and providing high-quality education. Rather than a blind, ham-handed tinkerer, Japan's government has been an astute, nurturing gardener.[20]

Local economies could contain a variety of models, including worker-owned cooperatives, individual proprietorships, partnerships, and corporations. Local currencies, like the LETSystem, could be used to stimulate local economic activity and keep the results of people's development efforts available to their community. Trading with local currency would be combined with the use of an international currency for transactions within the global marketplace. Establishing land trusts could reserve the control of vital local resources for the local community. The marketing and consuming of local goods and services could stimulate economic growth and help reduce energy use and environmentally costly transportation. Naturally, all these developments presuppose a new economic ethic of sharing and mutual growth and an environmental ethic of sustainability and restoration of damaged ecosystems.

Yet what is still missing is a comprehensive plan for systems of transportation, energy use, and resource reuse which requires that the destructive impact of our economic activities on the earth be severely limited. For this to be accomplished we will have to reward activities that conserve and restore the natural and biological systems, and make it prohibitively expensive to harm them. In *The Ecology of Commerce,* Paul Hawken promotes eliminating all taxes, and substituting carbon and energy taxes to open the discussion of how best to accomplish this.[21]

Economic thinking today is a reflection of the political system that interpenetrates it, and in turn economic ideas influence the structure of politics. The collapse of communism is the result of a decline in both an economic and political ideology that tried to control complex economic and political evolutionary processes, resulting in its own demise, as the life within the people revolted against such stifling dominance. The economic excesses of the Reagan/Bush era were a result of the political laissez-faire doctrine of the conservatives, which deregulated business while establishing even more special privileges for the wealthy elites, ignoring issues of fairness and equity. The consequences of these policies were seen in economic decline, racial unrest, and voter anger.

The political changes in Western Europe are leading to a gradual melting of the borders within the European Community—a prototype for a mutually beneficial economic commonwealth, which, with appropriate democratic controls on corporate and bureaucratic power, will likely bring greater prosperity to all its citizens. The opportunity for humanity to observe the benefits of the synergy that results from such cooperation is stimulating other attempts at regional cooperation. Efforts are already under way to develop a community of South American nations; a North American trading block is being established with the United States, Canada, and Mexico through NAFTA; and cooperation between the nations of the Pacific Rim is also growing. Ultimately, when humanity realizes that promoting the freedom, growth, and well-being of all people is mutually beneficial, regional groups will join together in new agreements that will become the framework for the new economic order that will eventually include a global currency.

The worldwide environmental crisis is also moving humanity and the nations toward greater cooperation and coordinated efforts. Careful monitoring of changes in the planet's atmosphere, forests, land productivity, and ocean resources will be among the many efforts handled by international teams of scientists and government specialists. This will require a two-pronged shift in the distribution of power and decision-making from its present concentration in the national executive and representative assemblies. Some of the power will devolve to local constituencies, where many decisions can be made by those most affected by them. Power will also gradually rise upward into international coordinating bodies like the UN. The power of local issues can be seen in the impact of the seven thousand local groups in the United States organizing around cleaning up toxic pollution in their areas and in the thousands of nongovernmental local groups in southern nations organizing to save their rivers, forests, or agriculture. International cooperation and coordination will develop from the compelling need to find global solutions to our world environmental crisis, for it cannot be solved by any one nation or bloc of nations.

With this wider perspective, we can now see in all our crises the beneficent principles of a Higher Power at work. Since human beings learn almost exclusively by trial and error, we sense that we're being helped to move, one step at a time, toward a more cooperative, just, and sustainable world. Through the awesomely inevitable karmic effects of the causes we humans set in motion, and the progress of evolution through the experiences of many lives, we are slowly learning to adjust our thinking and activities to live in greater harmony with cosmic law. This law, which grants us free will, brings us inevitably to the realization that we are part of the One Life and Consciousness, regardless of how real separation may seem to some. This realization of unity is another important step on our evolutionary journey, leading us inexorably ever closer to our Divine Source.*

---

*See Resources section on page 423 for listing of organizations, environmental and cooperative businesses, and ethical investment companies that are building the new planetary economy.

Chapter Thirteen

◆

INNER AND OUTER WORK FOR PLANETARY EVOLUTION

He or she who cannot change the very fabric of his/her thought will never be able to change reality and will never, therefore, make any progress.

—ANWAR SADAT, FORMER
PRESIDENT OF EGYPT

Inner Work for Planetary Evolution

Each of us can make a difference. Through our prayers and meditations, and by changing our negative mental and emotional states into positive ones, we contribute significantly to the well-being of the planet. If we want to be really effective at inner work, however, we have to make a major shift in orientation. We have to move from relying only on our physical senses to experience and affect the world around us and instead turn to our subtler senses to experience the vast worlds within. With our very active, outwardly focused Western life-style, this is not easy. But with practice we can increase our effectiveness.

CONTACTING AN INNER SOURCE OF GUIDANCE

To help the world in some way, each of us, wherever we may be, can contact an inner source of guidance from our own Soul, or Higher Self, through sincere motivation and practice. The two of us, for example, received clear inner guidance in meditation in 1978 to buy a particular piece of land to start a community, an ecological village in Massachusetts, and name it after the star Sirius. It has served thousands of people who have visited over the years, providing an inspirational experience of a cooperative, environmentally conscious, spiritual life-style.

The Findhorn Community in Scotland, where we lived for many years, was also developed on the inner spiritual guidance received by cofounders Peter and Eileen Caddy and Dorothy Maclean, and it now has become an internationally famous education center. Dorothy also received inner guidance from the Devas, with both inspirational and practical advice on their garden.

Our Founding Fathers, such as George Washington, followed their inner guidance, as have many great leaders. Mahatma Gandhi once said, "The only tyrant I will accept in this world is the still, small voice within." Senator Bob Kerrey (D-NE) makes his major decisions in the Senate by "meditating and appealing to a higher spirit," according to colleague Senator Trent Lott (R-MS). Kerrey says, "I make my decisions vertically, not horizontally."[1]

Many people are now receiving inner guidance to help them in their lives. According to a 1985 Gallup poll, 16 million Americans admit to hearing an inner voice in their minds that is distinctly different from the usual internal chatter. The voice of the Soul is often described as "the still small voice within" or "the Inner Teacher." To hear this voice, it helps to meditate and focus our attention on the region of our heart (not our solar plexus, as it only responds to emotional or astral energies), and inwardly call on our Soul. Not everyone hears a voice or sees a vision—some people simply feel a sense of peace and inspiration. But as a result of the meditation, spiritual help may come when it is needed—later in the day or week—perhaps in the form of inspiration at the time, or words that a friend happens to speak or from a passage found in a book.

We need to learn to carefully evaluate our guidance to be sure it is coming from the highest level and not just from our own subconscious desires, from others' thoughts, or from deceptive "astral" entities on the emotional planes of desire and illusion. Guidance from the Higher Self, or from the Angelic realms, will always be inspirational, concise, and loving. It will honor the good of the whole. It will never create fear or separation, demand obedience, or claim ultimate authority for itself. It will not conflict with our personal ethics but will always recognize a Higher Power and be in harmony with the essence of the world's major spiritual teachings. When we apply these criteria to the guidance received by cult leaders like David Koresh in Waco, Texas, we can see why it's not from the highest level.

However, the real purpose of guidance is not just to receive information from higher levels, but to learn to think like higher beings. It is our challenge now to learn to perceive events and indeed all of Life from a broader and more inclusive perspective—from the perspective of our Divine Soul rather than from our limited personality, with its self-centered desires and opinions.

For example, a friend of ours, Frances Oliver, who was a contractor for one of the major federal agencies, began applying the metaphysical concepts she was learning to her work and asked for spiritual guidance on how best to proceed. While working on a cabinet-level report to the U.S. Congress, she found that whenever she thought of her role as being a typical project manager—very controlling and a stickler for due dates and responsibility—things would not go well. But as soon as she remembered that her higher purpose was to bring light and love to the government agency and to its employees, everything would flow smoothly. She began consciously asking to be given extra help if her work was in alignment with God's will and the highest good of all—and she was. Her timing on everything was perfect, which seemed miraculous to her colleagues, and her entire business has benefited.

It's also helpful to pay attention to the guidance we receive in dreams, as many leaders down through the ages have done, as far back as the Pharaohs of Egypt and Joseph in the Bible. Scientists have received dream guidance as well, such as F. A. Kekule dreaming of the shape of the ring-shaped benzene molecules in 1865.

In writing or speaking for a cause that helps the world in some way, we can ask for help from higher spiritual levels to receive creative inspiration. Writers may often receive ideas from spiritual sources unknown to them. For example, in the 1951 science fiction film classic *The Day the Earth Stood Still,* a powerful speech was given by a visitor from outer space that warned the governments of earth about the need to stop violence: "We regret that you cannot live in peace. You are behaving like children, but that is your problem, and you must work it out. As long as you use your toy boats and planes and guns to kill each other, we cannot interfere. But when you begin to endanger the other planets, we will have to destroy this one in order to preserve the planetary system." Later, the film writer was told that this was word for word the same speech given twenty-eight years earlier by a spiritual teacher, Master Morya, who lived halfway around the world in the Himalayas—although the writer had never seen or heard it, nor did he consciously know the teacher.[2]

Another example is a mysterious book that appeared in 1933 entitled *Gabriel over the White House* by Thomas Frederic Tweed. Made into a major motion picture, it is the story of how a faltering president was transformed and endowed with dynamic genius to uplift the nation and guide it through a difficult time. Overlighted and guided by the Archangel Gabriel, the president suddenly succeeds in bringing the nations together in a plan for international union, disarmament, cancellation of war debts, and removal of tariff barriers. The normally conservative *New York Times* noted in a review that the "narrative treated with rare common sense a multitude of contemporary affairs and in a manner that seldom transcends the conceivable."[3] The film seeded inspirational ideas and solutions, some of which were later adopted by Franklin Roosevelt in his New Deal policies.

MEDITATION AND PRAYER

One of the primary ways we can help in world crises is through the power of meditation. While prayer is often referred to as talking to God, meditation is about listening to God, or to that higher, wiser part of ourselves that is the spark of Divinity within us. For us personally, learning to meditate was probably the single most important contribution to our spiritual growth and our inner peace, as well as to the effectiveness of our service. We have been meditating together daily now for over eighteen years.

Meditation is the mind's power to hold itself steady in the Light and in that Light to become aware of Divine Purpose. Meditation is called the Science of Light because it works with the substance of Light. Light is the result of the fusion of Spirit and matter. Meditation helps us develop a sense of detachment emotionally and mentally so we can be more effective in helping the world from the inner side. When we react emotionally to an event, we cannot be of help, as our emotional body is vibrating on the same level as the problem, rather than working from a higher level in order to help heal it and transmute it into something positive. Meditation also helps to purify us, bringing up long-suppressed emotional negativity within us, so that it can be burned up by the fire of the mind in contact with Spirit. It also burns up illusions and distortions in the mind—our fear, anger, and hatred—and this enables us to perceive the world more clearly.

Concentration and steadiness of mind is also developed by the practice of meditation. This allows us to think more clearly and creatively about personal and social problems and to find solutions. Meditation helps us develop our intuition and helps us manage stress. The inner peace we find in meditation helps to create more peace in the world. It also fills us with healing energy, for ourselves and others in need of healing.

Meditation develops inner resources and energizes us so more can be accomplished with less effort. Just as personal meditation can help us discover more clearly what our purpose is in life, group meditation can also help an organization, public interest group, or government agency align more directly with its mission. This enables it to fulfill its higher purpose and channels organizational resources in a more effective direction. Meditation in groups can also assist us in working together to bring about a more positive future.

We can use a reflective form of meditation to explore a new understanding of an idea—to expand it or refine it—or to find a creative solution to a particular social problem. This type of meditation actively engages the abstract mind or intuition by holding it steady in the Light and dedicating the exploration to the highest good.

Visualization

One of the doors to meditation in the early stages is visualization, since it works according to the occult law that form follows thought. The creative imagination pictures a form, and the mind gives energy, life, and direction to this form. Visualization builds a bridge from the emotional to the mental plane that can affect the physical world in positive or negative ways.

For example, if a loved one is late getting home, we often tend to picture something horrible happening to him/her. Instead we need to consciously visualize positive images in great detail. We can visualize our loved one traveling safely and happily and arriving home perfectly fine. In just this way we can visualize the healing and unification of those groups or nations involved in a conflict, asking first that this be for their highest good. Many people visualize a stream of white Light radiating from the center of their forehead—from their "third eye" center between the brows—which can be directed where needed, surrounding the person(s) and the situation in Light.

Now that we've all seen pictures from NASA of the whole Earth, we can easily visualize our planet surrounded by love and Light and at peace, as this strengthens all efforts toward world unity and synthesis, and also helps to heal environmental problems.

Effects of Meditation

The practice of meditation is growing in popularity. A Gallup poll has shown that as much as 19 percent of the population in the San Francisco area, for example, practice some form of daily meditation or yoga to still their minds, and 46 percent practice less frequently.[4] Even some police meditate to overcome their aggressive tendencies. The hundreds of thousands around the world who meditated at ancient sacred sites during the "Harmonic Convergence" on August 16, 1987, to help transform the planet received tremendous media attention, though mostly skeptical. With hindsight, however, some observers have reconsidered. As an article by Don

Oldenberg, a staff writer for *The Washington Post*, noted, "Maybe the fringe dwellers who resonated with the Sedona sunrise or echoed their *mani padme hums* in the ruins at Machu Picchu were onto something after all. Consider the mind-blowing and upbeat happenings since then: European communism goes belly-up, democracy spreads, freedom rings, superpowers become superbuddies, environmental consciousness is awakened.... [B]y golly, you've got the makings of a wholesale Age of Aquarius."[5]

Science has offered an explanation for the peace-promoting effects of meditation in terms of quantum field theory. Physicists Josephson, Domash, Hagelin, and Sudarshan believe that impulses of coherence in consciousness could move much like an electric current in a supercooled wire and jump gaps from brain to brain by traveling in a field of consciousness that is much like the vacuum state. Physicist Itzhak Bentov explained that a good meditator can charge the electrostatic field surrounding his/her body so that it will be resonant with the frequency of the Earth at 7.5 cycles per second. This enables the meditator to affect any body vibrating at a similar frequency range.[6]

The Institute for Nuclear Research in Russia found there was less radiation in the Kiev cathedrals near the Chernobyl nuclear accident than in other locations nearby. In conducting tests, they found that radiation seemed to be reduced by one-third in the churches, raising the possibility of a causal link with prayer and meditation.[7]

A Dutch insurance company now offers a 30 to 50 percent discount on auto insurance to those who practice meditation. Their statistics indicate that meditators are low risks due to low alcoholism, reduced anxiety and stress, quicker reaction time, and better perception. To qualify for the discount, people must meditate twice a day and take out a five-year policy.[8]

Studies on the power of meditation to affect social change have appeared in such prestigious publications as *Journal of Conflict Resolution*, edited at Yale University (December 1988), and the *Journal of Mind and Behavior* (December 1988), although these studies have not yet convinced skeptics and more research is needed. In 1983 Dr. Audrey Lanford, a Stanford Ph.D., conducted a scientific study on the effect of meditation on the crime rate in Washington, D.C., by studying police homicide statistics during the weeks when four hundred Transcendental Meditators (TM) meditated together regularly. TM is an Eastern form of meditation, based on the repetition of a particular sound or mantra, started by the Indian teacher, Maharishi Mahesh Yogi. Dr. Lanford found there were 22 percent fewer homicides—"statistically significant at the .02 level" during that time.[9] Transcendental Meditators also went to Iran during the 1978 revolution. According to John Davies, research coordinator at the University of

Maryland's Center for International Development and Conflict Management, war death and injuries declined dramatically—in some instances by 70 percent—during the times when the TM groups were meditating there.[10] TM meditators also claim to have helped quell violence while meditating over the years in trouble spots such as Lebanon, Nicaragua, Israel, Zimbabwe, and Zambia, but independent research is needed to verify.[11]

In July 1993, 4,000 TM meditators again descended on Washington, D.C., for three weeks to help "reduce violent crime and improve the success of the government." With what they claim as an independent scientific review board (but which includes several TM devotees and others who believe in TM's effects), they planned to document lowered crime rates and so convince the local government to allocate part of its budget to support this work. *The Washington Post* did report a 19 percent drop in robberies and an 11 percent drop in assaults during this period, but homicides increased 50 percent and rapes 9 percent, so depending on which statistics are emphasized, different effects can be claimed.[12]

TM has attracted hundreds of thousands of practitioners and had a significant effect on the spread of meditation worldwide. Although TM practitioners believe their particular technique of meditation is best for everyone, there are actually a number of effective and advanced techniques available for any serious seeker, many of which have been part of specific spiritual disciplines for many centuries, such as Buddhist Vipassana and Zen meditations. The effectiveness of meditation depends more on the level of ability of the individual, rather than on a particular technique, as some have practiced meditation for many lifetimes and so are quite potent.

From the perspective of the Ageless Wisdom, the problem with trying to do good in the world by insisting on the power of one's own developed discipline, whether meditation skills or anything else, is that our ego gets too identified with the fruits of the action and is not sufficiently detached from results to allow spiritual energy to flow through. What is encouraged in the Ageless Wisdom tradition is to first purify our motives for wanting to help, and then to align our personal will with God's will, asking for the highest good to come from our efforts, realizing we may not consciously know the deeper lessons and karmic purposes being played out in a given situation.

All the spiritual traditions warn that meditation can be dangerous if there is not right motive involved—a desire to serve the world in some way rather than to serve only the self or to achieve personal powers.

Much of the inner work to be done is for the future, not the present, to prepare the blueprint for the new consciousness and forms to manifest. In doing this kind of inner, meditative work, we need to remember that we may not see the fruits of our work for many years—in fact, we may never know the results of our work at all. There is no objective way to verify that any specific event is directly the result of an inner, meditative effort. And, in fact, we can only do this kind of work successfully if we develop a sense of detachment from the need to see results.

Affirmations and Mantras

The use of affirmations can also be very effective. An affirmation is a phrase briefly stating a spiritual or healing goal, repeated over and over. For example, over the years great numbers of people have repeated, "Every day, in every way, I am getting better and better." Repeating the affirmation aloud over and over helps us to bring that quality into our lives—and into the world. Repeating an affirmation is also a good technique for quieting the mind to enter a meditative state.

The power of group mantras is especially potent. A mantra is a combination of sounds, words, or phrases that achieves certain results through rhythmic effects. Mantras can be quite powerful as rhythmic sounds. They can create, purify, and harmonize—or they can destroy—depending on the consciousness of the person using them. The Buddhist prayer "*Om mani padme hum*," for example, is a series of powerful seed sounds with the potency to stimulate the good in us, protect us, and positively affect our environment.

"The Great Invocation" is a universal mantra invoking God's Light, love, and spiritual power that is now being used in over twenty languages all over the world. Rashmi Singh and others in the Philippines, for example, distributed thousands of copies just before the ouster of Marcos and repeated the invocation every day before the election and every hour on the hour on election day, and kept it up during the revolution that followed. The mostly peaceful transition of leadership was remarkable.

THE GREAT INVOCATION

From the point of Light within the Mind of God
Let light stream forth into the minds of men.
Let Light descend on Earth.

From the point of Love within the Heart of God
Let love stream forth into the hearts of men.
May Christ return to Earth.

From the centre where the Will of God is known
Let purpose guide the little wills of men—
The purpose which the Masters know and serve.

From the centre which we call the race of men
Let the Plan of Love and Light work out
And may it seal the door where evil dwells.

Let Light and Love and Power restore the Plan on Earth. *

*Please note: Although thousands of years old, this mantra was given out to the world in modern form in 1945 and the language uses the masculine word *men* in the generic sense to include both men and women. We haven't changed it to "men and women," as this interferes with the rhythmic and mantric quality of "men," which contains the feminine "ma" sound for matter, or earth.

During World War II there were many meditation groups in Britain and elsewhere that worked to defeat Hitler by invoking the help of spiritual Masters on the inner planes and by visualizing lines of Light to protect Britain. For example, Dion Fortune and the Society of the Inner Light in Glastonbury, England, linked together in meditation with the "group Soul of the race" and invoked Angelic presences to protect the country. Another metaphysician, Charles Seymour, tapped the traditional power centers of Britain to visualize a shield around the coastline.

Group Meditation

A project to strengthen the will of people on earth to create peace has been initiated as a technique of international attunement by the United Nations. The third Tuesday of September each year, the day the General Assembly of the UN convenes in New York, was proclaimed an International Day of Peace. At the moment the assembly begins at 3:00 P.M. (EST), a moment of silence is observed for world peace, and people everywhere are encouraged to join in. Pathways to Peace in Larkspur, California, was designated by the UN to promote this day. They are also encouraging people to observe a moment of silence for peace every day at noon. When thousands of people unite together at the same time, a powerful current of energy is created to express the purpose that is invoked.

Another approach is a walking meditation, to send healing energy to a place that is in need of it. For example, the Buddhist monk Thich Nhat Hanh led over four hundred people in a silent walking meditation at the Vietnam memorial in Washington, D.C., in 1990. Participants kept a meditative focus, silently breathing in and out, to release their own and other's negative feelings about the war in Vietnam and to bring healing to the resultant problems it created, both in Vietnam and in the United States.

Centers of Light

Just as the power of group meditation is very effective, so also is the power of people meditating together regularly in the same place, as this builds up a strong, high-frequency spiritual vibration. It creates a stronghold of Light, a storehouse of spiritual energy. These centers of Light help balance the places of extreme negativity, violence, and oppression on the planet, as the Light is a beacon of hope for humanity and for a better world emerging in the future. In *The Starseed Transmissions,* Ken Carey envisioned these centers as "islands of the future in a sea of the past . . . points of entry through which the healing energies of transformation will be channeled . . . to prepare the human species for its collective awakening."[13]

Many people are also building networks of Light around the earth as they connect with others of similar values and visualize themselves linked inwardly by lines of Light. This is mutually strengthening and helps break down the sense of isolation. Many of these people are later able to recognize each other when they meet in person—by the Light in their eyes and the fire in their hearts.

(At the end of this section on inner work, we have written guided instructions for several different types of meditations that we invite you to try.)

SENDING LIGHT TO GOVERNMENT LEADERS AND AGENCIES

It is important not to send world leaders negative emotional and/or mental energy when we don't like their policies, as this only makes it more difficult for them to express their higher qualities. While not being blind to their faults, we need to focus on their positive side.

We can visualize Light and Love being sent to leaders to help them connect with their own Soul, or Higher Self, which is concerned with the good of the whole, so that they may act from that higher awareness. Actor Richard Gere demonstrated this when he stopped in the middle of an Academy Awards presentation in 1993 and asked millions of TV viewers to send positive thoughts to Chinese leader Li Peng to free oppressed Tibetans. Also, it is very important that we do this kind of work only when we have a pure motive and when we know that we are aligned with our Higher Self or Soul.

Even more important, it's good to send Light to leaders who are already embodying spiritual values, asking that they continue to be guided and protected. In Native American societies, this was traditionally the role played by the medicine men and women of the tribe—protecting the leaders and warriors through prayer and rituals.

When we find ourselves physically in the presence of a leader, or are participating in an important event, or are in a place where a crisis is occurring, we can help by doing an "open-eyed" meditation. While being aware of everything going on around us, we make a deep contact with our Soul, and then visualize spiritual Light and Love flowing out from us into the environment. To do this, we must see ourselves as clear channels for Light to flow through and so must work first to release our own opinions and negativity and become more detached and impersonal. We then ask that our Soul work through us to bring the highest good to the situation.

Each event has an energy field surrounding it created by a combination of the people present, their karma, the energies of the earth in that place, the design of any physical structures in which it is taking place, the particular astrological timing, the thoughts and emotions projected on it by others, and the energy from higher beings on the inner planes. Therefore, if those present at an event—whether central actors or not—offer themselves as channels of Light, then spiritual beings functioning on the inner planes can use them as anchor points to stabilize and protect the energy field and charge the atmosphere with Light.

The unusually positive energy surrounding the meeting between Reagan and Gorbachev at Reykjavík, Iceland, may have been helped by this type of process, with a coordinated effort by many meditators around the country focused on sending Light to that event. Another example is to attend a session of Congress, sitting in the visitors' gallery above the chambers, sending positive energy to the proceedings below. Visitors can also go on a tour of the White House, the Pentagon, and other such significant forums, and visualize Light and Love everywhere they go.

A story of how effective an ordinary person can be in sending loving energy to leaders was told to us by Olaf Egeberg, a former member of the Sirius community. He said that his father, Dr. Roger Egeberg, former special assistant for health policy in the Nixon administration, was very inspired by the woman who ran the elevator in the HEW building where he worked. She consistently radiated such loving, positive energy that it always put him and other government leaders in a good mood before their important meetings and definitely helped the proceedings to be more aligned with the highest good.

Nancy Roof, of the Center for Psychology and Social Change, reported an experience of being instrumental in restoring communication between Serbian and Croatian delegates at the UN who weren't speaking to each other during negotiations between their factions in late 1991. Finding herself "coincidentally" placed between these two in a room with two hundred other people at a UN briefing, she prayed for God's help and inwardly sent them both Light and positive energy. She struck up a conversation with one and then turned to do the same with the other. She kept turning back and forth to speak to each of them, and soon one asked her to send a note to the other. They then agreed to speak to each other and began a discussion as soon as the UN meeting was over.

THOUGHT-FORM BUILDING

One subtle but effective way to influence public opinion is available to us all. We can learn to consciously invoke and receive inspiration and new, progressively better ideas from the inner planes—called "the raincloud of knowable things" by the Ageless Wisdom—and then form them into usable thought-forms that other minds can pick up.

A thought-form can be created from a vision, an abstract idea, or an archetype that is received intuitively, often in meditation or dreams, either consciously or unconsciously from the Enlightened Ones. After it is received, there must be a period of gestation, when we think out the idea clearly and concretely and fill it in with mental substance. Much reflection upon an idea will eventually produce a magnetic field that becomes increasingly potent through our desire to see the thought manifest as a living reality. Then our feelings and enthusiasm help give the idea form on an emotional level. It is then vitalized by our will and by our etheric body, giving it life and power through the breath.

In due time—when the processes of desire have adequately developed and we have released the thought-form, detaching ourselves from it in order that it may do its work—the idea will precipitate onto the physical plane. However, if we stay too attached and identified with the thought-form, we can seriously hinder it.[14]

THE LIFE CYCLE OF IDEAS

New evolutionary ideas begin as pure thought on the inner planes in the mind of an Enlightened One. However, when an idea is picked up by visionaries or abstract thinkers on earth, it becomes colored by their individuality and built into a concept that is not always as pure or wise as the original idea. This seed idea is then picked up by the intelligentsia, progressive thinkers, or artists who grasp the main outline of the idea. They step it down into a more definite shape that can be easily apprehended by everyone, and at this point the idea may attain mainstream respectability and become an ideology.

When it is seized upon as desirable by those focused on the emotional or astral plane, the idea takes on feeling substance and becomes a fashionable ideal, something for people to aspire to. Next it is stepped down to the energy of the physical plane, made practical, and adapted to the needs of daily life, where it is imitated, institutionalized, or mass-produced, finally becoming public opinion and "common sense." Eventually, as conventional wisdom or a fad, the idea will become crystallized and regressive, with its adherents fanatically resisting the next idea needed for human evolution.

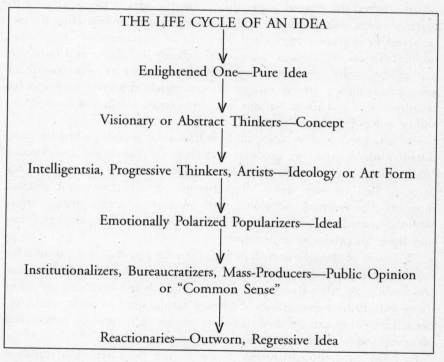

THE LIFE CYCLE OF AN IDEA

↓

Enlightened One—Pure Idea

↓

Visionary or Abstract Thinkers—Concept

↓

Intelligentsia, Progressive Thinkers, Artists—Ideology or Art Form

↓

Emotionally Polarized Popularizers—Ideal

↓

Institutionalizers, Bureaucratizers, Mass-Producers—Public Opinion or "Common Sense"

↓

Reactionaries—Outworn, Regressive Idea

Once a new thought-form reaches the masses and becomes public opinion, it has tremendous impact, because politicians and businesspeople carefully monitor public opinion polls to formulate their stands on issues, to direct government and business policy, and to develop new products.

A leverage principle of physics applied to social systems states that it takes only a small percentage of the population to be a fulcrum for change. Studies done at Stanford University show that when just 5 percent of society adopts a new idea, it becomes "embedded." When 20 percent adopt the idea, it is "unstoppable." However, it requires 50 percent of the population to be aware of the idea before it reaches the 5 percent who will adopt it and work with it.[15] Significantly, as pollster George Gallup notes, the people are usually ahead of legislators in accepting innovations and radical changes.

For example, the thought-form of protecting the sacredness of nature has become public opinion by going through the stages of germination—first by visionary environmentalists in the late 1960s; then through support by progressive thinkers and artists who created ideas and art forms around it; next through promotion of environmental ideals on Earth Day International on April 22, 1990, by activists, the media, and even corporations, which affected the general population. Now the idea is being adapted to practical needs, and environmentally correct products are becoming the latest trend in consumer marketing. The idea of "sustainability"—that economic practices and policies must be ecologically in balance and must not deplete the earth's resources—originally honored only by small groups of environmentalists a few years ago, is now widely discussed in corporate boardrooms. The United Nations has now created a Council on Sustainability as has President Clinton.

Just as a good-quality radio will broadcast clear sounds picked up from distant stations, when we meditate and clear our minds and emotions of "static," we can receive clear signals or new ideas relatively unimpeded. Our work is then to "step down" higher-frequency vibrations and abstract thoughts thus received and clothe them in more concrete mental forms. We look inwardly to see the new visions clearly so that we can then interpret them for others to understand.

This kind of thought-form building, for example, makes it possible for others to pick up these new ideas and create new cultural forms for peace and healing. As Alice Bailey said, "If the thinking and executive people of the world can have their minds 'illumined' by the spirit of wisdom and understanding, they can act as distributors of that light through enlightened planning and legislation and thus affect the entire world."[16]

Building new thought-forms is one of the purposes of Meditation Mount, an educational organization in Ojai, California, that coordinates the activities of a worldwide network of thirty thousand meditators. Their focus is to create thought-forms of a new planetary civilization and culture on the inner planes and thus make it easier for those who organize things on the physical plane to create the new forms and institutions. This group, as well as many other groups and individuals, thus seed the "morphogenetic field" with higher thought-forms to create "an idea whose time has come."

WORKING WITH THOUGHT-FORMS

We can connect with the hidden germ of Light in the heart of any thought-form, a spark of what's called the will to good. Projecting a line of Light from our minds, we penetrate the thought-form and go to its heart to touch the seed of the will to good. We see this expanding and gradually filling the entire thought-form, seeing all negativity and limitation falling away. Likewise we can link with the will to good at the heart of each event and of each person.

Another way of working with thought-forms is to use a concrete thought that's already in the public awareness, gather further information about it, and then allow it to be enlightened by the intuitive perceptions of the higher mind and so expanded into something more effective. This is currently being done, for example, by some transformational thinkers who have expanded on the New Paradigm policy ideas originally proposed by innovative policy thinkers in mainstream institutions.

In addition to creating new thought-forms, there is also important work to be done in destroying old thought-forms that have become limiting, negative, and incapable of serving their original purpose. Destroying these old thought-forms then becomes a matter of great concern and usefulness, since it allows a new form to take its place.

We have seen this process in the work of Mikhail Gorbachev. In calling for *perestroika* (restructuring) and *glasnost* (openness) instead of secrecy, he helped to destroy many of the old thought-forms of communism in his country. In fact, as American visitors to the former Soviet Union pointed out, Gorbachev was much better at destroying old thought-forms than building specific new thought-forms or policies, and the Russian people were frustrated with this. For a time he tended to get caught in some old thought-forms himself, such as a belief in the possibility of reforming communism, and so didn't see a coup of hard-line Communists brewing right under his nose.

In the last few years in the former Communist countries, we have witnessed the destruction of many old, negative thought-forms: Revolution cannot be peaceful; One person can't stop an army in its tracks; An army always serves the status quo; Police states cannot be overthrown; Change is always slow; The cold war will never end. Because of all the people working on inner levels to help change these limiting thought-forms, energy has been available for those with courage to demonstrate them outwardly. The actions of only a few brave individuals were key in catalyzing the revolutions of Eastern Europe.

Former President Reagan helped destroy an old thought-form—that government could somehow solve all social problems. He would have been more successful at creating real change, however, if instead of repeating over and over that government is bad and inefficient and crippling many programs, he had instead affirmed the creation of "efficient, effective government" and promoted new solutions for private-public partnerships. As the nation's leader, he could have helped create a constructive thought-form, which the mental and emotional energy of the American people would have energized and given form.

It's also essential to become aware of and work to eliminate the old, negative thought-forms each of us personally carry around with us, as they color and distort how we see the world and constantly re-create themselves. Those who can be most effective in creating new, positive thought-forms are the ones who have first cleared their own mental aura to some degree.

RITUAL AND CEREMONIES

Today many people are finding that the old familiar rituals and ceremonies in churches and synagogues have lost their meaning and power. This dissatisfaction has led to several responses. Some people are attempting to resacralize the religions of their birth by moving more deeply into the spiritual teachings that underlie the rituals. Others, however, are breathing new life into ritual by creating ceremonies that take participants into a deeper, inner state to help strengthen themselves spiritually to work for the planet.

A ritual is basically the rhythmic use of physical forms—sound, light, color, music, incense, dance, chanting, words of power, and so on—to invoke, transmit, and anchor spiritual energies from higher planes. Rituals embody abstract truths in forms that enable the mind to comprehend them. The secret of a good ritual is rhythm and timing—which maximizes the energies to invoke, build, and hold a point of tension, and then to distribute the energy. By appealing to all five senses, a ritual rivets attention upon a single focus and so creates a group mind and will. When conditions are right, energetic lightning strikes through the resistance of matter, and spiritual power is released. This spiritual power pours in through three subtle pathways—the etheric, the emotional, and the mental—and thus creates change in the physical world.

Many of those who identify with what have come to be called "New Age" philosophies have been for some years now creating their own participatory circle ceremonies for healing the earth and all life. These rituals often draw on elements of Native American, Christian, Jewish, Islamic, Hindu, and/or Buddhist ritual.

Standing or sitting in a circle in a ritual creates a sacred, protected space, with each participant a peer and equidistant from the center. In the center of the circle a symbol of the highest Divinity, such as a candle flame, is often placed. Flowers, feathers, crystals, seeds, water, herbs, and so forth are often used symbolically in rituals to connect the consciousness of participants to some aspect of life.

For example, in rituals we've created, we have used a rose to symbolize the heart, or candles to represent Spirit, as participants light each other's candles. We also have placed a lighted globe or a photograph of the whole Earth in the center of the circle, helping participants focus attention on the planet. If there is a national crisis, something symbolic of a particular country or political leader may be placed in the center. Candles symbolizing Spirit are lighted to invoke a blessing for a particular trouble spot on the earth. Quartz crystals that have been cleansed and blessed can be planted at particular places on earth for healing, as they hold energy. A friend of ours, for example, planted a number of crystals around Red Square before the collapse of communism.

However, we need to remember that the physical objects we may use in a ritual are merely the symbols of inner realities—not the essence. They have only as much energy as our consciousness places in them and can be empty forms if we don't energize them.

Rituals can be especially helpful in connecting us with the Divine Mother and with the Earth. Ceremonies to heal the Earth might include placing elements of nature, such as flowers, rocks, or leaves, in a mandala, or circular pattern in the center of the circle of participants, and blessing these elements. At the Spring Equinox we ask each person to plant a seed symbolizing a particular quality they'd like to develop, such as courage. Or we sprinkle water on the Earth to symbolize the blessings of Spirit and to help end drought or bring fertility.

A ceremony can be created to restore our lost unity and wholeness—symbolic of the Goddess Isis gathering up the dismembered remains of her husband, Osiris, which were scattered all over the earth. Pieces of a puzzle of the Earth can be scattered around and then searched for and reassembled to form a whole. Songs to the Earth and circle dances can bring a healing and unifying energy. Today a number of centers—such as Findhorn Foundation in Scotland, the Sufi Community of The Abode in upstate New York, the Lama Community in New Mexico, and our community, Sirius, in Massachusetts—are gathering traditional dances and creating new ones for healing the earth.

Rituals can also be as simple as "smudging ceremonies"—burning sage to clear out negative vibrations in a place, as Native Americans do. Two good friends of ours, who do international conflict mediation work, often perform a smudging ceremony and meditation in the room before a major negotiation, and have found it very effective for creating a clearer atmosphere—but they don't talk about this publicly!

Several Native American spiritual teachers have been leading ceremonies to stop the destruction of the earth's rain forests, home of two-thirds of the world's population where nearly half of the earth's oxygen is created. One of these teachers is Brooke Medicine Eagle. In her book, *Buffalo Woman Comes Singing,* she wrote that in 1986 she was standing in an Idaho aspen grove, and "without thinking, I opened my arms to the sky and said, 'Great Circle of Life, let me know what you need me to do. I am at your service.' Without a second's hesitation, there was an answer, which seemed to come from a chorus of ancient grandmothers' voices, 'Put a spiritual block on the cutting of trees in the Amazon, and other such acts that threaten the life and breath of the children of Earth!' " Within a week of a group ceremony she led—which included people of all colors and backgrounds—the World Bank and the United Nations Development Program announced an $8 billion, fifty-six-country plan to reverse the destruction of the tropical rain forests.[17]

Native Americans Harley Goodbear and Arlo Doss in full regalia performed a smudging ceremony with sage and sweetgrass at the swearing in of U.S. Secretary of Energy, Hazel O'Leary, in 1993. They tapped her with a sacred eagle feather to invoke the blessings of the Great Spirit on her and on the elements from which we derive all our energy.

An interesting example of ritual for political purposes was the work of Native American medicine people Wallace Black Eagle, Grace Spotted Eagle, and Marilyn Youngbird in early 1984 for Gary Hart. For a time Hart called Marilyn Youngbird his "spiritual adviser" and hung in his Senate office a prayer robe from her. The medicine people believed Hart's early dedication to the environment would help save nature from destruction, so they said prayers and performed ceremonies for him. His early success in winning the New Hampshire primary and coming in second in Iowa was a surprise to everyone. But as Youngbird says, "At the beginning, he was dedicated. He was in prayer, too. But once our desires were granted and he became known, swept up by fame, he didn't continue with his prayers. He forgot his original ideas. He lost his spiritual foothold."[18] Hart made some major personal and political mistakes, too—but could they have been the result of his neglecting his spiritual life?

Although modern people often see the ceremonies of native peoples as superstitious, the scientists who study these ceremonies have been amazed at how efficiently they are able to create rain or aid the fertility of their crops. Biologist Lyall Watson, for example, wondered at a drum that was beaten exactly every two minutes and thirty-five seconds for a full day by native drummers to insure crop fertility. Only years later did scientists discover that the cadence of this beat exactly matched the resonant frequency of the earth. Native peoples call this "the heartbeat of Mother Earth"—and this was apparently closer to literal truth than expected. Each of us can be guided inwardly to create effective ceremonies if we listen to our hearts for guidance—and to the heart of the earth—and are purely motivated.

CONNECTING ACTIVISM TO SPIRIT AND REAL NEED

A great deal of well-meaning activism often proves highly ineffective in solving social problems. Why this happens becomes clear when we think about the analogy of how electrical energy functions. In order for spiritual, transforming energy to make a complete circuit flow, three components must be present: a power source, a conductor, and a receiver. There needs to be something that produces the energy, something to channel it where it needs to go, and an effective mechanism such as a motor to absorb and make use of the power delivered.

Likewise, for spiritual work to be effective, there must be a good flow of energy from a higher voltage source of inspiration and creative ideas, an individual (or group) to channel or conduct it who is relatively free of emotional negativity and ego, and a person, group, or place in need of the energy to ground it. Otherwise the creative ideas and new service projects remain in the subtle world and are not useful in solving the problems we face today.

We can experience a short circuit—or burnout—in the energy flow when we are receiving too much "juice" from the power source and getting "over-amped" without sharing it or being connected to world need. This happens when we receive too much energy through meditation or other practices and do not share the energy with others. Or it can occur when we think too much about a social problem without doing anything about it.

Another type of short circuit in our energy flow is created when the conductor or individual channel develops a closed circuit—when all the emphasis is placed on our personal ego and processing our own psychological problems. When this happens the energy is blocked by the ego from flowing in from a higher source, and also doesn't flow out to where it is needed to help others. This also happens when we become too egotistically attached to having other people notice our good work rather than just getting the job done. Or it can occur when our self-worth becomes overly identified with the work.

We can also create a short circuit in the energy flow if we aren't plugged into a source of spiritual inspiration or power and are getting "grounded or shorted out"—becoming exhausted trying to meet the world need with no spiritual backup. A short circuit is also created when we get involved in service work to avoid dealing with difficult personal issues. Many of us doing service work don't take the time to renew and recharge ourselves spiritually and guilt-trip ourselves and others into being martyrs.

Service to others, personal psychological work on ourselves, and inner spiritual work are all needed in the world today. As Donald Keys, founder of Planetary Citizens, says:

> If you undertake meditative or spiritual practices as part of your spiritual life, you will soon . . . discover your essential identity with all persons and with humankind. If, on the other hand . . . you give your life to selfless service to humankind, you will find that you yourself are also on a path of self-transcendence and spiritual growth, because you will find the necessity for drawing on ever deeper aspects of yourself. The two approaches, vertical and horizontal, to our Soul and to humankind, are not at all separate paths. No matter which one you take initially, they will soon converge and eventually coincide. That they were ever separate was an illusion. They were one path from the beginning. . . . As the old aphorism says, "Advance without, retreat within."[19]

GUIDED MEDITATIONS FOR PLANETARY EVOLUTION

Basic Meditation Technique

This basic meditation technique can precede any of the other specific meditations that follow: We begin by choosing a quiet, comfortable, peaceful spot in our home where we won't be disturbed, turning off the ringer on the phone and the sound level of the answering machine if we have one. We might want to purify and dedicate the place where we meditate as a sacred space, attuning and aligning it with higher spiritual reality. Fresh flowers, candles, incense, or inspirational images can help uplift us.

We sit quietly with the spine erect in the manner most comfortable for us—in the cross-legged yoga position or on a chair with our feet flat on the floor and our arms at rest on our thighs or hands folded. The important thing is to sit with the spine erect rather than lying down (unless one has medical problems) so our chakras are perpendicular to earth's gravity and also so that we won't fall asleep. It's important to stay aware and awake and not become drowsy.

Alert but relaxed, we focus our mind on our breath—the sacred thread of life that links the above and the below, the inner and the outer. We inhale deeply, slowly, holding the breath for a moment. We then exhale very slowly. We repeat this cleansing, balancing breath several more times. If needed, we can breathe energy into all parts of our body to help us relax, beginning with the top of the head and moving slowly down through each part of the body to our feet.

Breathing regularly and evenly, we gently shift the focus of our attention to our feelings, observing them but not identifying with them. We can visualize our emotional energy rising up from our solar plexus center (just under the rib cage) to our heart each time we inhale, then imagine the feelings being balanced and transmuted into universal love through the heart as we exhale.

We then begin to still our minds, becoming a detached observer of our thoughts. We focus our attention fully in the present, letting go of past and future. We see the mind emptying its contents, until we experience pure awareness with no specific thoughts. Some people find it useful to repeat a mantra—a simple word or phrase, such as peace, love, or OM, over and over to still their minds. Others listen intently until they hear a sound inside their head and keep their attention focused on this. Other people may visualize an inspirational image such as a flower, a clear light, the ocean, and so on.

We then lift our awareness to connect with the highest and wisest part of ourselves, our Soul or inner Divinity. We remain relaxed and receptive, yet alert and aware, avoiding drowsiness. From this point of awareness, we can then proceed to any of the other suggested meditations given here.

WHITE LIGHT VISUALIZATION

We begin by visualizing a stream of pure white Light radiating out from our Third Eye center (in the center of the forehead between the eyebrows). We feel this beam of white Light growing stronger and brighter. Dedicating this Light to the highest good of all, we allow it to follow our intentionality.

We can visualize loved ones or important leaders and send out this beam of healing, protecting white Light to completely surround them. We can visualize an event or a troubled area of the globe and surround it with the white Light streaming from our third eye, asking that the highest good and God's will be done for this person or situation.

We can use this white Light as a powerful visualization for world peace. In our mind we call up an image of our beautiful, fragile, blue-white planet spinning through the darkness of space. Now we send a beam of pure white Light to totally surround the Earth with Love and Light and peace. We see the Earth healed and whole. This visualization strengthens all movements and efforts toward world unity and synthesis.

FULL MOON MEDITATIONS

The full moon each month is a very powerful time to meditate, individually or in a group, if possible. At this time, greater spiritual energy flows into the earth, as there is an unimpeded alignment between the earth and the sun when the moon is out of the pathway between them. If we can't meditate at the exact time of the full moon, then generally the evening before is the best time. There are full moon meditation groups in most cities around the United States and in many parts of the world, and these are usually advertised in local New Age newspapers and magazines.

We begin by aligning with our Soul, our Divine Self, and then link with the thousands of people around the world who are also meditating at this time. We align with the Enlightened Ones, the Masters of Wisdom on the inner level, and with the center of Divine Will, Shamballa, invoking an inflow of spiritual energy to help humanity and heal the planet. After a period of silence we then send out the energy for the greater good of the planet and close with The Great Invocation (see page 394).

EARTH AND SPIRIT MEDITATION

We sit alert and relaxed in our sacred space. Following our breath, in and out, in and out, in and out, we focus our attention on the soles of our feet. We sense a beam of white Light rising up from the center of the earth, entering our body through the soles of our feet. We feel this energy moving up through our legs, up our back, into our heart, filling it with the rich energies of the sacred earth.

Now we shift our focus of attention to the top of our head. We feel the flow of white Light descending down from the cosmos, pouring into the top of our head. The energy flows down into our heart center, where it meets and mingles with the upflowing energies of the earth. We feel the energies from the heavens and the earth merging, balancing and harmonizing with love in the sacred chalice of the heart.

Filled with love, we visualize ourselves blessing the earth, renewing and restoring the sacredness of our planetary home. We allow the energies flowing into and through us to continue circulating down into the earth and up into the heavens. We feel ourselves in perfect harmony with these ceaseless flows.

DIVINE MOTHER MEDITATION

This meditation is a very profound and sacred one, and this inner journey should only be taken when one is truly ready. We begin by visualizing ourselves entering a vast, ancient cave. We are carrying a torch, symbolizing our Soul or Higher Self. The way lies ever downward, into the womb of the earth, which feels warm and nurturing. We move deeper and deeper into the cave, deeper into the earth, until we find ourselves in the very center, the core, the heart, of the body of earth.

We sense that we are expected, that a very powerful being awaits us here in the heart of the earth. A sense of awe fills us as we enter into the veiled and mysterious presence of the Great Goddess, the Divine Mother. As we honor and embrace this Presence, we are in turn embraced by Her. We feel our conscious awareness blending and becoming one with the generative, form-giving energies of earth. Through this joining together, we feel the power of consciousness infusing and redeeming matter, and we likewise love and embrace the physical reality of our own body.

As we do, we see the veil of the Mysteries—the veil of phenomenal appearances, of matter—being lifted. We see before us the radiant face of the Queen of Heaven, illumined through the Light of human consciousness. We see Her radiate Light within the earth, healing imbalances, renewing its energies. We feel this sacred healing Light filling every part of our being.

Now, slowly, filled with Light, we begin to leave, taking the Love and Light of the Divine Mother with us, moving upward from the center of the earth. Up through the innumerable strata of rock, glistening with the radiant colors of crystals, of precious metals. Back to the entrance of the ancient cave. We feel ourselves totally filled with Light in every cell, every atom, of our being. Remaining in the Light, slowly we walk out of the cave and slowly open our eyes, becoming totally present, totally aware of our physical surroundings.

BALANCING THE MASCULINE AND FEMININE ENERGIES

This meditation helps women integrate their unexpressed masculine side, and men their unexpressed feminine. We begin by imagining our mind is

a blank screen and asking our Higher Self or Soul to spontaneously produce an image or a symbol representing our feminine side. We take the
first thing that appears spontaneously on our screen. We see it grow stronger and brighter. We watch it move and change and imagine how it feels,
letting it fill us. Then we release this image, and take a few deep breaths.
Next we ask our Higher Self to produce an image or symbol that represents
our masculine side and see it grow stronger and brighter. We watch it move
and change and imagine how it feels, letting it fill us. Then we release it
and take a few deep breaths.

Now we visualize these two symbols relating together, dancing with each
other, watching them blend together and harmonize. We ask our Higher
Selves to form them into a symbol of the inner synthesis of masculine and
feminine qualities. We allow this image to flow into us, to become us, to
create balance in our lives. . . . Then we slowly return our awareness back
to the room where we're sitting and open our eyes. We can call upon this
special symbol of synthesis any time we feel the need to rebalance these energies.

SYNTHESIS MEDITATION

This is a helpful technique for creating a higher synthesis out of any set of
polar opposites or conflicting views. We begin with brainstorming the positive aspects of each point of view from a typically rational, or left-brain,
perspective. Any and all ideas are elicited without any judgments about
their merit, and these are written down. Next the negative aspects or distortions of each point of view are brainstormed and written down, again
with no judgments.

Then we shift into a more intuitive, or right-brain, mode, and a visualization exercise is used to elicit a broader synthesis of the opposing perspectives. We relax, close our eyes, take a few slow, deep breaths, and allow our
minds to become like blank screens. Then we ask our Higher Self for
greater wisdom and understanding of the issues. We ask that an image or
symbol that represents the positive aspects of the first position appear spontaneously on our screen. We take the first image that appears, no matter
how strange, and keep watching it, noticing if it changes, grows, or reveals
more of itself, so it can be understood more deeply.

We then release this image, again allowing our minds to become blank
screens, and take a few deep breaths. This time we ask for an image or
symbol to appear that represents the positive aspects of the opposite position. The same process is followed as with the first image. Then this second image is released, the mind becoming a blank screen again, as we take
a few deep breaths.

We now imagine the two images appearing on the screen together, beginning to relate, creating some kind of relationship or dance together, and eventually blending together. Next we ask for a higher synthesis of the two to appear spontaneously on the mind's screen, incorporating the best aspects of both positions. This new image is then given the opportunity to change and grow and to reveal more of itself and how it applies in the practical situation. At the end of the process we open our eyes and write down what we experienced. (If meditation is done in a group, it can be shared with a partner.)

Note: This visualization can also include a movement component, if desired, and the participants can stand during the exercise. After each image is experienced, it then is translated in the body as a particular movement, allowing the image to flow into the body so we identify with it, and we move spontaneously however we feel inspired. After experiencing the two polar images, we move back and forth between the two, creating a blending that becomes a dance. We then let go of this and ask our Higher Selves for an image or symbol for synthesis. We then allow it to become a movement and feel it in our body, to understand it on a deeper level.

PEACE SHIELD MEDITATION

The peace shield meditation is part of a campaign for a "Spiritual Defense Initiative" (SDI) begun by our friend Ed Winchester, a former priest and Air Force captain. Winchester, who founded the Pentagon Meditation Club, says, "Every one of us has a personal peace shield around us. It can be stronger or weaker depending on your state of mind. When our peace shield is strong, it can protect us. But when we project divisive thoughts toward our adversaries, we weaken the peace shield and literally create mental barriers that have to be taken down."[20]

We begin this meditation by closing our eyes, directing our thoughts to the world of our inner being. We forgive ourselves for all our perceived wrongdoing to ourselves and to others. We ask for grace to experience our true nature, the God within us, love. We are a being of love. . . . We are Light. . . . Deep within us, we use the Holy Word, God's name, to quiet our mind and free us.

We mentally repeat, for a period of time that seems right, our favorite name or names of God. We might select from Creator, Source, All That Is, The Universe, Jesus, Adonai, Yhwa, Jehovah, Allah, Ram, Brahman, Satnaam, Radha-Krishna, Baha 'U'llah, Aum (Om), the Great Spirit, or any other name we have for God.

Then we feel into that place within us that yearns to love our self and other people more. We see our family, friends, and men, women, and children throughout the world in harmony with each other. We see influential leaders turning to God for direction and guidance. We see friends and adversaries joining together in fellowship to resolve issues, forgiving each other and praying together and for each other.

FOUNTAIN MEDITATION

This is a visualization recommended by Fountain International, an informal network of people around the world that grew out of a meditation group in Brighton, England. Many have noted remarkable changes in a town over a period of time from doing this kind of inner work.

We begin by concentrating on a focal point within a town, such as a church spire, a memorial, or some other well-known inspirational landmark, and see it radiating healing energy—love and Light, throughout the community. Any particular areas of disease needing healing within the community, such as crime, homelessness, or blighted areas, we can hold in mind during the meditation. We do this simple visualization for a few minutes each day, either individually or in groups.

THE RIGHT DIRECTION OF MONEY

Alice Bailey recommends this meditation on the right direction of money for the helping of humanity. Since money is crystallized energy, it can be moved only by greater energy. This meditation requires the right use of the will and an intense concentration of the mind, for the effectiveness of this meditation depends on the point of creative tension reached and on having an open heart afire with human need.[21]

We begin by reflecting on our personal attitude toward money. We ask ourselves, What is our responsibility toward the money that passes through our hands? Are we handling it in the most positive and beneficial way? Do we regard it as a great and possible spiritual asset or merely in material terms?

Next we visualize money as a great stream of flowing golden substance, passing out of the control of the forces of materialism where it is used mostly to satisfy personal desires, and into the control of the Forces of Light, where it can be used for spiritual purposes to help humanity. We see it being blessed and consecrated for higher work.

STATUE OF LIBERTY MEDITATION

We can use the evocative power of the Statue of Liberty to inspire us and generate healing energy for our nation.

We begin by visualizing ourselves climbing the spiraling stairs in the Statue of Liberty. When we reach the top we look out through the windows in the crown across the country in all directions. We see the great natural beauty of this country, the "melting pot" of all types of people, and all that they have created. This vision opens our heart to love for our country, and we feel inspired. From this expanded perspective we then open ourselves up even farther to perceive a deeper sense of our nation's special purpose. We focus on aligning ourselves with the Soul of the nation, visualizing Light and love radiating out from where we are standing in the crown of the statue all across America—to create healing, unity, and peace.

MEDITATION FOR THE SOUL OF A NATION

We can meditate on the Soul of a nation—our own or another nation—by reflecting on its highest qualities, its gifts to the rest of the world.

We begin by seeing the nation working to integrate and harmonize the many conflicting voices within—its subpersonalities. We see it beginning to transcend self-interest and express its full potential. We call on the nation's Soul and see it align with its spiritual destiny in the world. We can meditate on what this country can contribute to the world, to the family of nations, and visualize it doing this.

MEDITATION FOR AMERICA'S GOVERNMENT

As a Soul, we see ourselves as part of a network or latticework of Light, pulsating and circulating among all individuals and groups around the United States and the world, working to build the new civilization of Light and love, aligned with Divine Will.

We then align with those great Teachers, Saints, and Masters of all religions who guide human evolution.

Next we visualize the White House and within it see the president and vice president guided and protected by the great spiritual Masters, in a shield of Light and Divine protection that will allow them to carry out their mission, free from harm and aligned with the Divine Will for the United States. Then we see the president and vice president and all their administration working for the good of all humanity in accord with Divine Will.

We then see an aura of Light, guidance, and protection around the Congress and the people serving there. We see a channel of Light and cooperation flowing among the president, the vice president, and the leaders of Congress from both parties. We see them working together cooperatively and wisely for the highest good of all people, passing legislation that will support and empower people everywhere to take action to solve their problems.

Now we see Light and wisdom flowing into the Supreme Court, guiding and protecting those who serve there, helping to inspire decisions upholding those laws that are aligned with higher spiritual law.

Then we see Light flowing in a triangle among these three branches of government, circulating around the three points of the triangle—the White House, the Congress, and the Supreme Court—and infused with the all-seeing Eye of God (as atop the pyramid on our Great Seal), radiating Light throughout the United States and the planet.

We then close with the three Oms or whatever prayer we prefer.

MEDITATION/RITUAL FOR A WORLD CRISIS

David Spangler suggests the following meditation, which he created during the Persian Gulf war:

We begin by visualizing the creation of a circle around ourselves where we sit, and we light a candle in front of us. From each of the four cardinal directions, we summon a particular force or quality. From behind us we call upon the forces of history—the forces of karma and habit active in the situation, in the world, in our own life. We free these forces with mindfulness and offer our heart as a place for these habits to be transformed into liberation and wisdom.

From in front of us we call upon the forces of our future and ask for the Spirit of our possibilities to be present in this crisis, that suffering may be transmuted into joy and liberation. We ask to be a channel through which the potential of a new world may find expression.

From the left we summon the forces of the earth—the Spirits of plants, animals, and minerals—and ask for their assistance, protection, and wisdom, and their forgiveness for our destructiveness.

From the right we summon the Spirit of humanity and open our heart unconditionally to embrace its pain and possibility, that we may be an agent for humanity's liberation and growth.

We bring our right and left hands together to symbolize the union of humanity and nature. We open our hearts to past and future as a place where they can meet in mutual empowerment.

Then from above and below we invite the presence of the sacred to give wholeness and blessing to us all and pray for a peace that transforms us and takes us to a new world.

We then blow out the candle and close the circle.[22]

MEDITATION ON THE UNITED NATIONS

A meditation for the healing of nations and for strengthening the work of the UN helps us to be present there mentally, becoming "delegates by thought." Such subjective support can be of great service in strengthening the process of transmutation from national self-interest to international cooperation, creating the right atmosphere for change, and realigning outer appearance with inner purpose.

We begin by calling on our Soul. We then gently lift our consciousness to align with Divine Purpose. We hold the vision of the true purpose of the United Nations clearly in our mind, seeing it fully express the Soul of the One Humanity—unity in diversity. We then visualize the positive forces and energies already present to help the UN, both on the physical level and in the spiritual realms, where the Enlightened Ones are working continuously to guide and inspire its work.

Next, we "think through in the Light" the future development of the United Nations, asking that national self-interests be transmuted into international cooperation. We visualize humanity progressing toward global unity, then peace, and then plenty—in that order.

We then invoke the Spirit of synthesis on behalf of humanity, to further the manifestation of unity, oneness, and interrelation, seeing this great presence within the General Assembly of the United Nations, guiding and inspiring the delegates. We then say the Mantra of Unification:

> The sons of men* are one and I am one with them.
> I seek to love, not hate;
> I seek to serve and not exact due service;
> I seek to heal, not hurt.
>
> Let pain bring due reward of light and love.
> Let the Soul control the outer form,
> And life and all events,
> And bring to light the love
> Which underlies the happenings of the time.
>
> Let vision come, and insight.
> Let the future stand revealed.

> *Let inner union demonstrate*
> *And outer cleavages be gone*
> *Let love prevail.*
>
> *Let all men* love.*

*Can be changed to reflect more inclusive language—"all humanity."

Finally last, the Spirit of Peace is invoked to further the development of right human relationships and illumine the will of God in relationship to humanity.

MEDITATION ON COOPERATION WITH THE DEVAS AND ANGELS

We can clean up environmental pollution by consciously cooperating with the Devas, or Angels of nature. The Devas (see chapter 9) are the great invisible builders of all that we see in the world, producing form out of the substance of their own bodies. This process of "attunement" with the nature Spirits and Devas requires a deep, loving commitment and an inner sense of surrender. We may not get results the first time—it takes patience and practice. Sometimes a simple ritual like lighting a candle daily for the Deva can be helpful, as it's good to *do* something, some activity, to ground the experience.

To begin the process of cooperation or attunement with the Devas and Angels, we must first become inwardly still and commune with the deeper aspects of ourselves, with our inner essence or Soul. This in turn allows us to open to a deeper communion with nature. We tune in to the Soul essence or overlighting intelligence of a particular aspect of nature by feeling our love for it begin to flow. We then think Light and visualize Light, thus adding to that already existing, while also speeding up the growth and enhancing the beauty of nature.

Then we ask inwardly for the change we'd like to see happen—such as fertility returning to a barren area or a polluted stream of toxic dump clearing up. We hold an attitude of detachment from outcomes and open ourselves to receiving an impression of some kind from the Devas or Angels about how to help this process, making sure that any action taken is resonant with unconditional love. Any sense of impatience, ego, or ambition will block communication. After a time of silence, we close by affirming our willingness to work cooperatively as co-creators with the Devas.

TRIANGLES MEDITATION

If it isn't possible to meditate physically in a group, we can link up with two other people on an inner level in meditation and visualize a triangle, with lines of Light circulating through all three points, and then being distributed to the world for healing and peace. This "Triangles work," which was begun by the Lucis Trust in New York over fifty years ago, is very effective in generating spiritual energy for service and helps to create a network of Light around the earth. Many thousands of people link up regularly in their meditation in this way and send Light and love to people and places that need healing.

Outer Work for Planetary Evolution

FIFTEEN THINGS WE CAN DO TO HELP PLANETARY EVOLUTION

In addition to working inwardly through meditation and thought-form building, we can also take active, outer steps in the world that reflect our understanding of the inner causes of events. When we work from a consciousness of unity, with a compassion for those on both sides of an issue, we have more redemptive and synthesizing power. Below, we offer a list of suggested actions. We encourage you to develop additional creative ways to apply an understanding of how consciousness affects physical events. (See Resources in the appendix.)

• *Ask new questions.* In meetings of the PTA, church groups, political gatherings, and so on, ask questions that will help people think about a problem in new systemic ways. For example, if we change the structure of our organization or system, will this solve the problems we face? If not, what will? How are the problems interconnected and part of a whole system? What are the deeper causes of problems we're dealing with? What outworn or dysfunctional thoughts or beliefs are creating limitations?
• *Become more active in working on a social problem from a causal level.* Choose a problem area, educate yourself, and work to discern the deeper causes of the problem while looking for solutions that really deal with the causes. For example, in prison reform, motivate prison wardens and guards with financial rewards when the recidivism rate drops, while offering programs for inmates that deal with the psychological causes of their problems.
• *Host a coffee hour or informal "salon" in your home and invite over*

friends and colleagues to explore the inner meaning of events. Study social problems together from a spiritual perspective and develop causal-level solutions. Explore events from a symbolic, causal, karmic, or psychological perspective instead of in the usual political way. Develop communication skills and a commitment to talking about these new perspectives with people in your circle of contacts—family, friends, co-workers, and so forth—in an informal "salon" in your home.

• *Assist organizations and individuals who are working effectively to solve problems from a transformational perspective.* Donate money, volunteer time, and/or tell others about their work. For example, Foundation for Global Community and Earthstewards both have a variety of programs for getting involved in peace and environmental issues.

• *Adopt a leader who is carrying the seeds of a vision for the new world—whether local, national, or international.* Send him/her your prayers, positive thoughts, letters of support, and love. Keep up to date about your leader, studying his/her efforts, and work to bring progressive evolutionary ideas into human thinking. Leaders have many arrows of negativity directed at them, and inner support is crucial to their being able to carry out their vision effectively.

• *Create a home library of books, newsletters, and magazines that help people think about new solutions to problems.* Make your library available to friends and other people in your neighborhood to stimulate their thinking in new areas.

• *Use every opportunity available to express yourself as part of the "public opinion" that shapes the consensus of what is real and acceptable.* Call in on radio talk shows, write letters to the editor, or submit op-ed pieces to the editorial page of your local newspaper on issues from a New Paradigm perspective. You can send letters or faxes to the president and Congress on issues of concern or to corporations that produce products or engage in practices that are harmful to people or the environment. Corporate managers have acknowledged that it takes only twenty letters to a company for top management to take the expressed concerns very seriously. Join RESULTS, which trains people to express their opinions very effectively on key hunger or children's issues, or 20/20 Vision, which every month recommends a specific action that will take only twenty minutes of your time to complete.

• *Work with someone in need in a way that helps them overcome victim consciousness and develop self-reliance and self-esteem.* Volunteering to tutor or support a disadvantaged young person can be an opportunity to give of yourself and learn more about the real needs of human beings. For example, the BUILD Program in Baltimore has an innovative approach for helping high school students stay in school and develop self-esteem so they are guaranteed jobs.

• *Help melt down the walls of separateness among co-workers, neighbors, and people you meet on the street.* Organize a potluck dinner gathering for people in your neighborhood who may not know each other or for people you work with. Or attend a political meeting of those you generally disagree with and try to maintain an open mind and a readiness to learn something.

• *Do something every day that symbolizes your commitment to the entire planet and to humanity.* Find something that helps remind you that you are a citizen of planet Earth, as well as of your own country. Become a citizen diplomat by traveling and learning about other cultures and societies. Or send food to those in need in other countries, adopt a child overseas through financial support, or promote the basic rights of all people for food and shelter and opportunities to better themselves. Support the UN by visiting or learning about its work through a local UN Association, and let your congressperson know of your interest and support for it. It's important to give expression to your commitments through action and to learn more about organizations that deal with international issues, such as FINCA, which gives microloans to Third World people.

• *Apply a win/win approach to the next conflict you find yourself in at home or at work.* Read a book or take a course in conflict resolution so you can be a skilled facilitator. Make sure your children are trained in these skills and work to apply them.

• *Invest your money in one of the socially screened money market or mutual funds, or donate money to New Paradigm groups.* Invest in community development loan funds, such as the Institute for Community Economics, or give to meditation groups solving problems from the causal level, such as Meditation Mount in Ojai, California, or the School for Esoteric Studies in New York.

• *Study or write about the Soul of nations.* Explore their founding, history and culture, astrological chart, and the symbolism of their flag and heraldry. If possible, visit the country, interviewing their citizens, or visit their embassy. Study especially the interaction of the nation's personality and its Soul.

• *Promote a left-right synthesis on issues.* Help conservative friends appreciate positive aspects of liberalism and vice versa by asking direct questions and helping them transcend polarized positions.

• *Choose a political institution or branch of government, local or national, and work at making it more responsible to the needs of people.* Help focus it on solving real problems from a more transformational whole-systems approach that brings together all constituents in building new solutions together. Ideas for changing government can be found in chapters 3 and 4 and in books like *Reinventing Government* by David Osborne and Ted Gaebler.

These suggestions for inner and outer action are intended to help us think about how we can empower ourselves to be effective in contributing to our world. If more of us released our feelings of victimhood and instead asked inwardly for opportunities to be of help, we'd probably be surprised at how many interesting situations we'd suddenly find ourselves "coincidentally" drawn into. We all generally carry around so many limiting ideas about ourselves and our ability to "make a difference" that we create self-fulfilling prophesies. Instead we must constantly remind ourselves that our "thoughts create," that we are constantly affecting events. Inner and outer action inspired by an understanding of the deeper causes at work can catalyze dramatic and unexpected changes in the world around us.

THE HIGH ROAD TO PLANETARY WHOLENESS

It's time to wake up from the slumber of materialism, from the enchantment of the physical form side of life, and to experience the boundless energy hidden inside the form—the energy that has the power to transform our world. We can each let go of vague dreams, wishful thinking, and idealized utopias and think freshly and clearly about the problems before us. If we begin where we are to improve the lives of those around us we can help create "heaven on Earth." Each of us has a part to play—no one is unneeded. A trained and active citizenry that desires the highest good for all can truly transform our society.

The fate of the world is in our hands—or, more accurately, in our minds and hearts. As we begin to realize the creative effect of our individual thoughts and emotions on collective events, we will begin to use our God-given powers more consciously and wisely—to build a better world for all life on our beloved planet.

In a rapidly changing world, facing the challenges of major crises in the environment and the economy—not to mention explosive regional conflicts and violence—it is essential to remember that crises are opportunities for growth and learning. Earth is a schoolhouse, and we must remind ourselves that we have all signed up to study the curriculum. We are all here to learn the living alphabet of God written in the Book of Life.

Instead of responding with fear and clinging insecurely to the past, we can use the opportunities born of crisis to free ourselves of old ways and open to the new seeking to be born within us. The eternal Soul within us holds the answers to our confusion and uncertainty and is a trustworthy guide to the future.

Despite our concerns, the universe is unfolding in perfect timing, and the Divine Plan for human evolution promises a beneficent, even glorious outcome. Help is always available from the Enlightened Ones, the Masters of Wisdom, who guide humanity from the inner side—even when we're not conscious of their help. Their personal achievement of wisdom and compassion is an inspiring guarantee of our future, as we will each eventually evolve to become as they are.

The nations of planet Earth will be healed and made whole only through a unitive spirit that synthesizes the best in all opposing positions and finds win/win solutions to problems. Many great truths are paradoxes until we move to a larger perspective, a higher level of consciousness. Politics is not just the exercise of power; it is even more essentially the exercise of relationship and the science of synthesis. It is up to each of us to develop right relationships with others if we are to truly heal our world. The principles of unity, cooperation, and serving the common good can be our guideposts along the high road to planetary wholeness.

As we approach the millennium, social change will be far more effective as we begin to understand the hidden spiritual causes of world events and realize the power of turning politics "inside out."

Each of us has a thread to weave into the evolving planetary tapestry of Light. But we each have to make the effort to discover the threads we can offer, as well as to purify our own motivations and equip ourselves for the task. As more and more individuals around the planet awaken the fire within their hearts, the positive, loving energy field around the planet is strengthened and together we build a new world.

For Further Information

Gordon Davidson and Corinne McLaughlin lecture, consult and conduct seminars around the world. If you would like to contact them about presentations for your group or organization, or for information about their tapes, books, and slideshows, they can be reached at

Sirius
Baker Road
Shutesbury, MA 01072
(413) 259-1505

Sirius Educational Resources
P.O. Box 1101
Greenbelt, MD 20768
(301) 441-3809

If you are interested in visiting or attending programs at Sirius Community near Amherst, Massachusetts, or would like more information about their ecologically designed conference facilities for a retreat, conference, or other event, please contact

Sirius Guest Department
Baker Road
Shutesbury, MA 01072
(413) 259-1251

Resources

◆

Metaphysical Groups (offering information or courses related to the perspectives offered in this book):

Agni Yoga Society
319 W. 107th St.
New York, N.Y. 10025
(212) 864-7752

Arcana Workshops
407 North Maple Dr. #214
Beverly Hills, Calif. 90210
(213) 273-5949
(213) 540-8689

The Lucis Trust
113 University Place, 11th floor
New York, N.Y. 10013
(212) 982-8770

Meditation Mount
10340 Reeves Road
Ojai, Calif. 93024
(805) 646-5508

Other Dimensions Training Center
Box 2269
Salmon Arm, B.C.
CANADA V1E 4R3
(604) 832-8483

School for Esoteric Studies
40 E. 49th St. #1903
New York, N.Y. 10017
(212) 755-3027

Sirius School of Spiritual Science
Baker Road
Shutesbury, Mass. 01072
(413) 259-1505

The Theosophical Society
P.O. Box 270
Wheaton, Ill. 60189
(708) 668-1571

University of the Seven Rays
128 Manhattan Ave.
Jersey City Heights, N.J. 07307
(201) 798-7777

Political/New Paradigm Groups (highlighted in chapters 3 and 4):

Alternatives to Violence
2161 Massachusetts Ave.
Cambridge, MA 02140
(617) 661-6130

Center for Citizen Initiatives
3268 Sacramento St.
San Francisco, Calif. 94115
(415) 346-1875

Center for Living Democracy
RR #1 Black Fox Road
Brattleboro, VT 05301
(802) 254-1234

Center for Psychology and Social
Change
1493 Cambridge St.
Cambridge, MA 02139
(617) 497-1553

The Communitarian Network
2130 H St. NW #714J
Washington, D.C. 20052
(202) 994-7997

The Door
121 6th Ave.
New York, N.Y. 10011
(212) 941-9090

Earthstewards
P.O. Box 10697
Bainbridge Island, Wash. 98110
(206) 842-7986

The Elmwood Institute
2522 San Pablo Ave.
Berkeley, Calif. 94702
(510) 845-4595

The Findhorn Foundation
The Park, Forres
Scotland IV 36 OTZ
011-44-309-30311

Foundation for Global Community
(formerly Beyond War)
222 High St.
Palo Alto, Calif. 94301
(415) 328-7756

Global Communities
Institute for Policy Studies
1601 Connecticut Ave. NW
Washington, D.C. 20009
(202) 234-9382

In Context Magazine
P.O. Box 11470
Bainbridge Island, Wash. 98110
(206) 842-0216

Institute for Alternative Futures
108 North Alfred St.
Alexandria, Va. 22314
(703) 684-5880

Institute for Cultural Affairs
206 E. 4th St.
New York, N.Y. 10009
(212) 475-5020

Institute for Faith and Politics
110 Maryland Ave. NE #306
Washington, D.C. 20002
(202) 546-1299

Institute for Global Ethics
P.O. Box 563, 21 Elm St.
Camden, ME 04843
(207) 236-6658

Institute for Multi-Track Diplomacy
1133 20th St. NW #330
Washington, D.C. 20036
(202) 466-4606

Institute for Noetic Sciences
475 Gate Five Road #300
Sausalito, Calif. 94965
(415) 331-5650

Institute for Social and Economic Policy in the Middle East
John F. Kennedy School of Government
Harvard University
Cambridge, Mass. 02138
(617) 495-3666

ISAR
1601 Connecticut NW #301
Washington, D.C. 20009
(202) 387-3034

Moral Re-Armament
1156 15th St. NW #910
Washington, D.C. 20005
(202) 872-9027

The National Children of War Office
85 South Oxford St.
Brooklyn, N.Y. 11217
(718) 858-6882

Neve Shalom
Wahat as-Salam, D.N.
Shimshon, 99761 Israel
(02) 917160.02-917412

Pathways to Peace
P.O. Box 1057
Larkspur, Calif. 94930
(415) 924-2421

Peace Initiatives
10058 Calle de Cielo
Scottsdale, Ariz. 85258
(602) 860-4544

Political Restoration
12 Raglan Ave.
Toronto, Ontario
Canada M6C2K6
(416) 657-8837

Program on Negotiation
Psychologists for Social Responsibility
2607 Connecticut Ave. NW
Washington, D.C. 20008
(202) 745-7084

Project Victory
560 Oxford #1
Palo Alto, Calif. 94306
(415) 424-9622

Restorative Justice
Justice Fellowship
P.O. Box 17500
Washington, D.C. 20041
(703) 478-0100

RESULTS
236 Massachusetts Ave. NE, Suite 110
Washington, D.C. 20002
(202) 543-9340

Sarvodaya Movement
N. 77 De Soysa Road
Moratuwa
Sri Lanka

Search for Common Ground
1601 Connecticut Ave. NW #200
Washington, D.C. 20009
(202) 265-4300

Self-Esteem Task Force
State Capitol P.O. Box 942849
Sacramento, Calif. 94249
(916) 445-4253

Tikkun Magazine
251 W. 100th St.
New York. N.Y. 10025
(212) 864-4110

Transformational Politics Section
American Political Science Association
Prof. Jeff Fishel
American University
4400 Massachusetts Ave. NW
Washington, D.C. 20016
(202) 885-6225; 364-2665 or

c/o Doug Boyd
Program on Non-Violent Sanctions
Harvard University
1737 Cambridge St.
Cambridge, Mass. 02138

The *Utne Reader*
1624 Harmon Place
Minneapolis, Minn. 55403
(612) 338-5040

Economic Groups (highlighted in chapters 11 and 12)

ACCION International
130 Prospect St.
Cambridge, Mass. 02139
(617) 492-4930

Business Ethics Magazine
1107 Hazeltine Blvd., Suite 530
Chaska, Minn. 55318
(612) 448-8864

The Coalition for Environmentally Responsible Economics (CERES)
711 Atlantic Ave.
Boston, Mass. 02111
(617) 451-0927

Co-Op America
2100 M St. NS, Suite 403
Washington, D.C. 20063
(202) 872-5307
(800) 424-2667

Council on Economic Priorities
30 Irving Place
New York, N.Y. 10003
(212) 420-1133

E. F. Schumacher Society
Box 76, RD3
Great Barrington, Mass. 01230
(413) 528-1737

Franklin Research & Development Co.
711 Atlantic Ave.
Boston, Mass. 02111
(617) 423-6655

Institute of Community Economics
(ICE)
57 School St.
Springfield, Mass. 01105-1331
(413) 746-8660

LETSystem
Landsman Community Services
375 Johnston Ave.
Courtenay, B.C.
CANADA V9N 2Y2
(604) 338-0213/0214

National Association of Community Development Loan Funds
924 Cherry St.
Philadelphia, Pa. 19107
(214) 923-4754

The Rocky Mountain Institute
Drawer 248
Old Snowmass, Colo. 81654
(303) 927-3851
(303) 927-4178

Seikatsu Club Consumers' Cooperative
2-26-17 Miyasaka
Setagaya-ku
Tokyo, Japan

Social Investment Forum
P.O. Box 57216
Washington, D.C. 20037
(202) 833-5522

South Shore Bank
71st & Jeffery Blvd.
Chicago, Ill. 60649
800-NOW-SSBK
(312) 753-5636

Worldwatch Institute
1776 Massachusetts Ave. NW
Washington, D.C. 20036
(202) 452-1999

Notes

◆

Introduction

1. Robert Kennedy, University of Capetown Speech, South Africa, June 6, 1966.

2. For further information, see Natalie Banks, *The Golden Thread* (New York: Lucis Publishing, 1979); Helena Blavatsky, *The Secret Doctrine* (Pasadena, CA: Theosophical University Press, 1974); Edouard Schure, *The Great Initiates: A Study of the Secret History of Religions* (San Francisco: Harper and Row, 1961); Aart Jurriaanse, *Bridges* (Pretoria, South Africa: Bridges Trust, 1978); Manly Hall, *The Secret Teachings of All Ages* (Los Angeles: The Philosophical Research Society, 1972); Aldous Huxley, *The Perennial Philosophy* (New York: Harper and Row, 1944); Caitlin and John Matthews, *The Western Way: The Hermetic Tradition* (London: Routledge and Kegan Paul, 1986).

3. Michael Baigent and the other authors of a controversial and best-selling new version of religious history, *Holy Blood, Holy Grail,* reflect our experience also: "If one surveys any period of the past, one will find a number of ostensible anomalies, incidents, phenomena, groups, and individuals which call attention to themselves but do not seem to coincide with the 'mainstream' of historical development. Most historians, when confronted with anomalies of this sort, choose to ignore them—to dismiss them as transient aberrations, as peripheral and/or incidental. So Nostradamus, for example, is deemed an irrelevant oddity and receives only scant attention in studies of sixteenth-century France. So the Knights Templar . . . are regarded as a mere footnote to the Crusades. Secret societies by virtue of their very secrecy have often kept historians at bay, and the historians, reluctant to confess their ignorance, prefer to diminish the consequence of their subject . . . [They appear to believe that] if something cannot be exhaustively documented, it must be irrelevant and thereby not worth discussing at all . . . [T]ruth may not be confined only to recorded facts but often lies in more intangible domains—in cultural achievements, in myths, legends, and traditions; in the psychic life of both individuals and entire peoples." Michael Baigent, et al., *Holy Blood, Holy Grail* (New York: Dell Books, 1982), 19.

4. John Naisbitt and Patricia Aburdene, *Megatrends 2000* (New York: William Morrow and Co., 1990), 280.

Chapter One

1. Peter Marshall and David Manuel, *The Light and the Glory* (Old Tappan, N.J.: Fleming H. Revell Co., 1977), 172.

2. In *The Structure of Scientific Revolutions*, researcher Thomas Kuhn found that even in the hard sciences, when confronted with information that didn't fit their paradigms, scientists either distorted the information until it fit their rules or they just didn't see it at all. Researchers found, for example, that subjects who were briefly shown a deck of playing cards with red spades instead of black literally saw the red spades as black—in line with their deeply ingrained concept of what playing cards should look like. Thomas Kuhn, *The Structure of Scientific Revolutions* (Chicago: University of Chicago Press, 1970).

3. Rex Weyler, "The Global Brain," *New Age Magazine* (June 1983).

4. Adin Steinsaltz, "Becoming Unstable: Hierarchy and Evolution," *Parabola* (Winter 1984).

5. Nick Herber, *Quantum Reality* (New York: Doubleday, 1985), 227.

6. Deepak Chopra, *Quantum Healing* video (Cos Cob, Conn.: Hartley Film Foundation, 1991).

7. Robert Jahn and Brenda Dunne, *Margins of Reality* (Orlando, Fla.: Harcourt Brace Jovanovich, 1987).

8. *Survey of Science and Technology Issues Present and Future*, U.S. Congress Committee on Science and Technology, June 1981.

9. David Spangler and William Thompson, *The Reimagination of the World* (Santa Fe, N.M.: Bear and Company, 1991), 172.

10. *Los Angeles Times*, March 17, 1990.

11. Michael Crichton, "Greater Expectations," *Newsweek*, Sept. 24, 1990.

12. *The New York Times*, Feb. 17, 1989.

13. "Body and Soul," *Newsweek*, Nov. 7, 1988. See also: *The Relaxation Response*, Dr. Herbert Benson (New York: William Morrow & Co., 1975).

14. *Boston Globe*, July 25, 1988, 27.

15. Patricia A. Norris, Ph.D., "Clinical Psychoneuroimmunology: Strategies for Self-Regulation of Immune System Responding," The Menninger Clinic, Kansas. Peavey (1982), Keicolt-Glaser, et al., (1985, 1986); Hall (1983); Gruber, et al., (1986); and Velkoff (1988).

16. National Opinion Research Council of the University of Chicago, *American Demographics*, Sept. 1988.

17. Steven Kull, *Burying Lenin* (Boulder, Colo.: Westview Press, 1992).

18. Corinne Heline, *America's Invisible Guidance* (Los Angeles: New Age Press, 1949), 33.

19. Kull, op. cit., 26–27.

Chapter Two

1. "When Storm Got Tough, the Women Got Tougher," *The New York Times*, Sept. 10, 1992.

2. David Spangler, *Conversations with John* (Elgin, Ill.: Lorian Press, 1980), 7–8.

3. *The Washington Post*, Dec. 6, 1988, A-15.

4. "JFK," *Tikkun* (March/April 1992).

5. Fletcher Prouty interview, "The Diane Rehm Show," WETA, Washington, D.C., Jan. 14, 1992; see also "The Mind of L. Fletcher Prouty" video, Prevailing Winds Research, Santa Barbara, Calif., 1992.

6. "The Real Cover-up," *Newsweek*, November 22, 1993.

7. John Welwood, "Reopening the Wounds," *The Sun* (Winter 1992).

8. *The New York Times*, April 1, 1989; also "Princeton Scientists Set Fusion Record," *The Washington Post*, December 10, 1993.

9. "International Project to Build Fusion Reactor Moves to Next Stage," *The Washington Post*, July 11, 1991.

10. "Power for the 90s," *MRA: For a Change*, Washington, D.C., 1990.

11. The Bible, Revelation of St. John 8:1.

12. "Joanna Macy and the Nuclear Waste Project," *Utne Reader* (July 1990), 64.

13. "Another Fiasco," *Newsweek*, May 12, 1986.

14. "Project Censored," *The Valley Advocate*, Hadley, Mass., June 19, 1989.

15. "Heaven Can Wait," *Newsweek*, July 9, 1990.

16. "A New Mirror Problem for NASA May Stall Vital Weather Satellites," *The New York Times*, August 8, 1990.

17. "Star Wars Fails House Test," *Greenpeace* (July/August 1988).

18. *The Washington Post*, April 18, 1991.

19. "Memorial Day 1991: A New Mission for U.S. Troops," *The Washington Post*, May 27, 1991.

20. Mark Whitaker, "Thomas and Black-Victim Game," *Newsweek*, Oct. 28, 1991.

21. "Los Angeles Will Save Itself," *Newsweek*, May 18, 1992.

22. "Polls Uncover Much Common Ground on L.A. Verdict," *The Washington Post*, May 11, 1992.

23. "The New Age President," *Newsweek*, Jan. 25, 1993.

24. "Clinton Calls Packed Agenda 'One Goal' " *The New York Times*, September 5, 1993.

25. "Have You Heard the One About Clinton and the Homeless Tots," *The Washington Post*, May 23, 1993.

26. Speech at Cooper Union School, New York City, May 12, 1993.

27. "Bill Clinton's Hidden Life," *U.S. News & World Report*, July 20, 1992.

28. Walt Whitman, "I Sing the Body Electric," *Leaves of Grass and Selected Prose*, Lawrence Buell, ed. (New York: Random House, 1981), 83.

29. Helen M. Luke, *Woman: Earth and Spirit* (New York: Crossroads Press, 1984), 79.

30. Kevin McClure, *The Evidence for Visions of the Virgin Mary* (Wellingborough, England: The Aquarian Press, 1983).

31. "Sighting of Our Lady in Yugoslavia Lures Believers," *Washington Times*.

32. Susan Faludi, *Backlash: The Undeclared War Against American Women* (New York: Crown Publishers, 1991).

33. Marilyn French, *The War Against Women* (New York: Summit Books, 1992).

Chapter Three

1. Corinne McLaughlin and Gordon Davidson, *Builders of the Dawn: Community Lifestyles in a Changing World* (Summertown, Tenn.: The Book Publishing Co., 1990), 171–2.

2. Jeff Fishel, *Principles of the Transformational Section* of the American Political Science Association, Washington, D.C., 1990.

3. Theodore Becker, ed., *Quantum Politics* (New York: Praeger, 1991), 50–57.

4. Foundation for Global Community brochure, 1991.

5. Meg Greenfield, "The Hardest Judgement Call," *Newsweek*, Jan. 21, 1991.

6. Peter Senge, *The Fifth Discipline*, (New York: Doubleday, 1990), pp. 15, 73–5.

7. "The Inside Guerrilla," *Newsweek*, July 16, 1990.

8. "Forest Service Promises to Look Beyond the Trees," *The Washington Post*, July 31, 1990, A-23.

9. Dr. Louise Diamond, *Multi-Track Diplomacy: A Systems Guide and Analysis*, Iowa Peace Institute, Occasional paper no. 3, June 1991, 1–5.

10. Mark Satin, *New Options for America* (Fresno, Calif.: The Press at California State University, 1991), 167–68.

11. "Exploring New Ways of Resolving Conflicts," *Timeline* (May/June 1992), by Foundation for Global Community.

12. Mark Satin, *New Options for America* (Fresno, Calif.: The Press at California State University, 1991), 219–224.

13. Bejurin Cassady, "Tin Wis: An Experiment in Cooperation," *In Context*, no. 32 (1992).

14. "In Congress, a Cliche Is Worth a Thousand Speeches," *The Washington Post*, July 4, 1991.

15. "Clinton's Hard Lesson in Pragmatism," *The Washington Post*, May 26, 1992.

16. "Rare Pact Reached to Fight Smog," *The Washington Post*, August 16, 1991.

17. Roger Fisher and William Ury, *Getting to Yes* (New York: Penguin Books, 1983), 3–98.

18. Ibid., 42–43.

19. Karl-Henrik Robert, "Educating a Nation: the Natural Step," *In Context*, no. 28 (1991).

20. Richard Tarnas, *The Passion of the Western Mind* (New York: Harmony Books, 1991), 379.

21. Alice Bailey, *Discipleship in the New Age II* (New York: Lucis Publishing, 1955), 575.

22. E. J. Dionne, *Why Americans Hate Politics* (New York: Simon & Schuster, 1991), 11.

23. "Why We Hate Politics," *The Washington Post*, May 12, 1991.

24. "Rehatching the Chicken-Egg Debate," *The Washington Post*, April 18, 1991.

25. "Tough Love Comes to Politics," *Los Angeles Times*, Nov. 19, 1991.

26. "An Infusion of Vision," *Newsweek*, Dec. 3, 1990, 24–25.

27. "The Idea Man with a 'Vision Thing,'" *The Washington Post*, Dec. 5, 1990, C-1.

28. "The Democrats' Economic Heretic," *The Washington Post*, May 19, 1991.

29. Daniel Moynihan, *Family and Nation* (San Diego: Harcourt, Brace and Jovanovich, 1987), 189.

30. David Osborne, *Laboratories of Democracy* (Boston: Harvard Business School Press, 1988), 326–327.

31. Ibid., 12, 14.

32. David Osborne and Ted Gaebler, *Reinventing Government* (Reading, Mass.: Addison-Wesley Publishing, 1992), ix–x.

33. "Exploring Whether Left and Right Could Converge into a New Politics," *The Washington Post*, Oct. 31, 1991.

34. Mark Satin, op. cit., 183–184.

35. Alice Bailey, *The Externalisation of the Hierarchy* (New York: Lucis Trust, 1957), 572–573.

36. James McGregor Burns, *Leadership* (New York: Harper and Row, 1978), 4.

37. Donald N. Michael, "Neither Hierarchy nor Anarchy," *Rethinking Liberalism*, Walter Truett Anderson, ed. (New York: Avon Books, 1983).

38. Corinne McLaughlin and Gordon Davidson, op. cit., 154, 162–168.

39. Eva Pierrakos, "Evolution in Terms of Individual and Group Consciousness," study paper of the Center for the Living Force, New York, November 20, 1974, lecture no. 255.

40. "Battling the Rights Wings," *U.S. News & World Report*, Nov. 25, 1991.

41. "The Community in an Age of Individualism," *The Futurist* (May/June 1991).

Chapter Four

1. John Vasconcellos, et al., *A Liberating Vision* (San Luis Obispo, Calif.: Impact Publishers, 1979), 33.

2. Jerome Bernstein, *Power and Politics: The Psychology of the Soviet-American Partnership* (Boston: Shambhala, 1989).

3. *The Washington Post*, Dec. 5, 1988, A-8.

4. Deena Metzger, "Personal Disarmament: Negotiating with the Inner Government," *Revision* (Spring 1990).

5. Michael Henderson, *Moral Re-Armament: A Factor in World Affairs*, MRA pamphlet.

6. Christa Daryl Slaton, "Sources of Resistance to Political Transformation: Theory and Illustrations," paper presented to the American Political Science Association, 1991, 12–13.

7. David Ruben, "Have You Hugged Your Lawyer Today?" *New Age* (Nov./Dec. 1992).

8. Sam Keene, *Faces of the Enemy* (New York: Harper and Row, 1987).

9. Psychologists for Social Responsibility, *Dismantling the Mask of Enmity: Educational Resource Manual* (Washington, D.C., 1991), 1–15; 62–68.

10. Psychologists for Social Responsibility, op. cit., "Our Cultural Demon—the 'Ugly Arab,' " 1.

11. Ellen Goodman, "Concerns Across the Abortion Chasm," *The Washington Post*, May 30, 1992; also Tamar Lewin, "In Bitter Abortion Debate, Opponents Learn to Reach for Common Ground," *The New York Times*, Feb. 17, 1992.

12. "East German Spies Speak Up in Anger," *The Washington Post*, May 25, 1992.

13. "Hey, I'm Terrific," *Newsweek*, Feb. 17, 1992.

14. Gloria Steinem, "Gross National Self-Esteem," *Ms.* (Nov./Dec. 1991).

15. Gail Sheehy, *Character* (New York: William Morrow and Company, 1988), 159–60.

16. Jeff Fishel, "Leadership for Social Change: John Vasconcellos and the Promise of Humanistic Psychology in Public Life," *Political Psychology* (1992).

17. "Self Esteem: New Word for Goodness," *The Economist*, February 2, 1991.

18. Fishel, op. cit.

19. *Your Invitation to Participate in Generating a New California Politics*, pamphlet published by Vasconcellos office, Jan. 1991.

20. Teo Furtado, "Can Self-Esteem Fight Poverty and Drugs?" *Utne Reader* (Jan./Feb. 1992).

21. "Building Self-Esteem Through Service," *The Washington Post*, Dec. 9, 1990.

22. Fran Peavey, *Heart Politics* (Philadelphia: New Society Publishers, 1986).

23. Robert Axelrod, "The Evolution of Cooperation," *Breakthrough: Emerging New Thinking of Soviet and Western Scholars*, Anatoly Gromyko and Martin Hellman, eds. (New York: Walker and Company, 1988), 185–92.

24. Ibid., 187.

25. Alfie Kohn, "How to Succeed Without Even Vying," *Psychology Today* (September 1986); also, Alfie Kohn, "No Contest," *New Age Journal* (Sep./Oct. 1986).

26. Ed Schwerin, "Empowerment as a Paradigm for Transformational Politics," paper presented at the American Political Scientists Association Conference, San Francisco, 1990.

27. Leonard Duhl, *The Social Entrepreneurship of Change* (New York: Pace University Press, 1990), 13–19.

28. Clem Bezold, *Anticipatory Democracy* (New York: Random House, 1978).

29. Christa Daryl Slaton, *Televote: Citizen Participation in the Quantum Age* (New York: Praeger Publishers, 1992).

30. Paul Tsongas, speech to Democratic Convention, 1992.

31. Lee Atwater, "Last Campaign," *New Age Journal* (May/June 1992).

32. "Bush's New Life," *The Washington Post*, March 3, 1993.

33. William A. Henry III, "Dissident to President," *Time*, Jan. 8, 1990.

34. "The Effort to Exercise Power in Accord with a Vision of Civility," *The New York Times*, July 26, 1992.

35. Michael Lerner, "Can the Democrats Be Stopped from Blowing It Again in 1992?" *Tikkun* (July/Aug. 1992).

36. Mac Lawrence, "Exploring New Ways of Resolving Conflicts," *Timeline*, no. 3 (May/June 1992).

Chapter Five

1. Alice Bailey, *Education in the New Age* (New York: Lucis Publishing, 1954), 63.

2. The Bible, Proverbs 23:7.

3. "Archie Bunker, Alive and Well," *Newsweek*, Jan. 21, 1991.

4. Alice Bailey, *The Destiny of the Nations* (New York: Lucis Publishing, 1949), 121, 356.

5. Alice Bailey, *The Externalisation of the Hierarchy* (New York: Lucis Publishing, 1957), 453.

6. Alice Bailey, *A Treatise on Cosmic Fire* (New York: Lucis Publishing, 1951), 889.

7. Vice President Al Gore (D-TN), speech at Communitarian Conference, Washington, D.C., Oct. 30, 1991.

8. Alice Bailey, *Esoteric Psychology, Vol. II* (New York: Lucis Publishing, 1942), 660.

9. The International Society for the Study of Aggression *Manifesto*, Seville, Spain, May 1986.

10. William Blake, "Letter to Thomas Butts," ed. David V. Erdman, *The Poetry and Prose of William Blake* (New York: Doubleday and Co., 1970), 693.

11. Donella H. Meadows, et al., *The Limits to Growth: A Report for the Club of Rome's Project on the Predicament of Mankind* (New York: Universe Books, 1972).

12. Hunter S. Lovins, "Abundant Opportunities," *In Context*, no. 25 (1990).

13. Thomas Jefferson, letter to a friend, quoted on the walls of the Jefferson Memorial, Washington, D.C.

14. Peter Dawkins and Sir George Trevelyan, *The Pattern of Initiation in the Evolution of Human Consciousness* (Northampton, England: Francis Bacon Research Trust, 1981), 12.

15. Jerome Glenn, *Future Mind: Artificial Intelligence* (Washington, D.C.: Acropolis Books, 1989).

16. Willis Harman, *Global Mind Change* (Indianapolis: Knowledge Systems Press, 1988), 157.

17. John Marks and Igor Beliaev, eds., *Common Ground on Terrorism* (New York: W. W. Norton, 1991).

18. Bailey, op. cit., *Esoteric Psychology, Vol. II*, 662.

19. Jessica Matthews, "Our Leaders Used to Care About Posterity," *The Washington Post*, June 27, 1991.

20. Rudolf Steiner, *World History in the Light of Anthroposophy* (London: Rudolf Steiner Press, 1950), 97.

21. Alice Bailey, *Esoteric Healing* (New York: Lucis Publishing, 1953), 404.

22. Bailey, op. cit., *The Externalisation of the Hierarchy*, 347.

23. Three Initiates, *The Kybalion* (Chicago: The Yogi Publication Society, Masonic Temple, 1912), 142–143.

24. Alice Bailey, *Ponder on This* (New York: Lucis Publishing, 1974), 131–4.

25. The Bible, Deuteronomy 29:4.

26. Sign in the Whitney Museum, New York, by artist Barbara Kruger.

27. Elisabeth Sahtouris, *Gaia: The Human Journey from Chaos to Cosmos* (New York: Pocket Books, 1989).

28. "Studies Back Theories on Near Death Experiences," *The Washington Post*, Nov. 9, 1990.

29. *Utne Reader* (Jan./Feb. 1991), 2.

30. Garry Wills, *Under God: Religion and American Politics* (New York: Simon & Schuster, 1990).

31. William Raspberry, "The Desire for a Life That Makes Sense," *The Washington Post*, December 10, 1993.

32. Rushworth Kidder, *An Agenda for the 21st Century* (Cambridge, Mass: MIT Press, 1987).

33. Willis Harman, *Global Mind Change* (Indianapolis: Knowledge Systems Press, Inc., 1988), 129.

34. "Hayden to Combine Ecology, Theology, During Class at SMC," *Outlook Mail*, Santa Monica, Calif., August 7, 1991.

35. "Personalities," *The Washington Post*, July 6, 1991.

36. "The Return of the Fourth R," *Newsweek*, June 10, 1991.

37. "Therapists See Religion as Aid, Not Illusion," *The New York Times*, Sept. 10, 1991.

38. "Is TV to Blame for Violence?" *The Washington Post*, April 7, 1993.

39. Jess Stearn, *Edgar Cayce: The Sleeping Prophet* (New York: Bantam Books, 1967), 82–84.

40. Henry C. Roberts, ed., *The Complete Prophecies of Nostradamus* (Oyster Bay, N.Y.: Nostradamus Company, 1969), 235.

41. "Nostradamus Prophesies," show hosted by Charleton Heston, NBC Television, Feb. 20, 1991.

42. Erika Cheetham, *The Final Prophesies of Nostradamus* (New York: Perigee Books, 1989), 275.

43. David Spangler, *Links with Space* (Findhorn, Scotland: Findhorn Press, 1971), 16–18.

44. Russel Targ and Keith Harary, *The Mind Race: Understanding and Using Psychic Abilities* (New York: Villard Books, 1984).

45. Ronald McRae, *Mind Wars: The True Story of Government Research into the Military Potential of Psychic Weapons* (New York: St. Martin's Press, 1984).

46. John White, *Psychic Warfare: Fact or Fiction?* (Wellingborough, England: The Aquarian Press, 1988).

47. Wesley Bramshaw, "Washington's Dream," *National Tribune* 4, no. 12 (Dec. 1880).

48. Claudia Wallis, "Why New Age Medicine Is Catching On," *Time*, Nov. 4, 1991.

Chapter Six

1. John Graham, *In Context*, no. 10, (Summer 1985), 9.

2. Jeff Fishel, "Leadership for Social Change: John Vasconcellos and the Promise of Humanistic Psychology in Public Life," *Political Psychology* (Dec. 1992).

3. David Feinstein and Stanley Krippner, "Bringing a Mythological Perspective to Social Change," *ReVision* 11, no. 1.

4. Carl Jung, *Man and His Symbols* (New York: Doubleday, 1964), 85.

5. Joseph Campbell, ed., *The Portable Jung* (New York: Penguin Books, 1971), 145–146.

6. Jerome S. Bernstein, *Power and Politics: The Psychology of Soviet-American Partnership* (Boston: Shambhala, 1989), 16.

7. Christopher Dickey, "A 'Common Purpose'—Or a Common Enemy?" *Newsweek*, Sept. 24, 1990.

8. Rudolf Steiner, *The Destinies of Individuals and of Nations* (New York: Anthroposophic Press, 1987), 21–23.

9. Walt Anderson, "Good Guy—Bad Guy Syndrome Fuels Environmental Movement," *Context Institute* (June 8, 1990).

10. Alan Atkisson, "Guardians of the Future: An Interview with Joanna Macy," *In Context* (Spring 1991).

11. Senator J. William Fulbright, quoted in *The Institute for Psychiatry and Foreign Affairs* pamphlet, Washington, D.C., 1978.

12. " 'Realism' and Human Rights," *Newsweek*, Feb. 20, 1989.

13. "Minority Against Minority," *Newsweek*, May 20, 1991.

14. "The Making of a Usable Past," *The Washington Post*, Sept. 2, 1991.

15. Albert Einstein, in a letter to Sigmund Freud (July 1932), quoted in *The Institute for Psychiatry and Foreign Affairs* pamphlet, Washington, D.C., 1978.

16. William D. Davidson, M.D., *The Institute of Psychiatry and Foreign Affairs: A Report on the First Eight Years*, Washington, D.C., 1978.

17. "A Turning Point in History," *The Washington Post National Weekly Edition*, Aug. 26–Sept. 1, 1991.

18. "Roots of Addiction," *Newsweek*, Feb. 20, 1989.

19. Gail Sheehy, *Character* (New York: William Morrow and Company, 1988), 257.

20. Ivan Boesky, Commencement Address to the School of Business Administration, U.C. Berkeley, 1985.

21. "Wall Street's Watergate," *Newsweek*, Dec. 1, 1986.

22. "What's Wrong," *Time*, May 25, 1987.

23. Ibid.

24. Ibid.

25. "A GOP Wunderkind's Free Fall to Poverty," *The Washington Post*, April 19, 1991, 1.

26. Vaclav Havel, quoted in "Vaclav Havel and the Politics of Hope," by Jeffrey B. Symynkywica, *Noetic Sciences Review* (Spring/Summer 1991).

27. David Spangler, *Conversations with John* (Elgin, Ill.: Lorian Press, 1980), 23.

28. The Brandt Report, *North-South: A Program for Survival* (Cambridge, Mass.: MIT Press, 1980).

29. Viola Neal and Shafica Karagulla, *Through the Curtain* (Marina del Rey, Calif.: Devorss & Co., 1983), 154–55.

30. Malvin Artley, "The Wind and the Weathervane: Reflection of Occultism in the Atmosphere and Weather Patterns," *The Journal of Esoteric Psychology* 7, no. 1 (1991).

31. Alice Bailey, op. cit., *A Treatise on Cosmic Fire*, 888–889.

32. "Hurricane Rakes New England, Loses Some Force," *The Washington Post*, Aug. 30, 1991.

33. "Loan Guarantees for Israelis," *Miami Herald*, March 1, 1992.

34. Nicholas D. Kristof, "The End of the Golden Road," *The New York Times Magazine*, Dec. 1, 1991.

35. Christopher Bird, *The Secret Life of Plants* (New York: HarperCollins, 1989).

36. Michelle Lusson, *The Chakras and the Spiritual Stem* (McLean, Va.: American Metaphysical Society, 1971).

37. Bailey, op. cit., *Esoteric Healing*, 340.

38. Edith Fiore, *The Unquiet Dead* (New York: Ballantine, 1987), 140–152.

39. "Overload," *The Washington Post*, May 5, 1993.

40. "Searching for Nature's Message in a Bottle of Glowing Water," *The Washington Post*, Aug. 12, 1991.

41. Irwin Edman, ed., *The Works of Plato* (New York: Random House, 1928).

42. Christopher Bird, op. cit.

43. Steven Halpern and Louis Savary, *Sound Health* (San Francisco, Cal.: Harper and Row, 1985), 57–58.

44. *The Global Family Update* (June/July 1991).

45. Halpern, op. cit., 7–8.

Chapter Seven

1. Alice Bailey, *A Treatise on White Magic* (New York: Lucis Publishing, 1934), 35.

2. "Conventional Wisdom Watch," *Newsweek*, July 2, 1990.

3. "Personalities," *The Washington Post*, March 5, 1991.

4. "Rough Justice in the Greenhouse," *Newsweek*, Dec. 18, 1989.

5. W. Pater, *Plato and Platoism* (Westport, Conn.: Greenwood Press, 1970), 54.

6. Joseph Head and S. L. Cranston, *Reincarnation: The Phoenix Fire Mystery* (New York: Crown Publishers, 1977), 556–560; also Silvia Cranston and Carey Williams, *Reincarnation: A New Horizon in Science, Religion, and Society* (New York: Crown Publishers, 1984), ix, 18, 41, 44, 45, 333, 344–345.

7. *Newsweek*, March 27, 1989.

8. "Bay Area Interest in 'New Age' Mysticism," *San Francisco Chronicle*, April 24, 1990, A-8.

9. "Genius," *San Francisco Examiner*, Aug. 28, 1929.

10. Cranston and Williams, op. cit.

11. Roger Woolger, *Other Lives, Other Selves* (New York: Doubleday, 1987), 311–315.

12. Trevor Ravenscroft, *The Spear of Destiny* (New York: Bantam Books, 1973), xiii, 202.

13. Martin Blumenson, *Patton: The Man Behind the Legend, 1885–1945* (New York: William Morrow and Co., 1985), 29.

14. Bailey, op. cit., *Esoteric Psychology, Vol. II*, 261.

15. Rudolf Steiner, *The Destinies of Individuals and of Nations* (New York: Anthroposophic Press, 1987), 15.

16. *The New York Times*, Nov. 12, 1967.

17. The Dalai Lama, *My Land and My People* (New York: McGraw-Hill, 1962), 50–51.

18. *Young India*, April 2, 1931.

Chapter Eight

1. Rudolf Steiner, *The Driving Force of Spiritual Powers in World History* (North Vancouver, Canada: Steiner Book Centre, 1972), 51.

2. Alice Bailey, *The Light of the Soul: The Yoga Sutras of Patanjali* (New York: Lucis Publishing, 1955), 53.

3. Helena Blavatsky, *The Secret Doctrine* (Pasadena, Calif.: Theosophical University Press, 1974; orig. 1888), 274.

4. Bailey, op. cit., *The Externalisation of the Hierarchy*, 573, 699.

5. Ibid., 600 and 616.

6. Torkom Saraydarian, *The Hierarchy and the Plan* (Sedona, Ariz.: Aquarian Educational Group, 1975), 43–47.

7. Spangler, op. cit., *Links with Space*, 38.

8. Letters of Helena Roerich to Franklin D. Roosevelt, Roosevelt Library Collection, Hyde Park, N.Y., 1934.

9. C. Kerenyi, *Eleusis* (New York: Schocken Books, 1977), 7–11.

10. Amedee Thierry, *Histoire des Gaulois, I*, 246.

11. Will Durant, *The Life of Greece* (New York: Simon & Schuster, 1939), 197–198; see also Robert Flaceliere, *Greek Oracles* (New York: W. W. Norton and Co., 1965), 55–59.

12. Edouard Shure, *The Great Initiates* (San Francisco: Harper and Row, 1961; originally 1889), 269–270.

13. Rudolf Steiner, *The Destinies of Individuals and of Nations* (New York: Anthroposophic Press, 1986), 52.

14. Malcolm Billings, *The Cross and the Crescent* (New York: Sterling Publishing, 1990), 53.

15. Helena Roerich, *Agni Yoga* (New York: Agni Yoga Society, 1929), 29.

16. Letters of Helena Roerich to President Franklin Roosevelt, op. cit.

17. I. Cooper-Oakley, *The Comte de St. Germain: The Secret of Kings* (Wheaton: Ill.: Theosophical Publishing, 1982); also Manly P. Hall, *The Secret Teachings of All Ages* (Los Angeles: The Philosophical Research Society, 1958).

18. Manly P. Hall, *The Secret Destiny of America* (Los Angeles, Calif.: Philosophical Research Society, 1958), 165–172. Also Theodore Heline, *America's Destiny: A New Order of the Ages* (La Canada, Calif.: New Age Press, 1941), 7; and R.H.H., *Talk Does Not Cook the Rice, Vol. 1* (New York: Samuel Weiser, 1982), 30; Letters of Helena Roerich to President Franklin Roosevelt, op. cit., Oct. 10, 1934.

19. Robert Alan Cambell, *Our Flag* (Chicago: H. E. Lawrence & Co., 1890, reprinted in 1975 by Naconah's Patriotic Research Publications, Salt Lake City), 35–54; also Theodore Heline, op. cit., 7; also Eugene Coswell, *Letters to a Disciple* (Chicago: Ashram Press, 1935), 222–239; also Manly P. Hall, op. cit., *The Secret Destiny of America*, 147–154.

20. Norman Cousins, *In God We Trust* (New York: Harper & Row, 1958), 66.

21. Wesley Bramshaw, "Washington's Dream," *National Tribune* 4, no. 12 (December 1880), 1.

22. For more information on the Rosicrucians see Michael Baigent, et al., *Holy Blood, Holy Grail* (New York: Dell Books, 1982).

23. Robert Hieronimus, *American's Secret Destiny* (Rochester, Vt.: Destiny Books, 1989), 39; also Spencer Lewis, *Rosicrucian Questions and Answers: A Complete History* (San Jose, Cal.: Supreme Grand Lodge of AMORC Publishing, 1929), 165.

24. Helena Blavatsky, *The Theosophist*, 1883.

25. Andrew Rothovious, "The Dragon Tradition in the New World," *East/West Journal* (August 1977).

26. *The Franklin Papers, Vol. 9* (New Haven, Conn.: Yale University Press, 1966), 323–325.

27. Corinne Heline, *America's Invisible Guidance* (Los Angeles, Calif.: New Age Press, 1949), 16.

28. E. G. Alderfer, *The Ephrata Commune* (Pittsburgh: University of Pittsburgh Press, 1985).

29. Hieronimus, op. cit., *America's Secret Destiny*, 37.

30. Spencer Lewis, *Rosicrucian Questions and Answers: A Complete History* (San Jose, Calif.: Supreme Grand Lodge of AMORC Publishing, 1929), 165.

31. Some of these Masonic memberships are known by tradition or circumstantial evidence and some by tangible proof. (See next footnote.)

32. Ronald E. Heaton, *The Masonic Membership of the Founding Fathers* (Silver Spring, Md.: Masonic Service Association, 1965).

33. Sidney Morse, *Freemasonry in the American Revolution* (Washington, D.C.: Masonic Service Association, 1924), 51.

34. Michael Baigent and Richard Leigh, *The Temple and the Lodge* (New York: Arcade Publishing; Little, Brown and Company, 1989), 211.

35. H. C. Clausen, *Masons Who Helped Shape Our Nation* (Washington, D.C.: Masonic Service Association, 1976), 82.

36. Baigent and Leigh, op. cit., *The Temple and the Lodge*, 262.

37. Ibid., 145.

38. *Evening Courier*, Portland, Maine, March 8, 1862.

39. Garry Stewart, "Becoming Intimate with God," *The Quest* (Spring 1992).

40. David Knight, ed., *An ESP Reader* (New York: Grosset and Dunlap, 1969).

41. Corinne Heline, op. cit., 137–139.

42. Jennifer and Roger Woolger, *The Goddess Within* (New York: Fawcett Columbine, 1989), 57.

43. Charles E. Clark, *Maine: A History* (Hanover, N.H.: University of New England Press, 1977), 120–121.

44. Harold Laski in Walter Thilles's *Road to War, America, 1914–1917* (Boston: Houghton Mifflin Co., 1935); also George Sylvester Vierick, *The Strangest Friendship in History: Woodrow Wilson and Colonel House* (Westport, Conn.: Greenwood Publishing Group, 1976).

45. Theodore Heline, op. cit., 10.

46. Helena Roerich correspondence to F.D.R. (Roosevelt Library, Hyde Park, NY).

47. "The 'Guru Letters': Wallace Meets the Roerich Cultists," *Newsweek*, March 22, 1948; also Karl E. Meyer, "The Two Roerichs Are One," *The New York Times*, Jan. 22, 1988; also Jacqueline Decter, *Nicholas Roerich: The Life and Art of a Russian Master* (Rochester, Vt.: Park Street Press, 1989), 136.

48. Charles DeMotte, "An Esoteric History of Modern Times," unpublished paper, 1991.

49. Clara M. Codd, *The Way of the Disciple* (Adyar, India: Theosophical Publishing House, 1964), 44–45.

50. Guru R.H.H., *Talk Does Not Cook the Rice, Series II* (York Beach, Maine: Samuel Weiser, 1985), 66; also Codd, op. cit., 36; also, "Angels Among Us," *Time*, December 27, 1993.

51. Interview with authors, Feb. 17, 1989.

52. Carolyn Myss, "Guidance and Chaos," *Onearth* (Spring 1990) Findhorn, Scotland.

Chapter Nine

1. Alice Bailey, *The Rays and the Initiations* (New York: Lucis Publishing, 1950), 332.

2. "The Changing of the Guard," *Newsweek*, Dec. 4, 1989, 37.

3. Bailey, op. cit., *The Destiny of the Nations*, 107–110; 37.

4. Dion Fortune, *The Cosmic Doctrine* (Wellingborough, England: The Aquarian Press, 1971), 90.

5. Agni Yoga Society, "Supermundane," paper presented Feb. 14, 1991, at the Agni Yoga Society, New York, N.Y.

6. Bailey, op. cit., *Esoteric Psychology, Vol. II*, 577.

7. Neal and Karagulla, op. cit., *Through the Curtain*, 282–290.

8. Trevor Ravenscroft, *The Spear of Destiny* (New York: Bantam Books, 1973), 173.

9. Ibid., xiii.

10. Jackson Spielvogel and David Redles, "Hitler's Racial Ideology: Content and Occult Sources," *Simon Wiesenthal Center Annual, Vol. 3* (White Plains, N.Y.: Kraus International Publications, 1986), 233.

11. Agni Yoga Society, op. cit., *Leaves of Morya's Garden: The Call*, 17.

12. Alice Bailey, *A Treatise on White Magic* (New York: Lucis Publishing, 1934), 311.

13. Bailey, op. cit., *A Treatise on Cosmic Fire*, 488–489.

14. Ibid., 612–613.

15. The Findhorn Community, *The Findhorn Garden* (San Francisco: Harper and Row, 1975), 54–99; Dorothy Maclean, *To Hear the Angels Sing* (Elgin, Ill.: Lorian Press, 1982); William Bloom, *Devas, Fairies, and Angels: A Modern Approach* (Glastonbury, England: Gothic Image Books, 1986), 3–6; Michelle Small Wright, *Behaving As If the God in All Life Mattered* (Jefferson, Va.: Perelandra, Ltd., 1987); Bailey, op. cit., *Cosmic Fire*, 489.

16. The Findhorn Community, op. cit. 54–99.

17. Bailey, op. cit., *Treatise on Cosmic Fire*, 612–617; 670–682.

18. Bailey, *Esoteric Psychology I and II*, op. cit.; also Michael D. Robbins, *Tapestry of the Gods, I and II* (Jersey City Heights, N.J.: University of the Seven Rays Publishing, 1988).

19. "Bay Area's Strong Interest in 'New Age' Mysticism," *San Francisco Chronicle*, April 24, 1990, A-8.

20. "The Stargazers Strike Back," *Newsweek*, Jan. 15, 1990.

21. Ibid.

22. Chris Hedlund, "Uranus Neptune Conjunction," *Magical Blend*, no. 41, Jan. 1994.

23. "Morality Among Supply-Siders," *Time*, May 25, 1987.

24. Mark Lerner, "Saturn-Neptune Conjunction," *Welcome to Planet Earth*, 9, no. 5 (1989).

25. Donald Regan, *For the Record: From Wall Street to Washington* (New York: St. Martin's Press, 1989), 3–4.

26. Joan Quigley, *What Does Joan Say?* (New York: Birch Lane Press, imprint of Carol Publishing Group, 1990).

27. Marcia Montenegro, "George Bush: A Man and His Chart," *Welcome to Planet Earth* 9, no. 12 (1990).

28. Mark Lerner, "The Clinton Presidency," *Welcome to Planet Earth* 12, no. 9 (1993), "The Clinton Gore Victory," *Welcome to Planet Earth* 12, nos. 5 and 6 (1992), and "The Wounded King," *Welcome to Planet Earth* 11, no. 10 (1992).

29. Ibid.

30. *Springfield Advocate*, Oct. 31, 1991, 10.

31. Dane Rudyar, *The Astrology of America's Destiny* (New York: Random House, 1974), 70–71.

32. Lynn Koiner, "The Berlin Wall," *The Washington Astrology Forum Newsletter* (July 1990).

33. Mark Lerner, "The Clinton Presidency," *Welcome to Planet Earth* 12, no. 8 (1993).

34. Rudyar, op. cit., 86–88.

Chapter Ten

1. Rene Wellek, ed., *The Meaning of Czech History* (Chapel Hill, N.C.: The University of North Carolina Press, 1974), xxii.

2. Sri Aurobindo, *The Human Cycle,* (Pondicherry, India: Sri Aurobindo Ashram Publications, 1970), 29.

3. Donald Keys, "The Synthesis of Nations," *Synthesis: The Realization of the Self, Vol. 1,* No. 2, 1975, 8.

4. Donald Keys and Astrid Koch, *Voting in the General Assembly of the UN: 1970–1985* (Mt. Shasta, Calif.: Planetary Citizens, 1985), 11.

5. "Nation-State: An Idea under Siege," *The Washington Post*, Nov. 11, 1990.

6. Bailey, op. cit., *The Destiny of Nations*, 60, 101.

7. Helena Roerich, *Brotherhood* (New York: Agni Yoga Society, 1962), 173–174.

8. Helena Roerich, *Agni Yoga* (New York: The Agni Yoga Society, 1952), 141.

9. Spangler, op. cit., *Conversations with John*, 7-8.

10. Ibid., 19–20.

11. Jerry Mander, "What You Don't Know About Indians," *Utne Reader*, (Nov./Dec. 1991).

12. Corinne McLaughlin and Gordon Davidson, *America's Metaphysical Foundations* (Shutesbury, Mass.: Sirius Publishing, 1988), 11.; also Robert Hieronimus, *America's Secret Destiny* (Rochester, Vt.: Destiny Books, 1989).

13. Bailey, op. cit., *The Destiny of Nations*, 104–105.

14. Jacqueline Decter, *Nicholas Roerich: The Life and Art of a Russian Master* (Rochester, Vt.: Park Street Press, 1989); Nicholas Roerich, *Art and World Culture* (New York: World Unity Publishing, 1973), 5.

15. Nancy Seifer, *Face to Face with Freedom* (New York: Freedom Press, 1991), 9, 52.

16. Ibid., 23.

17. Melissa Everett, "Creative Disorderly, Determined, Citizen Diplomats Help Foil Coup," *Surviving Together* (Autumn 1991).

18. Rudolf Steiner, *The Destinies of Individuals and of Nations* (New York: Anthroposophic Press, 1987), 23, 26–27.

19. Edgar Cayce, "The Spirit of Nations," *Venture Inward* (Nov./Dec. 1989), Reading no. 3976–29.

20. Spangler, op. cit., *Conversations with John*, 6, 11.

21. Bailey, op. cit., *The Destiny of Nations*, 60–61.

22. Akio Morita, "Capitalism East and West: A Dialogue," *New Perspectives Quarterly* (Winter 1992), 36.

23. Terry McCarthy, "Akio Morita's Voice of Reason," *World Press Review* (April 1992), 12.

24. Karel von Wolferen, "The Unaccountable Superpower," *New Perspectives Quarterly* (Winter 1992), 46.

25. Ibid., 34.

26. "Africa, Crisis and New Life," *World Goodwill*, no. 2 (1991).

27. Ibid.

28. David Spangler, *Planetary Vision* (Forres, Scotland: Findhorn Press, 1977).

29. Alice Bailey, *Discipleship in the New Age, Vol. 1* (New York: Lucis Publishing, 1972), 161.

30. Robert Muller, "The United Nations and the World's Future," *Who is Who in Service to the Earth*, Hans J. Keller, ed. (Asheville, N.C.: Vision Link Educational Foundation, 1991), 102–103.

31. "U.N. Chief Restored Body's Reputation," *The Washington Post*, Jan. 1, 1992.

32. *CNN News*, Dec. 6, 1991.

33. Nancy Roof, "The Role of the U.N. in the New World Order," paper prepared for the International Society of Political Psychology Conference, July 8, 1992, 22.

34. Bailey, op. cit., *The Externalization of the Hierarchy*, 190–191.

Chapter Eleven

1. Bailey, op. cit., *Esoteric Healing*, 128.

2. "House Members Owe $300,000 for Hill Meals," *The Washington Post*, Oct. 3, 1991.

3. Hazel Henderson, "Beyond the Information Age," *Creation* (March/April 1988), 33–35.

4. Manfred Max-Neef, *The Living Economy*, Paul Ekins, ed., 49.

5. Willis Harman interview, *Business Ethics* (March/April 1992), 29.

6. Lester Thurow, "Communitarian vs. Individualistic Capitalism," *New Perspectives Quarterly* (Winter 1992), 41.

7. Philip Slater, *Wealth Addiction* (Santa Cruz, Calif.: University of California Press, 1972), 11.

8. Slater, op. cit., 27.

9. *World Goodwill*, no. 3 (1987), 3.

10. Eloise Salholz, "The Empathy Factor," *Newsweek*, Jan. 13, 1992, 23.

11. Thomas H. Greco, Jr., *Money & Debt: A Solution to the Global Crisis*, 2nd ed. (self-published pamphlet, 1989), 14–18.

12. "Capital Idea," *The Washington Post*, Dec. 30, 1991.

13. Ravi Batra, *Surviving the Great Depression of 1990* (New York: Simon & Schuster, 1988), 238.

14. Jamie Babson, personal interview with authors, July 27, 1990.

15. Chuck Collins, "Sharing the Wealth," *Community Economics* (Winter 1992), 3–4.

16. Mohammad Yunus, "Credit as a Human Right," *The New York Times*, May 15, 1990, 76.

17. "Development Assistance: What Works and What Doesn't," ACCION information packet (Boston: ACCION, 1987).

18. Paul Hawken, *Utne Reader*, no. 22 (July/August 1987), 3.

Chapter Twelve

1. Albert Gore, *Earth in the Balance*, (New York: Penguin/Plume, 1993), 242.

2. Allan Luks with Peggy Payne, *The Healing Power of Doing Good* (New York: Fawcett Columbine, 1991), 17.

3. Ibid., 18.

4. Ibid., 82–83.

5. Robert Ornstein and David Sobel, *Healthy Pleasures* (Reading, Mass.: Addison-Wesley, 1989), 235, 237.

6. Lester Brown, op. cit., *State of the World 1990* 149.

7. "A Social Assessment Guide," booklet published by Franklin Research & Development Co., 1987.

8. Lester Brown, op. cit., *State of the World 1990*, 150.

9. Ibid., 152.

10. Ibid., 190.

11. Robert Gilman, "Abundant Opportunities," *In Context*, no. 25 (1991), 21.

12. Huey D. Johnson and Peggy Laner, "The Dutch Green Plan," *Earth Island Journal* (Spring 1992).

13. Lester Brown, op. cit., *State of the World 1991*, 182.

14. Op. cit., *World Watch 1992*, 152.

15. "ABC Evening News," Oct. 1, 1991.

16. Guy Dauncey, *After the Crash* (Basingstoke, U.K.: Green Print, 1988), 52–53.

17. Ralph Nader, *Time Dollars* (Emmaus, Pa.: Rodale Press, 1992), Introduction.

18. Alisa Gravitz, "Cooperation," *Co-op America Quarterly* (Fall 1991), 2.

19. Paul Hawken, *The Ecology of Commerce*, (New York: Harper Business, 1993), p. xiv.

20. Michael Rothschild, *Earth Island Journal* (Spring 1992), 34.

21. Hawken, *The Ecology of Commerce*, op. cit., p. 170–175.

Chapter Thirteen

1. "Whew," *Newsweek*, August 16, 1993. also, *The Washington Post*, August 8, 1993.

2. R.H.H., *Talk Does Not Cook the Rice, Vol. 1* (New York: Samuel Weiser, 1982), 33.

3. Theodore Heline, *America's Destiny: A New Order of the Ages* (La Canada, Calif.: New Age Press, 1941), 8–9.

4. "Bay Area's Strong Interest in 'New Age' Mysticism," *San Francisco Chronicle*, April 24, 1990.

5. Don Oldenburg, "The Harmonic Convergence, Revisited," *The Washington Post*, May 4, 1990.

6. Elaine and Arthur Aron, *The Maharishi Effect* (Walpole, N.H.: Stillpoint Publishing, 1986), 72 and 170; see also Itzhak Bentov, *Stalking The Wild Pendulum*.

7. Maria Gritsay, "Prayer Cleanses Radiation," *Global Family Newsletter*, Winter 1992.

8. "Good News Briefs," *The Global Family Update*, June/July 1991.

9. Aron, op. cit., 130.

10. *Journal of Conflict Resolution*, Yale University, April 1990; also Aron, op. cit., 2.

11. Aron, op. cit., 92.

12. "Meditators See Signs of Success," *The Washington Post*, July 30, 1993.

13. Ken Carey, *The Starseed Transmissions* (Kansas City, Mo.: Uni-Sun Publishing, 1982), 61.

14. Bailey, op. cit., *The Externalization of the Hierarchy*, 263, and *A Treatise On White Magic*, 367–368.

15. Everett M. Rogers, *Diffusion of Innovations* (New York: Macmillan Free Press, 1983).

16. Bailey, op. cit., *The Externalization of the Hierarchy*, 466.

17. Brooke Medicine Eagle, *Buffalo Woman Comes Singing* (New York: Ballantine Books, 1991).

18. Gail Sheehy, "The Hidden Hart," *Vanity Fair* (July 1984).

19. Donald Keys, "The Synthesis of Nations," op. cit., 8.

20. "Pentagon Group Installs SDI Without Permission of Top Brass," *The Washingtonian*, February 1988, Vol. 23, No. 5.

21. Bailey, op. cit., *Discipleship in the New Age, Vol. II*, 228–231.

22. David Spangler, "The Spiritual Challenge of War," *New Age Journal*, March/April 1991.

Selected Bibliography

◆

Adams, John D., ed. *Transforming Leadership*. Alexandria, Va.: Miles River Press, 1986.

Aron, Elaine, and Arthur Aron. *The Maharishi Effect*. Walpole, N.H.: Stillpoint Publishing, 1986.

Ashe, Geoffrey. *Gandhi: A Study in Revolution*. London: William Heinemann, 1968.

Ayer, Fred, Jr. *Before the Colors Fade: Portrait of a Soldier George S. Patton Jr.* Boston: Houghton Mifflin Co., 1964.

Baigent, Michael, et al. *Holy Blood, Holy Grail*. New York: Dell Books, 1982.

————, and Richard Leigh. *The Temple and the Lodge*. New York: Arcade Publishing: Little, Brown and Company, 1989.

Bailey, Alice. *A Treatise on White Magic*. New York: Lucis Publishing, 1934.

————. *Esoteric Psychology II*. New York: Lucis Publishing 1942.

————. *Problems of Humanity*. New York: Lucis Publishing, 1947.

————. *The Destiny of the Nations*. New York: Lucis Publishing, 1949.

————. *Esoteric Healing*. New York: Lucis Publishing, 1953.

————. *Education in the New Age*. New York: Lucis Publishing, 1954.

————. *The Light of the Soul: The Yoga Sutras of Patanjali*. New York: Lucis Publishing, 1955.

————. *The Externalisation of the Hierarchy*. New York: Lucis Publishing, 1957.

————. *A Treatise on Cosmic Fire*. New York: Lucis Publishing, 1951.

————. *Discipleship in the New Age. Vols. I and II*. New York: Lucis Publishing, 1955.

Batra, Ravi. *Surviving the Great Depression of 1990*. New York: Simon & Schuster, 1988.

Benavides, Rodolfo. *Dramatic Prophecies of the Great Pyramid*. Mexico: Editores Mexicano Unidos, S.A., 1970.

Bergler, Edmund. *Money and Emotional Conflicts*. Garden City, N.Y.: Doubleday, 1951.

Bernstein, Jerome S. *Power Politics: The Psychology of Soviet-American Partnership*. Boston: Shambhala, 1989.

Bird, Christopher. *The Secret Life of Plants*. New York: HarperCollins, 1989.

Blavatsky, Helena. *The Secret Doctrine*. Pasadena, Calif.: Theosophical University Press, 1974; orig. 1888.

Bloom, William. *Devas, Fairies, and Angels: A Modern Approach*. Glastonbury, England: Gothic Image Books, 1986.

Blumenson, Martin. *Patton: The Man Behind the Legend, 1885–1945*. New York: William Morrow and Co., 1985.

Brandt Report, The. *North-South: A Program for Survival*. Cambridge, Mass.: MIT Press, 1980.

Brooke Medicine Eagle. *Buffalo Woman Comes Singing*. New York: Ballantine Books, 1991.

Brown, Lester. *State of the World 1993*. New York: W. W. Norton and Co., 1993.

Burns, James McGregor. *Leadership*. New York: Harper and Row, 1978.

Cambell, Robert Alan. *Our Flag*. Chicago: H. E. Lawrence & Co., 1890. Reprint, Salt Lake City: 1975. Naconah's Patriotic Research Publications.

Campbell, Joseph. *The Power of Myth*. New York: Doubleday, 1988.

————, ed. *The Portable Jung*. New York: Penguin Books, 1971.

Carey, Ken. *The Starseed Transmissions*. Kansas City, Mo.: Uni-Sun Publishing, 1982.

Carter, Stephen. *The Culture of Disbelief*. New York: Harper and Row, 1993.

Cheetham, Erika. *The Final Prophesies of Nostradamus*. New York: Perigee Books, 1989.

Clausen, H. C. *Masons Who Helped Shape Our Nation*. Washington, D.C.: Masonic Service Association, 1976.

Cleary, Thomas, ed. *The Tao of Politics*. Boston: Shambhala, 1990.

Codd, Clara M. *The Way of the Disciple*. Adyar, India: Theosophical Publishing House, 1964.

Cooper-Oakley, I. *The Comte de St. Germain: The Secret of Kings*. Wheaton, Ill.: Theosophical Publishing, 1982.

Coswell, Eugene. *Letters to a Disciple*. Chicago: Ashram Press, 1935.

Cranston, Silvia, and Carey Williams. *Reincarnation: A New Horizon in Science, Religion, and Society*. New York: Crown Publishers, 1984.

Dalai Lama, The. *My Land and My People*. New York: McGraw-Hill, 1962.

Dass, Ram, and Paul Gorman. *How Can I Help?* New York: Alfred A. Knopf, 1987.

Dauncey, Guy. *After the Crash*. Basingstoke, U.K.: Green Print, 1988.

Dawkins, Peter, and Sir George Trevelyan. *The Pattern of Initiation in the Evolution of Human Consciousness*. Northampton, England: Francis Bacon Research Trust, 1981.

De Castillejo, Irene Claremont. *Knowing Woman*. London: Hodder and Stoughton, 1973.

Decter, Jacqueline. *Nicholas Roerich: The Life and Art of a Russian Master*. Rochester, Vt.: Park Street Press, 1989.

Dionne, E. J. *Why Americans Hate Politics*. New York: Simon & Schuster, 1991.

Duhl, Leonard. *The Social Entrepreneurship of Change*. New York: Pace University Press, 1990.

Durant, Will. *The Life of Greece*. New York: Simon & Schuster, 1939.

Eisler, Riane. *The Chalice and the Blade*. San Francisco: Harper and Row, 1988.

Ekins, Paul, ed. *The Living Economy*. New York: Routledge, Chapman & Hall, 1987.

Etzioni, Amitai. *The Spirit of Community.* New York: Crown Publishers, 1993.

Faludi, Susan. *Backlash: The Undeclared War Against American Women.* New York: Crown Publishers, 1991.

Findhorn Community, The. *The Findhorn Garden.* San Francisco: Harper and Row, 1975.

Fiore, Edith. *The Unquiet Dead.* New York: Ballantine Books, 1987.

Fisher, Roger, and William Ury. *Getting to Yes.* New York: Penguin Books, 1983.

Flaceliere, Robert. *Green Oracles.* New York: W. W. Norton, 1965.

Fortune, Dion. *Sea Priestess.* York Beach, Maine: Samuel Weiser, 1938; 1978.

————. *The Cosmic Doctrine.* Wellingborough, England: The Aquarian Press, 1971.

French, Marilyn. *The War Against Women.* New York: Summit Books, 1992.

Gimbutas, Marija. *The Language of the Goddess.* San Francisco: Harper and Row, 1989.

Glenn, Jerome. *Future Mind: Artificial Intelligence.* Washington, D.C.: Acropolis Books, 1989.

Godwin, Joscelyn, trans. *Chemical Wedding of Christian Rosenkerutz.* Grand Rapids, Mich.: Phanes Press, 1991.

Gorbachev, Mikhail. *Perestroika.* New York: Harper and Row, 1987.

Greco, Thomas H., Jr. *Money & Debt: A Solution to the Global Crisis,* 2d ed. Self-published pamphlet, 1989.

Gromyko, Anatoly, and Martin Hellman, eds. *Breakthrough: Emerging New Thinking of Soviet and Western Scholars.* New York: Walker and Company, 1988.

R. H. Guru. *Talk Does Not Cook the Rice, Vol. 1.* New York: Samuel Weiser, 1982.

Hall, Manly P. *The Secret Destiny of America.* Los Angeles: The Philosophical Research Society, 1958.

————. *The Secret Teachings of All Ages.* Los Angeles: The Philosophical Research Society, 1958.

Halpern, Steven, and Louis Savary. *Sound Health.* San Francisco: Harper and Row, 1985.

Hammarskjold, Dag. *Markings.* New York: Alfred A. Knopf, 1968.

Harman, Willis. *Global Mind Change.* Indianapolis, Ind.: Knowledge Systems Press, Inc., 1988.

Harris, Sam. *Reclaiming Our Democracy.* Philadelphia: Camino Books, 1993.

Head, Joseph, and S. L. Cranston. *Reincarnation: The Phoenix Fire Mystery.* New York: Crown Publishers, 1977.

Heaton, Ronald E. *The Masonic Membership of the Founding Fathers.* Silver Spring, Md.: Masonic Service Association, 1965.

Heider, John. *The Tao of Leadership.* New York: Bantam Books, 1986.

Heline, Corinne. *America's Invisible Guidance.* Los Angeles: New Age Press, 1949.

Heline, Theodore. *America's Destiny: A New Order of the Ages.* La Canada, Calif.: New Age Press, 1941.

Henderson, Hazel. *The Politics of the Solar Age.* Indianapolis, Ind.: Knowledge Systems Inc., 1981.

————. *Paradigms in Progress.* Indianapolis, Ind.: Knowledge Systems, 1991.

Hieronimus, Robert. *America's Secret Destiny.* Rochester, Vt.: Destiny Books, 1989.

Jaikaran, Jacques. *Debt Virus.* Lakewood, Co.: Glenbridge, 1992.

Jung, Carl. *Man and His Symbols.* New York: Doubleday, 1964.

Keene, Sam. *Faces of the Enemy.* New York: Harper and Row, 1987.

Keller, Hans J., ed. *Who Is Who in Service to the Earth.* Asheville, N.C.: Vision Link Educational Foundation, 1991.

Kerenyi, C. *Eleusis.* New York: Schocken Books, 1977.

Keys, Donald. *Earth at Omega.* Boston: Branden Press, 1982.

————, and Astrid Koch. *Voting in the General Assembly of the UN: 1970–1985.* Mt. Shasta, Calif.: Planetary Citizens, 1985.

Knight, David, ed. *An ESP Reader.* New York: Grosset and Dunlap, 1969.

Kübler-Ross, Elisabeth. *On Death and Dying.* New York: Macmillan, 1969.

Kull, Steven. *Burying Lenin.* Boulder, Colo.: Westview Press, 1992.

Lewis, Spencer. *Rosicrucian Questions and Answers: A Complete History.* San Jose, Calif.: Supreme Grand Lodge of AMORC Publishing, 1929.

Luke, Helen M. *Woman: Earth and Spirit.* New York: Crossroads Press, 1984.

Luks, Allan, with Peggy Payne. *The Healing Power of Doing Good.* New York: Fawcett Columbine, 1991.

Maclean, Dorothy. *To Hear the Angels Sing.* Elgin, Ill.: Lorian Press, 1982.

Marks, John, and Igor Beliaev, eds. *Common Ground on Terrorism.* New York: W. W. Norton, 1991.

Marshall, Peter, and David Manuel. *The Light and the Glory.* Old Tappan, N.J.: Fleming H. Revell Co., 1977.

McLaughlin, Corinne, and Gordon Davidson. *Builders of the Dawn: Community Lifestyles in a Changing World.* Summertown, Tenn.: The Book Publishing Co., 1990.

Meadows, Donella H., et al. *The Limits to Growth: A Report for the Club of Rome's Project on the Predicament of Mankind.* New York: Universe Books, 1972.

Mogil, Christopher, and Anne Slepian. *We Gave Away a Fortune.* Philadelphia: New Society Publishers, 1992.

Moore, Thomas. *Care of the Soul.* New York: HarperCollins, 1992.

Morse, Sidney. *Freemasonry in the American Revolution.* Washington, D.C.: Masonic Service Association, 1924.

Muller, Robert. *New Genesis.* Garden City, N.Y.: Doubleday, 1982.

Murphy, Michael. *The Future of the Body.* Los Angeles: Tarcher and Co., 1992.

Nader, Ralph. *Time Dollars.* Emmaus, Pa.: Rodale Press, 1992.

Naisbitt, John, and Patricia Aburdene. *Reinventing the Corporation.* New York: Warner Books, 1985.

————. *Megatrends 2000.* New York: William Morrow and Co., 1990.

Neal, Viola, and Shafica Karagulla. *Through the Curtain.* Marina del Rey, Calif.: Devorss & Co., 1983.

Ornstein, Robert, and David Sobel. *Healthy Pleasures.* Reading, Mass.: Addison-Wesley, 1989.

Osborne, David. *Laboratories of Democracy*. Boston: Harvard Business School Press, 1988.

————, and Ted Gaebler. *Reinventing Government*. Reading, Mass.: Addison-Wesley Publishing, 1992.

Peavey, Fran. *Heart Politics*. Philadelphia: New Society Publishers, 1986.

Psychologists for Social Responsibility. *Dismantling the Mask of Enmity: Educational Resource Manual*. Washington, D.C., 1991.

Roberts, Henry C., ed. *The Complete Prophecies of Nostradamus*. Oyster Bay, N.Y.: Nostradamus Company, 1969.

Roerich, Helena. *Leaves of Morya's Garden, Vol I*. New York: Agni Yoga Society, 1924.

————. *Agni Yoga*. New York: Agni Yoga Society, 1952.

————. *The Mother of the World*. New York: Agni Yoga Society, 1956.

————. *Brotherhood*. New York: Agni Yoga Society, 1962.

Roerich, Nicholas. *Art and World Culture*. New York: World Unity Publishing, 1973.

Roszak, Theodore. *The Unfinished Animal*. New York: Harper and Row, 1975.

Rudyar, Dane. *The Astrology of America's Destiny*. New York: Random House, 1974.

Sahtouris, Elisabeth. *Gaia: The Human Journey from Chaos to Cosmos*. New York: Pocket Books, 1989.

Saraydarian, Torkom. *The Hierarchy and the Plan*. Sedona, Ariz.: Aquarian Educational Group, 1975.

————. *Earth-Quakes and Disasters: What The Ageless Wisdom Tells Us*. Sedona, AZ: Aquarian Educational Group, 1991.

————. *The Year 2000 & After*. West Hills, Calif.: T.S.G. Publishing Foundation, 1991.

Satin, Mark. *New Options for America*. Fresno, Calif.: The Press at California State University, 1991.

Schure, Edouard. *The Great Initiates*. San Francisco: Harper and Row, 1961; orig. 1889.

Seifer, Nancy. *Face to Face with Freedom*. New York: Freedom Press, 1991.

Senge, Peter M. *The Fifth Discipline*. New York: Doubleday, 1990.

Sheehy, Gail. *Character*. New York: William Morrow and Company, 1988.

Slater, Philip. *Wealth Addiction*. Santa Cruz, Calif.: University of California Press, 1972.

Slaton, Christa Daryl. *Televote: Citizen Participation in the Quantum Age*. New York: Praeger Publishers, 1992.

Spangler, David. *Links with Space*. Findhorn, Scotland: Findhorn Press, 1971.

————. *Conversations with John*. Elgin, Ill.: Lorian Press, 1980.

————. *Emergence, The Rebirth of the Sacred*. New York: Delta/Merloyd Lawrence, 1984.

————, and William Thompson. *The Reimagination of the World*. Santa Fe, N.M.: Bear and Company, 1991.

Sri Aurobindo. *The Human Cycle, The Ideal of Human Unity, War and Self-Determination*. Pondicherry, India: Sri Aurobindo Ashram Publications, 1970.

Steinem, Gloria. *Revolution from Within: A Book on Self-Esteem*. Boston: Little, Brown and Company, 1992.

Steiner, Rudolf. *World History in the Light of Anthroposophy*. London: Rudolf Steiner Press, 1950.

———. *The Driving Force of Spiritual Powers in World History*. North Vancouver, Canada: Steiner Book Centre, 1972.

———. *The Destinies of Individuals and of Nations*. New York: Anthroposophic Press, 1987.

Stone, Merlin. *When God Was a Woman*. New York: Harcourt Brace Jovanovich, 1976.

Tarnas, Richard. *The Passion of the Western Mind*. New York: Harmony Books, 1991.

Tester, Jim. *A History of Western Astrology*. New York: Ballantine Books, 1987.

Thompson, William Irwin. *Pacific Shift*. San Francisco: Sierra Club Books, 1986.

Three Initiates. *The Kybalion*. Chicago: The Yogi Publication Society, Masonic Temple, 1912.

Tweed, Thomas Frederick. *Gabriel Over the White House*. New York: Farrar and Rinehart, 1933.

Vasconcellos, John. *A Liberating Vision*. San Luis Obispo, Calif.: Impact Publishers, 1979.

Von Franz, Marie-Louise. *Shadow and Evil in Fairytales*. Dallas: Spring Publications, 1974.

Walker, Barbara G. *The Woman's Encyclopedia of Myths and Secrets*. New York: Harper and Row, 1983.

Woolger, Jennifer, and Roger Woolger. *The Goddess Within*. New York: Fawcett Columbine, 1989.

Wright, Michelle Small. *Behaving As If the God In All Life Mattered*. Jefferson, Va.: Perelandra, Ltd., 1987.

Index

◆

About the Authors

◆

CORINNE MCLAUGHLIN and GORDON DAVIDSON are co-
authors of *Builders of the Dawn* and are cofounders of Sirius,
an ecological village and educational community in Massachusetts and the Sirius School of Spiritual Science, which offers courses and workshops in the Ageless Wisdom. They are
also former members of the Findhorn Foundation in Scotland.

Corinne has taught transformational politics at American
University in Washington, D.C., and has worked with President Clinton's Council on Sustainable Development. Gordon
is a Director of Ally Capital Corporation, sponsors of the Environmental Allies Funds. He was formerly Executive Director
of the Social Investment Forum and the Coalition for Environmentally Responsible Economies (CERES) and is coauthor
of the CERES Principles.